The Architecture of the French Enlightenment

ALLAN BRAHAM

THE ARCHITECTURE OF THE FRENCH ENLIGHTENMENT

with 424 illustrations

THAMES AND HUDSON

For Helen

Text © 1980 Allan Braham

Plates and lay-out © 1980 Thames and Hudson Ltd, London

Filmset and printed in Great Britain by BAS Printers Limited, Over Wallop, Hampshire
Bound in Great Britain by Webb Son and Company Limited, Glamorgan

Contents

PART THREE: CLAUDE-NICOLAS LEDOUX (1735–1806)

PART FOUR: ARCHITECTURE BEFORE AND AFTER THE REVOLUTION

Preface and acknowledgments

THE HISTORY OF ARCHITECTURE in late eighteenth-century France has been treated in three important works: in volumes 3 to 5 of Louis Hautecoeur's *Histoire de l'architecture classique en France* (1950–53), in Emil Kaufmann's *Architecture in the Age of Reason* (1955), and in Michel Gallet's *Demeures parisiennes, l'époque de Louis XVI* (1964; revised and expanded as *Paris Domestic Architecture of the 18th Century*, 1972). Though my own approach to the subject is inevitably different, I am conscious of the great debt that is owed to these pioneering studies.

Since these books have appeared a resurgence of interest in the art of the later eighteenth century has fathered a multitude of exhibitions and publications, devoted either to such general themes as 'Neo-classicism' or to individual artists and subjects. A series of exhibitions in France has covered the festivals of the Revolution (1974), Piranesi and his French contemporaries (1976), garden design (1977), Charles de Wailly and Ledoux (both of 1979), and this is planned to continue with a conference and an exhibition highlighting the work of Soufflot (1980).

Amongst articles and books on general themes in the last twenty years there have been studies by Svend Eriksen on early 'Neo-classical' taste (1962, 1974), by Helen Rosenau on the Prix de Rome drawings of the later eighteenth century (1960), by Robin Middleton on ecclesiastical architecture and its theoretical background (1962–63), by Alain Gruber on festival decorations (1972), by Dora Wiebenson on gardens (1978), and the publication by Hans Ottomeyer of the autobiographies submitted by many architects seeking admission to the Academy. Individual artists, patrons and theorists have been studied by Michael Petzet (Soufflot, 1961), Johannes Langner (Ledoux, 1960 and 1963), Wolfgang Herrmann (Ledoux, 1960, and Laugier, 1963), François-Georges Pariset (Louis, 1958, 1959, 1973, and Brongniart, 1957–62), Michel Gallet (de Wailly, 1965, Ledoux, 1970, 1974–75, 1979, and Trouard, 1976), J.-M. Pérouse de Montclos (Boullée, 1969), Daniel Rabreau (de Wailly, 1972, 1973, with Monika Steinhauser, 1977), Monique Mosser (Antoine, 1971, and the patronage of Marigny, 1972), Christopher Tadgell (Gabriel, 1978).

Like new possessions these studies have also served to show how much else still needs renewal. There are still no monographs on architects as important as Peyre, de Wailly, Antoine, Chalgrin and Gondoin, while Louis, Ledoux and Brongniart lack comprehensive up-to-date studies, and the works on Soufflot (by Monval, 1918) and on Belanger (by Stern, 1930) would both benefit from new editions with a full corpus of illustrations.

In attempting to survey the architecture of pre-Revolutionary France I have tried to take account of most of the literature available on the subject, but I am aware that it has become almost impossible to master all that has been written on so wide a theme, and regret the omissions in the notes and bibliography of the present work, especially amongst nineteenth-century books. Similarly in pursuing especially Ledoux and de Wailly through surviving documents in the Archives Nationales, I have become conscious of how much awaits discovery there, particularly in the Revolutionary dossiers and in the notaries' papers in the Minutier Central.

I have also become increasingly aware that the architecture of late eighteenth-century France is one of many art-historical subjects which have suffered from an excess of generalization, or from an obsessive search for underlying principles, as pursued to an extreme degree by Kaufmann. Without questioning the very real importance of such general principles, it seems to me that the discovery of what is common to the artistic manifestations of a particular age should be only the first step towards the more essential and more humane task of distinguishing what is special about the outstanding work of the period. In the later eighteenth century architecture was the subject of great public interest and I have been able to draw upon many memoirs, diaries and letters to illustrate the social and intellectual background of the great masterpieces of the age, and likewise the personal contributions of the architects and patrons involved in their creation.

In a period where so much background information is readily available I have been especially struck and not a little relieved to find confirmation of how relatively unlearned was the approach to their art of most architects and critics of the time. The majority were not essentially philosophers or trained in abstract thought, but had active professions of their own and a living to earn, and though they shaped and were shaped by the key theoretical issues of the day, their commitment to theory seems by and large to have been instinctively practical and emotional, and at times surprisingly casual. This is especially striking in the case of Soufflot, for example, or Belanger, and even with those who were more deeply committed to the written word, like Blondel and Le Roy.

I should like to think that my approach to the subject is deeply indebted to my colleague, Michael Levey, whose conversation and whose books, including an inimitable account of painting and sculpture in eighteenth-century France, are themselves works of art which also seem to me to reveal the true priorities of the art historian. At all stages of my work the support and encouragement of Robin Middleton has been invaluable to me; he has most generously shared with me his extensive knowledge of the subject and helped me unfailingly both with points of information and criticism, and with the provision of photographs. My interest in the subject was greatly stimulated by John Newman, who invited me to give a series of lectures and classes at the Courtauld Institute on French architecture in the later eighteenth and early nineteenth centuries. At Thames and Hudson, Emily Lane, and Simon Marks, on whom the burden of an over-long manuscript and so many illustrations has largely fallen, have been continuously alert and patient, and it would be wrong of me, in spite of their scruples, not to acknowledge their consistently helpful and friendly support. The attractive lay-out of the illustrations and design of the jacket are benefits due respectively to Mrs Pat Mueller and Mr Shalom Schotten, and the elegant maps have been drawn by Mrs Hanni Bailey.

In France I have been privileged to discuss the pleasures and problems of pre-Revolutionary architecture with many friends and colleagues, and two conferences I attended were particularly memorable, one in Bordeaux in 1974, organized by Professor Pariset, on the theme of 'Neo-classical' architecture, and the other at the French Academy in Rome in 1976 on Piranesi and the French. The great generosity of Mlle Monique Mosser has extended to helping me to obtain many illustrations for the present book, including the series of photographs of the Monnaie, and M. Michel Gallet has also been particularly kind in lending me photographs and in answering over the years many questions about a subject that is largely his own. Among others in France to whom I am especially grateful are M. Daniel Rabreau, a generous host who has also shared with me his detailed knowledge of de Wailly and of theatre architecture, M. Pérouse de Montclos, who most kindly put at my disposal a series of annotated photographs of the Prix de Rome drawings at the Ecole des Beaux-Arts, and M. Olivier Choppin de Janvry, the skilful restorer of the Chinese pavilion of Cassan and the Désert de Retz.

At the Bibliothèque Nationale I have enjoyed the unfailing help of M. Jean Adhémar, Mlle Nicole Villa and Mme Françoise Jestaz, and at the Archives Nationales that of M. Michel Le Moel, Mme Nicole Felkay and Mme Rochas, and M. Louis-Henri Collard. My thanks are also due to Mme Wanda Bouleau-Rabaud and Mlle Annie Jacques at the Ecole des Beaux-Arts, and to the staff of the Bibliothèque Historique de la Ville de Paris, the Bibliothèque de l'Institut and the Musée Carnavalet. At the Louvre Mme Sylvie Béguin most kindly facilitated my research and took much trouble to help me procure photographs. Work in Bordeaux was greatly assisted by M. Jean-Pierre Mouilleseaux and pursued with the help of M. Jean-Paul Avisseau and Mme de Vignan of the Archives Municipales, and in Dijon M. Yves Beauvalot, and M. J.-C. Garretta of the Bibliothèque Municipale were especially kind and helpful. Amongst many others, finally, with whom I have had the pleasure of lengthy discussions or who have allowed me to borrow photographs and sent me copies of their work, I should like especially to thank Mme Hélène Fustier, Professor Joseph Rykwert, Dr Dora Wiebenson, Professor Johannes Langner, Richard Chaffee, Christopher Tadgell, Peter Smith, Martin Meade, Werner Oechslin, Mr John Harris, Mr Geoffrey de Bellaigue, Dr Helen Rosenau-Carmi, Professor Tom McCormick and Mme A. Voronikhine.

Allan Braham, 1979

Introduction

THE ARCHITECTURE of the early Renaissance in Italy, which so clearly mirrors the emergence of humanism and the rediscovery of antiquity in the fifteenth century, has long been the object of popular interest and affection. The dome of Florence Cathedral, the Malatesta Temple at Rimini and the church of St Peter's in Rome are all well-known masterpieces, celebrated for their visual and technical virtuosity, and for the story they tell of human pride and aspiration in the service of man and of God. The remains of antiquity continued to be a source of inspiration during four centuries of architectural development, but not until the later eighteenth century was the scope of classical architecture fully explored and its power in consequence gradually loosened. The closing stages of the Renaissance tradition in architecture, occurring in France in the later eighteenth century, and reflecting the variety of thought in the 'Age of Enlightenment', though much less familiar than the history of its origins, is no less inspiring a record of human achievement.

Art in the later eighteenth century in France only gradually relinquished the standards of the earlier part of the century, which had arisen from a conscious effort to impart visual pleasure and excitement, even if by the mid-century most works of art had come to seem empty of much feeling or depth of thought. It was realized at the time that radical changes were long overdue, and these changes when they came inevitably followed the transformations in thought and behaviour that were to culminate in the outbreak of the Revolution. It fell to architecture, more than to painting and sculpture, to provide the most immediate and most profound expression of this new outlook, inspiring a series of masterpieces that were fashioned, and many of them built, long before the visual sophistication of the earlier eighteenth century was finally extinguished.

In reflecting the intellectual preoccupations of the age architecture may even be felt to have clarified the main issues of the day by providing simple visual equivalents, assimilable by the populace at large, to ideas that would otherwise have been freshly available only to an articulate

minority. The church of Ste-Geneviève (now the Panthéon), begun by Soufflot in 1757, reflected throughout its long building history that reappraisal of tradition in a mood of optimism and apparent rationality which is fundamental to the pages of the *Encyclopédie*. Swiftly following this reappraisal came the freedom to repudiate the notion of human progress, fundamental to the thought of Rousseau, and used to great architectural advantage above all in the works of Ledoux. Architects became more articulate and more conscious of their responsibilities than before, and many committed their views, sometimes disastrously, to print. They wrote not treatises on the orders or pattern books of the traditional kind, but mostly books and articles dealing with their own works that show a new awareness of what should constitute good architecture both in theory and in practice.

The social transformations linked with this revolution in thought are expressed in the many new types of building that began to assume increasing importance – theatres and hospitals, law courts and prisons – and in the use to which artistry and knowledge could be put in distinguishing between buildings so varied in function. In domestic architecture social distinctions, which had been strictly regulated in France according to the rules of *convenance*, were dramatically eroded, and the very basis of architectural design gradually altered. Stages of transition between masses, which had been codified in the Renaissance in relation to the God-given design of the human body, were of little relevance to a community increasingly resentful of all social and religious authority.

The political and social climate that affected architects and their buildings in the later eighteenth century is clearly reflected in architectural fashions and in the evidence that patronage supplies. The relative tranquillity of the earlier part of the reign of Louis XV under the administration of Cardinal Fleury came to an end in the middle years of the century with the intervention of France in the War of the Austrian Succession (1740–48), closely followed by the Seven Years' War which ended in the humiliating Treaty of Paris (1763). These years marked the ascendancy of the king's most influential mistress, Mme de Pompadour, who had been presented at court in 1745. Mme de Pompadour ruled not only in matters of taste, having her brother, Abel Poisson, later Marquis de Marigny, appointed Surintendant des Bâtiments du Roi (effectively Minister of Arts), but she also wielded undisguised political power, and manipulated the careers of the king's ministers, particularly the Duc de Choiseul, whose political supremacy began in 1758.

A bridge was formed between the court and the freer intellectual life of Paris largely through the agency of Choiseul and Mme de Pompadour. Both corresponded with Voltaire, and it was under the protection of Choiseul, the friend of the 'philosophes', that the volumes of Diderot's *Encyclopédie* continued to appear after the storm that had greeted the publication of the first volumes in 1751–52. Choiseul supported the Parlement in its opposition to the fanaticism of the Jesuits, and witnessed the expulsion of the order from France (1764). Though himself a distinguished collector, he initiated little of architectural significance, in either his private or his official capacity, but left the initiative for public buildings with Marigny and his sister, or with the king himself.

In matters of taste there had been isolated signs of rebellion against what was considered the triviality of fashionable art throughout the earlier part of the century. To the extent that writers (including Voltaire himself) and artists called for a return to the standards that had glorified the reign of the king's predecessor, Louis XIV, no immediate threat to conservative values was implied. Indeed, these sentiments were echoed by some of the more intelligent courtiers, who linked the taste for elaborate decoration with the newly rich financiers, and called for a return to the standards of their grandparents, the 'bon vieux goût' that is recommended, in preference to recent manifestations of taste, in the amusing *Souvenirs* supposedly written by the Marquise de Créquy: 'Lately,' she says, 'all forms of ornaments tortured themselves on woodwork, in the reliefs on panels, jewellery, silver, and everything of that kind. They were contortions and broken twirls against the rules of good sense and good old-fashioned taste . . .'

Once the need for change had been appreciated developments became increasingly radical. The character of English architecture and garden design seemed to mirror the values of a society that many in France had begun to envy for its political liberties. The opposition to the Rococo style embraced the good sense and sobriety of bourgeois taste, associated with Mme Geoffrin and her circle, as well as the more lavish experiments of a new generation of financiers and bankers, and it was very shortly to affect many of the most illustrious members of the court, especially those related to the royal family, whose patronage is of the greatest historical interest.

The final years of the reign of Louis XV were marked by open antagonism to the Crown as widespread as the hostility that had greeted the accession of the Hanoverians to the throne of England. Almost the entire aristocracy was alienated by the presentation of a commoner at court in 1770 in the person of the king's new mistress, Mme du Barry, who was to introduce fashions more extreme than anything her predecessor could have imagined. Choiseul left the court, exiled to Chanteloup, and political power was transferred to the Chancellor, Maupeou, who saw the Parlements banished and new ones of his own set up. This unpopular measure brought into the open the antagonism of the king's own family, the Duc d'Orléans and his son, the Duc de Chartres, the Prince de Condé and the Prince de Conti. But with the death of Louis XV in 1774 a new beginning was made, more nearly in line with the growth of liberal opinion. The new king, Louis XVI, recalled the Parlements and, having chosen the aged Maurepas as Premier Ministre, he asked Turgot to become Contrôleur des Finances.

The famous reforms that Turgot attempted to implement affected architecture to the extent that he and the Comte d'Angiviller, Marigny's successor as Surintendant des Bâtiments du Roi, brought order to the many earlier proposals for the improvement of Paris and the other major cities of the realm. As a former local administrator, Intendant of the province of Limoges, Turgot was sympathetic to the needs of the provinces, and he encouraged in particular the building of the theatre of Bordeaux. In Paris he gave his attention to projects that reflected public awareness of the need for social amenities, like the building of a new royal library and the transformation of the Louvre into a public museum. But the growing financial insecurity of the Crown prevented most such well-intentioned projects proceeding far.

Private rather than public building flourished in Paris and the other major French cities. Patronage shifted from Versailles and became a monopoly, or so it seemed, of the bankers and tax farmers. They comprised the group of sixty (until 1780) who controlled the Ferme Générale (the tax farm which gathered the indirect taxes in return for loans to the Crown), the Receveurs des Finances for the different provinces, usually fifty in number, the treasurers of the different state departments, and private and official bankers. The development of property brought a good return on capital and Sébastien Mercier, writing of Paris in the later eighteenth century, asked: 'who do they belong to, all those fine houses? To money lenders, to concessionaires, to speculators, to the tireless agents of oppression.' Yet Mercier acknowledged that the city had benefited from such speculations: 'The passion for building is much preferable to that for pictures, to that for girls: it stamps the town with an air of grandeur and of majesty.'

What Mercier overlooked was that all those who owned land in Paris, including the royal princes and distinguished aristocrats, joined with the financiers and the municipality in speculative projects, despite the social opprobrium that such profiteering attracted. Above all the Duc de Chartres was ridiculed at court for what was admittedly the most spectacular of all such developments, the reconstruction of the Palais-Royal, which was eventually to become a kingdom that challenged the very existence of the court, but many of those who mocked were themselves involved in less extravagant speculation. Architects also took part as agents in such developments to augment the small percentage they would otherwise receive as a fee, though they were thereby debarred from membership of the Académie Royale d'Architecture. Established in the reign of Louis XIV, the Academy was itself one of the principal causes of a surfeit of architects in the later part of the century. 'Louis XIV', as one observer noted, 'having, by his establishments, multiplied architects, a half-century after him, more architects were created than architecture.'

The social confusion that arose, more in Paris than in the country, from this new distribution of wealth, is described in many of the memoirs of the time, but perhaps nowhere as vividly as in the Créquy *Souvenirs*:

It was thus what was most natural and most simple that was in fashion. You saw wives and husbands embracing: you saw brothers and sisters calling each other *tu*: Ladies no longer escorted each other or rose for a greeting. People said *women* instead of *Ladies*, and the *men* of the court instead of Nobles. The greatest Ladies were invited to supper and mixed with the wives of financiers.

Architects too undoubtedly benefited from this social levelling, and many enrolled amongst the ranks of the freemasons. Imported from England in the earlier part of the century, freemasonry had become fashionable, despite the mistrust of the Crown, especially after the peace of 1763, but only in rare instances was it a direct source of architectural inspiration.

Speculation ensured the remarkable growth of Paris and the other main French cities, Lyon, Bordeaux and Marseille. It was calculated that Paris, with a population of over half a million, had increased in size by a third in the later eighteenth century. The old centre of the city, the Ile-Notre-Dame and the Ile-St-Louis and the quarters to the north and south, were largely neglected, while building moved westwards on both sides of the Seine, in the early part of the century, across the Faubourg St-Honoré and the Faubourg St-Germain. The squalor of the old town was as much a surprise to visitors as the luxury of the new. 'It is the ugliest beastly town in the universe,' wrote Horace Walpole in a mood of depression in 1765; 'I have not seen a mouthful of verdure in it, nor have they anything green but treillage and window shutters.' The Scottish gardener, Thomas Blaikie, complained ten years later that

. . . most of the streets in Paris is remarkable narrow and no pavement for people a foot, so that Paris may be said to be very unconvenient especial for the lower Class of people who goes a foot, who is constantly in risk of there lives by the numbers of Coaches carts &c . . . The town is lighted in the night by lamps which is suspended upon a cord fixed across the street.

Later in the century the city spread far beyond the walls of the seventeenth-century capital, which follow roughly the line of the present inner boulevards, especially towards the west and north, beyond the Place de la Concorde and towards Montmartre, and on the south bank of the Seine mainly in the environs of the Invalides. The quality of the late eighteenth-century town can now scarcely be appreciated amongst the depredations of the following

century, but a collection of isolated monuments still survives and the growth of the town can be discerned along certain roads, like the rue du Faubourg-St-Honoré itself or the rue du Faubourg-Poissonnière, where proceeding west and north from the centre the houses of the 1750s and 1760s make way for the looser and more varied designs of the pre-Revolutionary capital. The final definition of the city was marked by the customs barriers of the tax farmers, designed by Ledoux in the 1780s to protect the boundaries of the capital.

To the writer of the most useful and popular guide-book to Paris, Luc-Vincent Thiéry, there was no doubt about the excellence of the new town:

The arts, brought alive again, are fathering masterpieces to rival those of Greece and Rome; Architecture takes on its primitive purity, and joins to the nobility of its origins greater elegance, greater taste and more convenient planning. A new town built on the land formerly occupied by gardens, offers straight roads, and every house is so to speak a mansion.

Many visitors endorsed this opinion, including Mrs Thrale, visiting Paris in 1775, who noted that 'the Extremes of Magnificence & Meanness meet at Paris'. She was struck by the quality both of the air and of the local stone:

The purity of the Air in a Metropolis so crowded is truly surprizing : no Sea Coal being Burned, the Atmosphere of the narrowest part of Paris is more transparent & nitid than that of Hampstead hill . . . The Stone Quarries all round the town make Building very cheap, & of course invite the enlargement of Paris, which from the whiteness of the Ground & Houses resembles Bath more than London – on the whole.

The magnificence and growing confidence of the financiers received encouragement from the choice of a Genevan banker, Jacques Necker, to replace Turgot when he was dismissed, partly through the jealousy of Maurepas, in 1776. The new Parlement was unwilling to ratify the more equitable tax system that Turgot favoured, but Necker, relying on loans, was scarcely more successful than his predecessor in improving the financial administration of the state, and he was confronted with the additional burden of the intervention of France in the War of American Independence (1778). Like Turgot, Necker was concerned with schemes of public welfare which had important architectural consequences, especially with hospital and prison reform, and with the reorganization of the Ferme Générale, but he too found his position, especially as a Protestant denied entry to the council of state, untenable and in 1781 he resigned.

Economy was the ruling passion of the king, his main hobbies being hunting and clockmaking, and the expensive distractions of his grandfather, Louis XV, ceased to flourish at the court. Queen Marie Antoinette was constrained to follow the example of her husband, and, despite her reputation for thoughtless extravagance, she was responsible for little of architectural importance. More significant was the patronage of the king's two brothers, the Comte de Provence and the Comte d'Artois (the future Louis XVIII and Charles X). The king was notoriously indulgent towards the extravagance of his more fashion-

11

1 The salon of the Hôtel de Maisons, Paris. Designed by Nicolas Pineau about 1750 and a late example of the style of decoration that began to provoke criticism in the 1740s and 1750s

able brothers, who remained heirs to the throne until the belated birth of his first son in 1781. With their cousin, the Duc de Chartres, they were amongst the most active builders, benefiting from speculations in the capital and creating three of the earliest 'English' gardens (Brunoy, Bagatelle and Monceau).

Interest in English customs and institutions, from being a notional sympathy entertained by the 'philosophes', became with the Comte d'Artois and the Duc de Chartres a socially acceptable fashion. The influence of England was not less pervasive for being concerned with the more superficial aspects of English life, betting, horse racing, simplicity of dress, and even deportment. 'Some young men', according to the Marquise de la Tour du Pin, 'went so far as to affect an English accent and made a study of all the awkwardness of manner . . . of an Englishman, so that they could adopt them for their own use.'

On his visit to Paris in 1765 Horace Walpole wrote of the Anglomania of the French, and he elucidated the term 'philosophes': 'In the first place it comprehends almost everybody; and in the next, means men who, avowing war against popery, aim, many of them, at the subversion of all religion, and still many more, at the destruction of royal power.' He asserted that Anglomania, spreading to France after the peace of 1763, had 'had its day', but his prediction proved entirely false. The 'English' garden, then only in its infancy in France, was a social phenomenon that touched upon the deepest preoccupations of the age and profoundly affected architecture. The gardens of the Duc de Chartres at Monceau, begun before the death of Louis XV, and the later park of the Comte d'Artois at Bagatelle, while they were not the earliest examples of the 'English' style, provide a point of reference because of the social consequence of their owners.

The 'philosophes' themselves on the comparatively rare occasions when they commented upon architecture seem to have been revolutionary only to the extent of expressing admiration for the 'bon vieux goût', the monuments of seventeenth-century France and the rules which had governed their construction. Voltaire was one of the first to show such a preference, in his *Temple du goût* (1733), and Diderot, whose sympathies were more for painting than for architecture, despite his interest in techniques of construction, seems unconvincing when his remarks on buildings advance the position of Voltaire: 'A piece of architecture is beautiful when it is strong and seen to be strong, and when it is visibly appropriate to its purpose. Strength is here the equivalent of health in living creatures; appropriateness to a purpose is the equivalent of suitability to a given way of life in human beauty.'

There is no special reason why the 'philosophes' should have taken more than a cursory interest in architecture. Few had the time or the money to concern themselves directly with building, and Voltaire was almost alone in the extent of his architectural patronage. The relatively modest buildings he constructed, mainly at Ferney, were architecturally unremarkable, and not by any of the more famous architects of the period. 'My church', he wrote in 1760, 'will not be built until the Spring. You want me to dare to consult M. Soufflot about this village church, and I have made my château without consulting anyone.'

The one subject that united enlightened opinion was the growing sympathy, largely inspired by Rousseau, for the unspoilt beauty of nature. The informality of the English garden was linked with the prevalent taste in the decorative arts for the irregularity and exoticism of Chinese art, and the 'Anglo-Chinese' or 'picturesque' garden, as it was called, revolutionized the concept of a

2 Holkham Hall, Norfolk, begun 1734, by William Kent. 'Palladianism' was rarely directly influential in France, where it was considered a derivative style

building as a work of art existing in opposition to the country that formed its setting, while also popularizing more informal patterns for domestic housing that were to proliferate during the course of the following century and beyond.

In architecture and the visual arts English influence appears to have been considerably less profound than is sometimes supposed, despite the effect of England on habits of thought and behaviour in France. Although the French were aware that their own standards of decoration seemed excessively elaborate when compared with the Palladian severity of English houses (1, 2, 3), they were also conscious of the beauty of their own seventeenth-century buildings, which seemed to them unrivalled by anything English. English books were generally available, but very few Frenchmen had actually visited England before the peace of 1763. The Prince de Croÿ remarked in 1755 on how little those of his own social level had travelled abroad. The occasional French visitor with a special interest in the arts found little to admire. Rouquet in his book on the arts in England (1755) singled out for praise the portico of St Martin-in-the-Fields (4), 'but the English', he said, 'have no architecture, they take their architecture from Italy and antiquity'. A more generous comment of 1768 allowed that 'Architecture is the fine art that has for a long while made the greatest progress in England ... However, the architects are producing in London buildings that are heavy and massive, rather than male and majestic ...'

The 'philosophes' too, much as they may have admired Locke and Newton and the relative liberty of English thought, seem to have found no real equivalent in the English scene. Diderot described the disappointment of the Baron d'Holbach on his return from England in 1765.

3 Holkham Hall, the staircase. The public character of such a staircase in a private house offended French notions of decorum (*convenance*), but the design is paralleled in theatres *(193)*

4 St Martin-in-the-Fields, London, 1721–26, by James Gibbs. The columned portico, but not the 'Gothic' steeple, was admired in France

behaviour of the Parisians: 'a Crowd here is far less rude & dangerous than in London, & you are sure to meet no Insults from the Populace of Paris where every Man thinks himself the Protector of every Woman'. Philip Thicknesse came to dislike the capital: 'Walking the streets is extremely dangerous, riding in them very expensive; and when those things which are worthy to be seen, (and much there is very worthy) have been seen, the city of *Paris* becomes a melancholy residence for a stranger, who neither plays at cards, dice, or deals in the principal manufacture of the city; i.e. *ready-made love*.' Thicknesse also noted that 'The Frenchman is always attentive to his own person, and scarce ever appears but clean and well dressed; while his house and private apartments are perhaps covered with litter and dirt, and in the utmost confusion; – the Englishman, on the other hand, often neglects his external appearance; but his house is always exquisitely clean.'

However dirty their houses may have appeared inside, the French were also famous for their sumptuous taste in decoration and furnishings. As Mercier explained, 'the wonders of architecture, are, in Paris, in the interior of the houses', and he is echoed by Walpole at his most malicious in describing (at the banker Laborde's) the excessive formality of a French household.

Lord! Madam, how little and poor all your houses in London will look after his! In the first place, you must have a garden half as long as the Mall, and then you must have fourteen windows, each as long as t'other half, looking into it; and each window must consist of only eight frames of looking-glass. You must have a first and a second antechamber, and they must have nothing in them but dirty servants. Next must be the grand cabinet, hung with red damask, in gold frames, and covered with eight large and very bad pictures, that cost four thousand pounds – I cannot afford them you a farthing cheaper ... Then there must be immense *armoires* of tortoise-shells and *or moulu*, inlaid with medals – and then you may go into the *petit cabinet* and then into the great *salle*, and the gallery, and the billiard-room, and the eating room; and all these must be hung with crystal lustres and looking-glass from top to bottom; and then you must stuff them fuller than they will hold with granite tables and porphyry urns, and bronzes, and statues, and vases, and the Lord or the devil knows what ...

Walpole may have been oppressed by the lavish furnishings of the richest French houses, but the craftsmanship of French furniture and decoration was without parallel in the later eighteenth century. Manufacturing in France had been notoriously neglected until Calonne took over the control of the Finances shortly after Necker's resignation, at a time when it was no longer fashionable to believe, like Turgot, that land was the only source of national wealth. It has been estimated that in 1775 out of a population of twenty-five million only half-a-million Frenchmen were engaged in the production of goods; the rest worked mainly on the land. The manufacture of iron and the process by which it began to strengthen and slowly to supersede stone in the construction of buildings constitutes the most important undercurrent of architectural development in the later eighteenth century in France, but little of architectural distinction appeared as an immediate result of the good intentions of Calonne.

He went off prejudiced in favour of the country, he had a very warm welcome there and enjoyed excellent health. Even so, he came home discontented: discontented with the country, which he found to be neither as populous nor as well-cultivated as he had been led to expect, discontented with the architecture, which is almost all odd and Gothic, discontented with the gardens, where the affected imitation of nature is worse than the monotonous symmetry of art, discontented with the people ... discontented with the dinner parties, where everyone is seated according to rank and where formality and ceremony sit by the side of every guest ...

Admiration for the work of Wren and for the technical virtuosity of the dome of St Paul's *(5, 6)* appeared only fitfully in France, influencing Servandoni at St-Sulpice and Soufflot in the latest stages of the design of Ste-Geneviève, while the freer designs of Wren's associates, Vanbrugh and Hawksmoor, were of little importance to French architects in comparison with the buildings of antiquity or of the Renaissance.

The reactions of English visitors to France in the later eighteenth century, apart from their direct comments on the buildings of the time, supply an amusing commentary on French ways of life. Mrs Thrale admired the orderly

5 St Paul's Cathedral, London, 1675–1711, by Christopher Wren. An influence on Servandoni's façade of St-Sulpice *(23)* and on the final design for the dome of Ste-Geneviève *(98)*

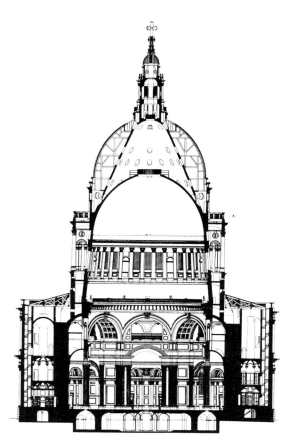

6 St Paul's, section of the dome (after Poley). The dome is composed of three shells, like the final designs for Ste-Geneviève *(96)*

The urban developments associated with Calonne included the formation of new rules for the control of building in Paris which regulated the height of the houses and the width of streets, the clearing of the old houses from the bridges and the building of the *barrières* of Ledoux. In France itself Calonne was concerned with the modification of the ports, especially Cherbourg, which the king visited in 1785. Calonne was probably more deeply interested in the arts than any of his predecessors, though he built little for himself, and he was criticized for a civilized and generous manner that concealed a professional vacuity. 'M. de Calonne', wrote the Comte de Ségur, 'united in himself all that could please at the court, displease the people, foster illusions of authority and reawaken the fears of the Parlements . . . Perceiving everything quickly, but nothing deeply, no obstacle disturbed him, or halted his presumptuous confidence.' It was Calonne, conservative in his approach to the financial crisis of the country, who finally proposed the calling of the Assembly of Notables in 1788, which led to the summoning in the following year of the States General.

The Revolution marked a serious decline in building throughout the country, accompanied by an increasingly doctrinaire approach to all aesthetic matters. With the notable exception of theatres and small houses little was actually built before the advent of Napoleon. Hardship faced the many architects who failed to gain a post in the reorganized public administration of buildings, and occasional public competitions, which scarcely ever resulted in firm commissions, drew many contestants. Architects turned increasingly to writing and to the drafting of idealized projects, just as the courtiers of the Ancien Régime settled down to write their memoirs. The transformation of Paris into a new Rome under its new Emperor, Napoleon, inspired buildings which, though they derived in principle from the architecture of the Enlightenment, seem quite alien to the later eighteenth century in their pedantry and in the monotony of their appearance.

The priority that architecture and certain of the applied arts assumed over painting and sculpture in the later eighteenth century in France has not won widespread

7 The Interior of the Pantheon, Rome, by Giovanni Paolo Panini (National Gallery of Art, Washington, Samuel H. Kress Collection). Panini (c. 1692–1765/8) taught perspective at the French Academy in Rome and his paintings circulated widely in French collections

recognition, but it was a phenomenon that was noted at the time. As Mercier wrote, 'Two arts have been regenerated at the same time, music and architecture' (in music he must have been thinking of the famous conflict between French and Italian styles that was later overshadowed by the advent of Gluck). Only later did painting and sculpture

8 The Tomb of Cecilia Metella, Rome, etching by Piranesi, 1762, from the *Vedute di Roma*. French architects who failed to visit Italy were inspired by Piranesi's plates of Roman antiquities

catch up with the advances that architects had made, coming into prominence in the works of David and Canova in the years when the Ancien Régime was perishing aesthetically, as it had perished politically. The Renaissance tradition ended less coherently in France than it had begun in Italy, and this is apparent from the largely misleading terms that are popular as a means of comprehending the artistic developments of the age.

'Neo-classicism' is the term at present most in favour for the artistic manifestations of the later eighteenth century, a period of transition between the 'Rococo' and the more carefully defined movements of nineteenth-century art. 'Romantic classicism' also has its adherents, who argue that the classicism of the age is only part of a greater movement of liberation that lasted into the following century. Or there is the now unfashionable 'Late Baroque classicism', which acknowledges the persistence of tradition in the later eighteenth century. Building in France enlarges upon these terms and is itself clarified by their implications.

'Neo-classicism' has the advantage of stressing the importance of antiquity for the architecture of the time, even if the prefix 'Neo-' carries implications of the merely derivative which are more suited to the academic classicism of the early nineteenth century. Few of the buildings of ancient Rome, and still less those of Greece, had ever been exploited to the same extent as the sculpture of antiquity, or the meagre remains of antique painting. Many were unsuited to the needs of Renaissance patrons and they had not been visually brought to life until recreated in the work of Panini and Piranesi (7, 8), who responded as eighteenth-century artists to the pictorial character of ruins and to the glories of the pre-Christian past of Rome – Panini with the well-mannered detachment of the early part of the century and Piranesi with much greater psychological intensity.

Hand in hand with the exploitation of antiquity for its pictorial resonance went the growth of classical studies, including greater knowledge and appreciation of antique art, which came slowly to maturity in Rome from the early years of the century and found its most eloquent advocate in Winckelmann. For the French, heirs of a native classical tradition that embraced the work of the Mansarts, the theoretical disputes of Blondel and Perrault and the archaeological explorations of Desgodetz, Rome had an aesthetic and practical relevance denied to architects of all other nationalities, and it was they who understood how antiquity could be harnessed as a new stylistic force. Indeed, the first artist to whom the word 'Neo-classical' might seem relevant is the sculptor, Bouchardon, who produced in Rome in the 1720s works of surprising fidelity to some simpler antique patterns (9). They remained without any obvious sequel until after the architectural revolution of the mid-century had begun. In architecture the influence of antiquity extended further than is sometimes admitted, affecting planning in French buildings as much as decoration; yet knowledge of antique architecture was only part of a much wider understanding of past achievements, and to encourage the belief that it had a magical sovereignty is to place undue emphasis upon the most derivative works and the weakest artists.

The term 'Romantic classicism' expresses something of the variety of inspiration that art commanded in the later eighteenth century, properly stressing the function of antiquity as a means rather than an end. It focuses attention upon a basic psychological distinction that had always been present in matters of artistic choice, though not clearly defined until the later eighteenth century. When Bernini, for example, visited Paris in the 1660s to plan the rebuilding of the Louvre his methods of creation deeply shocked the French, who witnessed in his procedure care for detail being sacrificed to the inspiration of the moment. In relation to the buildings of Ledoux, in all their imaginative freedom, or to the drawings of Boullée, where even the simplest practical considerations are disregarded, the word 'Romantic' has an obvious relevance.

Yet Romanticism is associated above all with developments in literature and painting in the early nineteenth century. There is little in the architecture of that time in France to compare with the achievements of writers and painters, and the architectural monuments of the preceding age are not well understood in relation to the work of Delacroix or Chateaubriand. Architecture was unable to command the freedom that painters or writers then enjoyed. Its own technique, based upon developments in engineering, could not yet be frankly exploited, and the imitation of past styles became increasingly academic, rather than 'Romantic' in any obvious sense. The academic style that accounts for most painting and sculpture in the nineteenth century shows something of the dislocation that also troubled architecture: as technique in both painting and engineering grew increasingly sophisticated, subject-matter and decoration became all the more superficial and anecdotal.

'Revolutionary' though architecture became in the later eighteenth century, not the least source of its qualities was paradoxically the persistence of traditions that had their origins in the art of the seventeenth century, a concern for the effects of light and shade to lend dramatic emphasis to buildings and a preoccupation with conceits that conferred a liveliness absent for the most part in buildings of the nineteenth century. These symbolic and witty ideas, recalling the *concetti* of Bernini, account for the 'Romantic' character of much of the building of the time, that imaginative expressiveness summed up, though only recently, in the words 'architecture parlante', and usefully acknowledged in the phrase 'Late Baroque classicism'.

These same problems of terminology have their relevance to painting in the later eighteenth century, the transformation of traditional techniques into a new means of expression being recalled by the greatest artist of the new age, Goya. Working far from the artistic centre of Paris and well into the following century, he can be likened to Ledoux in the imaginative freedom of his work and in his traditional ('painterly') style, which only the most revolutionary nineteenth-century painters took to heart. A further parallel between architecture and painting

9 Portrait of Baron Philipp von Stosch, marble bust by Edmé Bouchardon, completed 1727 (Staatliche Museen, Berlin-Dahlem). Bouchardon anticipated Soufflot in the intensity of his response to classical art, which is to be seen especially in his early portrait sculpture

can be seen in the relation of both with the everyday, practical world, which proved the touchstone for the most moving work of the time. If the representation of nature, in portraiture and landscape, carries much greater conviction than so many of the scenes of classical history painted at the time, so too in architecture buildings designed for daily use, houses, palaces and even churches, as well as all the less familiar types of structure, seem essentially more lively than the many idealized designs which have enjoyed more than their fair share of critical attention.

Since the most forward-looking architects were not necessarily those most endowed with artistry or the most ambitious projects truly representative of excellence, the difficulties of analysing the architecture of the time are more than usually acute. Of the main figures, Soufflot and Ledoux have a claim in their very different ways to a certain priority, despite the rival attractions of Boullée and the more practical achievements of many other architects, like de Wailly, Gondoin and Chalgrin. The general direction of stylistic change and technical progress within the period can be traced in the evolution of Soufflot's church of Ste-Geneviève, beginning with the first design of 1757, and covering the transformations of the 1770s and the alterations that took place after the Revolution. Whatever name is chosen to describe the architecture of the age the rule that seems especially relevant is that antiquity was indeed of importance at a time when it could be imaginatively exploited to best possible visual advantage.

10 Portrait of Jacques-Germain Soufflot, by Louis-Michel van Loo, 1767 (Musée du Louvre, Paris). Soufflot wears the *cordon noir* of the Order of St-Michel and is shown at work on an early design for Ste-Geneviève *(34)*

Part One

JACQUES-GERMAIN SOUFFLOT (1713–1780) AND HIS CONTEMPORARIES

1 The early years of Soufflot: training and background. Soufflot in Paris; the first design for Ste-Geneviève

'THE RESTORER of architecture in France', 'The author of the greatest monument that France has seen built in the eighteenth century', 'the finest building since the Renaissance of the arts': these are some of the opinions of Soufflot's contemporaries on his importance as an architect and the supremacy of his church of Ste-Geneviève. He was considered during his lifetime to have been chiefly responsible for initiating a new phase of architectural development, and though his achievement is now sometimes treated as no more than a symptom of change and transition, the church of Ste-Geneviève should rather be regarded as a great work of art, personal to its creator, and one which provided a standard of excellence that few of Soufflot's contemporaries could hope to equal.

Though much is known of Soufflot's professional career after the design of Ste-Geneviève had made him a famous and controversial figure, and severely tested his character, his origins and early work are still very obscure. In the portrait of 1767 by Louis-Michel van Loo *(10)*, Soufflot is seen in his years of triumph; it is an image not far removed from the same artist's portrait of Diderot, showing the newly confident professional of the time, amused and benign, and buoyant in the assurance of private achievement.

Jacques-Germain Soufflot was the last but one of fifteen children born to a lawyer living at Irancy, a small town near Auxerre, midway between Paris and Lyon. Baptized on 22 July 1713, and destined, according to his early biographers, for a career in law, he was sent to Paris to study. Here, however, he showed an instinctive interest in architecture, which led him at the age of eighteen to undertake the journey to Rome. In the epitaph that Soufflot later composed for himself, he claimed that he had no formal training in architecture but followed his natural taste, and there is a rare reference to Soufflot as a young man studying not any of the monuments of his own age but a chapel that had been built in the previous century by François Mansart in the Château of Fresnes, not far from Paris *(11)*. The reason for Soufflot's precocious journey to Rome probably arose from the enthusiasm he

11 The chapel of the Château of Fresnes, late 1640s (now destroyed), by François Mansart (engraving from Mariette). One of the monuments of the seventeenth century that Soufflot studied in his youth

12 Versailles, the chapel, 1688–1703, by Jules Hardouin Mansart. An interior that resembles the colonnade of the Louvre *(16)* in the presence of columns and lintels

had developed for the achievements of the seventeenth century, which had isolated him from current architectural practice in his own country.

For a young architect contemplating ecclesiastical architecture in France Fresnes was an intelligent but not an obvious choice of monument. More famous buildings were the chapel of Versailles *(12)*, designed by Jules Hardouin Mansart, the court architect to Louis XIV, with its colonnaded upper storey where the king attended Mass, and in Paris itself the church of the Invalides, designed by the same architect *(13)*. By François Mansart there was also the small domed church of the Visitation *(14)*, known as the Temple de Ste-Marie, and its later sequel, the church of the Assomption, begun by Charles Errard, with its colonnaded portico and swollen dome *(15)*. And, most famous of all French monuments, Soufflot would have known the colonnaded east front of the Louvre, attributed to Claude Perrault *(16)*, with its paired columns and straight lintels, which approaches closer to the spirit of an antique temple than any other building of its age.

In Rome, after two years, Soufflot was given a place at the French Academy there through the agency of the Duc de St-Aignan, a notably cultured French ambassador to the Papal court. He soon won the esteem of the Director of the Academy, the painter Nicolas Vleughels, who described him in a letter of 1735 to the Surintendant des Bâtiments du Roi, the Duc d'Antin: 'young as he is, there is reason to believe that he will bring no dishonour to the Academy'. And indeed in 1738, at the age of twenty-five, Soufflot returned to France to become municipal architect to the town of Lyon.

Soufflot spent much of his time in Rome studying and measuring the most important churches, especially St Peter's and S. Carlo al Corso, a building which had been

13 The church of the Invalides, Paris, 1680–91, by Jules Hardouin Mansart. The most famous seventeenth-century church in Paris and an influence on Soufflot's early designs for the dome of Ste-Geneviève *(34)*

14 The church of the Visitation, Paris, 1632–34, by François Mansart. An early work by Mansart, unusual for its unaccented hemispherical dome

15 The church of the Assomption, Paris, 1670–76, by Charles Errard (engraving from Blondel, 1752–56). Conspicuous amongst the seventeenth-century churches of Paris for the large scale of the dome and the colonnaded portico

16 The Louvre, Paris, the colonnaded east façade, 1667–70, by Louis Le Vau and Claude Perrault. Admired in the eighteenth century for its 'classical' design based upon columns and straight lintels

17 The Corso, Rome, and the Palazzo Mancini (engraving from Vasi). Built in the 1690s and attributed to Sebastiano Cipriani, the Palazzo Mancini (on the right) was the home of the French Academy for most of the eighteenth century

18 The Palazzo della Consultà, 1732–37, by Ferdinando Fuga. Fuga's inspired development of seventeenth-century Roman architectural styles is paralleled by the work of Gabriel in France

19 St Peter's, Rome. The subject of measured drawings by Soufflot and many other students who followed him at the French Academy in Rome

completed in the middle of the preceding century by Pietro da Cortona. At the Academy, housed in the Palazzo Mancini on the Corso (17), he also enjoyed the company of other promising students, including the painter Subleyras and the sculptor René-Michel Slodtz, but there were few other architects in residence. The Academy had begun to receive architects only after 1720 and they formed a minority amongst the painters and sculptors who had been sent since the time of Colbert to finish their education in Rome. Though Soufflot may have realized that his values had little in common with those of his fellow students, and still less with those of the director, he must have been aware in the city itself of the presence of Bouchardon, whose stay in Rome overlapped his arrival by one year. And in the work of Bouchardon (9), he would have discovered the gulf that existed between the taste of the early eighteenth century and the art of the classical past that students were sent to Rome to encounter at first hand.

At this date, in the 1730s, it had not become the fashion to doubt the excellence of prevailing taste. In Rome itself many of the most elegant monuments of the city had recently been designed – the Spanish Steps, the Piazza S. Ignazio and the Trevi Fountain – although a return to the more regular geometry and heavier forms of the preceding century is marked in the early masterpieces of Ferdinando Fuga (18). It was amongst scholars and antiquarians, rather than practising architects, that a greater knowledge and appreciation of antique art noticeably flourished.

At the beginning of the century the Albani Pope, Clement XI, had encouraged the study of the early past of the city and restored many of its Early Christian basilicas; the chief architect at the start of his reign, Carlo Fontana, had designed a church for the arena of the Colosseum in honour of the Christian martyrs who had been slain there. Fontana had published in 1694 a detailed monograph on St Peter's (19) which referred in detail to the church's antique past, and in architecture he had pioneered simplified variations of the work of his great predecessors in Rome, loose compositions often based upon the use of free-standing columns, which his chief Italian pupil, Juvarra, had developed in Turin. The monuments of Roman architecture were being recorded with all the eighteenth century's sense of visual grandeur in the paintings of Panini (7, 156), who had begun his career in Rome in 1711. As Vleughels' brother-in-law, Panini taught perspective to the French students at the Academy and glamorized in his paintings not only the classical past of the city but also its modern festivals.

In France too, when Soufflot returned to his native land, there was no absence of talent amongst practising architects, though many of the greatest buildings of the early eighteenth century date from before Soufflot's departure. Germain Boffrand was still active and one of his last works was the great orphanage, built in the later 1740s, that lay beside the main Paris hospital, the Hôtel-Dieu (20). Court architecture was in the hands of Hardouin Mansart's cousin and successor, Jacques Gabriel, whose major work was the building of the Place Royale at Bordeaux (21). This and the transformations that Héré was

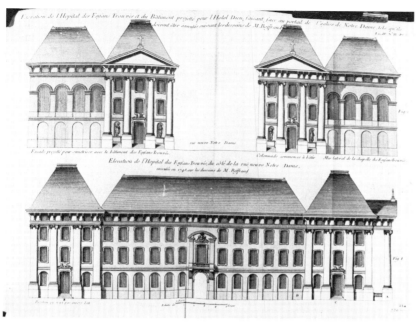

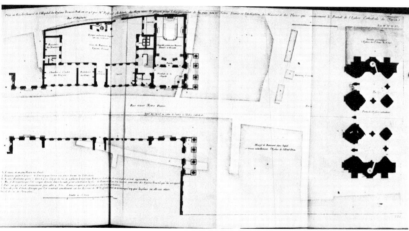

20 The Hôtel-Dieu, Paris, project by Germain
Boffrand, elevations and plan (engravings from
Blondel, 1752–56). Of Boffrand's project for the
Hôtel-Dieu, sited opposite Notre-Dame, only the
orphanage, begun in 1746 and thus later than
Soufflot's Hôtel-Dieu in Lyon (26), was built

21 The Place de la Bourse, Bordeaux, by
Jacques Gabriel, the north corner from
the rear. Begun in 1735, the Place was the
masterpiece of Ange-Jacques Gabriel's
father, who was Premier Architecte du
Roi until his death in 1742

22 Portrait of Giovanni Niccolò Servandoni, attributed to Servandoni (Musée de Versailles). The artist holds up the second version (1736) of his winning design for the façade of St-Sulpice (23)

23 The church of St-Sulpice, Paris, project by Servandoni, 1736, elevation (engraving from Blondel, 1752–56). The design of 1732 was modified in 1736 to one resembling more closely the façade of St Paul's (5), and it was further altered in execution (171)

24 The house of Servandoni, Place St-Sulpice, Paris, 1752. The only part of Servandoni's design for the square before the church that was carried out

to undertake at Nancy are amongst the most ambitious and effective urban developments of the century. In France the style known as 'Rococo' had remained largely confined to decoration; this became increasingly elaborate in the 1730s in the work of Oppenordt and Meissonnier. Planning too might become complex, as in some of the town houses of Boffrand, but in the articulation of external walls the architectural repertoire of the seventeenth century was still much in evidence (116).

Yet in France, as in Italy, a closer adherence to the spirit of the seventeenth century, itself more nearly related to the public grandeur of classical architecture, had begun to affect the appearance of buildings. It was an Italian, Giovanni Niccolò Servandoni (22), who showed how far taste was changing when his design for the façade of St-Sulpice was accepted in 1732. His project, based upon the use of free-standing columns and straight lintels (23), recalls both the colonnade of the Louvre (16) and the west front of Wren's St Paul's (5). Even in the early nineteenth century the façade was praised as one 'formed of straight lines with a single regular sequence of free-standing columns', and favourably contrasted to seventeenth-century Italian church façades 'where bizarreness was given the freest rein'.

Servandoni had been born in Florence in 1695 and had trained as a painter, assimilating architecture in Rome; he was accepted as a member of the French Academy of Painting in 1731. Though active as an architect and teacher of architecture, he was chiefly famous for his stage and festival decorations, which he constructed not only in France but also in England, in Portugal and at Stuttgart. Towards the end of his life, in 1754, his own house, forming part of an ambitious project for the square in front of St-Sulpice, was begun *(24)*, a domestic building directly recalling the crisp geometry of Italian palace design, but shaped by its rusticated windows and corner quoins into a French pattern.

Beginning in the 1740s, these hints of radical change were to have more powerful advocates in Soufflot himself, in Ange-Jacques Gabriel, who succeeded his father as Premier Architecte du Roi in 1742, and in Jacques-François Blondel, who in the following year opened a private school of architecture that was to become one of the most influential of all such establishments. Blondel praised the work of Servandoni, of whom he said that 'he knew how to sustain the Greek style in all his productions', and he admired the buildings that Soufflot had begun to create in Lyon. Yet very little is known of the relations between Blondel, Gabriel and Soufflot during the crucial decade of the 1740s, when Soufflot himself was in a position to take the practical initiative.

That the French as a nation approached architecture with such coherent aesthetic standards and technical expertise was in a large measure due to the existence of the Académie Royale d'Architecture. Soufflot was later to become a distinguished member of this body, which had given him shelter during his years in Rome. Founded by Colbert in 1671, the Academy was under the control of the Surintendant des Bâtiments du Roi and directed by the Premier Architecte. From 1756 it consisted of sixteen members of the first class and sixteen second class members, with further places for corresponding members in the provinces and abroad. Members were appointed by the king, who chose one of three names submitted by the Surintendant when a vacancy occurred in either class. The Academicians met once a week in the Louvre, when the secretary minuted their discussions. Collectively the Academy was often a passive spectator of change, and hidebound in its discussion of precedent and theory, but as new members were appointed it renewed itself in response to their ideas.

Students were trained principally in the studios of the Academicians, but they could also attend a twice-weekly course of lectures, also open to the public, given by the Professor of the Academy. A committee of Academicians judged each year the students' competition drawings for the Prix de Rome, choosing the winner of the gold medal who would have the privilege of a three-year stay in Rome, and committees were also set up to advise and report on projects for official and municipal buildings throughout the kingdom.

In many ways the French Academy differed from the Roman Accademia di San Luca, where the membership was wider, the teaching less disciplined and the competitions (principally the Concorsi Clementini, established by Pope

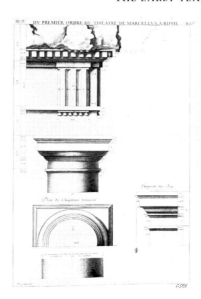

25 The Theatre of Marcellus, Rome, engraving of the Doric order from Desgodetz, 1683. Desgodetz clearly shows the absence of transitional mouldings at the base of the order

Clement XI) open to students of all nationalities. If Italian architects took somewhat for granted the classical remains that were an everyday experience for them, their colleagues in France were brought up with far greater notional respect for these remote monuments. They may not have seemed useful or relevant to the practice of architecture in proportion to the attention they commanded, but the Academy ensured that the pre-eminence of antiquity was continually endorsed, and that the single surviving architectural treatise from Roman times, by the first-century architect, Vitruvius Pollio, was not forgotten. When Claude Perrault challenged the architectural code that the Academy observed and tried to set up yet more stringent rules of his own, a famous battle ensued, the Ancients against the Moderns. The Professor of the Academy, François Blondel, upheld the authority of antiquity and traditional practice, and Perrault falsely gained a widespread reputation as an architectural libertarian.

The issue seems the more academic since it had little practical relevance to the architectural masterpieces of the time and the partisans on both sides were comparatively ignorant of the infinitely varied architecture of antiquity. It was a Frenchman, Antoine Desgodetz, who later published the most accurate survey that had yet been attempted of the antiquities of Rome, *Les Edifices antiques de Rome* (1683). Desgodetz spent eighteen months in Rome measuring and recording, and he was for example the first to illustrate adequately the curious columns of the lower storey of the Theatre of Marcellus, columns of the Tuscan order with an unsculpted entablature and no base mouldings of any kind *(25)*. Peculiarities such as these in antique architecture had not been seriously considered before. They challenged the very basis of the traditional Renaissance view that man himself was the measure of architectural proportions. A column without a base would have undermined the whole hierarchy of values that architects of the early eighteenth century so ingeniously manipulated, stages of transition between one form and another, pedestals, pediments, even the very presence of the orders themselves. By the end of the century this hierarchy lay in ruins, like the social order it had served. The Academy meanwhile passed over in virtual silence the disturbing discoveries that Desgodetz had made in Rome.

Soufflot kept in touch with the Academy during his early years in Lyon, and he must have aspired to work in the capital, though he would not have received there the same opportunities he was offered in the provinces in the 1740s: the chance to carry out important public commissions, and to voice his ideas in the less daunting setting of the Lyon Academy. Lyon was one of the largest towns of provincial France, rivalled in size only by the ports of Marseille and Bordeaux. Described by Rousseau as 'Trésor de l'univers, source de l'abondance', it lay on the main route between Paris and Italy, and enjoyed a conspicuous prosperity that was largely due to its silk industry. Noting that the town 'stands nearly in the centre of Europe', Philip Thicknesse came to prefer it to Paris: 'at *Lyons* every thing, which man can wish for, is in perfection; it is indeed a rich, noble, and plentiful town, abounding with every thing that is good, and more *finery* than even in *Paris* itself'.

Lyon was ruled in the eighteenth century by a council of five aldermen, the Consulat, a royal governor (by heredity a member of the Villeroy family), and an Intendant, though it remained without its own Parlement, falling under the legal jurisdiction of Paris. It was the scene of active architectural enterprise throughout the eighteenth century, the possessor of the oldest and most venerable hospital in the kingdom, the Hôtel-Dieu, and a town whose considerable intellectual activity was centred upon its Academy of Science, Literature and Arts.

Soufflot was employed by the Consulat for the most important public buildings of the city from soon after his arrival until long after he had taken up residence in Paris, and in 1773 he was honoured with the title of Contrôleur-Général des Bâtiments. He also worked for many private patrons, although domestic architecture was never a real strength of his, and the houses attributed to him in Lyon, like his later private commissions in Paris, are disappointing. Nevertheless Soufflot clearly found no difficulty in impressing important patrons, and at Lyon the most considerable of these was the archbishop, Cardinal de Tencin, who had himself been in Rome as ambassador shortly after Soufflot's departure. Charles Natoire, on his way to Rome to take over the directorship of the Academy in 1751, hints at Soufflot's friendship with Tencin:

The little visit which I made in Lyon was very agreeable . . . M. Soufflot, whom I know not how to praise enough, took every possible care to provide me with everything agreeable; he procured me the honour of saluting a Cardinal, an Eminence, the Cardinal Tancent [*sic*], who kindly invited me to see his country house [Oullins], where I had the privilege of dining in very good company.

During his early years in Lyon Soufflot made known his architectural ideas in a series of papers read to the Academy, modest in tone and showing some very unexpected architectural preoccupations. Speaking of proportions in September 1739 he referred in simplified terms to the quarrel of the Ancients and the Moderns, explaining that 'for myself I have always deferred to the opinions of M. Blondel more than to those of M. Perrault'. After a subdued attack on modern architecture, Soufflot went on to discuss churches he had measured in Rome and to defend, like Blondel before him, variations in proportions with reference to the rules that nature had imposed on architecture: 'We see everyday with admiration plants and fruits and trees very different in their proportions. The same variety is found in animals and finally in men and women.' From the churches he knew in Rome Soufflot concluded that 'there are for churches proportions that are founded less on custom than on something natural and that as there are in music perfect relations to which we cannot refuse our appreciation there are also in architecture certain proportions which necessarily provoke pleasure'.

In 1741 Soufflot's theme was the surprising one of Gothic architecture, an interest apparently springing from his obsession with churches. The subject is apologetically and rather tentatively advanced, muted in deference to the prejudices of his audience or perhaps not entirely clear in his own mind. Soufflot discussed the structure and proportions of Gothic churches in relation to Renaissance practice; while critical of their decoration he praised the lightness of their interiors, which he compared with antique basilicas. 'Vitruvius in his basilica at Fano had no frieze or cornice . . . the Goths without wishing to follow them [the ancients] in that, believed like them that projections, interrupting the sight lines, encumbered the plan of their churches.' The Gothic churches that Soufflot mentions are St-Jean and St-Nizier in Lyon, St-Maxence at Vienne, and the cathedrals of Paris and Milan.

Soufflot was not to be asked for a church design while he was at Lyon, but his public buildings there are remarkable for their time, the first being an extension for the Hôtel-Dieu *(26, 27)*, designed in 1740 and begun in January of the following year, and the second the Loge-au-Change (the Exchange), begun in 1748. No drawings for these buildings have been discovered, and little more is known of their origins than of Soufflot's other works at Lyon, but taken at their face value the buildings show a disturbing talent at work, both in their general character and in their decoration.

At the Hôtel-Dieu Soufflot added a new wing to the river front, a scheme made possible after the Consulat had charged the architect Delamonce to construct this part of the quay of the Rhône, and he thereby concealed the miscellaneous earlier buildings of the hospital on the river bank beyond. Open by the terms of its charter to the sick of all countries, the old hospital had become shamefully inadequate by the relatively exacting standards of the mid-

26 The Hôtel-Dieu, Lyon, river wing by Soufflot, begun 1741.
The major work of Soufflot's first Lyon period

27 The Hôtel-Dieu, Lyon, detail of main frontispiece.
The statues represent King Childebert and Queen
Ultrogotte, the sixth-century founders of the hospital

28 The Hôtel de Ville, Lyon, detail of main façade. The major secular building of the later seventeenth century in Lyon and a source of inspiration for Soufflot's decorative ornament

eighteenth century. It was estimated that after Soufflot's work there had been completed the patients were reduced to being two to a bed from their former total of four. They also had four new wards and a chapel that occupied the central pavilion of Soufflot's extension.

In appearance Soufflot's wing has little of the agitated and almost domestic sophistication of Boffrand's later Paris orphanage (20). Horizontal in emphasis and a little flat in appearance, it unfolds along the west bank of the Rhône, a façade punctuated by three pavilions and a central square dome. The basis of the design goes back to the palace of the Louvre, more especially to the south front and its central dome, as built by Louis Le Vau for the young Louis XIV. It is not, however, a direct copy; a more spacious, eighteenth-century, sense of interval marks the placing of the windows, and the ground floor is a rusticated pedestal pierced by round-headed openings originally allocated to shops. In decoration the building is not greatly indebted to any single prototype, for Soufflot invented a wide-ranging repertory of forms as an alternative to the elaboration he had grown to despise, a repertory that is as much Italian as French and which goes back even beyond the seventeenth century.

Instead of the elaborate French Ionic order that was everywhere to be found in contemporary architecture (21), where small garlands hung vertically from the ears of the capital, Soufflot has an unusual order which is distinguished only by a raised moulding well below the level of the volutes (27). Occasionally used in Italy, this type of capital is much more severe than its French counterpart and moderates the vertical stress of the column. The upper windows of Soufflot's façade are oval and garlanded, and derive, except for the lions' heads, from the Louvre. There follow, in descending order, the uncommon Greek key motif that Soufflot would have seen in Italy, then broad and flattened swags of drapery over the main floor windows that recall the rather clumsy decoration of French architecture in the later sixteenth century. For the central window of the main pavilion Soufflot chose a lion's head with heavy ropes of leaves attached, a design that was later to become popular as a well-rope (corde-à-puits). Some of these decorations recall parts of the old Hôtel de Ville of Lyon, a building of the later seventeenth century that is almost Gothic in its eccentric verticality, but one that represented neverthe-less something of the grandeur of the reign of Louis XIV in the provincial setting of Lyon (28).

Soufflot's decoration gives his hospital a certain historical authority, and its 'antiquity' was finally emphasized in the choice and placing of the sculpture, to which the architect gave the same careful consideration as to the decoration as a whole. Precedence is given not to such general allegories as Charity or Mercy, but to the sixth-century founders of the Hôtel-Dieu, King Childebert and Queen Ultrogotte, who stand guard over the main entrance – possibly the earliest of the long series of medieval heroes to be glorified in the art of the later eighteenth century.

In 1748 work on the Hôtel-Dieu came to a halt when funds ran temporarily short, and the building with all its decoration was not completed for many years. Engravings suggest that Soufflot made relatively few alterations during the course of its construction. He changed some details of the decoration and enlarged the central dome, which was then apparently diminished to its present squat proportions by his successors. While supervising the hospital and designing the Loge-au-Change Soufflot kept in touch with Paris, and he was one of the many architects who submitted plans for a public square there in honour of the king (1748). The competition led finally to the construction of the present Place de la Concorde, designed by Gabriel who used a site given by the king at the end of the Tuileries gardens. Soufflot's ambitious idea (recorded in Pl. 41) was to join the two main islands in the Seine together to form a public square flanked by pairs of matching buildings. He had already shown his drawings for the Hôtel-Dieu to the Academy in 1747; Blondel subsequently prepared an engraving of the main façade of the hospital and two years later Soufflot was chosen to fill a vacant place at the Academy.

The late 1740s were the years when Mme de Pompadour was establishing her ascendancy at court, following her presentation in 1745, and it was to the mistress of the king, who 'loved the arts, and gave all the orders', according to one courtier, that Soufflot owed the sudden change in his fortunes. Anxious to promote the interests of her family, Mme de Pompadour destined her young brother, Abel Poisson (not yet Marquis de Marigny), to succeed to the post of Surintendant des Bâtiments, which was meanwhile held by an older relation of hers, Charles-François Le Normand de Tournehem. It was a position that demanded no political ambition and one that had already been occupied by courtiers of the greatest distinction, like the Duc d'Antin, who was one of the bastards of Louis XIV. Perhaps most important of all, it brought its occupant into frequent contact with the king, who found in architecture a means of alleviating the tedium of his existence.

Marigny, then aged eighteen, was to be sent on a journey to Italy to complete his education in anticipation of his eventual promotion and it was decided that Soufflot (fluent in Italian) should accompany him as instructor in architecture, together with the engraver Charles-Nicolas Cochin and the Abbé Le Blanc, a writer and protégé of Mme de Pompadour. Born in 1706, Le Blanc was the oldest of the travellers and one of the few Frenchmen who had visited England, of which he published an unflattering account, the *Lettres d'un françois*, in 1745. Cochin, at thirty-four, was already well known as a draughtsman and engraver; Marigny later appointed him Secretary of the Académie Royale de Peinture et de Sculpture, and he became one of the most vociferous opponents of the Rococo style. The tour of 1750 was to be modelled on the journeys to which English gentlemen were customarily exposed in their youth, but organized with all the formality – befitting Marigny's rank – that the French observed in social matters.

Soufflot had come to the notice of the court allegedly through Blondel's engraving of the Hôtel-Dieu, and a special importance attached to his presence since one aim of the journey – to study the design of Italian theatres – was primarily architectural. Italy still dominated Europe in music and opera, and possessed a long tradition, going back to Palladio, of expertise in the construction of theatres, of which the most recent and most celebrated was the court theatre of Turin. Versailles had no permanent theatre, while in Paris the Comédie-Française occupied a small and inconvenient building of the late seventeenth century *(123)*, and the Opéra was lodged at the Palais-Royal. By 1749 Gabriel had for some time been considering the construction of an opera for the palace of Versailles.

Marigny and his three companions travelled south through Lyon to Italy, where they stopped first at Turin. Cochin kept and later published a journal of the tour, an account of the works of art which they saw that is too earnest to accommodate any information about the travellers themselves. In architecture the taste of the party extended to all that was relatively pure in design, the works of antiquity, of Palladio, even of Juvarra, while confidently deprecating the more imaginative architects of the seventeenth century, Guarini and especially Borromini. Rome was the ultimate goal of the travellers and

they passed through Parma, Modena and Florence on their way there. In Rome Soufflot renewed his relations with the Academy and was admitted as a member of the Accademia di San Luca on presenting a design for a triumphal arch.

Many changes had occurred at the Academy in Rome since Soufflot had last been there in 1739. Especially amongst the architectural students a new spirit of experiment, based more closely upon the example of antiquity, had begun to prevail. Younger architects had respected no more than Soufflot himself the values of their immediate predecessors, and Soufflot would soon join

29 The Temple of Neptune, Paestum, engraving by Dumont, 1764. Based on sketches made by Soufflot in 1750, Dumont's inaccurate engravings were the first illustrations of the Greek temples at Paestum to be published

30 'Lycurgus wounded', by Charles-Nicolas Cochin, 1750 (Musée du Louvre, Paris, Cabinet des Dessins). In this scene of Spartan history Cochin introduced baseless Tuscan and Doric columns in the background

31 Section of Mount Vesuvius, engraving by Dumont, 1764. A measured section of the volcano, based on sketches made by Soufflot and Dumont on 9 June 1750

them in transforming the character of architecture as it was practised in Paris, providing in the church of Ste-Geneviève a focus for the reforms they sought.

Soufflot formed a friendship with one of the older students, Gabriel-Pierre-Martin Dumont *(64)*, who had remained in Rome after the term of his pension at the Academy had expired, and together with Cochin they travelled south from Rome to visit Naples and the Greek temples at Paestum, which had been discovered in the earlier years of the century. The temples were published for the first time in 1764 by Dumont from sketches that Soufflot made there *(29)*, but the plates are neither accurate nor expressive of the primitive nature of the temples, and Dumont's book was superseded in the following year by an English publication devoted to Paestum, by Thomas Major. Cochin too showed an immediate interest in the style of the temples, and he included primitive Greek and Roman columns in the background of a drawing of 1750 showing 'Lycurgus wounded' *(30)*.

Soufflot and Dumont must also have seen the excavations that were then beginning at Herculaneum, of which Cochin published an account in 1754 after his return to Paris. They also stopped to measure Mount Vesuvius and probably regarded the temples of Paestum as natural phenomena not far removed in character from the mountain itself *(31)*. The measured drawings of Vesuvius that Dumont published in his book on Paestum seem more than a little bizarre, but the interest of the two architects in the volcano is a symptom of that spirit of detached enquiry which was to lead to the more emotive interpretations that Paestum and Vesuvius were later to inspire in both architecture and painting.

Soufflot fell ill on his return to Rome – he was always apparently troubled by his stomach – and he travelled to Viterbo to take the waters. Marigny meanwhile returned to Paris, passing by way of the Veneto and Venice itself, and Soufflot returned temporarily to Lyon. With the

sudden death of Le Normand in 1751 Marigny was appointed his successor, and in the following year Marigny provided Soufflot with a house in Paris, which he shared with Cochin. Late in 1754 Soufflot became architect of the new church of Ste-Geneviève and took up permanent residence in the capital. But before his move to Paris Soufflot had become a well-known figure and, probably through Cochin, who was later to engrave one of the frontispieces of the *Encyclopédie*, his reputation had already impressed Baron Grimm, a spokesman for the views of the 'philosophes'. He is one of the very few architects mentioned in the *Correspondance littéraire*, making an impressive first appearance in its pages in 1753: 'we should mention that the only architect famous today in France, by his genius and his taste, is M. Soufflot, a citizen of Lyon'.

The main work of Soufflot's last years in Lyon was the theatre *(32)*, the first of the great theatres of late eighteenth-century France, and a building of which Soufflot himself always remained particularly fond, calling it 'a child that is dear to me'. Begun in 1754 on a restricted site that formed the garden behind the Hôtel de Ville and designed for as many as 2,000 spectators, the theatre survived for only seventy years before being entirely rebuilt. Engravings and drawings suggest that Soufflot made few innovations in the plan, but he introduced improvements in heating, lighting and fire precaution. Unlike a court theatre his was also a free-standing building equipped with cafés and a foyer for the convenience of a public audience. Soufflot followed the Turin theatre in choosing an elliptical shape for the auditorium (considered by many to be the best for audibility), which was articulated in the customary way through the presence of tiers of boxes. The principal boxes which would seat the governor and the consuls were presumably those set into the proscenium arch, distracting attention – as was normal – from the stage itself, and most of the space in the stalls was given over to standing-room, as was also customary in France. Soufflot was proud of the vaulting of the theatre (presumably the vaults that supported the high roof over the stage), but he was criticized for the poor acoustics of the building.

If the plan of Soufflot's theatre seemed to offer little that was new, except in the provision of its public rooms, the restrained elegance of the external decoration in a building that formed a free-standing block, and the relative austerity of the interior, were both far from usual in a type of building traditionally festive in appearance. On the main façade most of the windows were plain and actually recessed, while the decoration was confined to the frames of the three larger windows, to the reliefs between the storeys, and to the statues of Apollo and *amorini* on the balustrade. Here at least Soufflot had contrived a visual *rapprochement* to the reforms that were then beginning to affect the drama in France, as described by Marmontel: 'Thus, from that time, all the actors were obliged to abandon their fringed gloves, their voluminous wigs, their feather hats, and all the fantastic paraphernalia that had so long shocked the sight of all men of taste.'

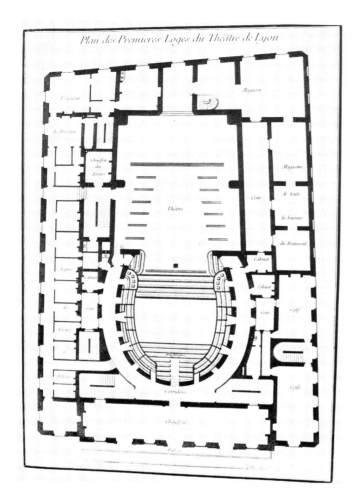

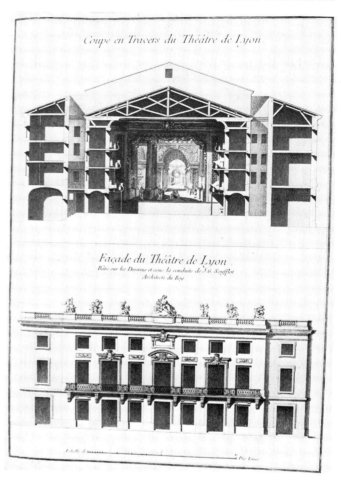

32 The Grand-Théâtre, Lyon, plan, elevation and sections (engravings from Dumont). The major work of Soufflot's second Lyon period, the theatre (begun in 1754) matches the greater 'simplicity' and 'naturalism' that had started to affect acting and the presentation of plays and operas

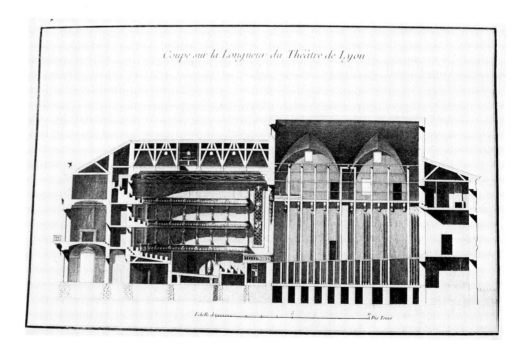

On his arrival in Paris in 1754 Soufflot's first appointment was as Contrôleur of the royal Château of Marly, one of about eighteen such posts in the Bâtiments du Roi, but soon the controllership of Paris, the most active post after that of Premier Architecte, fell vacant, and Soufflot was promoted by Marigny to this more senior position. As Contrôleur of Paris Soufflot occupied a house near the Tuileries palace and, working in conjunction with Gabriel and with the support of three subordinate Inspecteurs, he took charge of all the royal buildings in the capital, an onerous administrative duty that he fulfilled with characteristic patience. In 1755 Soufflot was elected a member of the first class of the Academy and in the next year he was knighted, receiving the cordon noir of the Order of St-Michel, a low rank of the order that was open to artists and men of letters.

Soufflot made his way in Parisian society, and, praised by Grimm, he inevitably found a warm welcome at the Salon of Mme Geoffrin, where he became a regular visitor at the Monday luncheons which she provided for her artist friends. Herself an habituée of the Salon of Mme de Tencin, the sister of the archbishop, Mme Geoffrin had known Mme de Pompadour long before her own Salon became famous, following the death of M. Geoffrin and Mme de Tencin in 1750. It was she, according to one contemporary, who had formed the ideas of Marigny, who 'having all the arts at his command, surrounded by artists, could have perpetuated that bad style which was tiresome to real connoisseurs. Mme Geoffrin made all the advances to introduce him to her society. It is there that he acquired a sound judgment and that, despite himself, he purified his taste.' The excellence of Mme Geoffrin's taste was a byword during her lifetime, as was the soundness of her judgment and the bourgeois sobriety of her appearance, and Marigny would have found in her society support for the counsel that Soufflot had imparted to him in the judgment of architecture.

Soufflot's social life in Paris is referred to by Diderot, who flippantly mentions his indigestion, and by Marmontel, who described him more sympathetically as he appeared at Mme Geoffrin's: 'a man of sense, very circumspect in his conduct, a skilful and learned architect; but his ideas were all commensurate by the rule and the compass'. The other guests at these Monday gatherings listed by Marmontel included the painters Boucher and Vernet, who was a close friend of Soufflot, the pastellist La Tour, and Jean-Baptiste Lemoyne, the sculptor.

The artists at Mme Geoffrin's were dominated by the Comte de Caylus, a distinguished aristocrat, who had in his youth visited the Middle East and studied the ruins of Ephesus; he was famous for his collection of classical and pre-classical antiquities, of which he published a seven-volume catalogue (1752–56). Though Caylus had a reputation as a protector of artists, he was deeply hated by the 'philosophes', who gathered at Mme Geoffrin's on Wednesdays, and Marmontel suggests in an evidently biased portrait that Caylus, whose benefactions were motivated largely by self-interest, had unjustly claimed for himself the title of restorer of good taste in architecture:

He insinuated himself into the company of men of information, and persuaded them to write memorials on the toys he had bought at his brokers; . . . and with this charlatanism of erudition, he crept into the academies, without knowing either Greek or Latin. He had so often said, he had so often published, by those whom he paid to praise him, that in architecture he was the restorer 'of the simple style, of simple beauty, of beautiful simplicity', that the ignorant believed it.

Soufflot was one of the artists on whom Caylus conferred the apparently doubtful honour of his interest, and it may have been partly through his influence that the architect was chosen as Marigny's travelling companion. In 1757 the Abbé Barthélemy, stopping at Lyon on his way to join the embassy of the Duc de Choiseul in Rome, reported to Caylus:

We have been very pleased with everything that M. Soufflot has done in Lyon: apart from the larger buildings which mark a man who is consummate in his art, we have seen the evidence of his spirit in the smallest objects. For example, on the altar of the chapel of the archbishop's palace, is a bas-relief that represents the angel delivering Saint Peter; a small window has been arranged at the side from which the angel is invested with a shadow that seems to belong to him, and that he communicates to Saint Peter and the guard.

However enlightened was the taste of the Comte de Caylus or Mme Geoffrin, or of the many other theorists and patrons who wished to see a new kind of architecture, the claims they made for themselves and for each other as pioneers of the new style cannot be taken very seriously since they lacked the ability to put their ideas into practice. Soufflot on the other hand could fashion his own ideas and those of his circle into acceptable and indeed beautiful works of art, and his early years in Paris, before the acceleration of the Seven Years' War halted most public building, were amongst the most productive of his career. He was brought in in an advisory capacity to assist with plans for the restoration of Rennes Cathedral, and for the royal squares at Reims and at Bordeaux. His elegant reconstruction of the sacristy and treasury of Notre-Dame dates from these years, as does the beginning of his work under the supervision of Gabriel on the completion of the Louvre, which had been left unfinished in the seventeenth century. And in addition to these tasks there was the start of work on the crowning achievement of Soufflot's career, the church of Ste-Geneviève.

It had been decided in November 1754 to rebuild the medieval church of the patron saint of Paris, creating a monument that would rival the great cathedrals of St Paul's in London and St Peter's in Rome. The church and the attached monastery, forming the headquarters of the Augustinian order in France, had been founded according to popular belief by Clovis, the first Christian King of France; the shrine of St Geneviève (in the crypt) and the tomb of Descartes formed the principal attractions of the old church. The idea of creating a new monument went back to the reign of Louis XIV, when Perrault had made proposals for the reconstruction of the church on the lines of an antique basilica (33). The project was revived by Louis XV, in 1744, in thanksgiving for his recovery from a serious illness. On that famous occasion fears for the king's life were

33 The church of Ste-Geneviève, Paris, project for reconstruction by Claude Perrault, 1697. Drawing by Sébastien Leclerc (Bibliothèque Ste-Geneviève, Paris). Columns and lintels appear in Perrault's design in conjunction with an otherwise conventional plan

entertained, and he had publicly adjured his sinful life and dismissed his current mistress, Mme de Châteauroux.

It cannot have aroused happy memories for the king, or indeed for Mme de Pompadour, but the foundation of a new ecclesiastical monument must have seemed wise as a political move some ten years later, when criticism of the Church was becoming intensified; and Marigny, conscious of the talents and interests of Soufflot, his protégé, would no doubt also have urged the building of a monument that would glorify the memory of his own administration. In January 1755 Soufflot, rather than Gabriel, was chosen as the architect of the new building. Two years later his project for the church was given official approval and made known to the public in a series of engravings, and very different it must immediately have seemed from any church that had been constructed before (34).

Churches in Paris had been tied throughout the seventeenth and eighteenth centuries to a relatively dull and inflexible formula; with a few notable exceptions, they have nothing like the same lively appeal as contemporary town houses and châteaux, and they are consequently less well known. The most important church under construction before Ste-Geneviève was St-Roch, in the rue St-Honoré, which had been begun in the seventeenth century but was not given its façade until 1736 (35). Its general type is that deriving from the main

Jesuit church in Rome, the Gesù, with a nave lined with side chapels and articulated with masonry piers relieved by pilasters. The nave is supported by heavy flying buttresses left visible from the street (36), and the façade has a double order of small columns applied to the surface of the wall. Only in its decoration, which was never completed, and in its sense of interval, could the real date of the façade easily be guessed.

Soufflot's design for Ste-Geneviève marks a decisive break with the tradition represented by St-Roch – an expulsion of the Jesuits in visual metaphor that prefigures by some years the political banishment of the order from France. His study of Roman churches is here largely superseded by a growing appreciation of the architectural achievements of antiquity and the Middle Ages, as well as by a new confidence in his ability as an engineer, and all are happily united with the complexity and visual sophistication of the French classical tradition as it had developed in the middle years of the eighteenth century.

Just how high Soufflot had set his standards is shown in the plan of the church. The form of a Greek cross with its four equal arms is to be associated not with any obvious French precedent, but with such monuments of the history of architecture as the designs of Bramante and Michelangelo for St Peter's, and with Wren's Great Model for St Paul's. And the setting itself is commensurate with these prototypes; in the site plan published in 1757 (34) the church faces a new road that stretches to the gardens of the Luxembourg Palace and opens into a rectangular square before the portico. The old church of Ste-Geneviève lies behind the new building, flanked to the north by the larger church of St-Etienne-du-Mont.

Though Soufflot's church may suggest comparisons with the great cathedrals of Rome and London, it differs from them fundamentally as a design based largely upon the use of free-standing columns and straight lintels in preference to pilasters and piers. The portico, in the first place, is composed of twenty-four columns, taller than the columns of the Roman Pantheon and largely free-standing, which form a temple front far more extensive than any that had distinguished a Christian basilica in the past. The plan of the portico is, however, French rather than antique in its complexity, with two pairs of columns extracted from the centre and added for emphasis at the sides (a new road was to be pierced facing the south side of the portico). The complexity of the plan gives the portico a degree of independence, as a centralized design of its own with steps on all sides, that hints at the autonomy of a complete classical temple, and in scale it exceeds in height as well as in breadth the nave of the church which it was designed to serve, rising to a giant pediment destined by Soufflot for a relief showing the Elevation of the Host.

A smaller order of columns reigns inside the church, columns set on low bases and supporting not arches but a straight entablature. This aspect of the design has been singled out for particular comment, since in these respects the interior constitutes a decisive break with the Renaissance tradition and its reliance upon the wall, the pilaster and the arcade. Though Perrault had proposed a

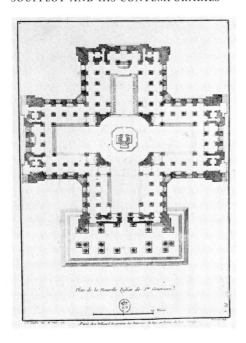

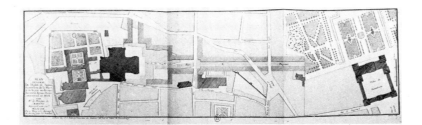

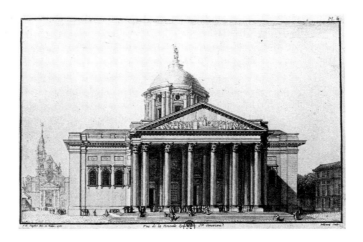

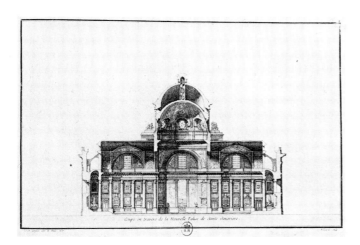

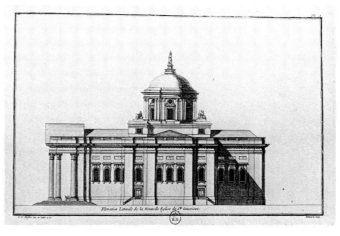

34 The church of Ste-Geneviève, Paris, Soufflot's project of 1757, plan, site plan, perspective view, cross-section and side elevation (engravings by Bellicard). The church, a Greek cross in plan, was to have a rectangular square in front and a road extending to the gardens of the Palais du Luxembourg

36 St-Roch, detail of south transept. The system of flying buttresses, supporting the nave and transepts, is left untidily apparent

35 The church of St-Roch, Paris, the façade and the nave. The major Parisian church under construction in the earlier eighteenth century; its plan had been designed by Lemercier in the seventeenth century, while the façade was carried out (minus its ornamentation) by 1736

similar idea in his project for Ste-Geneviève many years earlier, and the chapel of Versailles, together with the Louvre colonnade, had been designed on the same principle but with a much greater sense of spaciousness, not since the dawn of the Renaissance (in the church designs of Brunelleschi) had such a columned interior been seen in a metropolitan setting.

The columns of the interior are not only an essential part of the classical repertoire, used for the articulation of temples, but they also give an effect of spaciousness like that of a Gothic cathedral. Springing from low bases to support the vaults of the church, they offer, as Soufflot had recommended in his speech to the Lyon Academy, the least possible resistance to the lines of sight that cross and recross the interior. And again, as in a Gothic church, the outer walls are closely packed with windows, which in the absence of side chapels shed their light directly into the interior. The columns are arranged in double lines along the sides of the four arms of the cross, though with two of their number missing from each inner row, an arrangement recalling the plan of the portico and giving each arm of the cross a suggestion of the same autonomy.

In pursuit of his dream of spaciousness Soufflot reduced to the very minimum the size of the piers which were to support the dome. They are free-standing as in Gothic churches, allowing uninterrupted vistas along the sides of the four arms of the cross, and each consists of a masonry core articulated with three engaged columns. The columns are assisted in their work of supporting the vaults, and ultimately the dome, by a system of flying buttresses concealed behind the outer wall of the building. The use of flying buttresses is an aspect of Gothicism that had never died out in France – such buttresses are still plainly visible on the exterior of St-Roch *(36)* – but what Soufflot contrived at Ste-Geneviève, as had Wren before him at St

Paul's, was the provision of a screening wall behind which buttresses could proliferate without apparent untidiness.

Just as Soufflot avoided pilasters inside the church, so too he rejected them for the exterior. He stopped short of making the walls entirely plain, but he employed only narrow projections to strengthen the corners of the block, where the cornice, carried round from the portico, breaks forward twice to define each corner of the cross. The dome is small in proportion to the church below, as Soufflot's critics noted, but this must have seemed inevitable at the start since the piers which carry its weight are set forward from the walls of the church. Since the plan itself is dispersed in emphasis, the portico and each arm of the cross having its own implied centre, a small and relatively unemphatic dome may have seemed more suited to the design than a cupola of seventeenth-century proportions, uniting the different elements below by its dominating size. And in its design too the dome has an intricacy that echoes the complexity of the church plan, though it fails to match the church below in directly recalling the dome designs of antiquity.

The relative scarcity of antique domes, compared with the abundance of temples and basilicas, longitudinal and relatively unaccented in design, was a source of difficulty and also of challenge to architects throughout the later eighteenth century. The most famous of classical domes was that of the Roman Pantheon, a single shell coffered on the interior and rising externally in a shallow curve from a rim of steps to a central open oculus. As a feat of engineering it may have daunted Renaissance architects, but it was not a shape that had seemed generally useful for the propagation of the Christian message. The dome of St Peter's – constructed as a double shell with a strong vertical stress, strengthened and emphasized by a series of ribs – had become a more venerable model and one more easily copied by architects of the seventeenth century. In France, where the technical virtuosity of medieval architecture remained a living tradition, in roofing no less than in masonry, the pattern established by St Peter's had been subjected to various subtle variations which Soufflot had taken to heart.

In the first design for Ste-Geneviève *(34)* the dome is relatively conventional, to be constructed as a double shell over a columned drum, and in this familiar setting the garlanded oval windows are a conspicuous concession to the elegance of contemporary taste. The ovals of the drum cast light between the two shells of the dome, while the rectangular windows below, themselves transformed into ovals in the interior, light the crossing of the church. In the articulation of the drum Soufflot follows an unusual plan, with pairs of projecting columns on the four diagonal axes, which he has taken from the domed church of the Invalides *(13)*. Based upon the omission of pairs of columns on the central axes of the plan, the dome plan expresses something of the character of the church below and its four columned arms. But whereas the dome of the Invalides has a ribbed cupola, as was normal practice in association with a columned drum, Soufflot's dome is a smooth hemisphere of a more regular, and in that sense classical, shape. Such cupolas were not unknown in France, but they were usually, as in the church of the Visitation *(14)*, reserved for smaller churches where an accented drum was not needed.

The name 'Temple de Ste-Geneviève', by which Soufflot's church quickly became known, is above all justified by the architect's daring substitution of a huge statue of the saint for the lantern that would normally crown such a dome as his. As a goddess might preside in effigy within a classical temple, so here the patron saint of Paris, bearing her cross, stands watch over the shrine that has been designed for her. Such discriminating use of sculpture in relation to architecture, already apparent in the design of the Lyon hospital *(27)*, was to become one of the hallmarks of late eighteenth-century design, and is closely related to the manipulation of structure itself for its expressive potentialities, 'architecture parlante', as it later came to be known.

Symbolic ideas, however, had never been neglected by architects of the past. *Convenance*, the suitability of a building to its rank and function, was a commonplace of architectural theory (and is particularly stressed in the criticism of Diderot), but if all architects had instinctively distinguished a castle from a palace or a church, the nuances of these distinctions and the cross-fertilization of patterns evolved for different functions provided openings for the artist of genius. In the use of sculpture for architectural decoration it was Bernini who had been the most radically inventive, and in a drawing for the dome of S. Andrea al Quirinale in Rome he too had suggested substituting an image, in this case the cross of St Andrew, for the lantern.

The ecclesiastical programme of Soufflot's church, culminating in the statue of St Geneviève, began with the pediment of the portico, and embraced groups of the four Fathers of the Church, including St Augustine, the patron of the adjacent monastery, at the base of the dome. Inside the church the four arms of the cross were to be decorated with respective reference to the Old Testament, and the Greek, Roman and Gallican Churches. The cupola was to show the apotheosis of St Geneviève and the pendentives the four Evangelists. A group of three altars occupied the centre of the crossing, while the high altar at the east end was to be set before a brightly illuminated glory of painted rays and clouds. This was a devotional aid, also originating with Bernini, and already manipulated by Soufflot in the chapel of the archiepiscopal palace at Lyon, that persisted in France with diminished intensity right up to the time of the Revolution. Elsewhere in the church the walls are made over to carefully defined rectilinear wall-memorials.

The church of Ste-Geneviève was to undergo many alterations before its final completion in the early years of the nineteenth century, and its long building history mirrors the rapid changes in taste in the later eighteenth century. Soufflot's first design may not be perfectly consistent in character – the architect himself was to make many modifications – but it remains a moving and succinct expression of the artistic and intellectual aspirations of the mid-century, retaining as a work of art a kind of visual integrity that was to become increasingly rare as the years passed. The integrity of Soufflot's design resides above all in the sense of order and spaciousness he was determined to achieve, deriving from the effects that he admired in classical architecture. 'The principal aim of M. Soufflot in building his church', his successor, the architect Brébion, wrote, 'was to reunite in one of the most beautiful forms, the lightness of the construction of Gothic buildings with the purity and magnificence of Greek architecture.'

The sense of space is the element in the design of Ste-Geneviève that marks Soufflot as an artist of the same generation as Boucher and Pigalle, rivalling in his use of columns the effects that these artists achieved in paint and stone, while at the same time paying due honour to the architecture of antiquity. In isolating the piers supporting the dome in order to accentuate the lightness of the interior, Soufflot was to bring about a reassessment of the scope of engineering that affected future architectural development, but it was not his intention to facilitate the mere imitation of Gothic or indeed classical forms.

Similarly Soufflot cannot have intended to undermine the practice of religion in considering how best to fashion his church, however much he was influenced by the scepticism of the 'philosophes' with whom he associated. Yet because he had broadened the sources of ecclesiastical architecture and given so important a place to the antique temple in his designs for Ste-Geneviève it was obviously that much easier to deconsecrate his masterpiece when the Revolution abolished traditional religion. If the church can be assigned a role in the history of architecture equivalent to that of the *Encyclopédie* it is essentially for the new architectural questions it raised, and for the standard of excellence it set. It was not a project on paper that could easily be forgotten but a building of monumental proportions actually under construction from the late 1750s until just after the outbreak of the Revolution.

2 Official taste of the mid-century: Blondel and Gabriel; Marigny and Soufflot

THOUGH GRIMM HAD WRITTEN of Soufflot in 1753 as the 'only architect famous today in France', it was too late by that time to allude to his work in the *Encyclopédie*, of which the first volume, covering architecture, had appeared two years earlier. The main articles dealing with architecture were entrusted to Jacques-François Blondel *(37)*. Blondel was the chief spokesman for a return to the great traditions of seventeenth-century French architecture, the nourishment that had sustained the early work of Soufflot, and through the influence of Blondel these traditions were to shape the thought of many of Soufflot's younger contemporaries. Though Blondel could write in the *Encyclopédie* that 'It is only in the last two centuries that the architects of France and Italy have applied themselves to rediscover the early simplicity, the beauty and the proportions of ancient architecture', there was little he could illustrate of recent architecture that justified the tenor of this statement. He included in the illustrations designs of his own, many by his friend François Franque (who later wrote an obituary of Blondel), and others by Boffrand and Contant d'Ivry.

Blondel was some eight years Soufflot's senior, being born in 1705; he died in 1774 and thus lived to see some of the more extreme works of his former students. He published his first work in 1738, a book dealing with the country house and its planning (*De la distribution des maisons de plaisance*), and there followed in 1752–56 the publication of his monumental four-volume encyclopaedia of French building, the *Architecture françoise*. Meanwhile in 1743, in the face of initial hostility from the Academy, he had opened the first independent school of architecture in Paris. This was an establishment in the rue de la Harpe that young architects preferred to the Academy with its more conservative teaching, and which numbered among its graduates not only French students but also foreigners, like William Chambers, who spread the ideas of Blondel in their native countries. The scope of Blondel's courses is outlined in a prospectus that he published in 1747, the *Discours sur la manière d'étudier l'architecture*. What had

37 Portrait of Jacques-François Blondel (1705–74), by an unknown French artist (Musée Carnavalet, Paris). Influential as a teacher of architecture, Blondel was also the main architectural contributor to the *Encyclopédie*

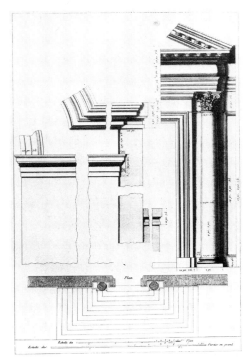

38 The main doorway of the church of the Visitation, Paris *(14)*, engraving from Blondel, 1771–77. Blondel stressed the achievements of seventeenth-century French architecture in his teaching and publications

39 The Château of Maisons, 1642–46, the main staircase. One of the most famous creations of François Mansart, whom Blondel regarded as 'the god of architecture'

not been done before, he pointed out, was to teach the young architect all the skills he needed, to mould his ideas into a coherent pattern: 'The consequence is that a young man who takes up architecture, is often ignorant of the proportions of the human body, Perspective, Mathematics, Ornament and almost always design in general.'

Blondel's method was later adopted by the Academy when in 1762 he was himself appointed to be its professor, the post that his famous namesake François Blondel had occupied in the late seventeenth century. The range and method of his teaching can be appreciated in the twelve-volume *Cours d'architecture*, based on his lectures, which was completed by his assistant Pierre Patte in the 1770s. Blondel himself revised the first two sections, dealing with decoration and planning, while Patte composed most of the final part, which was concerned with construction.

The general rules that Blondel passed on to his students seem in the abstract as vague and unhelpful as most such academic recipes. There is 'taste united to rule', 'symmetry', 'simplicity', 'liveliness in planning and in silhouette', and *bienséance*, which implies (like *convenance*) the suitability of the building to its function or the rank of its occupants. All are general ideas which, with only a little common sense, could be grasped instinctively by the students, but which in no way defined the masterpieces studied by them or guaranteed the excellence of their own productions. The few buildings that Blondel himself constructed, mainly in the 1760s in eastern France, including the Place d'Armes at Metz, are well-mannered according to his own principles, but unremarkable for their date.

It is mainly in the wide scope of his method and in his devotion to the French classical tradition that Blondel must have been a source of inspiration to his students. He recalled appreciatively the work of their great seventeenth-century predecessors, especially François Mansart, whom he regarded as 'the god of architecture' *(38, 39)*, and twice a week in April and May he conducted sightseeing tours to visit his favourite buildings, which he also used to illustrate his lectures:

the Mansarts, the Debrosses, the Merciers, the Perraults and other architects appear successively upon the scene, and give in their works useful lessons to young architects, principally if they are accompanied by a man versed in the Art, and who serves, so to speak, as interpreter to these designs of a different time, and the different reasons for which buildings have been constructed, and the differences that are to be found in buildings of the same type.

But in passing on his knowledge and enthusiasm for his seventeenth-century heroes, Blondel was forced to acknowledge, like many of his contemporaries, an architectural style that he had helped in part to instigate, but of which he was too conservative to approve. His final book, a collection of dialogues which he entitled *L'Homme du monde éclairé par les arts*, shows both disillusion and grudging admiration for the most successful works of his former pupils.

Blondel's tastes are embodied to a large extent in the buildings of Ange-Jacques Gabriel, and just as Blondel is

40 Portrait of Ange-Jacques Gabriel
(1698–1782), marble bust by Jean-Baptiste
Lemoyne (Musée du Louvre, Paris). Gabriel
succeeded his father as Premier Architecte du
Roi in 1742

41 Plan of Paris, showing projects for the Place
Louis XV (engraving from Patte, 1765). As well
as the Place which was built (Gabriel's Place de
la Concorde), the plan shows many of the rival
projects submitted by other architects,
including Boffrand, Servandoni, Contant
d'Ivry, and Soufflot, who proposed joining the
two main islands in the Seine (A on plan)

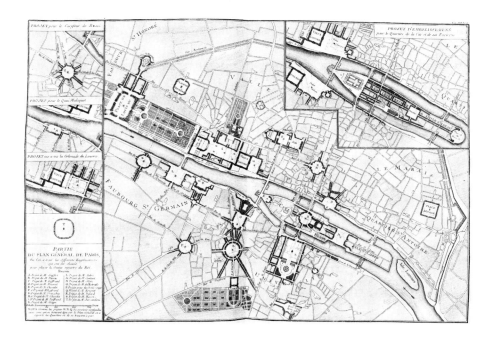

the last great theoretician of the Renaissance tradition so
Gabriel is its last great architect (40). His work, together
with the buildings of Fuga in Rome, may be likened to
other great movements of consolidation that prelude
widespread change. An older man than Blondel, Gabriel
was born in 1698, the son of Jacques Gabriel, whom he
succeeded as Premier Architecte du Roi in 1742. He held
this post until 1775, the year after the death of Louis XV,
while remaining head of the Academy until his own death
in 1782. The Gabriels were a dynasty of architects directly
related to the Mansarts, Ange-Jacques being the great-
great-great-nephew of François Mansart, whose small
house in the east of Paris he is known to have inherited,
although he never lived there.

Gabriel's work must be understood in the context of the
court which he served, implying a kind of flattery to the
Crown in the sense that the glorious reign of Louis XV's
great-grandfather, Louis XIV, is consciously perpetuated
in his designs. Architecture was one of the principal
distractions of the king and on occasion he acted in
collaboration with his own chief architect. The Prince de
Croÿ was given in 1754 plans of the octagonal pavilion in
the Trianon gardens that the king and Gabriel 'had made
together in the same style', and when de Croÿ had made a
sketch of his own garden king and architect worked on it
in collaboration, suggesting improvements. Unlike Soufflot, Gabriel was not affiliated with the Paris of the
'philosophes', and in his relations with Marigny and
Soufflot there was inevitably an undercurrent of tension
that occasionally erupted. Gabriel's commitment to the

court of Louis XV was later to bring its share of criticism,
and a passage in the gossipy Mémoires secrets speaks of him
at the time of his death with surprising acrimony: 'All his
pompous titles will not prevent him passing, justly
appreciated by posterity as a mediocre artist, of the most
ordinary kind.'

Gabriel was rarely inclined to experiment, even on the
few occasions when he was not working directly for his
royal master, and there is in his work a sense of
predictability that sets him apart both from younger
contemporaries, like Soufflot, and from the architects of
the past whom he admired, who were themselves amongst
the most radical innovators. Gabriel's style appears to have
developed little in the course of his long career, and
attempts to divide it into separate phases, sometimes with
reference to Palladio, are unpersuasive and even misleading. Taking into account the different functions of the
buildings that he designed, and their degrees of status,
there is a tendency towards a greater austerity, shared by
most other architects, a reliance less upon decoration and
more upon simplicity of design.

Gabriel's style was manifested publicly in Paris in the
1750s by two of his most important buildings, the Place
Louis XV (Place de la Concorde) and the Ecole Militaire,
works that slowly came into being during the early stages
of the construction of Ste-Geneviève. Following the
commission of Bouchardon's equestrian statue of the king
and the initial competition of 1748 for a suitable site for the
statue (41), when Soufflot submitted his design for a
square between the Ile-St-Louis and the Ile-Notre-Dame, a

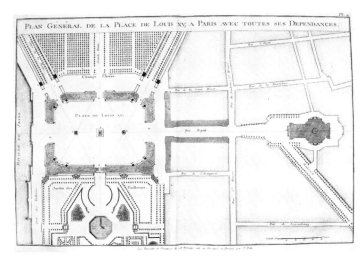

42 Plan of the Place de la Concorde and the church of the Madeleine (engraving from Patte, 1765). The plan shows the pedestal of Bouchardon's now destroyed equestrian statue of Louis XV in the centre of the Place, the moat, which is now filled in, and the first design for the Madeleine, by Contant d'Ivry *(58)*

43 The Place de la Concorde from the Tuileries Gardens. The Place was inaugurated in 1763, the designs for the buildings, which resemble the Louvre colonnade *(16)*, having been approved in 1755

site was finally donated by the king at the western extremity of the city as it then was, at the end of the gardens of the Tuileries, and a second competition was held. Soufflot was again a competitor but Gabriel was finally asked to take up the commission on the basis of the different ideas that had already been supplied. His final design was approved in December 1755, and the square inaugurated eight years later, though the work continued for some time thereafter.

Gabriel provided a rectangular setting for Bouchardon's statue, surrounded by moats and with pairs of small pavilions at each corner *(42–45)*. Its positive architectural interest was supplied by two colonnaded buildings on the northern edge of the site, the maximum effect thus being obtained with a minimum of building. The present rue de Rivoli was not then in existence and the main route from the Champs-Elysées into Paris led between the colonnaded buildings to the rue St-Honoré. And at a short distance to the north was the site where the old church of the Madeleine, grown too small for the greater population of the area, was to be rebuilt. Elsewhere the land was sold for speculative building, which helped to finance the construction of the square.

Gabriel's buildings refer consciously to the colonnade of the king's palace of the Louvre *(16)*, and his reaction was

more festive, more suited to the decoration of a public square, than the severer scrutiny which underlies Soufflot's design for Ste-Geneviève. Gabriel turned the formula of the colonnade into a much richer composition, one which is paradoxically closer in spirit to a lively drawing by Le Vau on which the colonnade was originally based. Gabriel's eleven-bay open colonnades are more classical than the east front of the Louvre in having single rather than double columns, but each is confined by large pavilions of the traditional French pattern (five bays in extent with four central columns supporting a pediment). The design has no central focus beyond that provided by the Madeleine, and in this it complements Bouchardon's statue which originally formed its centrepiece.

The elaboration of Gabriel's decoration, far from being the manifestation of a chosen style at this particular moment of his life, clearly refers to the public character of the design and the distance at which its effect had to be appreciated. Supporting the colonnades is a lively rusticated basement, densely patterned in the English Palladian manner, which increases in richness beneath the end pavilions where great consoles project to support the central balconies. Deeply channelled, and ending in guttae, the consoles recall those of Fuga's Palazzo Corsini, and they too derive ultimately from the style of Michelangelo. Above the basement the decoration is more restrained, with smaller consoles linked by drapery beneath the upper windows, and blank niches in the side bays of the pavilions below oval garlanded medallions that directly recall the Louvre. Compared with the decoration of Soufflot's Lyon hospital (27), the effect is less austere, more professional in the choice of ornaments, but perhaps in consequence less inventive.

The guard-houses of the square below seem almost weighted down with ornaments of a similar character (45). In proportion to their size, these sentry-boxes are the most densely articulated parts of the design, in keeping with their notionally defensive function, while the buildings that lead away from the colonnades, whose design was also supervised by Gabriel, form in contrast a gentle de-crescendo (166).

Gabriel's critics, while they applauded the revivalist spirit of the work, sensed many weaknesses in the elaboration of the project. The basement was considered too high and the scale of the component parts too small for the size of the buildings, and inevitably Gabriel suffered more than Soufflot from the doctrinaire criticism of the post-Revolutionary period, one writer going so far as to say that 'defects without number will always prevent this important production from being ranged amongst the masterpieces of architecture'. But the nature of Gabriel's achievement was not so easily forgotten by members of his own profession, and Ledoux himself, in one of the clearer passages of his book on architecture, noted the modest scale of the buildings and described the Place – perhaps not entirely without irony – as 'a sumptuous building where the inexhaustible spirit of French architecture shines forth'. Anti-royalist feeling had an easier target in Bouchardon's statue of the king, with the Four Virtues at

44 The Place de la Concorde, detail of doorways, In detail Gabriel's buildings are more elaborate than the Louvre colonnade

45 The Place de la Concorde, sentry-box. Originally guarding the passages across the moat, the sentry-boxes also serve as pedestals for statues

46 Versailles, the Petit Trianon, the front façade. The most celebrated of Gabriel's buildings, designed for Mme de Pompadour and completed in the year of her death (1764)

its base, which Pigalle had sculpted: 'Grotesque monument, infame piédestal/Les vertus sont à pied et le vice est à cheval.'

Gabriel's work for the court, on the various châteaux and hunting-lodges of the king, was, like his Parisian building, spread over many years. Versailles, Choisy, Fontainebleau and Compiègne were the main centres of his activity. For Versailles Gabriel produced several in the series of 'grands projects', designed to lend the building some semblance of coherence, but most of his executed work was concentrated in the interior. His two masterpieces there are the Opéra in the main château and the palace of the Petit Trianon, built for Mme de Pompadour, in the grounds.

The Petit Trianon is perhaps the most famous of all Gabriel's buildings, a paradigm of elegance that architects in France are still today asked to copy for their clients *(46)*. It is a large pavilion where Mme de Pompadour could escape periodically from the ceremony of Versailles. Completed in the year of her death (1764), it seems to possess a chilling perfection that evokes the personality of the owner, who had long since repudiated the physical intimacy of the king. Separated from the king's palace, yet partaking of the same architectural formality, it is based upon a type of villa design, deriving ultimately from Palladio, that had come into fashion in France with the decline of the feudal château in the preceding century. While English architects may have looked closely at Palladio's own designs in their schemes for such buildings, Gabriel's villa is a variation of the traditional French pavilion, of which indeed it is the crowning monument.

Gabriel provides three variations on the theme: a frontispiece of pilasters over a rusticated basement for the main entrance, full columns for the rear façade, and half-columns at the sides. No pediment interrupts the horizontal line of the cornice, no statues punctuate the line of the balustrade, no garlands enliven the window frames, and in these ways the villa marks the most austere point that the taste of the court, in the person of Mme de Pompadour, reached during the reign of Louis XV.

It was not until after the death of the king's mistress that the theatre of Versailles was begun *(47)*. The second of the great theatres of eighteenth-century France, it too is a variation on a theme that derives ultimately from Palladio. Though the need for a court theatre had become increasingly acute since the 1740s and, following the visit

47 Versailles, the Opéra. Completed by Gabriel and his assistants in 1770, the Opéra overwhelmed Mrs Thrale by its splendour during her visit to Paris in 1775

of Marigny to Italy, several architects had been instructed to make further studies of the theatres there, nothing permanent came of these preparations until the late 1760s, on the eve of the marriage of the Dauphin to Marie Antoinette. The building was then constructed rapidly with the help of a team of assistants both from the Bâtiments du Roi and from the Menus-Plaisirs, the body responsible for temporary decorations and stage scenery carried out for the court.

As finally constructed the auditorium recalls the most famous of all earlier theatres, the Teatro Olimpico of Palladio, in its semicircular plan and in the free-standing columns that ring the gallery, columns which derive from the design of antique theatres, but which appear at Versailles in conjunction with tiers of boxes. The decoration too lacks the austerity of the classical theatre, with its reliefs by Pajou and its mirrors behind the wooden columns reflecting the ostentatious chandeliers suspended from the ceiling. The building was one of the few royal commissions discussed in the press, and in a letter to the *Mercure de France* Gabriel gave the names of his assistants and described the character of the building: 'The object was . . . particularly to give an idea of the progress of the

arts under the reign of Louis XV.' The technical virtuosity of the stage machinery, a source of special interest and admiration, was the work of Arnoult, who described his art at length to the Prince de Croÿ.

As de Croÿ admitted, the theatre 'does much honour to M. Gabriel, and it is the first building [of his?] that I have seen generally praised'. Its reputation was undiminished some years later when it impressed two visitors familiar with the stage in England, Mrs Thrale and Dr Johnson:

The Theatre was the fine Thing we were then carried to admire, & so fine it is that Imagination itself can add but little to its Splendour – I had never known what Expence could do when pushed to the utmost had I not seen the King of France's Theatre. We walked on the Stage to look at the House – & now, says I to Dr Johnson, what Play shall we act? – the Englishman In Paris? No indeed, says he, – we will act Harry the fifth.

Gabriel's masterpieces were all secular buildings, produced in the service of the king, but amongst his few, mainly modest, ecclesiastical designs the little-known projects for the Frederikskirke in Copenhagen suggest how he might have handled such a commission as that for Ste-Geneviève *(50)*. The Copenhagen church had been started by a Danish architect, Niels Eigtved, in 1752, as a circular domed cathedral with high bell-towers to each side *(48–49)*. Eigtved died soon after work had begun and later architects were constrained to follow his awkward design, based upon projects by Juvarra and on German Protestant church types which had never in any case recommended themselves in France.

It was presumably as a political concession that Gabriel was permitted in 1754 by the French king to work for his Danish counterpart, Frederick V, whose ambassador in Paris had recommended the architect to the Danish prime minister, Count Bernstorff. Two designs of Gabriel's are known, but neither was followed, and in the end a much younger French architect, Nicolas-Henri Jardin, who was a student at the French Academy in Rome in the 1740s, was invited to Copenhagen to continue the building, which was damaged when Nelson blockaded Copenhagen and not finally completed until the nineteenth century *(69)*.

Despite its German form Eigtved's project for the church is indebted to French domestic architecture of the earlier part of the century in its decoration, whereas Gabriel's drawings seem less overtly French, deriving more directly from the tradition of St Peter's, which Gabriel must have studied in drawings and engravings. A giant Corinthian order spans the three storeys of the façade, forming a coherent base for the dome and bell-towers. Gabriel closely follows Eigtved's articulation, although this may not be apparent at first, so subtly is the transformation to a less vertical composition achieved. But whatever the limitations that Eigtved had imposed, Gabriel would presumably have produced a design not unlike this, had he received the commission for Ste-Geneviève: a great cathedral in the style of St Peter's with a tall ribbed dome and giant Corinthian pilasters.

In the development of French architecture in the eighteenth century the division between the standards that Gabriel so capably maintained and the more experimental, more influential ideas of Soufflot cannot be disassociated from the taste and patronage of the Marquis de Marigny, Soufflot's protector and friend. Marigny was not an active instigator of change, but a passive arbiter, influenced by his sister, Mme de Pompadour, probably by Mme Geoffrin and certainly by Soufflot and Cochin; according to the obituary that appeared in 1782 in the *Journal de Paris*, 'he never took a decision without having consulted several artists whom he had taken into his confidence and especially the companions of his journey [to Italy], whom he called his eyes'.

At court Marigny had a reputation for great modesty, in keeping with his obscure origins; 'a very modest simplicity and almost fearful', was one description of his manner, and Mme d'Oberkirch mentions that 'He called himself simply Poisson, and was not at all inflated by his elevation.' But those who worked closely with him found Marigny an insecure and difficult man. One enemy described him as 'A great egoist, brutal and very presumptuous', and also accused him of too great a liking for the bottle, which may indeed have been true.

Evidently Marigny was at ease with those, like Soufflot,

48 The Frederikskirke, Copenhagen, elevation by Niels Eigtved, 1754 (Royal Archives, Copenhagen). Shortly after the start of building, the Danish king, Frederick V, sought advice in France about his church; Gabriel and Jardin *(68, 69)* provided alternative proposals

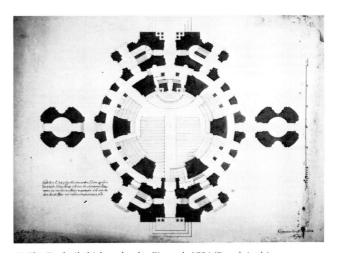

49 The Frederikskirke, plan by Eigtved, 1754 (Royal Archives, Copenhagen)

50 The Frederikskirke, elevation and section by Gabriel (Royal Archives, Copenhagen). Altering Eigtved's plan very little, Gabriel proposed a more monumental building in the tradition of St Peter's *(19)*

with whom he had already formed an attachment, and Marmontel, who served for a while as secretary of the Bâtiments du Roi, gives the following picture of the progress of their relations:

Attentive to watch the opinion that was entertained of him, it often happened that he spoke of himself with a feigned humility, to see whether his auditors would be pleased to hear him undervalue himself; and then, if the least smile, the least equivocal word escaped, the wound was deep and without remedy . . . from the moment I ceased to be his secretary . . . no one expressed more eager desire to have me for his companion and friend. Yet, as long as I held the place of secretary under him, he never once permitted himself to invite me to dinner.

Marigny's name is above all associated with the style known as the 'goût grec' that became widespread in Paris during the 1750s and 1760s: 'everything today is *à la grecque*' are the famous words that appeared in the *Correspondance littéraire* in 1763. The term is a confusing one, as it has come to embrace almost all the artistic manifestations of the time, including the buildings of Gabriel, and a new style in decoration and furniture, and even in dress, as well as the church of Ste-Geneviève, a building which is classical not only in its decoration but also on a more serious level of principle. In the official portrait of Marigny made in 1761 by the Swedish artist Alexandre Roslin *(51)* and hung at the Academy of Architecture, the sitter is presented in a setting that includes the most modern

furniture, a chair and table with straight legs, and a rectilinear picture frame; on the table is a plan and a drawing of the colonnade of the Louvre, which Gabriel and Soufflot were engaged in completing.

From a number of celebrated phrases of his it appears that Marigny indeed disliked the extremes of Rococo decoration and of classical severity: 'I want no modern foliage (*chicorée*), I want no antique austerity', he said, referring to frames for paintings by Boucher, and the Academy of Architecture, he hoped in 1756, would 'correct the bad taste of today'. For his official residence near the Louvre, he asked for panelling 'in good taste, half-Greekery (*mi-partie grecquerie*)', and in a letter of 1762 to the Director of the French Academy in Rome he wrote, 'I would wish that our architects occupied themselves more than they do with things that are more suited to our customs and to our usages than to Greek temples. They are straying from their object in applying themselves to that kind of architecture.'

For his own private 'usages' Marigny employed Soufflot, and in a lesser capacity several younger architects who had been students in Rome. The positive hallmark of his personal taste appears to have been a devotion to building styles of the sixteenth century that he had learnt to value in Italy, a predilection that formed only a part of Soufflot's much wider range of sympathies. On the death of Mme de Pompadour in 1764 Marigny inherited the

51 Portrait of the Marquis de Marigny, by Alexandre Roslin, 1761 (Musée de Versailles). Brother of Mme de Pompadour and Director of the Bâtiments du Roi since 1751, Marigny here holds a plan of the Louvre colonnade (16), which Gabriel and Soufflot were then in the process of completing

Château of Ménars, near Blois, and he began to make improvements to the building, which Gabriel had already enlarged for his sister. Soufflot who, with Cochin, was a frequent guest there built a salon to link the château with the garden, a circular pavilion dedicated to Apollo, where the statue of Abundance by Lambert-Sigisbert Adam was placed, and a grotto that Marigny, perhaps thinking of a joke he had shared in Italy, called 'piccola ma garbata' ('small but pretty') *(52)*.

'Garbata' seems to be a surprising choice of word considering the severity of the little building, with its plain piers and central arch (a variant of the Venetian window pattern). The interior is based in plan upon a Greek cross with short arms, while the central pool is in the same ecclesiastical shape, and the vault is supported by baseless Tuscan columns, appropriate to the subterranean informality of the site, and amongst the earliest columns of this type to appear in France. Some of the other improvements that Marigny contemplated Soufflot could not bring himself to approve, and when his patron asked for a Chinese pavilion, Soufflot in vain recalled to Marigny a sense of his position: 'a Director General under an administration in which good architecture has reappeared in France after an almost complete absence of more than thirty years, should not, I think, build at his house either

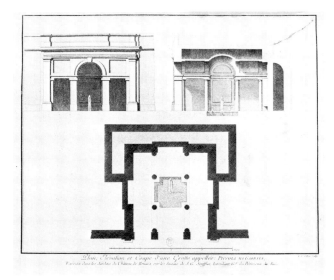

52 The grotto of the Château of Ménars, near Blois (engraving by Sellier). Built by Soufflot for Marigny after 1764 and incorporating Tuscan columns without base mouldings

in the Chinese or the arabesque taste'. To this rebuke Marigny replied: 'I agree with you, Sir, about what a leader in the arts should do; but you will agree with me that it is my person and not my position that resides at Ménars.'

At Marigny's official residence in Paris Soufflot had installed in 1764 the panelling 'mi-partie grecquerie' that his patron required, and in the later 1760s Marigny asked Soufflot for additions to a private house on the western extremity of Paris, at the very end of the rue du Faubourg-St-Honoré. Marigny had come into a considerable fortune on his marriage in 1766, though the alliance was much less grand than Mme de Pompadour had hoped for and, according to Marmontel, it became clouded by Marigny's jealous disposition. With part of the fortune Marigny and Soufflot planned the alteration of the house. Soufflot built an entrance leading from the main road to a narrow courtyard closed by a pavilion *(53)*.

The pavilion gave the impression of being a small and isolated dwelling, though it formed part of a larger and more complex building (with stables on the other side of the rue de Monceau) more befitting the rank of its occupant. It was the most conspicuous manifestation of the mature taste of Marigny, as advised by Soufflot, and it fits very uncomfortably into the pattern of Paris domestic architecture in the 1760s. The precise character of its eccentricity, which probably reflects Soufflot's own

uncertainty in domestic practice, seems to reside in an austerity that prefigures developments of the 1780s in the design of town houses, combined with a dependence on sixteenth-century architecture that is more frankly apparent than was normal. According to Thiéry, Soufflot was asked to make the doorway leading from the street 'male and square in the manner of Michelangelo', and the pavilion itself is not inconsistent with such a formula.

The plan accommodated a staircase in the centre and two slightly projecting rooms on either side, expressed externally in the three-part division of the façade. The cubic mass of the block is relieved only in the design of its six openings. The side windows of the first floor have full tabernacle frames, with columns placed in advance of the wall, supported from below by large consoles, and each was given a full Doric entablature and a curved pediment. Where the façade breaks back in the centre two full tiers of the Venetian window motif appear, with columns and short sections of entablature matching at a distance the articulation of the side windows. The conflict between an almost ecclesiastical austerity and the richer decoration needed in a private dwelling seems only partly resolved, reflecting the patron's own nostalgia for the art that had touched him most deeply in Italy: 'as I judged by my own experience that the study of Florence and Venice are very useful and in some ways indispensable, above all for those who have taken the part of painting'.

VUE DE LA MAISON DE M. LE M^guis
DE MARIGNY, RUE DU FAUB^g
St HONORÉ

53 The house of Marigny in the rue du Faubourg-St-Honoré, Roule, Paris (engraving by Janninot after Durand). Soufflot extended an existing house for Marigny, creating an unusual and austere façade, that appears Venetian in character

3 Theory and practice in church architecture: Laugier and Contant d'Ivry. Students in Rome in the 1740s; the exponents of the 'goût grec'

54 The frontispiece of Laugier's *Essai sur l'architecture*, 1755 (engraving by Eisen). The Genius of Architecture, accompanied by fragments of classical architecture, points to the primitive cabin which Laugier recommended as a model of structural integrity

WHEN SOUFFLOT began working on his projects for Ste-Geneviève he must already have known the *Essai sur l'architecture* that Père Laugier, a Jesuit priest, had published in 1753. Indeed so closely are the ideas of the two men related that it would be surprising if they had not exchanged views long before their respective works became publicly known. This is not to say that Soufflot was merely the instrument of the more articulate Laugier, as is sometimes assumed. Impressive though Laugier's book undoubtedly is – consistent, eloquent and deriving from a standpoint that intelligibly invokes the two deities of eighteenth-century thought, Reason and Nature – there is nothing in its wording that conveys the visual sophistication of Soufflot's style.

An exact contemporary of Soufflot, Laugier was born at Manosque in Provence and served his novitiate at Avignon, transferring later to the province of Lyon, where he may have encountered Soufflot's earliest work. He moved to Paris in 1744 and established himself as a preacher and a writer on artistic matters. The *Essai* of 1753, which ran to a second edition two years later, was followed by a review of the Salon of the same year and a defence of French music against the Italian style favoured by Rousseau. As a preacher Laugier was engaged for the chapel of Versailles until, in 1754, the radical tone of his sermons gave offence to the king. He was sent away to Lyon for a while and successfully petitioned to transfer from the Jesuit to the Benedictine order. Laugier returned to architecture in one of the many literary projects that occupied his last years when in 1765 he published his *Observations sur l'architecture*, a book dealing with the subject of proportions that is chiefly interesting for the many comments it contains on new buildings in Paris.

In his most influential book, the *Essai*, Laugier argued for a reform of architecture based on the concept of the 'primitive hut', which is illustrated as the frontispiece of the second edition in an elegant engraving by Eisen *(54)*. All architecture, Laugier felt, should be based upon the use of the column, the entablature and the pediment, a ludicrous proposition which he nevertheless argued with extraordinary persuasiveness. Pediments should only appear at the ending of the roof, not at its sides or anywhere else on a building. Entablatures which include a cornice should only appear at roof level, since the cornice represents the eaves of the roof, and so on. Laugier strongly disapproved of arcades, of cantilevering and of the use of structural members supported on the crown of an arch, which he regarded as an extreme case of irrational design (*porte-à-faux*). For him each part of a building should have a clearly visible support immediately beneath it.

A large part of the *Essai* is devoted to the description of an ideal church, based upon the principle of the primitive hut, and combining the spaciousness of a Gothic cathedral with the use of classical columns – precisely the formula that underlies Soufflot's Ste-Geneviève. Laugier was not, however, the first to describe such a church, for a much earlier book, the *Nouveau Traité de toute l'architecture*, written by the Abbé de Cordemoy and first published in 1706, advocated a very similar building. Cordemoy applied to architecture many of the rules that Laugier advocated and he too dreamed of a church articulated with columns. He spoke of being seized with admiration for Gothic churches, buildings which can be grasped in their entirety at a glance. He wished that the church of St Peter's had been built in the same style as Bernini's Piazza so as to incorporate the best features of Gothic practice. His ideal church was one built in the style of the colonnade of the Louvre.

Though their views on churches are in many ways so similar, Cordemoy and Laugier justified their liking for columns in very different ways. Cordemoy says, with engaging disingenuousness, that this taste of his is perhaps a foible, but one which he shared with the ancients, while Laugier, like other thinkers of his generation, built his views into a complete system, and by referring to the origins of architecture could assert that his taste, far from being a foible, was one sanctioned by Reason and by Nature.

If Laugier was influenced by Cordemoy and by the rationalist philosophers of the eighteenth century, he must also have known something of the ideas of Rousseau. It was in 1749 that Rousseau composed his revolutionary essay for the Dijon Academy on the theme that mankind had regressed from the purity of its natural primitive state: 'our souls have gradually become corrupt as our sciences and arts have advanced towards perfection'. Though Laugier's primitive hut implies no direct nostalgia for the primitive state of man, despite the pastoral felicity that Eisen conveys in his engraving, the conventional notion of architectural progress at least during the Renaissance is measured against primitive standards that are held to be better.

In spite of the precocity of much of Laugier's thinking, of his recommendations for churches and also of his dislike of the rigid formality of French garden planning (which transpires from a later chapter of the *Essai*), there is a danger of making him too thoroughgoing an apostle of subsequent change, for he would have disliked much that

took place after his death. He had condemned, for example, evenly articulated elevations, and disapproved of the use of the giant order in domestic architecture, since in his view the separate floors of a building should be expressed on the exterior.

The importance of the *Essai* was, however, immediately recognized at the time of its publication. In the *Correspondance littéraire* Grimm noted that the book had enjoyed a great success in Paris at the time of the author's prudent exile in Lyon, and he gave a lengthy summary of Laugier's views, adding that 'all those who join in to supply principles for the fine arts should learn from Father Laugier how to simplify them, to lead them back to nature, the mother of all the arts'. Blondel reacted at first with approval but he later considered that Laugier's influence had been disastrous, and condemned his writings with incoherent abusiveness in 1774: 'Most of our young architects are thinkers, but do not think; and most clients are ignorant and presumptuous. Because they have read the *Essai of Father Logier* [sic], they believe themselves very learned; from there that prodigality of monsters, often allied with reptiles [has arisen].'

In considering the design of churches supposedly based upon the recommendations of Laugier and Cordemoy, care has to be taken in relating their words to any real buildings. There was in France, in the provinces bordering upon Holland and Germany, a long tradition of hall churches, buildings that had developed from Gothic architecture and which were articulated with pillars or columns though not with straight entablatures. There are also the great Protestant churches of Holland and England, encompassing the work of Wren, where columns are much in evidence, and even straight lintels, often used to support balconies.

Gothic architecture, quite apart from its structural qualities, which architects increasingly admired, was not in any case unrelated to the Rococo fashions of the early eighteenth century, and though architects might qualify their opinions of medieval buildings, the non-professional public still loved a Gothic cathedral. Mme d'Oberkirch, for example, wrote movingly of Toul, and Philip Thicknesse expressed admiration for Reims, while for Mrs Thrale Canterbury was 'truly grand and majestick'. Even architects and masons could, when necessary, make passable designs in imitation of medieval architecture, a notable case in France being the façade of the cathedral of Ste-Croix at Orléans, which was the most important Gothic building completed during the later eighteenth century.

Though Soufflot and Laugier were to give the weight of their approval to the structural and visual achievements of Gothic architecture, it need occasion no surprise that Ste-Geneviève was not the first church of the mid-eighteenth century by a French architect that incorporated free-standing columns and a straight entablature. This notional honour is apparently due to an older architect, Pierre Contant d'Ivry, with his church of St-Wanson at Condé-sur-l'Escaut in northern France, begun probably in 1751, which was followed by a more ambitious but similar design four years later, St-Vaast at nearby Arras (57).

49

55 Portrait of Pierre Contant d'Ivry (1698–1777), frontispiece of Contant's *Oeuvres d'architecture*, 1769. The large plan shows Contant's revised project for the Madeleine *(58)*

56 The garden façade of the Palais-Royal, Paris. Part of the remodelling of the interior and exterior of the palace carried out by Contant for the Duc d'Orléans from 1756

Contant d'Ivry was one of the most gifted of that generation of French architects whose works were all too swiftly overtaken by the architectural revolution of the mid-century (others were his pupil, François Franque, and Le Carpentier). An exact contemporary of Gabriel, but less well placed in the architectural hierarchy, Contant lacked the background that sustained the consistency of Gabriel's style to the extent that he seems on closer acquaintance a gifted eccentric. A quality of quirkiness even seems apparent in the engraved portrait that Contant published as the frontispiece of a book of his architectural designs (*Oeuvres d'architecture*) which appeared in 1769 *(55)*. But Contant was nevertheless one of the most successful architects of his time.

Described as 'my friend Contant' by the Prince de Croÿ, who gives details of several of his works, Contant was also Premier Architecte to the Duc d'Orléans and created much of the present Palais-Royal. In his interiors there, illustrated by Blondel in the *Encyclopédie*, Contant showed a precocious liking for columns in place of 'chicorée', and on the garden façade of the palace *(56)* he made extensive use of free-standing columns, though only for the main floor and with capitals of the ornate French variety; and columns are also a feature of his famous staircase there. Yet Contant was also capable in his fluent architectural drawings of matching the elaborate effects of the most lively Rococo decoration, and the beauty of the Palais-Royal staircase owes much to its complex shape and to the intricate design of the balustrade.

Contant's ecclesiastical buildings, beginning with the church of the fashionable abbey of Panthémont in the rue de Grenelle in Paris (1748), where he had already shown a preoccupation with structural innovation in the use of brick vaulting (*à la Roussillon*), cannot be separated from the work of Soufflot. In the interior of St-Vaast at Arras *(57)* an order of Corinthian columns supporting a straight entablature is the main feature of the articulation, and the effect is notably austere as well as being brilliantly illuminated, the light flickering between the columns and reflected from the plain vault. Contant, like Soufflot, has groups of three columns at each corner of his crossing, but in his case two in each group project forwards to strengthen the corners of his colonnades and the entablature above is surmounted for emphasis by flaming urns.

Contant's St-Vaast was a reconstruction of a medieval abbey church and it seems likely that the earlier building marked its character more deeply than anything the architect had read by Cordemoy, or even at this date by Laugier. Indeed the projecting columns, used so conspicuously in the crossing, are a feature that was singled out for condemnation by Cordemoy and Laugier, since according to their theories such columns were not seen to serve a useful purpose. They recall the projecting columns of classical triumphal arches which Contant himself had employed extensively in earlier designs.

Whatever Contant's view of Laugier, Laugier certainly had no love for the most important of Contant's ecclesiastical works, the rebuilding of the church of the Madeleine, designed to close the northern vista from Gabriel's Place

57 The nave of St-Vaast, Arras. Designed in 1755, and the second of two churches by Contant with an articulation of columns and lintels

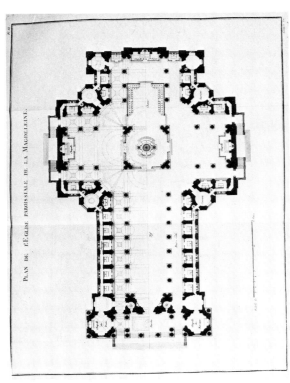

58 Project for the church of the Madeleine, Paris, elevation and plan (engraving from Patte, 1765). Contant's first project for the Madeleine, 1763, which failed to win the approval of Laugier, who realized that Ste-Geneviève *(34)* corresponded better with his own theories

Louis XV *(58)*. The origins of the Madeleine have not been studied in depth, and why it should have been Contant who received the royal approval for this project (in February 1763) is uncertain. A passing reference to his design in the *Observations* of Laugier is far from flattering: 'The plan of the new church of the Madeleine is very inferior to that of Sainte-Geneviève. It is with some changes, the old form of the Latin cross, with nave, choir, crossing and aisles. There is nothing special except the kind of baldachin constructed for the altar, in the centre of the crossing.'

Though columns and lintels are used by Contant in the interior of his church, his articulation seems awkwardly related to the plan, which is indeed as unoriginal as Laugier implies, with its side chapels and even crossing chapels in the customary French manner. From the exterior the dome, placed over the *baldacchino* in the crossing, is smaller in relation to the scale of the church than Soufflot's dome, and it recalls more closely the dome type of Mansart's Visitation *(14)*. The portico, to be seen in relation to the colonnades of the Place Louis XV, combines the giant order of Ste-Geneviève with flanking towers, like the lower storeys of Servandoni's towers at St-Sulpice.

A more unusual design for the front of the church appears in a later plan of Contant's, which he displays in the engraved portrait *(55)*. Here the church is disposed like Soufflot's on a cross plan with a much truncated nave. The façade has no towers, and the portico projects deeply with the approach from the sides marked by curved flights of steps. The plan was further modified by Contant's successor, Joseph-Abel Couture, who lengthened the

internal colonnades, and encased the whole exterior of the nave with columns matching those of the portico *(59)*. This appears to be the first instance of a real church, as opposed to an idealized project, with the columns of a classical temple lining part of the sides of the building, in accordance with the more rigid archaeological approach of the later decades of the century. From here to the doctrinaire vacuity of the Madeleine as finally constructed for Napoleon is but a short step *(345)*.

The decade of the 1740s, which witnessed the earliest works of Soufflot and the opening of Blondel's school in Paris, also saw the spread of an undercurrent of more radical, more irrational, architectural design by students sent to complete their education in Rome. Indeed, the revival of classicism in eighteenth-century architecture was attributed by some writers of the time to yet another author, a certain Jean-Laurent Legeay. According to no less an authority than Cochin, 'The truly decisive epoch [of change], marked by the return of M. de Marigny and his company from Italy' had been preceded by an earlier phase of 'the return to a better taste' marked by the appearance of Legeay after his stay in Rome. In Cochin's view, Legeay 'was one of the finest geniuses in architecture that there has been, but otherwise, without discipline, and so to say, without reason. He could never submit to the demands made upon him, and the great Moghul would not have been rich enough to construct the buildings he planned.'

Legeay was the winner of the architecture Grand Prix in 1732, and spent the years 1737 to 1742 in Rome, overlapping by one year Soufflot's stay at the Academy.

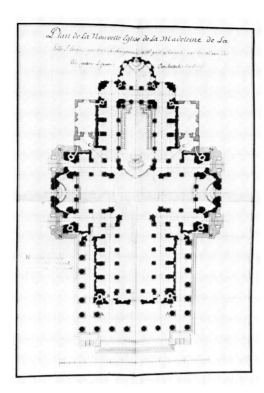

alternative to the fare supplied at the Academy in Paris, or indeed at the school of Blondel. Legeay and those who followed him in Rome, themselves inspired by the example of Piranesi, appear as the fathers of that more frankly imaginative approach to architecture which ultimately prevailed over the rationalism of Laugier and Soufflot. 'He is a young man who has much talent,' de Troy wrote of Legeay on his departure from Rome in 1742, using a phrase that he had employed to describe the work of other *pensionnaires*, 'he brings [with him] many very beautiful drawings, as many studies he has made after public buildings as of his own compositions, [and] in these last there is fire and genius.'

Legeay's first known building is the cathedral of St Hedwig in Berlin, commissioned by Frederick the Great in 1746 and engraved in the following year *(61)*. Making allowances for any local conventions that Legeay was constrained to respect, there is little that is particularly startling about the work. Something of the Roman Pantheon and something of Bernini's churches (especially the one at Ariccia which Cochin later admired) are combined in a design that in a Parisian context might be regarded as a descendant of the Assomption *(15)*. Unusual perhaps in this guise is the smooth dome, rising from a rusticated wall surface, and the paired columns of the interior carrying an unaccented entablature around the circumference of the church, which is otherwise decorated in a manner that again recalls Bernini.

The service buildings of the Neues Palais at Potsdam *(62)*, where a breach occurred between the architect and his employer, must – if they indeed faithfully represent the intentions of Legeay – be closer in spirit to the imaginative drawings that de Troy had seen in Rome. They seem to reflect more intelligibly the character of the patron in the

On his return to France he came into contact with a number of younger students, especially the two great architectural draughtsmen of the later part of the century, de Wailly and Boullée. But by 1748 he had left Paris to follow a career in Germany, first at Schwerin, and then from 1756 in Berlin. He returned to Paris in the early 1760s after a short stay in England, and then moved to southern France where he probably died in poverty and obscurity in the later 1780s.

Legeay's years in Rome brought him to the notice of the young Piranesi, who had recently arrived there from Venice, and it has been assumed that even Piranesi was indebted artistically to him. Legeay indeed published a number of engravings, views of Rome in books with which Piranesi was associated, and fanciful views of urns and tombs *all'antica* that appeared even as late as 1767. These designs vary in quality and seem to become increasingly simplified in their architectural forms. Some are more strictly architectural than others *(60)* but none of them stand the test of comparison with the work of Piranesi. Only in the French nationality of the author are they distinguished from a tradition that was by no means rare in Rome by the time they were produced.

The importance of Legeay seems to have been not so much his ability as an architect, but that – like Servandoni before him – he combined in his admiration of the antique past of Rome the approach of the draughtsman and of the practising architect. Though he may not have been outstanding in either branch of his art, this need not have prevented him from fostering in Paris in the 1740s a climate of opinion that directed impressionable students to explore for themselves what Rome had to offer as an

60 A circular temple in a landscape, engraving by Jean-Laurent Legeay (published by Dumont). One of the more attractive of Legeay's architectural caprices; his earlier designs are believed to have deeply influenced Boullée and de Wailly

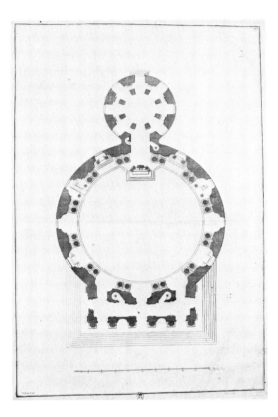

61 The cathedral of St Hedwig, Berlin, elevation, plan and section, engravings by Legeay, 1747. The major ecclesiastical building carried out by Legeay during the course of his employment with Frederick the Great

unexpected innovations that underlie their traditional grandiloquence. Service buildings that recall the elaboration of early eighteenth-century palace designs (by Juvarra and even Vanbrugh), they rely largely on the repetition of free-standing columns for their effect.

Legeay's style appears to have altered in conformity with the changes that he had himself helped to initiate in his youth, and his design for a church dedicated to the Trinity engraved in 1766 is far more austere than St Hedwig which it otherwise resembles in its shape and gawky appearance *(63)*. The plan of the interior derives from Borromini, the triangular symbol of divine wisdom that determined the plan of S. Ivo della Sapienza here referring to the Trinity. In section, however, the church is remarkably severe, and even more so the exterior with its stepped dome, its open oculus, directly recalling the Pantheon, and its ring of free-standing columns.

'It is to be hoped', runs the inscription on the engraving, 'that a similar church will be built in Paris:

nothing is more needed in that capital than an example of this type to reunite in that great town the beauty in architecture of the Greeks and the Romans.' Nothing comparable had indeed been built in Paris, but by 1766 such a design must have seemed more than a little provincial in its form, if not in principle, to the architects who had known Legeay in the 1740s. When Legeay returned to Paris a few years later he was said to have been astonished to see that his pupils were designing buildings with columns everywhere; no longer in sympathy with these new developments, he is alleged to have reflected sadly that columns were 'good . . . in the designs for decorations or firework displays which I gave them to copy'.

In the years following Legeay's departure from Rome, other students at the Academy, becoming in turn acquainted with Piranesi, had begun to follow his example, and when Soufflot returned to Italy in 1750 he must have become intimately aware of their experiments

62 The service buildings of the Neues Palais, Potsdam, detail. Legeay quarrelled with Frederick the Great over his project for the Neues Palais, but the extravagant colonnaded service buildings were probably carried out to his designs after his departure from Berlin in 1763

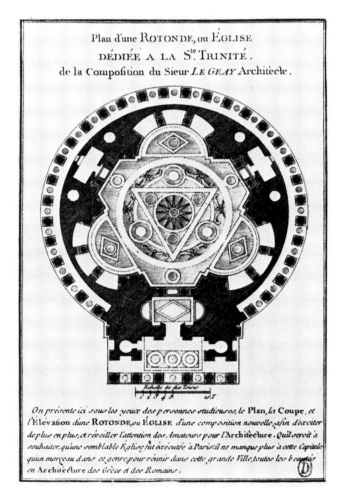

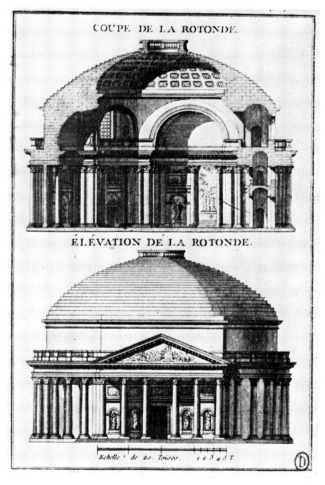

63 Project for a church dedicated to the Trinity, by Legeay, 1766, plan, section and elevation (engravings by Legeay). The inscription explains that the architect wished to see a church of this character constructed in Paris

64 Portrait of Gabriel-Pierre-Martin Dumont (c. 1720–after 1790) (engraving by Baron after Kucharski). Professor at the Ecole des Ponts et Chaussées and the author and editor of many engraved architectural designs, Dumont had been befriended by Soufflot in Rome and accompanied him to Paestum

through his friendship with Dumont (64), who had won the Prix de Rome in 1737. Dumont's departure to Rome was delayed for five years, but he spent almost the whole decade of the 1740s there. After his return to Paris he became the professor of the royal engineering department, the Ecole des Ponts et Chaussées, and he brought out several collections of architectural engravings, which comprised many projects of his own, a quantity of vignettes by the different architects who had been with

65 Project for a Temple of the Arts, by Dumont, perspective view, engraving after Dumont. According to the inscriptions, the temple, inspired by Voltaire's *Sémiramis*, was Dumont's reception piece at the Roman Accademia di S. Luca in 1746

him in Rome, and many of the works of Soufflot, including the engravings after his Paestum sketches. Dumont's volumes cover a spectrum of much that was considered advanced in the architecture of the mid-century.

Otherwise Dumont's own contribution to architecture in the later eighteenth century was perhaps made rather through the range of his contacts and through his work as a teacher than through his practical work. He is the author of only one known work in France, although his designs for buildings were numerous, especially in the 1770s. All are influenced by his experiences in Rome, but they must have seemed, like Legeay's later designs, unacceptably old-fashioned by the time that they appeared in print.

The difference between the drawing that won Dumont the Prix de Rome and a design he offered ten years later to the Accademia di San Luca (65) suggests something of the greater freedom that French-trained architects enjoyed in Rome, and which they later took back to Paris. The French competition in 1737 was for a staircase, a task modestly and competently discharged by Dumont. In Rome, however, Dumont's programme was the more amusing theme, recalling Voltaire, of a Temple of the Arts, which lent itself to the unusual triangular form familiar in Rome from several earlier ideal projects. The temple is severe enough (recalling in its use of columns Michelangelo's Capitol palaces), but not profoundly radical, and in a later version of the same building (1765) Dumont introduced a plainer articulation. The part of his earlier design that most clearly shows an experimental attitude of mind is the low dome that crowns the building, formed of a mound of shallow steps. Several other architects took up the idea at the same time as Dumont, and a dome of a similar character was built in Rome in 1750 by Girolamo Teodoli, the President of the Accademia di San Luca, on a small church not far from the Colosseum, SS. Pietro and Marcellino.

The most successful of Dumont's contemporaries at the Academy in Rome was Nicolas-Henri Jardin (66), the designer of the Frederikskirke in Copenhagen, who had won the Prix de Rome in 1741 with a project nearly as modest as Dumont's, the subject being the choir of a church. He produced in 1765 a book of engravings of his works which included several projects drawn in Rome, one of which was his design for a sepulchral chapel (67). Though it resembles a fanciful vignette by Legeay or Piranesi, this is also a building seriously considered as an architectural structure: a pyramid modelled on Roman tombs (especially the monument of Gaius Cestius), and equipped with open porticos and attic windows. It is defined in space – with that generous sense of interval characteristic of the later part of the century – by means of four rostral columns emitting smoke, themselves perhaps suggested by a design used in the first place for a catafalque or a firework display.

In the same years as Soufflot was meditating his design for Ste-Geneviève Jardin took over the project for the Frederikskirke after the failure of Gabriel's drawings (50). Jardin had returned to France in 1748 with the commendation of de Troy and he followed the sculptor Saly to Copenhagen six years later. Saly was to design an

66 Portrait of Nicolas-Henri Jardin (1720–99), by Peter Als, 1764 (Academy of Arts, Copenhagen). Jardin won the Prix de Rome in 1741 and moved to Denmark in 1754 to undertake the building of the Frederikskirke

67 Project for a sepulchral chapel, perspective view, engraving from Jardin. A design, based upon the Roman monument of Gaius Cestius, made by Jardin in Rome and published by him in 1765

68 The Frederikskirke, Copenhagen, elevation of Jardin's first project, drawing by Jardin (Royal Archives, Copenhagen). Designed after Jardin's arrival in Copenhagen in 1754, the drawing shows alternative projects, both of which failed to win approval

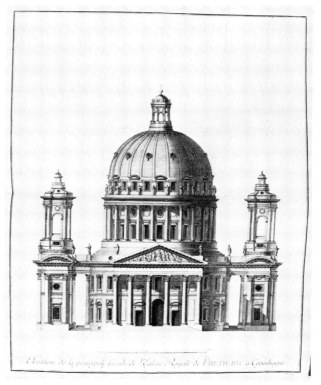

69 The Frederikskirke, Copenhagen, elevation of Jardin's final project, engraving from Jardin. The less experimental final project, designed before 1756, on the basis of which the present church was constructed

70 The villa of Marienlyst, near Elsinore, Denmark. One of several smaller commissions carried out by Jardin during his years in Denmark

equestrian statue of King Frederick for the square of the Amalienborg Palace, laid out by Eigtved, which stands in relation to the church rather as the Place Louis XV, with its statue by Bouchardon, was related to the Madeleine.

Jardin produced several projects for the church (68, 69) which, with all their incoherence, usefully define the differences that an architect of Jardin's background, working in friendly rivalry with Gabriel and Soufflot, hoped to see in a major commission for a real building, as opposed to a fanciful design. He respected Eigtved's basic plan (49), but his early projects are otherwise a riot of columns and heavy decoration based approximately upon sixteenth-century precedent. The oval garlanded medallions, deriving from the Louvre colonnade, which mark the building as French in inspiration are entirely flat discs, and the attic storey as a whole is largely plain. Most curious of all in their effect are the steps on which a dome so large is mounted and the plain bell-towers, punctuated by panels containing windows.

The Danish reaction to Jardin's first project was understandably unflattering. His work (perhaps on his own admission) was taken to be a reflection of Laugier's thought: 'Because Father Laugier dislikes pilasters, it should not be assumed that they are always wrong and misplaced' runs the memoir on his project, and Jardin's final design is less aggressive (69). There are still no pilasters on the exterior and the decoration is almost as heavy as before, but the general appearance of the building is more traditional, its proportions recalling the church of the Assomption (15). In 1756 Jardin sent copies of his drawings to Paris, where the Academy gave its approval to his second design, and also to Rome where he touchingly sought the opinion of the students then in residence at the Academy there.

Other buildings by Jardin in Denmark suggest that he, like Legeay and Dumont, would have seemed something of a traditionalist later in life. Though he did construct a pyramid with smoking vases at the corners, this served as a catafalque for King Frederick. In his domestic architecture, as at the villa of Marienlyst, near Elsinore (70), the order of pilasters, the discreet decoration and the round-headed openings lend an air of old-fashioned French good manners to an otherwise severely rectilinear building. Jardin was elected to the French Academy in 1771, and he became an active member on his return to France shortly thereafter. He travelled to England to investigate experiments in fire prevention and he then worked on a number of small commissions before his death in 1802.

Amongst Jardin's contemporaries and immediate successors in Rome were several other artists who began active careers in the 1750s, including Potain, whose work forms part of a later chapter (chapter 8), Ennemond Petitot, who became architect at the court of Parma, Barreau de Chefdeville, a slightly later visitor to Rome whose distinctly minor talent proved no handicap to an interesting career in France, and the painter Jean-Joseph Le Lorrain, who is the most closely associated with the 'goût grec' in furniture and interior decoration. Le Lorrain had won the Grand Prix of the Academy of Painting in 1739; he arrived in Rome in the following year and spent nine years at the Academy there making copies for Louis XV of Raphael's decorations in the Vatican. 'He is a young man who has infinite talents in all branches of painting' was the opinion that de Troy had formed of his work.

Le Lorrain's abilities were not, however, confined to painting, for he also made designs for some of the annual firework displays that attended the feast of the Chinea. This was a celebration whereby the city of Naples paid homage to the Pope with the presentation of two white horses. By tradition the presentation was accompanied by a grand firework display in the Piazza Colonna, and most of the early eighteenth-century designs for the festival are recorded in engravings. For occasional architecture such as this little-known, often young, artists were employed, working in wood and stucco, and not surprisingly experimental ideas sometimes made a brief appearance in such displays. Several French architects were invited to participate in the Chinea celebrations and the designs of Le Lorrain, which were amongst the most radical, closely reflecting the architectural fantasies of Piranesi, are of particular interest because of his later activity in Paris and the movement of which for a short while he played so important a part.

In a design of 1747 the *machina* was a circular Corinthian temple dedicated to Venus Genetrix (71). Modelled on the temples of antiquity, it also included a dome with oval garlanded windows and a stepped cupola with a statue at the summit. Obelisks were placed at the four corners with fountains at their bases, and steps led up to the temple platform whose smoking urns seem to relate the fireworks themselves to the burnt sacrificial offerings of antiquity. De Troy was able to claim with some pride: 'There is room to flatter ourselves by the justice that the Italians

71 The *machina* for the firework display for the festival of the Chinea, 1747, by Jean-Joseph Le Lorrain (engraving by Le Lorrain). For temporary decorations in Rome younger architects, both French and Italian, built experimental structures; Le Lorrain's design is a circular temple dedicated to Venus Genetrix

72 The salon of the castle of Åkerö, Sweden. A painted decoration, incorporating columns and lintels, carried out to designs furnished by Le Lorrain in 1754 after his return to Paris

73 Portrait of Ange-Laurent La Live de Jully, by Greuze, 1757 (The National Gallery of Art, Washington, Samuel H. Kress Collection). The heavy architectural furniture is part of the set designed for La Live by Le Lorrain (now in the Musée Condé, Chantilly)

themselves do to several of our *pensionnaires*, who, whether for decoration, or for architecture, are well fitted to honour the nation.'

During the few brief years of Le Lorrain's activity in Paris after his arrival there in 1748 (he died in St Petersburg in 1759) taste was slowly changing in the wake of the assault mounted in the previous decade. On the recommendation of Caylus, Le Lorrain designed the painted decoration for the dining-room in the castle of Åkerö in Sweden for Count C. G. Tessin *(72)*. This room, different in appearance from the interiors of Contant at the Palais-Royal, has been taken to be the first 'Neo-classical'

interior, in the sense that it is decorated with an order of columns and a straight entablature and is also notably austere in its effect. Yet more surprising is the furniture that Le Lorrain designed about 1757 for a room decorated to Barreau's designs in the house of a rich dilettante, Ange-Laurent La Live de Jully *(73)*.

La Live is one of the earliest representatives of a type of patronage that made its appearance in the later part of the century and was itself allied to the new sense of self-consciousness that the artists experienced. No longer content to follow the lead of aristocratic taste, some patrons now positively sought to differ, to express their

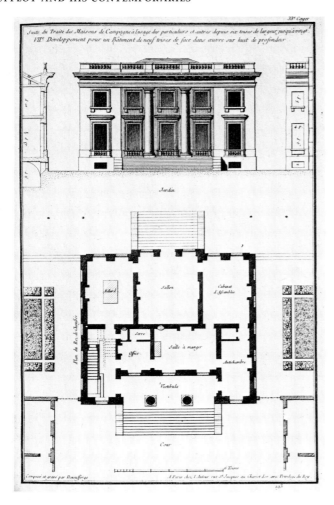

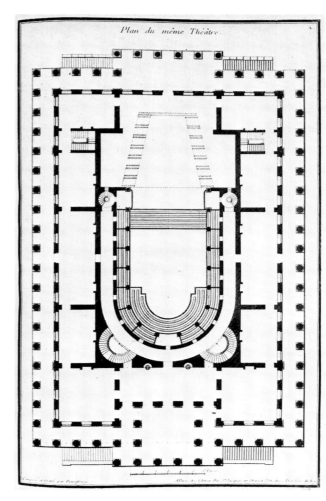

own often eccentric personal character. La Live was the son of a financier from Lyon; the brother-in-law of Mme d'Epinay, he too was a friend of Rousseau, who sought his advice on the illustrations for *La Nouvelle Héloïse*. He was an amateur engraver, who became an associate member of the Academy in 1754, and he attended with Caylus the Salon of Mme Geoffrin. A protégé of Mme de Pompadour at the court, he bought the position of Introducteur des Ambassadeurs, but his career came to a tragic end in 1764 when he succumbed to a form of melancholia and retired to the country, where he died in 1779.

In an earlier age the son of a tax farmer would not so confidently have indulged in pretensions that might have offended established taste, but in Greuze's portrait of 1757 La Live sits with studied informality playing his harp *(73)*. He is posed to show off his furniture; the chair he sits on and the table behind him, forming part of the suite that Le Lorrain had designed, are severely rectilinear, with a decoration of rosettes and *cordes* found earlier in buildings rather than in furniture designs. Cochin found Le Lorrain's designs 'very heavy', but La Live himself proudly wrote: 'It is since the execution of this Cabinet that this taste has spread for works in the Greek style, which is now

ridiculously employed for everything, in vessels, in jewellery, in materials, in hair styles, etc. and as far as shops, whose signs are now nearly all *à la grecque* . . .'

In architecture this indiscriminate diffusion of the 'Greek' style is associated with the books of the Flemish engraver François de Neufforge. Born in Liège, Neufforge had moved to Paris and found employment as an engraver, and in 1757 he brought out the first part of a collection of six hundred architectural prints, entitled *Recueil élémentaire d'architecture*, which was to appear in eight parts during the following eleven years.

The *Recueil* is traditional in being a pattern book, with examples of buildings of all types, some shown in different sizes to suit richer and poorer. The range of buildings is, however, much wider than in any earlier pattern book, with such buildings as lighthouses and prisons appearing in the later volumes. And in style Neufforge's patterns are based upon a new range of ideas, especially the use of free-standing columns and sixteenth-century decorative motifs *(74)*.

A house from the first volume of the *Recueil* shows an Italianate villa of a type that became increasingly popular in the later eighteenth century, with stone balustrades

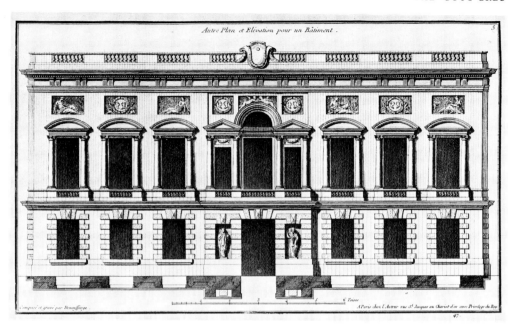

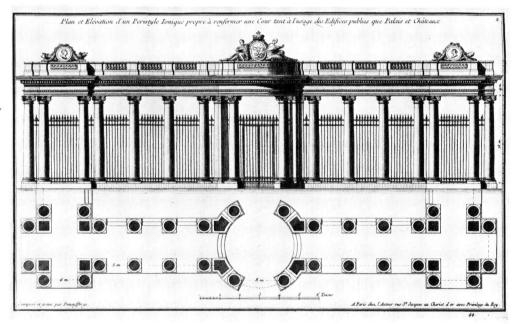

74 Designs for a villa, a theatre plan, a town house façade and an Ionic screen, by François de Neufforge. Four plates from Neufforge's *Recueil élémentaire d'architecture*, which appeared in eight parts from 1757 to 1768

instead of iron railings beneath the windows and a central loggia screened by two giant free-standing columns. Some of Neufforge's larger town houses might almost – so heavy is their style – be Italian palaces of the sixteenth century; their date is betrayed only by the extensive use of columns and rectangular reliefs. Columns are also the means whereby Neufforge transforms the screening wall of the traditional Parisian town house. Neufforge's theatre is a transcription of a temple, but with the addition of a suite of rooms around the central cella, and his cathedral is a version of the church of Ste-Geneviève.

Many of the undiscriminating and predictable patterns of Neufforge were taken up for real buildings in the years that followed the publication of his books, and it is sometimes assumed that the great architects who followed after him plundered his books for their own buildings. Neufforge may indeed have proved a useful elementary source, but his heavy Flemish style has little in common with the visual elegance of eighteenth-century art, and the work of later architects is no more encapsulated in Neufforge's clumsy plates than is the church of Ste-Geneviève in the writings of Laugier.

75 The foundations of the Castel S. Angelo, Rome, etching by Piranesi from the *Antichità romane*, 1756

4 The face of the land: archaeology, engineering and early 'English' gardens

THE CLOSE RELATIONSHIP between archaeology, engineering and garden design, however obscure it may seem today, would have appeared self-evident in eighteenth-century France, and it was indeed fundamental to the development of architecture in the period. The engineering techniques of Greek and Roman architects had never been fully comprehended in earlier centuries and they were only in part relevant to the buildings of the Renaissance. Methods of vaulting were important, but very few architects wished to emulate the long colonnades of classical architecture or to construct roads and bridges on the scale practised by the Romans, and no one had considered that the gardens of their estates could be transformed into parks resembling a classical site long overtaken by neglect and the pressure of nature. Archaeology in these ways nourished the most rational works of the eighteenth century as well as the extremes of irrationality that followed swiftly after.

The greatest archaeological work of the century, apart from Fischer von Erlach's early *Entwurf einer historischen Architektur* (1721), are the four volumes of Piranesi's *Antichità romane*, which appeared in 1756, marking a revolution in the development of all such publications. Being himself both architect and draughtsman, Piranesi covered a far wider range of buildings than had been surveyed before and he neglected no means of making them visually exciting. Buildings are shown by him within their landscapes, viewed from the most advantageous point, and set off against the agitated figures that they dwarf both physically and psychologically *(75)*. At the same time Piranesi produced more technical engravings – plans, sections, reconstructions of the techniques of Roman building *(76)* – and even town-planning is not overlooked by him.

Though Piranesi showed little interest in Roman methods of vaulting in his books, he covered the construction of roads and bridges, and included plates that show the foundations of the Pons Aelius, the bridge leading to the Mausoleum of Hadrian (now the Castel S. Angelo), down to the bedrock *(77)*. Piranesi cannot have

76 The construction of the Tomb of Cecilia Metella, etching by Piranesi from the *Antichità romane*, 1756. Piranesi's imaginary reconstruction of Roman building methods used in the construction of the tomb *(8)*

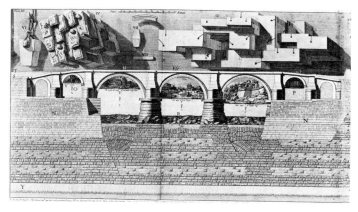

77 Section of the foundations of the Pons Aelius, Rome, etching by Piranesi from the *Antichità romane*, 1756. A reconstruction of the foundations of the Tiber bridge which leads to the Castel S. Angelo

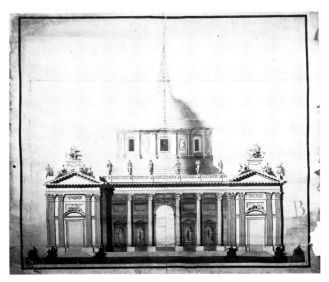

78 Project for a Temple of Peace, drawing by Julien-David Le Roy (Ecole des Beaux-Arts, Paris). One of the set of drawings which gained Le Roy the second place in the 1749 Prix de Rome competition, which he won in 1750

observed in such detail the construction of the bridge, and he was notoriously inaccurate in many of his illustrations, but his works, like the volumes of Gibbon's *Decline and Fall of the Roman Empire* (1776–88) are not less moving because of the partiality and imaginative resourcefulness of their author.

After Rome had been resurrected by Piranesi, it was the turn of Herculaneum and Pompeii, which were more carefully investigated and made known in a series of publications that influenced especially the decorative arts and painting. The relative weakness of surviving classical paintings in comparison with the architectural remains was, however, noted at an early date, and the subject of comment in Grimm's review of the account of Herculaneum that Cochin and Bellicard had published in 1754.

The leaders in archaeology in the later eighteenth century were undoubtedly the English, who produced accurate and painstaking surveys of many of the major sites of the eastern Mediterranean, of which the first was Robert Wood's *Ruins of Palmyra* (1753). The buildings of Athens, however, were first made known to the public in a French publication of 1758, the *Ruines des plus beaux monuments de la Grèce*, which was written by a young architect, Julien-David Le Roy, who had been a student at the French Academy in Rome in the early 1750s. Despite its impressive appearance and the range of its illustrations, the book was hastily put together and quickly shown to contain major errors, but its attractive plates and unpedantic perspective views define the visual character of the buildings with something of the intensity of Piranesi's eye, and even in the later years of the century, whatever scholars may have thought, architects in France spoke with reverence of their initiation to Greek architecture through the work of Le Roy.

Born in 1724, Le Roy was from a distinguished scientific family, his father and one of his brothers being clock-makers to the king, another brother a doctor, and the fourth a scientist and mechanical engineer. He was trained by Blondel and Legeay, and, sponsored by the then Professor of the Academy, Louis-Adam Loriot, he won the Prix de Rome in 1750, having won second place in the preceding year. His drawings of 1749 are amongst the Prix de Rome drawings that have survived and almost the only architectural designs by him that are known *(78)*. The competition in that year, won by Barreau de Chefdeville, was for a Temple of Peace, a theme that marked the first departure from the strictly practical subjects customarily set at the French Academy and which recalled the ideal projects created by students in Rome. Le Roy's temple shows a close affinity to their work in its decoration, use of columns and experimental dome, and it suggests how far his mind had already been opened at this early date to the influence that Rome had exerted on his older colleagues.

Le Roy arrived in Rome in 1751 and became involved in an escapade that alienated the sympathy of the new Director of the Academy, Natoire, who subsequently spoke of his 'arrogance and undocile character, which set a bad example to his colleagues'. Le Roy was a draughtsman as well as an architect and he made sketches in Rome of the Carracci frescoes in the Palazzo Farnese. At the start of 1754 he obtained permission to visit Athens, an idea that indeed argues a degree of single-minded determination, and he left Rome early in April. No doubt he was encouraged by the knowledge that two members of the English community in Rome, James Stuart and Nicholas Revett, were planning a book on the antiquities of Athens, where they had travelled three years earlier. Le Roy sailed via Pola to Constantinople and arrived in Greece several weeks after the departure of Stuart and Revett. After visiting Delos he spent some months in Athens sketching and measuring, and he travelled to Corinth and Sparta before returning via Rome (July 1755) to Paris, where he began the preparation of his book. With the assistance of the Comte de Caylus and the help of a team of draughtsmen and engravers, which included Le Lorrain and Neufforge, the work was prepared for the press and appeared in 1758.

The book is divided into two sections, the first describing Le Roy's travels in Greece, and the second outlining his views on the development of Greek architecture. He was the first to publish the Greek Ionic order in detail *(79)* and the first to discuss at length the development of the Greek Doric order. Beginning with the sturdier proportions of the earliest columns, he distinguished three phases of the Doric, with the Parthenon appearing in the second. His plan of the Acropolis includes the entrance (the Propylaea), the Parthenon and Erechtheum beyond, and all three are illustrated in detailed architectural plates *(79)*, special attention being devoted to the decorated Ionic of the Erechtheum. Le Roy also described monuments of the Roman occupation of Athens, which he believed to be much earlier in date, like the Arch of Hadrian – his 'Arch of Theseus' *(79)*.

For Soufflot the book must have elucidated the temples he had seen at Paestum some eight years previously, and the publication won general acclaim in France. But in

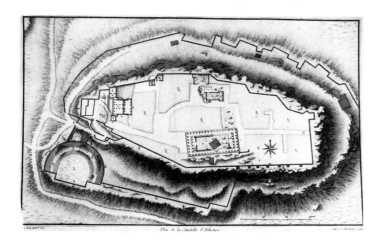

79 Plates from Le Roy's *Ruines des plus beaux monuments de la Grèce*, 1758, plan of the Acropolis, view of the Parthenon, reconstruction of the Propylaea, detail of Ionic order of the Erechtheum and view of the 'Arch of Theseus'. Following a visit to Greece in 1754, Le Roy was the first to publish a detailed, though not completely accurate, survey of Grecian monuments, which led in 1764 to his appointment as assistant professor to Blondel at the Academy of Architecture

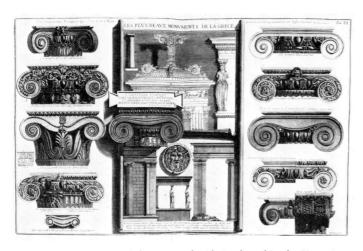

80 Roman Ionic capitals contrasted with Greek, etching by Piranesi from the *Della magnificenza*, 1761. Referring to Le Roy's book, Piranesi compared the variety of Roman Ionic capitals, shown at the side, with the Grecian Ionic in the centre

England and in Italy dissenting voices were heard. Stuart and Revett, when the first volume of their own *Antiquities of Athens* appeared (1762), pointed out many inaccuracies in Le Roy's work; he later defended himself from their attacks in a booklet of 1764, and in a second edition of the *Ruines*, which appeared in 1770. Criticism of a different kind came from Piranesi, who deeply resented the assumption that was prevalent in France of the superiority of Greek over Roman architecture. In his *Della magnificenza ed architettura de' romani* (of 1761) he stressed the early origins of Roman architecture and the greater variety it offered *(80)*.

In France almost immediately after the appearance of his book Le Roy became a member of the Academy and was appointed assistant to Blondel, the professor, succeeding to Blondel's position on his death (1774). Le Roy was aware of the relevance of his research to the main architectural developments that were taking place in Paris, and in a book of 1764, a simplified history of Christian 'temples', he lent the weight of his approval to the church of Ste-Geneviève, speaking also of the 'excellent principles' of Laugier, though he felt that these were not consistently developed by the author.

Later in his career Le Roy's interests moved beyond architecture and he became deeply interested in methods of shipping in antiquity and their application to modern navigation. He spoke to Benjamin Franklin about his ideas, and constructed a boat suitable for navigation on sea and river waters, which he sailed across the Channel in 1787 and along the Seine to the Louvre with a cargo of lead. These experiments were influenced by his Greek voyages, and probably also supported by his brother, as Mrs Thrale, who was entertained by Le Roy in Paris in 1775, suggests: 'The *People* who have pleased me best were I think all Foreigners except old Mons[r] Le Roy the Mechanist & his Brother who has travelled into Greece, Asia, &c, & is a pleasing Man enough, & vastly friendly with his Brother of whose Machines he seems very proud & very confident.' After the dissolution of the Academy in the early years of the Revolution Le Roy continued to teach (see chapter 15) and he was one of the founder members of the Institut; he died in Paris, a still respected teacher and scholar, in 1803.

Le Roy's book on the monuments of Athens was the most influential publication of its kind in France, but it was not the only important volume on travel and archaeology that the French, in competition with the English, produced. The Comte de Choiseul-Gouffier, a cousin of the minister, published in 1782 the first volume of a yet more elaborate survey of Grecian remains, while the antiquities of Sicily became widely known through the works of the Abbé de St-Non (1781–86) and later of Jean Houel (1782–87), and the classical remains of Nîmes were published by Clérisseau in his *Antiquités du Midi de la France* (1778).

Clérisseau had been a student at the Academy in Rome at the same time as Le Roy, and he too had tried the patience of Natoire, in refusing to observe the Easter regulations of the Academy, an act of irreligion that Marigny condemned. Leaving the Academy in 1753, he stayed on in Italy and formed friendships with Piranesi, with Robert and James Adam, and with Winckelmann. In company first with Robert and then with James Adam he explored Italy and went to Spalato to survey the Palace of Diocletian, which formed the subject of an archaeological publication by Robert Adam (1764).

Clérisseau returned to France in 1767 and was admitted as a member of the Academy of Painting and Sculpture. He was active in architecture as the designer of the governor's palace at Metz and late in life as Jefferson's adviser in the construction of the Virginia Capitol, but his chief importance lay in his interior decorations and his drawings in gouache. His book on the antiquities of Nîmes was the only volume that appeared of a more general survey of French antiquities which he planned, though it contains some of the most notable Roman remains in France, like the Maison Carrée. Other Roman monuments in France,

81 View of the antique remains at St-Rémy, engraving from La Borde's *Description de la France*, 1781. One of the many publications of the later eighteenth century in France in which little-known classical remains, both native and foreign, were illustrated

including the tomb of the Julii at St-Rémy *(81)* and several of the more famous works of Roman engineering, were described and illustrated in the volumes of the *Description de la France*, edited by Jean-Benjamin de La Borde which began to appear in 1781.

Yet in spite of all these publications, the development of archaeology in eighteenth-century France seems more than a little haphazard compared with that of engineering, for there was no central authority for archaeologists such as existed for engineers in the Ecole des Ponts et Chaussées. This was a government department that had been founded by Colbert and directed as much for military as for civil convenience. It was largely based upon the *corvée*, a form of service later curtailed by Turgot, that required the poorer country folk to work unpaid for a certain number of days each year upon the construction of roads.

The department was reorganized in 1716, and again in the 1740s by Daniel Trudaine who, as Intendant des Finances, transformed the Ecole with Jean-Rodolphe Perronet as its head *(82)*. After his early death Trudaine's equally energetic son, Trudaine de Montigny, supervised the work of the department. It had its headquarters where Perronet lived, in the rue Vieille-du-Temple in the east of Paris, and Perronet as Premier Ingénieur had the services of a professor (a post later occupied by Dumont), and a number of inspectors and engineers posted in each Généralité or county. The work the engineers were called upon to undertake was by no means confined to bridges and roads. In many Généralités they were charged by the Intendant with supervising a wide range of architectural projects, imposing a standard of practical and elegant

82 Portrait of Jean-Rodolph Perronet (1708–94), marble bust by François Masson (Musée Carnavalet, Paris). Perronet directed the work of the Ecole des Ponts et Chaussées, the royal department responsible for the construction and maintenance of bridges and roads in France

83 The Construction of a Highway, by Joseph Vernet, 1774 (Musée du Louvre, Paris). The principal figure on horseback may be a representation of Perronet

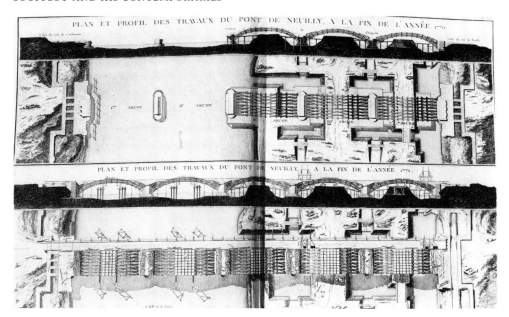

84 Plans showing the course of construction of the bridge at Neuilly, 1770–71, engraving from Perronet's *Description*. The methods used by Perronet in his famous bridges to combine wide arches and a level roadway are illustrated in the plates of his book

85 The Opening of the Bridge at Neuilly, by Hubert Robert, 1772 (Musée Carnavalet, Paris). In the presence of the king, the scaffolding supporting the arches of the bridge is cast into the Seine

simplicity that spread to the provinces the aesthetic of the most advanced Parisian architecture.

The work of the engineers in transforming the roads of France to a standard unknown since the decline of the Roman Empire was a source of great pride to the French: 'No nation possesses such magnificent works of this kind, and we are not equalled or surpassed in this respect by the most famous peoples of the universe' *(83)*. Foreigners endorsed this opinion, even if it seemed to them at the same time an instance of the extravagance that marked the excessive centralization of the French governmental system. Arthur Young, who took particular interest in the transformation of the French landscape, speaks of the roads he used in 1787 in Languedoc in this way:

The roads here are stupendous works . . . Enormous sums have been spent to level even gentle slopes. The causeways are raised and walled on each side, forming one solid mass of artificial road, carried across the valleys to the height of six, seven, or eight feet, and never less than 50 wide . . . we have not an idea of what such a road is in England. The traffic of the way, however, demands no such exertions; one-third of the breadth is beaten, one-third rough, and one-third covered with weeds. In 36 miles, I have met one cabriolet, half-a-dozen carts, and some old women with asses . . . In Languedoc, it is true, these works are not done by *corvées*; but there is injustice in levying the amount not far short of them. The money is raised by *tailles*, and, in making the assessment, lands held by noble tenure are . . . much eased . . .

The development of architectural principles in eighteenth-century France, the close unity that prevailed in style, technique and function, is nowhere more clearly seen than in the design of its many famous stone bridges. This was a branch of architecture that had always answered the same basic need, and it was a speciality of Perronet himself, the designer of the bridges at Orléans, Mantes, Château-Thierry, Nogent-sur-Seine, Pont-Ste-Maxence, Neuilly, and of the Pont Louis XVI, which was to cross the Seine on the central axis of the Place Louis XV. Most of these designs are illustrated in the official publication of Perronet's works, his *Description des projets de la construction des Ponts de Neuilly . . .*, of 1782–83.

The three closely related principles that guided Perronet in the planning of his bridges were to ensure that the road, instead of rising in a hump over the river, should remain level, that the arches of the bridge, instead of observing a hierarchy of size, should be equal in width, and obviously as widely spaced as practicable, and that the piers supporting the arches should disturb as little as possible the flow of water beneath the bridge. The similarities with Ste-Geneviève in the character of its design and the demands of its construction are clear enough, since there the articulation was to consist of columns and straight lintels, with the dome supported on piers that interrupted as little as possible the sight lines across the church.

The course of construction of the bridge at Neuilly (1768–72), the bridge over the Seine that linked the Champs-Elysées with the road to St-Germain-en-Laye and the west, is shown in a series of illustrations in Perronet's book *(84)*. The narrow piers, rounded at each end and heavily supported with iron braces, were constructed first, then wooden platforms were fixed in the river bed for the building of the arches. The masonry was laid evenly across the whole span of the bridge, until in 1772 its five low stone arches were fixed in position and the wooden centering cast into the river. The 'décintrement' of the bridge was a moment of public celebration, which took place in the presence of the king, and a great crowd gathered to witness the scaffolding carried away by the river *(85)*.

Perronet's achievements were the subject of general public acclaim. Among the many eulogies of the Neuilly bridge is one by Blaikie:

from thence we descended to the new and fine bridge at Neuilly which is supposed one of the finest existing; it is quite level and

about 750 feet long composed of 5 large Arches each 120 feet wide and quite flat; there is at each side a smaler arche; the stones of which this Bridge is built is exceeding large we measured some of them 34 feet long.

For Young the bridge was 'by far the most beautiful I have anywhere seen . . . incomparably more elegant, and more striking than our system of different sized arches'. He also noted that the bridge at Orléans was 'the first experiment of the flat arch made in France, where it is now so fashionable', and he comments too on another of Perronet's experiments in the construction of the Pont-Ste-Maxence, 'a handsome bridge, of three arches, the construction uncommon, each pier consisting of four pillars'.

The nature of their employment prevented Perronet and his subordinates from establishing full commercial practices, and the prospect of abandoning the relative security of an established post became less and less attractive as the market became flooded with architects, but this did not prevent them from undertaking a wide range of public and occasionally private buildings. The names of the engineers of the Ecole des Ponts et Chaussées became famous in most parts of the country; Mathieu Hue, Emiliand Gauthey and Louis Le Masson were three of the foremost. And as buildings became increasingly simplified in character, their elegance residing in shape and structure more than in decoration, the engineer was well placed to set an example.

An early instance of a modern design of unusual elegance constructed outside Paris by a representative of the Ecole des Ponts et Chaussées is the Bourse of La Rochelle, designed by Hue and built in the early 1760s *(86)*. In plan the building recalls the type of a large private town house, with three wings around a court which is closed at the front by a screening wall. The rear façade, where an open arcade supports a chamber above for general public meetings, is more closely related to a

86 The Bourse, La Rochelle, the rear façade. Designed by Mathieu Hue in the early 1760s, the Bourse is an early example of the distinguished architecture of the engineers of the Ecole des Ponts et Chaussées

traditional exchange plan. Hue's design is simpler and more economical than Soufflot's Loge-au-Change at Lyon, but discreetly enhanced by simple decoration.

The modest window frames, consisting of rectilinear mouldings with ears at the top corners and a raised moulding at the base, are by no means perfunctory in design, and they are tied to the surface of the wall by flat keystones of a Michelangelesque pattern that Gabriel and Soufflot had employed. The three central bays of the façade, projecting slightly, have their windows set into projecting panels mounting to the level of the entablature and decorated with a Greek key pattern instead of ornamental keystones. The central window is not in any way distinguished from those to each side, and only as a group of three do the central bays hint at the presence of a passageway beneath leading to the court of the exchange. A high entablature gives a strong horizontal emphasis to the façade, linking its three sections, while high volutes, recalling triglyphs, are placed in pairs above each window, occurring singly at the corners of the central projection and at the ends of the façade. Only on reflection is it apparent how far the understatement of the façade depends on the adaptation, in the hands of an engineer, of decorative forms that were employed sometimes even in Paris with much less discrimination.

English visitors to France in the later eighteenth century were struck not only by the splendour of the roads and bridges that the engineers had constructed but by the contrast they made with the still feudal way of life in the country. At Chanteloup, where Choiseul had spent his years of exile, Arthur Young reflected how 'Great Lords love too much an environ of forest, boars, and huntsmen, instead of marking their residence by the accompaniment of neat and well-cultivated farms, clean cottages, and happy peasants.' Between the house and the forest the French had traditionally laid out their gardens with all the formality that marked the construction of their roads and bridges, and the example of Le Nôtre's work for Louis XIV at Versailles remained an understandable source of enormous pride, as Blaikie related:

allthough those Architects has a great taste in their buildings yet they are extreemy defective in the arranging of their gardens allthough [through?] their vanity of Lenotre of which every French man braggs and certainly his plans was noble allthough the reverse of Nature, allways those Stiff terrasses and extravagant Staires as they emagined nothing could answer or be noble without Statues terrasses &c.

Inspired by contemporary English ideas, the 'philosophes', later joined by Rousseau, had begun to extol the greater virtues of unspoilt nature. Diderot's *La Promenade d'un sceptique* (1747) provides an early instance of this change of heart in France. 'I realized that Cléobule had evolved a sort of philosophy related to his surroundings, that the whole countryside appeared animate and articulate to him and that each object supplied him with thoughts of a particular kind and that the works of nature were for him an allegory from which he deduced a thousand truths of which other men were unaware.'

Transferring such sentiments to garden architecture,

Laugier had written in his *Essai* with only qualified praise of Le Nôtre: 'That great air of symmetry suggests nothing of the beauty of nature.' Laugier mentions the Chinese taste in gardening, known in France since the early eighteenth century, which seemed to him preferable to the French, but he is silent about the changes that had been introduced in England, beginning with the garden designs of William Kent. During the 1750s the style of Kent had been developed at Stowe and at Hagley, where Stuart had worked, and in Chambers' transformation of Kew, with its celebrated garden buildings, including the Chinese pagoda *(87)*. Though gardens slowly altered in France it was still possible as late as 1774 for an English visitor to feel that 'The French Taste in Gardening, I see, exactly resembles the English Taste [of] Fifty Years ago. High Walls, straight Lines, & Trees tortured into ugly and unmeaning Forms compose all the Variety of which these People's Imagination seems Susceptible . . .'

The development of the garden in late eighteenth-century France, which was important for architecture in relation to the work of Soufflot at Ménars and to Ledoux's whole conception of the role of his buildings, is clear enough in principle but notoriously vague in detail and in its wide historical ramifications – social, philosophical and political. The 'Rococo' garden, of which the most famous was the park of King Stanislas of Lorraine at Lunéville, already admitted a wide range of garden buildings and ornaments, including pavilions in the Chinese style, so that the more rigid manner of Le Nôtre was already declining by the time that so-called 'English' gardens came into fashion in France, and even these retained for many years much of the artificiality of the earlier eighteenth century.

In many French parks and gardens, even at Versailles, part of the site was in any case often left uncultivated, for reasons of economy or to provide a contrast with the formality elsewhere, and though owners may have taken only a limited interest in the 'natural' corners of their estates, these closely resemble in plan the wooded parks of the later eighteenth century. To complicate the picture still further very little is known about the appearance or the exact dates of the earliest 'English' gardens in France, despite all that was published on the subject of garden design at the time. It is, however, clear that the transformation of parks was a very gradual process. The earliest 'English' gardens were laid out at first with formal avenues usually at some distance from the house, and the formal garden rarely disappeared entirely even at the end of the century.

By the time of Mrs Thrale's journey to Paris in 1774 several French gardens had been fashioned in what seemed at the time an 'English' style. Amongst the first were the estates of 'Moulin Joli', created on an island in the Seine to the west of Paris by the financier Henri Watelet, the gardens at Ermenonville, laid out by the Marquis de Girardin, those nearby at Morfontaine, designed for Le Pelletier de Morfontaine, and in Paris itself a small garden known as 'Tivoli' which the financier Charles-Robert Boutin had laid out in the north-western outskirts. Not far from Tivoli the Duc de Chartres had begun, slightly later,

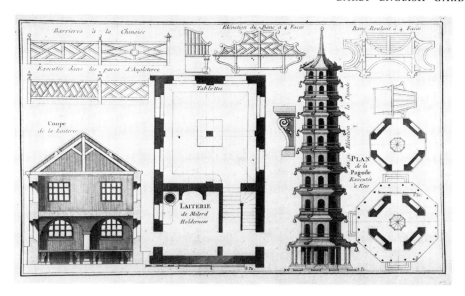

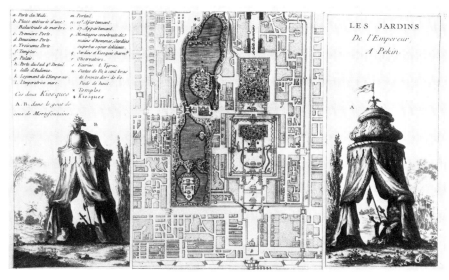

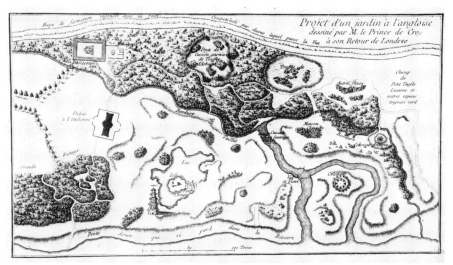

87 Plates from the *cahiers* of Le Rouge,
studies of English garden buildings,
including Chambers' pagoda at Kew,
studies of the gardens of the Emperor at
Peking, and plan of a garden 'à
l'angloise' designed by the Prince de Croÿ

the Parc de Monceau, which is, with Ermenonville, one of the few such gardens to survive in part. The names of two designers are connected with these gardens: Morel, who worked for Watelet and Girardin, and Carmontelle, the designer of Monceau.

Whatever the degree of English informality possessed by such gardens, they were nearly all abused by English visitors for their patent artificiality. The climate itself was unsuited to the creation of lawns, and, as Blaikie remarked, shade was more necessary in France than in England. Coming to France to work in the 1770s, Blaikie was appalled by the destruction of famous botanical gardens and by the widespread ignorance he discovered. Henry, the main Paris nurseryman, he found 'has got a fine Catalogue but hardly any scarce plants . . . this nurseryman which they look upon as the first about Paris does almost [all] his business in the Publick house'.

Of all the many gardens he visited Blaikie approved only of the work of Girardin and Morel at Ermenonville. The early gardens he saw were philosophical rather than horticultural in intention. Many were scattered with inscriptions designed to create a suitably pensive mood, or they were frankly amusement parks, for the pleasure of the owners, if not for the servants who pushed the swings and roundabouts. The rather self-conscious pleasure that the French had newly discovered in country life was attributed by Arthur Young as much to Rousseau as to the example of England:

The present fashion in France of passing some time in the country is new; at this time of the year [September], and for many weeks past, Paris is, comparatively speaking, empty. Everybody that have country seats are at them; and those who have none visit others who have. This remarkable revolution in the French manners is certainly one of the best customs they have taken from England; and its introduction was effected the easier, being assisted by the magic of Rousseau's writings.

For the type of garden that accompanied this change of fashion Young had nothing but scorn. 'As to the garden,' he wrote of M. du Barry's house in Toulouse, 'it is beneath all contempt, except as an object to make a man stare at the efforts to which folly can arrive. In the space of an acre, there are hills of genuine earth, mountains of pasteboard,

rocks of canvas; abbés, cows, sheep, and shepherdesses in lead . . .; nothing excluded except nature.' Horace Walpole had written in similar terms in his famous description of Boutin's Tivoli: 'There are three or four very high hills, almost as high as, and exactly the shape of, a tansy pudding. You squeeze between these and a river, that is conducted at obtuse angles in a stone channel, and supplied by a pump; and when walnuts come in, I suppose it will be navigable . . .'

Though most of these early French gardens have now been completely destroyed, several are recorded in the books of Le Rouge, which began to appear in 1774, and Le Rouge also shows comparative plates of real Chinese gardens and several English parks, including Stowe and Kew (87). Whatever English visitors may have thought, it was the artifice of such gardens that held the fascination of the French throughout the later years of the century. Mme Vigée Lebrun explained that at Morfontaine 'I always preferred the picturesque part of the park which is not set out in the English way . . . All artists accord it the front rank in its kind', and Moulin Joli remained for her a 'delightful spot, with which I have never seen anything to be compared'. Ermenonville she liked less, not because it resembled more closely a real English park, but because she found the inscriptions there 'at almost every step – a veritable tyranny over the mind'. On the Island of Poplars there Rousseau himself was buried in a classical sarcophagus in 1778 (88).

Though it was mainly financiers who planned these informal gardens in the 1750s and 1760s the fashion rapidly spread to the aristocracy, who had themselves come to appreciate the writings of Rousseau. Many visited him in Paris where he lived in obscurity and poverty, copying music in the years before his death. In the great parks of these later years engineering and archaeology played an increasingly large part, as new techniques were applied to the diversion of real rivers, the shaping of mountains of rock, the building of bridges and the imitation of classical ruins, and some of the greatest architects of the time became deeply involved in the designing of gardens.

88 View of the tomb of Rousseau at Ermenonville (engraving from Le Rouge). Dying in 1778 at Ermenonville, Rousseau was buried in a sarcophagus on the Island of Poplars there; his remains were later taken to the Panthéon

5 The later career of Soufflot; the completion of Ste-Geneviève

THE LATER CAREER OF SOUFFLOT was taken up with the effort of seeing his church completed, a task that came to require a heroic persistence on the part of the architect in the face of growing criticism and opposition. Though the significance of Soufflot's ideas was well understood, as well as his genius in translating them into visually acceptable forms, all the more was he subjected to public scrutiny. As Grimm reported on the first project for Ste-Geneviève of 1757, 'very beautiful things are to be found in the ideas of M. Soufflot, but several are also being criticized'.

The great phase of building activity that had begun in Paris at the end of the War of the Austrian Succession was interrupted a few years later by the outbreak of the Seven Years' War, just after Soufflot's first design for the church *(34)* was engraved (1757). The site itself, extensively quarried in the past, was unsuited to so heavy a building and foundations of unusual depth were required. As Laugier mentions, criticism of the church had extended to the plan, for the Greek cross that the architect preferred for its regular shape conflicted with liturgical tradition, as had occurred in the past at both St Peter's and St Paul's. By 1764, when the king formally laid the foundation-stone of the high altar, Soufflot had made many alterations to the plan, partly in response to the views of his critics *(89)*. He lengthened the church by adding extra bays to the choir and the nave, designed in such a way as to leave the shape of the Greek cross largely unaffected. He moved the high altar from the crossing to the east end and to each side of the new chancel he added bell-towers, though this was an architectural form distasteful – and scarcely less troublesome than a cupola – to all classically-minded architects.

Soufflot was forced to consider the provision of a crypt, a feature that he had omitted from his first project; in early drawings of about 1758 the shrine of St Geneviève, consisting of a statue and a tomb, is placed in a small chamber directly beneath the eastern recess of the church *(90)*. This design shows the first known attempt to employ the Greek Doric order in an eighteenth-century French building, but though the context is suitably subterranean

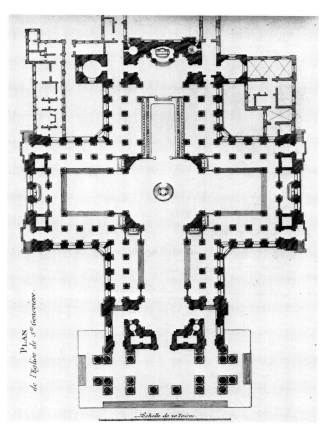

PLAN de l'Eglise de s.^{te} Geneviève.

Echelle de 20 Toises.

89 The church of Ste-Geneviève, Paris, Soufflot's revised plan (engraving from Piganiol de la Force, 1765). The plan shows the extensions to the nave and choir that Soufflot had introduced about 1758

(and historically remote) for an order that implies strength and venerable antiquity, Soufflot was unable to abandon himself at this date to all the primitive characteristics of the order, and he supplied it with a base, rather awkwardly contrived. Yet the squat proportions, deep channelling and prominent abacus over each stunted capital show that this

90 Ste-Geneviève, section of the crypt, drawing by Soufflot (Archives Nationales, Paris). Soufflot's first design for the crypt, of c. 1758, where columns based on the Greek Doric order he had seen at Paestum (29) are introduced

91 Ste-Geneviève, view of the crypt. More extensive than in Soufflot's early project and articulated with Tuscan columns, the crypt as built was criticized for being too like a prison

is cousin to the order Soufflot had himself seen at Paestum (29) and to those which are engraved in the plates of Le Roy's book (79). To accompany the order he invented an entablature consisting of an enlarged key ornament punctuated with rosettes which also forms part of the decoration of the vaulting.

By the time of the foundation ceremony in 1764 the crypt had been constructed to a different design (91), and Soufflot had introduced other variations in his scheme for the church, attending especially to the appearance of the cupola (94). The ceremony itself, with the presence of the king endorsing the importance of the building, is recorded in a picture by de Machy (92). A full-scale painting of the portico had been constructed on the site, and before it stands the architect, dressed in violet and wearing the cordon noir of the Order of St-Michel. The figure beside Soufflot, dressed in black, must be Marigny, no doubt in mourning for his sister, while the king advances towards Soufflot to inspect the plan that the architect holds up. Diderot, criticizing de Machy's painting at the Salon of 1765, noted that the 'portico, which is large and noble, has become a little house of cards'.

The portico was part of the building that Soufflot had not altered, but the crypt now extended below the whole eastern arm of the cross, articulated with pairs of Tuscan columns (91). In place of the altars originally in the centre of the crossing Soufflot intended to place staircases leading down to the crypt, their presence marked by a free-standing sculptural group on a huge circular base, showing the Four Cardinal Virtues with a reliquary casket (94). This was an idea that consciously referred to the heart of

the Catholic church, deriving from Bernini's *baldacchino* in the crossing of St Peter's, which marks the site of the saint's tomb in the crypt, and from the chair of the saint in the choir, which is carried in Bernini's bronze casing by the four Doctors of the Church *(114)*. Soufflot's final ideas for the crypt, though praised by Laugier, seem to have met with a mixed reception. Grimm expressed the view that the crypt was too like a prison, 'this forest of columns . . . which makes the space so narrow and squat', while the stairs in the crossing reminded him of a well. It was anticipated, according to Grimm, that the main doorway of the church would also be too narrow, but Soufflot had justified its width with reference to Greek and Roman buildings.

For the Virtues in the crossing Soufflot intended not modern sculptures but statues that had been made by the sixteenth-century French sculptor Germain Pilon *(93)*. This decision marks him as one of the first artists to associate himself with what was to become a general interest in the sculpture of the French Renaissance. It was a taste shared by artists and the general public and one that is well expressed in the Créquy *Souvenirs* in a passage referring to monuments of the Valois dynasty: 'I have always loved above all the compositions of the time of the Renaissance, in which I find neither the coldness of antiquity, nor the clumsiness of Gothic, nor the affected grimaces and torment of the monuments of today.' The revival of Goujon's style in the later eighteenth century, matching the revival of interest in early Renaissance architecture, is perhaps at its clearest in interior decoration, in reliefs like those that Métivier carried out to

92 The Foundation of the Church of Ste-Geneviève, detail of painting by de Machy, 1764 (Musée Carnavalet, Paris). In front of a full-scale painted model of the portico, Soufflot holds up a drawing to show Marigny (wearing black) and the hatted king, who went on to lay the foundation stone for the high altar

93 A Cardinal Virtue, by Germain Pilon (c. 1531–1590) (Musée du Louvre, Paris). One of four wooden statues of the Virtues by Pilon which supported a reliquary casket in the crossing of Ste-Geneviève *(94)*

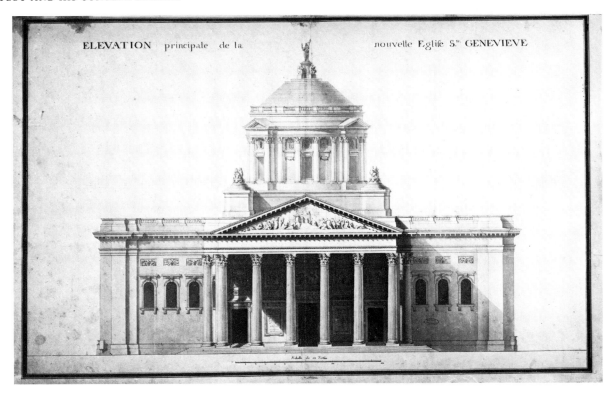

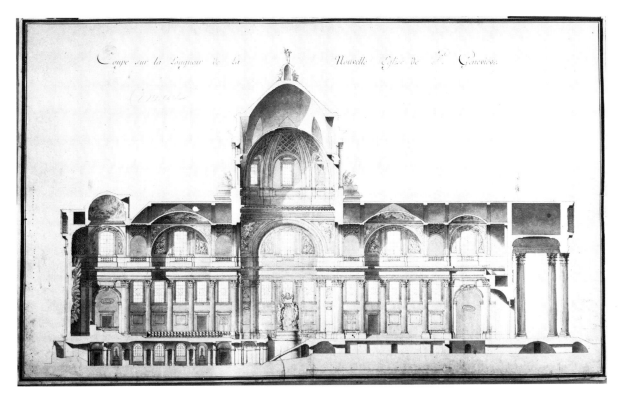

94 Ste-Geneviève, elevation and section of revised project of 1764, drawings by Soufflot (Archives Nationales, Paris). The dome in the revised project is a stepped cone with the statue of St Geneviève at the summit; the section shows the intended method of access to the crypt, from stairs in the crossing

Ledoux's designs *(223)*, where the intricate patterns and restrained outlines of the sixteenth century suit the architectural restraint of the time more effectively than the dynamic designs of the earlier eighteenth century.

In the decoration of Ste-Geneviève Soufflot gradually relinquished the Berninesque features present in his first proposals. The section of his 1764 project shows only the high altar surrounded by a glory of heavenly rays *(94)*. Elsewhere in the interior the effect is more austere than before and two important changes have been introduced. The columns now have much lower bases throughout, those of the 'aisles' standing almost directly on the floor, while in the vaults that enclose the shallow domes of the four arms of the cross, and which serve as buttresses for the crossing, balconies have been hollowed out over the entablature, making the interior still more light and spacious in appearance – and further weakening the support needed to sustain the dome.

Most radical of all in his proposals of 1764 was Soufflot's new design for the exterior of the church, as shown in his elegant drawing of the front elevation *(94)*. The drum has an articulation of groups of four columns between the projecting diagonal bays, which are now accented by means of pediments, and in place of the hemispherical cupola is a cone of steps forming a pedestal for the statue of St Geneviève that surmounts the composition. Statues of the four Evangelists are placed at her feet, taking precedence over the Fathers of the Church who remain below the cupola. A dome of this character, recalling the experiments of the French artists in Rome in the 1740s *(65)*, brings the design into conformity with the interior in the important sense that both now look directly to antiquity, bypassing the conventions of the Renaissance. But in style, in this the first of Soufflot's later experiments with the dome, the structure began to assume a simplified shape that expresses less well the complexity of the plan, established in essentials only seven years previously *(34)*.

The decade of the 1760s, before the celebrated dispute about Soufflot's handling of the dome of Ste-Geneviève began in earnest, was a busy time for the architect. The church itself was built to the level of the main cornice and with it rose the Ecole de Droit that occupied the northern half of the square in front of the church *(95)*. With its pedimented Doric portico on a curved plan facing across the square to the Corinthian portico of Ste-Geneviève, this forms a transition in scale and relative formality between the town and the church itself.

Soufflot's other duties in Paris included the continuation of work on the Louvre and the Tuileries, and commissions that came to him through his appointment as Director of the Gobelins tapestry factory. One of the innovations credited to him in this capacity is the invention of the oval-backed chair, for tapestries in this shape were produced at the Gobelins as early as 1763. At the Tuileries Soufflot altered the theatre, made famous by Servandoni's decorations, to accommodate the Opéra, but this second essay of his in theatre design was regarded as a failure. More significant were the designs he made for a large new opera house on the opposite bank of the Seine,

95 The Ecole de Droit, Place Ste-Geneviève, Paris, begun 1763. The curved façade of Soufflot's Ecole de Droit, with its Ionic order, occupies the north-west corner of the square in front of Ste-Geneviève

where the Monnaie now stands. Descriptions suggest that it had a circular auditorium and a projecting curved colonnade for its frontispiece – and it was thus a source for many later theatre designs.

At the Louvre, where he had collaborated with Gabriel, Soufflot was active until the year of his death and his last work there embodied the most important of his structural experiments. Having developed for the fabric of the portico of Ste-Geneviève a system of iron braces more extensive than those which had been used for the colonnades of the Louvre and the Place Louis XV, he designed in 1779 for a staircase that survived for only a few years a wrought iron roof, just over 50 feet (15 metres) wide, and believed to be the earliest of its kind. In addition to all these special commissions and the work undertaken for Marigny, the day-to-day routine of administration continued. A typical entry from Soufflot's letter book is a note sent by Marigny from Compiègne in June 1764: 'The Prince de Tingry, Sir, has asked me on behalf of the Marquise de Valory for some repairs at her apartment in the Palais du Luxembourg – take the trouble to go there and discover what they are.'

At Ste-Geneviève Soufflot not only altered the interior of the church preparatory to its construction, but in the later 1760s he also made adjustments to the exterior walls *(96)*. He abolished the relief panels over the windows, substituting a frieze of decoration just below the level of the entablature. This was a change, in line with the evolution of Soufflot's style, which made the decoration of the exterior less fragmented in appearance. A classical precedent existed for the alteration in the Tomb of Cecilia Metella, a building that had in common with the church the absence of an order *(8)*. Soufflot also strengthened the corners of his building by adding fluted channelling to the projections of the frieze. He may have remembered this unusual motif, which is unrelated to any well-known

96 Ste-Geneviève, diagonal section, drawing by Soufflot (Archives Nationales, Paris). Datable about 1770 and showing the first of Soufflot's experiments with a triple-shelled dome

classical precedent, from the Hôtel de Ville at Lyon *(28)*. It allowed the architect the advantages that pilasters would have contributed to the definition of the building, without exposing him to the criticism that real pilasters would inevitably have attracted at this date.

Soufflot's difficulties at Ste-Geneviève began in earnest in 1769, when Pierre Patte drafted a memoir (published in 1770) questioning the stability of the dome. Patte, though he worked in association with Blondel, had already gained a reputation as a troublemaker, and he had caused problems for Diderot over the publication of the plates of the *Encyclopédie*. Grimm attacked him in the *Correspondance littéraire*: 'he doesn't know how to create, but he wants to obstruct the creations of others'. Whatever his real fears for the stability of the church, Patte appears to have been motivated partly by personal antagonism to Soufflot. He argued that for a dome that was 63 feet (19 metres) wide the supporting walls of the drum would have to be 8 feet (2·4 metres) thick and that the pillars intended to support the drum, being just over 3 feet (0·9 metres) wide were insufficient to carry its weight. Ste-Geneviève was sufficiently experimental for such criticism to spread alarm, but the dome was defended by most of Soufflot's colleagues and by Perronet and the engineers of the Ecole des Ponts et Chaussées. During the preceding fifteen years

Soufflot had studied the construction of many earlier domes and drafted reports to the Academy, and Patte himself had been to London in 1768 (where he had delivered a letter from Soufflot to Chambers) to survey the dome of St Paul's, the model on which the dome of Ste-Geneviève was ultimately to be based.

Deeply wounded by the criticism of Patte and his supporters but undeterred by their attacks, Soufflot produced in the early 1770s a series of different designs for the dome in which its bulk was gradually increased and its support strengthened. The earliest, recorded in one of the liveliest of Soufflot's drawings *(96)*, is a design of about 1770, a diagonal section taken through the crossing, which demonstrates two new ways of supporting the dome. Clearly Soufflot himself entertained fears for the safety of the type of structure he had planned in 1764, and he returned in this drawing to a type of dome that is more traditional in character. It is a tall double-shelled cupola with a lantern at the summit in place of the statue of St Geneviève. The scheme derives ultimately from the church of the Invalides *(13)*, especially in the presence of the central oculus affording a view of a painting on the underside of the lower shell, but it also recalls St Paul's in the steep conical shape of the lower shell, supporting the root of the lantern *(6)*. In this design Soufflot further weakened the walls of the church by glazing throughout the lunettes of the clerestory, but in compensation he introduced tall pyramids in place of the statues of the Church Fathers to weight down the corners of the dome plinth. Seen in elevation these pyramids, which serve visually to define and limit the scale of the central dome, must have recalled not any earlier church designs, but rather mausoleum projects in the antique style that younger architects had produced in Rome *(67, 71)*.

In 1774 work was resumed on the dome to an enlarged design and Soufflot produced several new projects *(97)*. He introduced an attic storey, a further step towards a traditional solution, which allowed him to start the two shells of the dome at a higher level where they would not interfere with the main windows of the drum and the illumination of the crossing. In conjunction with the attic storey Soufflot used the plinth of the dome for a continuous colonnade that greatly increased the apparent width of the drum. But in these projects Soufflot hesitated before settling upon the circular shape that was finally chosen. In following Wren's design for the dome of St Paul's, Soufflot allowed free-standing columns to play as important a part in the crowning of the church as they had done in the interior, but the regularity of the circular shape conforms better with the taste of the 1770s than with the intricacy of his twenty-year-old plan, which seems to demand a more ingenious and certainly a more original dome than the one finally constructed.

In 1776, almost immediately after the dome was begun, two of the piers of the crossing were discovered to be cracking and the whole dispute about the stability of the church broke out again. Soufflot was finally exonerated and the cracks identified as being due to faulty workmanship. Building was resumed and the church had reached the level of the cupola by the time of Soufflot's death in 1780.

Setbacks in the construction of the church had not been the only cause of distress to the architect in the last years of his life. Equally mortifying had been his failure to succeed to the post of Premier Architecte on the retirement of Gabriel in 1775. Marigny had resigned as Surintendant des Bâtiments du Roi two years before and was succeeded briefly by the Abbé Terray, Turgot's predecessor as Contrôleur des Finances. In the reorganization of administration that marked the accession of Louis XVI, when d'Angiviller was appointed to direct the Bâtiments du Roi, the responsibilities of the Premier Architecte were curtailed and three posts of Inspecteur-Général created. Soufflot filled one of these posts, while the position of Premier Architecte went to Richard Mique, the personal architect of the daughters of Louis XV and of the new queen, Marie Antoinette, and an architect who respectfully followed the style of Gabriel right up until the time of the Revolution.

Soufflot's embitterment in the last years of his life is reflected in the short epitaph which he wrote for himself. Here, after stressing the absence of formal training in his first years, he continued: 'he liked talent to be joined with integrity; more than one jealous rival who was his enemy, if he had known his heart, would have been his friend'.

Nevertheless Soufflot enjoyed the respect of his contemporaries right up to the time of his death, and friendship was not lacking. In 1773, at the time when he again visited Lyon, Soufflot had gone with François Tronchin to pay his respects to Voltaire at Les Délices. Confined by illness at Ferney, Voltaire was unable to greet his distinguished visitors, but Soufflot slept in Voltaire's bed and this inspired him to compose a poem that alluded in jest to their brotherhood as freemasons. The architect also enjoyed the respect of those who worked for him at Ste-Geneviève and his obituary in the *Journal de Paris* contains a moving story that relates how the workmen from the church stopped the architect's funeral procession to insist that his remains be buried in the monument which he had created.

Though Soufflot had no immediate family, his young nephew, called Soufflot 'le Romain', was one of several younger architects whom he trained and protected. Brébion and Rondelet, his other successors at Ste-Geneviève, were also pupils, and so too, more surprisingly, was Lequeu, who left to the Bibliothèque du Roi, together with the volumes of his own bizarre drawings, a book of engravings of the works of Soufflot. The architect's closest friends in his later years were the painter Vernet (whose family included the architect Chalgrin) and the Bishop of St-Brieux, both of whom are mentioned in his will.

97 Ste-Geneviève, elevation (engraving by Sellier). The width of the drum is enlarged in this project, published in 1776, by the introduction of an octagonal colonnade

98 Ste-Geneviève, view of the church from the south west, *c.* 1790. The building is shown before the blocking of the windows and the demolition of the bell-towers

Soufflot's possessions are recorded in the catalogue of his collection which the dealer Lebrun, the husband of Mme Vigée Lebrun, compiled for the sale that took place shortly after his death. Many paintings are listed, mainly works by contemporary French artists, Boucher, Robert and Vernet, but also several works by Panini. There were drawings and engravings by French artists, and two engraved portraits, one of Marigny and one of Bertin, a former Intendant of Lyon, who had later become the minister with responsibility for the affairs of Paris. Bertin was celebrated for his collection of Chinese art, and

Soufflot had perhaps modified his hostility to the Chinese style when in 1775 he showed the Academy drawings of Chinese work that belonged to Bertin. Together with his nephew he is recorded as working on the estate that the minister owned at Chatou on the western outskirts of Paris.

Most interesting of all in the sale of Soufflot's possessions were the books he owned. They comprised none of the standard Renaissance treatises, such as Palladio and Serlio, but many French books, including the works of Le Roy, Clérisseau and Dumont, as well as several English architectural publications, including the works of Inigo

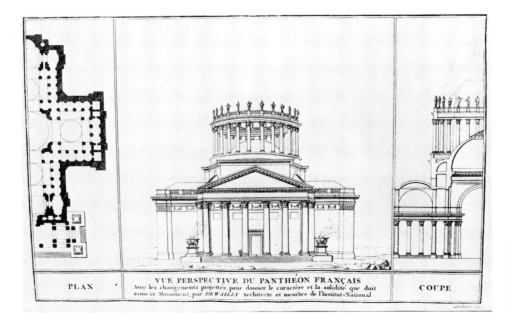

PLAN   VUE PERSPECTIVE DU PANTHÉON FRANÇAIS
Avec les changements projettés, pour donner le caractére et la solidité que doit
avoir ce Monument, par *DEWAILLY* Architecte et membre de l'Institut-National.   COUPE

99 Ste-Geneviève, project for alterations, by Charles de Wailly (engraving by Delettre). In de Wailly's design, one of many projects of the 1790s for altering the building, the dome is omitted while the circular colonnade is retained

100 Ste-Geneviève, view of the church from the south-west. The building as it appears today after the alterations of the 1790s

Jones and William Chambers. Though the catalogue lists no books of other than architectural interest Soufflot had an abiding interest in music and literature and he translated from the Italian poems by Metastasio, the celebrated librettist of the earlier part of the century. One further work owned by Soufflot was the *Encyclopédie*, but this he had presented to the Academy of Architecture shortly before his death.

On Soufflot's death Brébion and Soufflot 'le Romain', later assisted by Rondelet, took charge of the completion of Ste-Geneviève. Of Rondelet Soufflot had said 'he has all my secret', and following Soufflot's final ideas the fabric of the church was at last completed in 1790 *(98)*. But in 1791 a further group of alterations was carried out when the church was secularized for the first time and became the Panthéon. The changes were the work of Antoine-

Chrysostome Quatremère de Quincy, one of the most rigid and long-lived (1755–1849) theoreticians of his time. A failed sculptor and a friend of Jacques-Louis David, Quatremère made a considerable reputation as a writer on archaeological and artistic affairs. As Secrétaire Perpétuel of the Académie des Beaux-Arts later in his life, he pronounced the funeral discourses on several architects, and in a book of 1830 on the lives of famous architects Quatremère described the 'lightness' that Soufflot wished to achieve at Ste-Geneviève as a 'vice' ('le vice de légèreté'). He acknowledged the historical importance of the building, and the elegance and variety of Soufflot's style, but asserted that this was inappropriate to the function of a church. 'The sacred building should produce a quite different sensation. The great simplicity of lines and details, the severity of forms, the density of

101 Ste-Geneviève, view of the crossing. The interior of the church as it appears today after the reinforcement of the piers of the crossing carried out by Rondelet in 1806

colonnades, the economy of ornaments, that is what a church demands and that is what is not provided by the church of Sainte-Geneviève.'

Quatremère suppressed the bell-towers and had the windows filled in, for the 'Gothic' lightness of the interior was indeed no longer of any consequence at this late date. And the original sculptural decoration of the exterior was destroyed at the same time: Coustou's pediment relief of 'The Elevation of the Host' and the portico reliefs by Houdon, Julien, and others, of scenes from the lives of Sts Geneviève, Peter and Paul.

In the later 1790s many architects suggested projects for the alteration of the building, including several who had worked with Soufflot in earlier days. In one design *(99)* the cupola was to be suppressed altogether, leaving the columns of the drum to suggest a circular open temple crowning the crossing, and in another the building was apparently to be encased by a pyramid. None of these proposals was carried out, but in 1806 it was discovered that the piers of the crossing were again cracking, and Rondelet increased their size, cleverly adding pilasters and a solid core of masonry to Soufflot's groups of columns. The sculpture was also supplied mainly in these years so that in the decoration too the style of the later eighteenth century is scarcely apparent within the church.

Ste-Geneviève had become by the time of the Revolution a monument of collective national pride rather than the achievement of a single architect, though it was not so far transformed in character that the intentions of its author were wholly obscured. This may seem the inevitable fate of a building that had always been less a church for the worship of God than a symbol of intellectual endeavour, from the time when the first plans were projected in the 1750s to the emergence of the imposing but bleak and monotonous building that the visitor sees today *(100, 101)*.

Part Two

BUILDINGS OF THE 1760S AND THEIR ARCHITECTS

6 The Roman background: Peyre, de Wailly and Moreau-Desproux

THE ARCHITECTS who represent the first extreme of the classical revival in French architecture were nearly all *pensionnaires* at the French Academy in Rome during the decade of the 1750s. It was in relation to the work of these architects that Marigny, without realizing what further excesses their successors would commit, expressed his concern to Natoire about the neglect of 'our customs and usages'. It remained for them, following the example of Soufflot, to translate the buildings they admired in Italy not into engravings or temporary decorations, but into workable architectural designs. Their buildings began to appear in France from the late 1750s until well into the 1780s.

Though the buildings of antiquity had not been neglected by French students in Rome in the 1730s and 1740s, the supremacy of antiquity was established on an international basis in the following decade, with Winckelmann, who arrived in the city in 1755, as its principal spokesman. In painting clumsy attempts to emulate more closely the style of classical art had their beginnings in the work of Gavin Hamilton, who had been in Rome since 1748 staying with Stuart and Revett, and in the work of Anton Raphael Mengs. English 'Neo-classical' architecture was represented by Robert Adam, present in the city in the same year as Winckelmann, and by George Dance, who arrived there later in the decade.

In the early 1750s, shortly after Le Roy's departure from Rome, there were at the French Academy three students who are amongst the most important architects of the later eighteenth century in France. They all later practised in Paris and became interrelated in various ways. They are Marie-Joseph Peyre, Charles de Wailly and Pierre-Louis Moreau (Moreau-Desproux). The first to win the Prix de Rome was Peyre *(102)*, who had been born in 1730 and trained principally at the school of Blondel. His winning design of 1751 followed a programme for a public fountain.

Peyre arrived in Rome in 1753 and the work he undertook there as well as in the first years after his return to Paris was made known in a book he published in 1765, the *Livre d'architecture*. A second edition was brought out

102 Portrait of Marie-Joseph Peyre (1730–85), by an unidentified French painter (Ecole des Beaux-Arts, Paris). Given by Peyre's son to the Ecole des Beaux-Arts

thirty years later by Peyre's son, with a short biography of the architect and a collection of his later discourses. These form a commentary on the architectural projects, and show above all a profound awareness of the problem of matching classical architecture and modern customs, which had disturbed Marigny.

Following a dedication to Marigny Peyre explained in the introduction to his book that he had tried to imitate the character of the most magnificent buildings constructed by the Roman Emperors, which he names as the Baths of

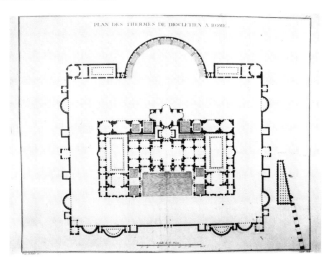

Diocletian, Caracalla and Titus, the Palace of the Emperors and the Villa of Hadrian. 'During my stay in Rome, the remains of these famous buildings inspired me to such an extent that I bent all my efforts to imitate the types of these great plans in several projects.' His own reconstructions of the Baths of Diocletian and Caracalla are illustrated in the book *(103)*, providing visual confirmation that the sources of his inspiration were indeed not any of the newly discovered classical sites nor the monuments of Greek architecture, but buildings that had been available for all to see and study throughout the Renaissance.

While in Rome Peyre entered for one of the architectural competitions held annually at the Accademia di San Luca with a design for a cathedral and two palaces *(104)*. The project is one that derives from the church and colonnade of St Peter's, but it is here adapted to a circular plan. The architect explained his idea as follows:

103 Plan of the Baths of Diocletian, Rome, reconstruction, engraving from Peyre, 1765. After winning the Prix de Rome in 1751, Peyre arrived in Rome in 1753 and made a survey of several of the major archaeological sites in and around the city

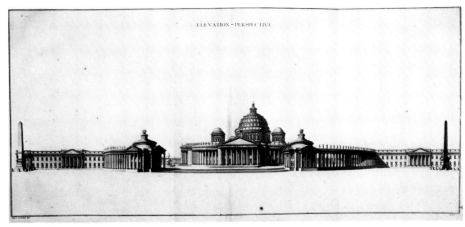

104 Project for a cathedral and two palaces, perspective view and plan, engravings from Peyre, 1765. Peyre's entry for the 1753 competition of the Accademia di San Luca in Rome

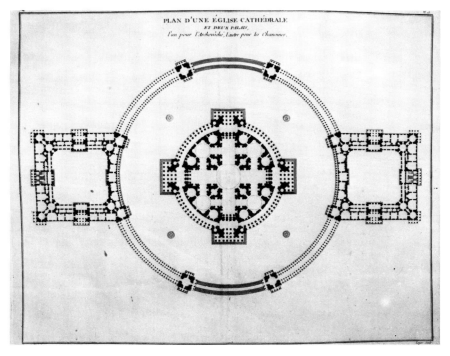

I have linked as far as possible the two palaces, with the general plan, by a magnificent boundary, which seems to unite them. The colonnades it is formed of, protecting the church from encumbrance and noise, would prepare, as in some ancient temples, for the respect that should be observed in entering there. There would be underground communications between the two palaces and the cathedral.

The visionary character of the project, with its mixture of Christian and pagan references, and its disregard of practical considerations, may well have astonished a French public but such ambitious designs, deriving from the town-planning projects of seventeenth-century Rome, had been a commonplace of the competitions at the Roman Academy since the time of their inception. Peyre showed himself to be not the instigator of the so-called 'megalo-mania' in later eighteenth-century French architecture but the first architect to publish such designs and one of the earliest to transform this familiar academic tradition into a relatively manageable and coherent style.

Peyre illustrated in his book two other designs comparable in scale with his cathedral project, a large building for Academies (suitably impractical in character) and a palace for a sovereign, and there are several more modest schemes – a mausoleum, a church portico (105), a small church – all of which are more viable architecturally than the more pictorial designs of his predecessors at the Academy in Rome. Throughout his projects Peyre was nevertheless committed to many of the features of Roman design that he later used to advantage in his real buildings in Paris; this is seen especially in his concern with symmetry and with the extensive use of colonnades and circular rooms.

Peyre's career after his return to Paris has not been investigated in detail, but it is known that he became Inspecteur, under Soufflot, of the Luxembourg Palace, and Contrôleur, under Gabriel, of the royal Château of Choisy, and he was chosen in 1767 to be a member of the Academy. Two important projects of the early 1760s are illustrated in his book, a small villa that the architect constructed on the southern outskirts of the city (106, 107), and his designs for the town palace of the Prince de Condé, the architect's masterpiece (108).

The villa was built for a member of one of the less well-known 'financial' families of the time (Le Prêtre de Neubourg), on the road forming the south-eastern boundary of the city (now the boulevard de l'Hôpital). Sited almost in the country, the house incorporated the remains of an earlier building, and it was evidently conceived by Peyre more as a villa than as a town house. 'I have decorated the façade', he wrote, 'with columns forming a peristyle, like most Italian casinos, in order to provide the relief and movement which in general make the effect of this kind of building very agreeable.'

Like an Italian casino, the building was indeed informal in its design, in plan, and in its setting, in spite of the presence of a small formal garden in front of the house. The main entrance lay at the side, marked by a pair of Tuscan columns which matched the order of the peristyle (106). The main façade was thus the garden elevation, pedimen-ted at each end but not in the centre, and the 'peristyle'

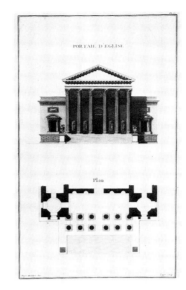
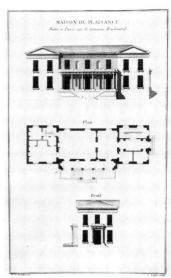

105 Design for a church portico, elevation and plan, engraving from Peyre, 1765. A portico resembling the front of a classical temple, but with the addition of side windows; the design is one of the more modest projects of Peyre's Roman years

106 The Neubourg house, Paris, elevations and plan, engraving from Peyre, 1765. Designed in the early 1760s for a site on the southern outskirts of Paris, the house was consciously modelled on Italian villas

107 The Neubourg house, perspective view showing gateway (engraving by Pierre Panseron). The semi-rural character of the site is shown in Panseron's view of the house

Élévation perspective du Projet de l'Hôtel de Condé.

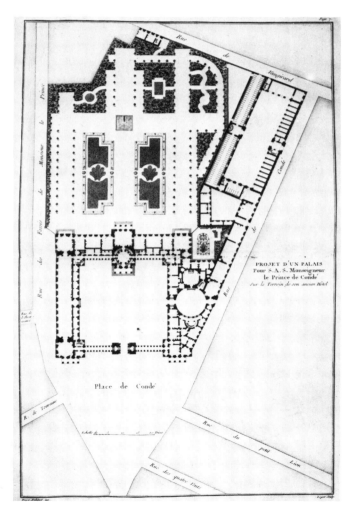

PROJET D'UN PALAIS
Pour S. A. S. Monseigneur
le Prince de Condé
Sur le Terrein de son ancien Hôtel

Place de Condé

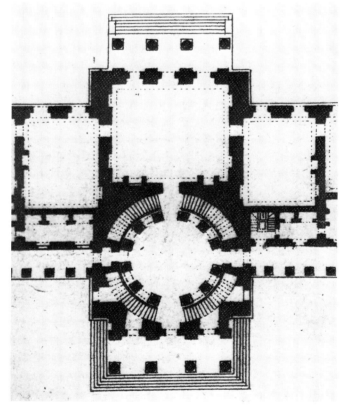

108 Project for the Hôtel de Condé, Paris, perspective view, plan, and detail of plan showing staircase, engravings from Peyre, 1765. Designed before 1763, Peyre's project shows a domestic building type, traditional in Paris, transformed by the influence of antiquity; the circular stairchamber with its central ring of columns, sited on the main axis, is exactly symmetrical in plan

marked the transition from the salon to the staircase leading down to the garden. The simplicity and unpretentious informality of the house, appropriate to its semi-rural setting, guaranteed the popularity of the building in the later years of the century. It made its appearance in many of the collections of engravings that recorded the most celebrated monuments of the day, and in one such vignette the pastoral felicity of the setting is emphasized in a view that also shows the main gateway and its relation to the façade (107).

Peyre's project for the Hôtel de Condé, which was shown to the Academy in 1763 and much liked, is in contrast a reinterpretation of a familiar French building type, showing for the first time how the traditional appearance of a large Parisian town house could be interpreted in a Roman style (108). The organization of the plan is relatively conventional, with three wings around a court, a stable court at the side and a stable nearby. But the plan is composed for the most part of relatively simple shapes, with the circle in particular used to advantage for the stable court and the main vestibule, where the principal staircase is placed.

The stairs lead upwards in matching curved flights visible behind a ring of columns that encircles the ground-floor vestibule. The main staircase in Parisian houses was not merely a utilitarian structure, but a semi-public room that had come to be regarded as a showpiece where the structural ingenuity associated with the French classical tradition invariably appeared to advantage. Since the very beginning of the seventeenth century the staircase had become separated from the vestibule – for reasons of show and convenience – and allowed to proliferate in a room, or even several rooms, of its own. But the complexity of such grand staircases was the cause of considerable difficulties in the later eighteenth century, since antiquity provided almost no guidance except in the design of wide and straight public stairways.

At the Hôtel de Condé Peyre reunited once again the vestibule and staircase, inventing an exactly symmetrical circular plan which also incorporated free-standing columns – and all this he contrived without diverting the route of access from the court to the state rooms on the garden side of the ground floor. The sources of his design lie not only in Roman architecture but also in seventeenth-century France, in Le Vau's staircase in the Château of Meudon (which had been developed in Germany especially by Balthasar Neumann). Peyre's own mausoleum design had narrow semicircular staircases concealed between the inner and outer walls of the building, and his reconstructions of Roman baths supply the regular and symmetrical geometry that underlies the plan.

The exterior of the hôtel is shown in a view (108) that gives an idea of the scale of the building within its setting (the site lay just to the south of the Palais du Luxembourg where Peyre was Inspecteur), and which also incorporates the fanciful addition of a markedly Berninesque fountain. Externally the building shows much of the formal elegance of the French vernacular tradition, embodied less in domestic than in public architecture (43), while remaining

109 Portrait of the Prince and Princesse de Condé *en berger*, by François-Hubert Drouais (Private Collection). Painted about 1760, Drouais' portrait shows Peyre's patron as an early devotee of 'naturalism' in dress and behaviour

far more geometric in appearance. The windows are equipped with well-defined frames which incorporate stone balconies and ranks of triangular pediments. The main emphases are defined largely by free-standing columns, a giant Ionic order for the frontispieces of the principal pavilions, and a smaller Tuscan order inside the court and across the screen and small triumphal arch that closes the court from the street. A screen of columns was a device that had been recommended by Laugier and engraved by Neufforge (74), and was apparently first employed by Robert Adam at the London Admiralty (1759). But the incorporation of a classical triumphal arch, in deference to the status of the owner, appears to be an innovation in the context of a Parisian town house.

Peyre must indeed have been conscious of the rank of his client, Louis-Joseph de Bourbon-Condé, a cousin of the king and one of the princes of the blood. Condé was not yet thirty when this design of Peyre's was commissioned, and he was evidently not afraid to associate his name with an architectural style that caused even Marigny qualms. He had returned from the war, in 1762, following the death of his wife, and turned, like many of his fellow officers, to the cultivation of learning, public charities and the arts, neglecting the court at Versailles and creating, at Chantilly, gardens of his own and a cabinet of natural history for the pleasure and amusement of his own circle of friends. A portrait by Drouais (109) shows the prince and his wife at Chantilly dressed in rustic clothes in an informal country

110 Portrait of the Duc de Nivernais, after Allan Ramsay, with frame drawn by Charles de Wailly, 1764 (The National Trust, Waddesdon Manor). A great-nephew of Cardinal Mazarin, Nivernais was a patron of de Wailly and Peyre, who designed the famous decoration of his Paris house in the rue de Tournon

setting. In 1764, after the death of his grandmother, the prince acquired her Paris house, the Palais-Bourbon, and Peyre's project remained unexecuted. Peyre was one of several architects who submitted proposals for the restoration of Condé's new home, but the work was finally entrusted to Le Carpentier.

Despite the relative austerity of his architectural style Peyre was also well known as a decorator, and he was thus brought into contact with a client who was the paragon of his age in matters of taste and breeding, the Duc de Nivernais *(110)*. A great-nephew of Cardinal Mazarin, Nivernais had been the ambassador in Rome shortly before Peyre's arrival there, and he later travelled as ambassador to Berlin and to London, where Horace Walpole described him on a visit to Strawberry Hill: confused by the neo-Gothic style of the house, 'he removed his hat in deference to the ecclesiastical shadows of the Tribune'. Walpole had earlier conceded that Nivernais 'has parts, and writes at the top of the mediocre . . . He would think freely, but has some ambition of being governor of the Dauphin', and he described his life in Paris, where he lived, as later at his Château of St-Ouen, 'in a small circle of dependent admirers'.

Nivernais' house in Paris was also near the Palais du Luxembourg, a building in the rue de Tournon that is now stripped of the decoration that Peyre had designed. As described by Thiéry there was a 'magnificent salon, ornamented with Corinthian pilasters', mirrors and the emblems of the patron's arms, a dining-room with an order of Ionic columns, and a billiard-room, decorated with paintings by Robert, that also doubled as a theatre and concert hall. Though no records of this interior are known,

111 The church of the convent of the Visitandines, Paris, views of the exterior and interior (engravings by Janninot after Durand). Peyre showed drawings for the church to the Academy in 1767, and the building, though not begun until later, was probably based on Peyre's project

its importance can be guessed from the reactions of visitors, one guest, overawed by its splendour, declaring that he 'would never have the courage to inhabit a room that resembles the salon of the Duc de Nivernais'.

The single known ecclesiastical commission of Peyre's career was for a small chapel and the adjacent monastic buildings at the convent of the Visitandines in the rue St-Jacques, not far from the site of the church of Ste-Geneviève (111). Though the chapel was not constructed until about 1780, Peyre had shown drawings of a project for the building at the Academy as early as 1767, and if they at all resembled the chapel as finally built, it must be counted amongst the earliest ecclesiastical monuments in the basilican manner (see chapter 8). The exterior was relatively simple, though not as austere as other chapels of the 1780s, with a pedimented façade and a central recess containing the doorway within a frame of Tuscan columns and a windowed lunette above. Inside, a short nave lined with Ionic columns and pilasters, supporting straight lintels, opened on to a coffered rotunda where the high altar stood, encircled by a larger order of Corinthian columns.

These small commissions which came to Peyre in the years preceding his relatively early death in 1785 may in part have alleviated the disappointment he had suffered in his design for the Hôtel de Condé, but this set-back was not entirely without profit to Peyre, for it led in 1767 to his involvement in the designing of the most important Parisian theatre of the Ancien Régime, the Théâtre de l'Odéon, which was built on the Hôtel de Condé site. In this work Peyre collaborated with the friend of his Roman years, Charles de Wailly (112), whose very different style was to prove a valuable complement to the precocious austerity of Peyre's own architectural manner.

De Wailly, unlike Peyre, was one of the most prolific and successful of the architects of the later eighteenth century. He ran a busy studio where many younger architects received their training, including several Russians, and he gradually established an international reputation, in Russia, in Germany and later in Belgium. De Wailly was above all known for his ability as a draughtsman, and for his consequent enthusiasm for a wide range of earlier art, particularly for the more extreme manifestations of the seventeenth century that he saw at first hand in Rome. Part of his work lay on the fringe of what is strictly architectural, for he excelled, like Servandoni, in the design of stage scenery, but he was able to transfer to his buildings much of the drama and elegance that distinguished his more strictly decorative projects.

Indeed the work of de Wailly and its relation to the style of his greater contemporaries, Soufflot and Ledoux, raises in its acutest form the question of what constitutes the artistry of later eighteenth-century architecture. De Wailly was the only architect who became a member of the Academy of Painting and Sculpture (1771), and he exhibited regularly at the Salon, drawing upon himself the criticism of Diderot and others, who failed to appreciate how inventive architecture had become in the aftermath of

112 Portrait of Charles de Wailly (1730–98), terracotta bust by Augustin Pajou, 1789 (present whereabouts unknown). De Wailly and Pajou were lifelong friends, and they occupied adjacent houses both designed by de Wailly (132, 133)

Soufflot's achievements. There were those, on the other hand, who felt that de Wailly was a great draughtsman, but not an architect, and according to one obituary, 'with more purity in his works, he would have been the Palladio of his century'. The truth is that the buildings of de Wailly, when presented in the architect's drawings in the dramatic manner in which he intended them to be seen, show the extent to which the manipulation of light and shade and the lively conceits of seventeenth-century art were beneficially transmuted into the 'architecture parlante' of the later eighteenth century.

De Wailly was born late in 1729, in the year before Peyre; according to his early biographers he was trained by Blondel, influenced by Legeay and befriended by Servandoni. Such a mixture of influences mirrors many of de Wailly's later strengths, his technical accomplishment as architect and draughtsman, his dedication to the architecture of antiquity, and his outstanding ability as a designer. One biographer attributes the architect's 'grand and picturesque' manner of drawing to the example of Legeay, and though Legeay may indeed have encouraged de Wailly's own gifts as a designer, the influence of Servandoni was possibly greater. Speaking of the decorations of Servandoni, Peyre might almost have been thinking of de Wailly, when he noted that though Servandoni 'merited the greatest reputation in such work, he often employed the severest architecture of the ancients, and it is thus that he had best succeeded'.

The dramatic drawing that won de Wailly the Prix de Rome in 1752 (113), despite the academic aimlessness of its

113 Design for a palace, drawing by de Wailly (Ecole des Beaux-Arts, Paris). The elevation of the project which won de Wailly the Prix de Rome in 1752; though a strict architectural elevation, the lighting provides dramatic contrast and suggests recession

theme, already shows the hallmark of his genius. It is a palace design with a colonnaded semicircular façade rising in the centre to a circular drum without a dome. An elaborate triumphal arch, complete with four-horse chariot, dominates the forecourt, which recalls the Piazza of St Peter's as interpreted in Peyre's slightly later project for a cathedral. In its expressive use of light and shade and in its variations in technique and focusing, admissible in a perspective view, but not, as here, in a true elevation, a receptivity to the visual grandeur of the seventeenth-century tradition, as it had survived especially in stage designs, is already apparent.

The third prize in 1752 was won by de Wailly's friend, Moreau-Desproux, and the architect won for himself the reputation for exceptional generosity in offering to share with Moreau the three-year pension in Rome to which he was entitled. This was the first of two famous breaches of the rules of the Academy associated with the name of de Wailly. The two architects arrived in Rome in November 1754 and stayed for just over two years, returning early in 1757. They joined with Peyre in his exploration of classical architecture and Peyre himself recorded in his later writings that the three of them had studied together the Baths of Caracalla and the Villa of Hadrian. But antique architecture was not de Wailly's only discovery in Rome; his admiration for the work of Bernini was recorded in many drawings, including a surviving study of the Cathedra of St Peter's, where the technique and viewpoint positively enhance the dramatic impact that Bernini intended *(114)*.

At the time of the departure of de Wailly and Moreau from Rome the Abbé Barthélemy singled out their work to Caylus:

you will see this summer two architects of the academy Moreau and Doilly [*sic*] who have done an admirable work on the Baths of Diocletian . . . They have entered the basement, have climbed on the roofs, have excavated in the earth . . . they seem to me to have revived the wise, intelligent and precise method that is admired in Desgodetz . . . Both of them are hard working, intelligent, without guile or jealousy, they would be able to add a supplement to the work of Desgodetz if M. de Marigny had had the goodness to give them three full years like the others here.

114 View of the Cathedra of St Peter, drawing by de Wailly, 1755 (The Hermitage, Leningrad). The art of seventeenth-century Rome, exemplified by Bernini's presentation of the throne in St Peter's, was as important for de Wailly during his stay in Rome as the work of antiquity

Of de Wailly's work in the first few years after his return to Paris little is known, but the decade of the 1760s was one of the most productive of his whole career. Like Peyre, he obtained a post in the Bâtiments du Roi at Versailles where he became Contrôleur-Adjoint. He is first mentioned there in 1762, and he worked with the friend of his Roman years, the sculptor Augustin Pajou, on the planning and building of Gabriel's Opéra. But according to one early biographer the atmosphere of the court was unsympathetic to the architect, and too much a distraction from the pursuit of his art.

While active at Versailles de Wailly also enjoyed a close association with the Marquis de Marigny, and he was asked for designs for the garden buildings, including the Chinese pavilion, at Ménars. He also became the unwitting source of considerable friction between Marigny and Gabriel, when in 1767 Marigny had him created a member of the first class in the Academy, thus bypassing the normal channels of promotion. The Academy finally registered the appointment, but not until the king had been forced to concede that such abuses would not occur in future. De Wailly himself lost no credit in the affair: 'He is a very modest young man,' as the *Mémoires secrets* reported, 'who had not at all asked to enter that company.'

Apart from his work for the king and Marigny, de Wailly began, as early as 1761, to exhibit at the Salon, ten years before he became an associate member, and amongst his earliest exhibits were drawings for a table in the simplified style that had become fashionable in furniture, one of many designs for the applied arts for which the architect also became famous. In these years he began to enrol his earliest pupils, of whom the Russian, Bajenev, is the first recorded. The first known architectural scheme of de Wailly was a design for the transformation of the choir of Amiens Cathedral, the vogue for improving Gothic churches then being at its height. De Wailly's ideas are described by Laugier, who was himself invited to intervene, proposing a form of decoration that, as he was pleased to explain, 'nowhere obscures the view of the aisles and the chapels'.

De Wailly's most famous works of the early 1760s were carried out for two private patrons, the Marquis de Voyer, a member of the distinguished d'Argenson family, and Jean-Philippe Fyot de la Marche, the Premier Président of the Parlement of Burgundy. The d'Argensons are described in the Créquy *Souvenirs* as the only ancient family that had 'abandoned the sword, in modern times, to enter into the magistracy'. The Marquis de Voyer *(115)*, 'One of the foremost connoisseurs of Europe', according to one contemporary, had enjoyed a distinguished career in the army during the Seven Years' War and he was later appointed head of the royal stud farms, where he was responsible for importing English racehorses to France. A frequent visitor to the court, he was also well known for his libertarian views, as a friend of Choiseul, and as one of the circle which, with Caylus and La Live de Jully, gathered at Mme Geoffrin's on Mondays. He was the elder son of the Comte d'Argenson, the enlightened Minister of War, to whom the first volume of the *Encyclopédie* is

115 Portrait of the Marquis de Voyer, pastel by Maurice-Quentin de la Tour (Musée A. Lecuyer, St-Quentin). Distinguished as a soldier and a man of taste, de Voyer commissioned de Wailly's refurbishing of his Paris house *(117)*

dedicated and the nephew of the Marquis d'Argenson, Minister for Foreign Affairs and author of the d'Argenson *Mémoires*. Following a celebrated intrigue against Mme de Pompadour (1757) the Comte d'Argenson had been deprived of power and banished to his estate of Les Ormes in Touraine, where he died in 1764. De Wailly carried out alterations on the château there apparently for de Voyer's father, who thus seems to have been the first member of the family to appreciate his talents.

The later transformation of the d'Argenson Paris house, undertaken by de Wailly for de Voyer, brought the architect into contact with Le Roy who mentions the building in his *Observations* of 1767. It was a relatively small house that had been constructed by Boffrand on the eastern edge of the gardens of the Palais-Royal *(116)*. Remodelled by de Wailly with the collaboration of Pajou, it became famous in the later eighteenth century for the elegance of its decoration, and more especially because de Wailly had employed for the garden frontispiece four columns of the Greek Ionic order *(79)*. This was the first and almost the only occasion that the order appeared in France, though in England and Russia it was to become a very common sight and had already been employed for interior decoration by Robert Adam.

In defending himself against the attacks of Stuart and Revett, Le Roy noted with some pride the influence of his engraving of the Erechtheum at the hôtel, and he later took Mrs Thrale and Dr Johnson to admire the building: 'The Capital which I show largest of all in my work, because it seemed to me worthy of it for its beauty, has just been executed in Paris, at the Hôtel* [*de Voyer] of a most distinguished man, known for his great talent in war and his taste for the arts.' But quite apart from the presence of

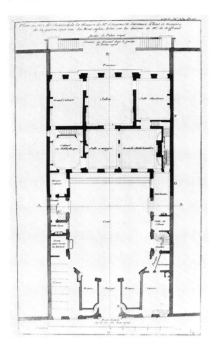

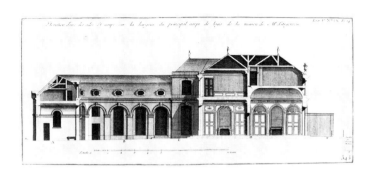

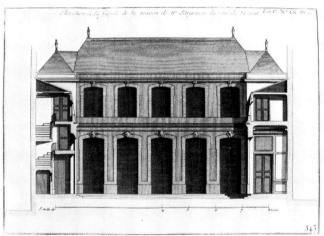

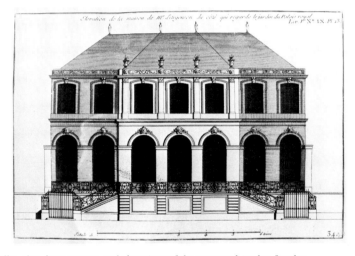

116 Engravings of the Hôtel de Voyer before the alterations of de Wailly, plan, long section, and elevations of the court and garden façades (engravings from Blondel, 1752–56). The house was built to the designs of Boffrand in 1704–05 on a site along the eastern edge of the gardens of the Palais-Royal *(199)*

the Greek Ionic order, the house is of more than unusual interest in showing how far standards of taste had changed since the time of Boffrand's original building. The house was tragically demolished as late as the 1920s, but it was a source of evident delight to William Chambers and is fortunately recorded in some detail in his Parisian sketchbook *(117)*.

The nature of de Wailly's transformations were proclaimed in the passage leading to the court from the street, with its boldly sculpted niche and plain coffered barrel vault, modelled on the *entrone* of the Renaissance palaces of Rome. Boffrand's simple court façade, accented

only in the framing of the slightly round-headed windows, is replaced by a densely rusticated elevation almost in the English manner, that, instead of implying the precedence of the interior over the exterior, calls attention to the outer wall. The new façade is also a rare instance of a centralized composition replacing an earlier design that was evenly articulated. The new frontispiece, with its four Tuscan columns, recalls (like the vestibule) the palaces of Rome, and more particularly a type of entrance much in favour around the turn of the century, as used by Fontana in his remodelling of Bernini's Palazzo di Montecitorio, and at the French Academy itself *(17)*.

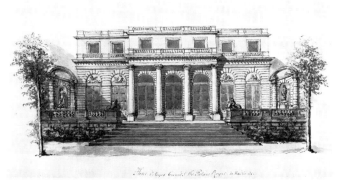

117 Views of the Hôtel de Voyer after de Wailly's alterations, the garden façade, the court façade and passage to the street, the dining-room and the salon, drawings by William Chambers (The Royal Institute of British Architects, London). Altered by de Wailly in the early 1760s for de Voyer (and demolished in the 1920s), the house was celebrated for the Greek Ionic order of the garden façade and for its interior decoration

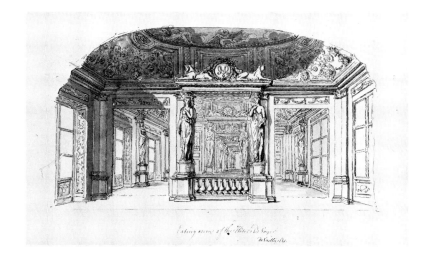

The rear façade, overlooking the gardens of the Palais-Royal, echoed in a suitably richer harmony the disposition of the court. A rectangular flight of steps, flanked by sphinxes on the garden balustrade, replaced the twin flights of Boffrand and served to define the famous frontispiece. On this elevation de Wailly retained the round-headed openings, but the arches became the background for four reliefs that Pajou provided on the appropriate theme of the Four Seasons. The lower part of the façade was sealed with a full entablature, a version of the type normally used with the conventional Ionic order, and set off against a plain attic storey and the rusticated Doric niches enclosing the terrace.

Internally de Wailly's transformation was no less elaborate, with mirrors placed in confrontation with each other in several of the rooms to achieve effects of almost theatrical perspective. The hôtel was the first building that Le Roy took Mrs Thrale to see in Paris, and to her it seemed

all Gold & Glass: his [Voyer's] Bed was a Tent of the most costly Tissue, with a ty'd up bundle of Spears for Posts; & a Helmet with Plumes at the Top – Bows, Arrows, Battle Axes, &c. forming the Back Frame behind his Head. This Bed was repeated eight times by Mirrors placed accordingly . . . Minucci . . . said that to reflect a Bed eight Times over could create no Pleasure except [what] the Idea of a Hospital [could give].

118 The Hôtel Bouhier de Lantenay, now the Préfecture, Dijon. The most up-to-date Dijon building of the 1750s, the hôtel was designed by Samson-Nicolas Lenoir 'le Romain', who later worked for Voltaire and then moved to Paris (323)

Dr Johnson, finding little to his liking in Paris, was more interested in how the mirrors were made. 'They come from Normandy', he reported, 'in [cast] plates, perhaps the third of an Inch thick. At Paris they are ground upon a marble table, by rubbing one plate upon another with grit between them.'

Some idea of how the exterior of the hôtel might have appeared before its tragic demolition is indicated by the surviving fragment of de Wailly's nearly contemporary Château of Montmusard, near Dijon, the first château of eighteenth-century France where the influence of antiquity played a preponderant part in the design. De Wailly's proposals for the château are attractively transcribed in two paintings by a local artist, Jean-Baptiste Lallemand, which show the building in its entirety (119). Less than half the château survives today (121), and it seems doubtful that much more than this was built.

Though it was a far smaller town than Lyon, Dijon too was the scene of active architectural endeavour in the middle years of the eighteenth century, and it was not backward intellectually – a competition of its Academy of Sciences having prompted Rousseau's essay on the progress of mankind. As the capital of the former Kingdom of Burgundy, Dijon was embellished less through the initiative of the municipality than by the patronage of a distinguished local aristocracy, centred for the most part upon the local Parlement.

The most remarkable buildings of the time were those carried out by a young architect, Samson-Nicolas Lenoir 'le Romain', who had been in Rome under the protection of Marigny shortly before de Wailly's arrival there. Attached to Dijon by family ties, he spent several years there in the later 1750s, and then worked for Voltaire at Ferney before pursuing a very active career in Paris (see chapter 14). His largest building in Dijon (118), the hôtel (now the Préfecture) constructed for Jean Bouhier de Lantenay, Président of the Parlement, is, despite its high and old-fashioned shape, not only more imposing in scale than most domestic architecture in Paris at this time, but also, in its reliance on bold architectural form in the decoration of the walls, considerably in advance of Parisian taste.

Amongst the other parliamentary families of Dijon that of Fyot de la Marche was the most outstanding. Claude-Philibert Fyot, the father of de Wailly's patron at Montmusard, had been a fellow boarder with Voltaire at the Collège Louis-le-Grand in Paris. Famous for his learning and wide culture, he became Premier Président of the Dijon Parlement in 1745, and continued to correspond with Voltaire throughout his life. He too was a patron of Le-noir, and he had created at Montmusard the most famous garden of the region. The old château he demolished to begin a new building, but suddenly he retired from public life, passing on his office and his château to his son, Jean-Philippe.

Like his father, the new owner of Montmusard was well known as a man of letters, and like his famous predecessor in the Dijon Parlement, the Président des Brosses, he wrote an account of his travels in Italy. In the year before de Wailly's drawings for Montmusard were produced, the

119 View of the Château of Montmusard, Dijon, by Jean-Baptiste Lallemand (Musée de Dijon). One of a pair of paintings of the château designed by de Wailly in 1764 for Jean-Philippe Fyot de la Marche, Premier Président of the Burgundy Parlement

architect had travelled to Dijon to inspect the medieval church of St-Bénigne on behalf of the Academy, and it may have been on this occasion that he and his patron met for the first time, though Fyot was also related through one of his sisters to the d'Argenson family.

The historical importance of de Wailly's château, which is immediately apparent on comparison with Gabriel's Petit Trianon *(46)*, finished in the year when Montmusard was begun, is partly due to chance, since opportunities for such buildings became increasingly rare in the later years of the eighteenth century. Owners preferred to invest in the embellishment of their estates and to build smaller and more informal houses, while wealth became increasingly concentrated in Paris and in the other major towns.

At Montmusard de Wailly followed the pattern of the traditional feudal château, itself a development of the keep of the medieval castle, in incorporating a projecting circular salon on the garden front, but as a compact block of only one main storey the design also recalls the design of large Parisian town houses of the earlier part of the century. Even so the emphasis upon the circular form and

the strict symmetry along the central axis of the building must derive from the plans of the Roman baths that Peyre and de Wailly had studied in Rome. Most unusual of all in the planning of the château *(120)* is the 'Odeum' or 'Temple d'Apollon', that projects forwards at the front of the building to provide the main portico, an open semi-circular colonnade that has no obvious precedent in Renaissance architecture. This lightens the bulk of the château, providing a negative circular space to counter-balance the domed 'Salon des Muses' beyond, and is chiefly instrumental in lending a spurious air of antiquity to the building.

Circular colonnades had been known in France since the famous example constructed by Hardouin Mansart in the gardens of Versailles; in juxtaposition with a building the motif appears in Peyre's reconstruction of the Baths of Diocletian *(103)*. At Montmusard the classical basis of the architecture is adumbrated in the amusing conceit whereby the building is dedicated to Apollo and the Muses. This notion probably derives from the name of the estate – Montmusard: the mountain of the Muses – and in

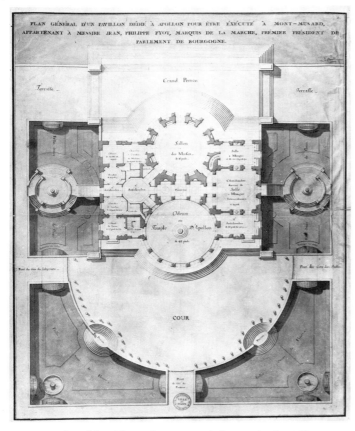

120 Plan of the Château of Montmusard, drawing by de Wailly, 1764 (Bibliothèque Municipale, Dijon). The geometrical planning of the house, 'a pavilion dedicated to Apollo', is related to the layout of the adjacent gardens

121 The Château of Montmusard, view of the surviving fragment from the west. The view shows four of the columns of the circular 'Temple of Apollo'; the château was probably never completed

consequence the château is probably the earliest domestic building of the century that was conceived, not unlike Soufflot's 'Temple de Ste-Geneviève', as the shrine of an antique deity.

The walls of the surviving wing are enlivened by rustication in the traditional French manner (121) that was associated especially at this time with the work of Gabriel, and the typical complexity of the style is apparent in such details as the double recession of the windows and the treatment of the keystones. The construction of the château probably came to a halt at the time of the death of Jean-Philippe Fyot in 1772, and financial problems may already have arisen since de Wailly apparently prepared an alternative design for the château that dispensed with the Salon des Muses and the Temple d'Apollon.

This alternative design is the project known in engravings (where the patron is misleadingly named as de Voyer) (122), which probably corresponded with a model for 'the staircase of Montmusard' that de Wailly exhibited at the Salon in 1771. According to Diderot it was 'very decently made' and 'has, it is said, an additional merit in its composition, that of being Roman'. In this second project, whether or not it was really for the same site, de Wailly indeed encountered the difficulty of providing a main staircase for the building. His answer was an ingenious variation of Peyre's design for the Hôtel de Condé, a staircase rising to an open Doric temple on a circular plan embedded in the fabric of the château, which seems correctly defined as 'Roman' in inspiration.

During the later 1760s de Wailly was fortunate in receiving commissions for two public buildings. The first was a small chapel that he constructed in the town of Versailles, which recalled, in its use of columns on a circular plan, Peyre's chapel of the Visitation as well as the larger basilican churches of the time. The second building was de Wailly's most celebrated work, the commission that he shared with Peyre for a new theatre for the Comédie-Française. The two architects were asked as early as 1767 to provide designs for this building on the site of the Hôtel de Condé which the state was to acquire from the prince, who had by then moved to the Palais-Bourbon. Their first design was approved by the king on the last day of 1769 (124), but it was quickly followed by a second proposal, approved by the king in the following May (125).

Until the cost had been met from the development of the site, the theatre was to be financed by the municipality of Paris acting in conjunction with two departments of the royal household, the Bâtiments du Roi and the Menus-Plaisirs, the body under the direction of four dukes (the Premiers Gentilshommes de la Chambre), which was responsible for festivals and temporary decorations at the court and also for the troupes of Parisian actors and singers. Still socially underprivileged though jealous of the great popularity they enjoyed, the companies remained few in number – the three principal ones being those of the Comédie-Française, the Comédie-Italienne and the Opéra – and under royal patronage until the time of the Revolution.

Despite the royal approval given to their early projects,

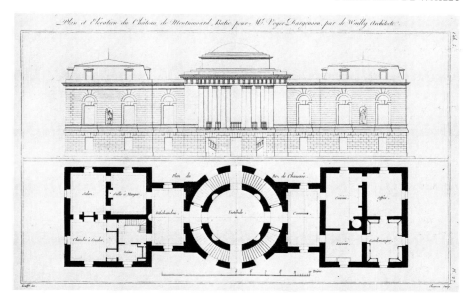

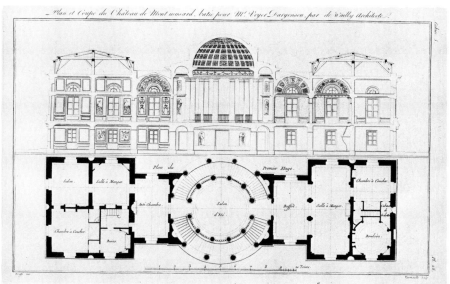

122 Project for the Château of Montmusard(?),
elevation and ground-plan, section and main-floor
plan (engravings from Krafft, 1812). Probably a
variant project for Montmusard, of which a model
for the staircase, deriving from Peyre's Hôtel de
Condé design (108), was exhibited at the 1771
Salon

almost a decade was to pass before work on the Odéon
began. The political climate during the last years of the
reign of Louis XV was unfavourable to a decision involving
so many influential parties. De Wailly himself travelled
abroad to study the design of theatres, visiting Italy, and
apparently England and Germany. Late in 1771 he was in
Geneva, where he spoke to Voltaire about the theatre. His
approach to Voltaire was made through Pierre-Michel
Hénin who announced his arrival in a letter:

I have here a man of genius who has especially to consult you
about a subject in your competence. He is M. Dually [sic],
architecte du Roy, regarded as the greatest draughtsman in this
genre. He is charged to construct the new theatre of the Com.
française and has carried out some very interesting research on
this question . . . It is from your works that M. Dually has drawn
many new ideas which he has realized . . .

Like Soufflot, de Wailly lost the protection of Marigny
when he resigned in 1773, and by this time many rival
projects for the Comédie had appeared. Under the
administration of Marigny's immediate successor, the
Abbé Terray, work was started on a design that had been
supplied by Moreau-Desproux, who had succeeded to the
post of Maître des Bâtiments de la Ville de Paris. This blow
to the two architects was the harder to bear since Moreau,
deeply in de Wailly's debt, was also the brother of Peyre's
wife. De Wailly was said to have forgiven Moreau his
ungrateful conduct, but never to have pardoned 'the
authority of Versailles for the perfidy committed'.

Under the new régime of Turgot and d'Angiviller a new
royal library seemed a more suitable building for the Hôtel
de Condé site than a theatre, and further designs were
made for transferring the theatre to the Place du Carrousel,

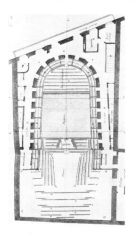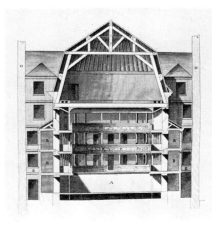

123 The old Comédie-Française, Paris, detail of plan, and section (engravings from Blondel, 1752–56). Designed by François d'Orbay in the late seventeenth century, the old Comédie was too small and inconvenient by the middle years of the eighteenth century

near the Tuileries. De Wailly again visited Italy in the late 1770s, but shortly after his return it was decided that the site should be developed as a speculation on behalf of the new king's brother, the Comte de Provence, who had received the Palais du Luxembourg as his official residence. The design of Peyre and de Wailly, modified for d'Angiviller in 1778, and switched from the north to the south of the site, where Moreau's foundations had been laid, was finally begun in 1779 and the theatre opened its doors for the first time on 9 April 1782. In the development of the site access and profit were reconciled by five roads which met in the semicircular Place in front of the theatre.

In the years following the opening of the Comédie-Française de Wailly became known as a specialist in theatre design; he was called in to modify the Théâtre-Italien, newly built by Heurtier, and later summoned to Brussels where he made several proposals for a new theatre. Much to the irritation of Peyre's son, it was generally assumed that the Comédie was the unassisted work of de Wailly, and the latter had to write to the press on at least two occasions to remind the public that the theatre was not his alone, although all the drawings, he declared, had been produced in his studio. De Wailly was reticent about the precise division of work, but the ideas of the two men were closely in accord since the time of their years together in Rome, and no great compromise was presumably necessary when they worked together. Yet if the drawings for the Brussels theatre show how de Wailly might have coped with the commission for the Comédie on his own, it seems that Peyre must have exercised a restraining influence upon his more exuberant collaborator in order that so happy a compromise should have been achieved.

Like the church of Ste-Geneviève, the building of a new theatre for the Comédiens du Roi was a subject of widespread public interest and debate, all the more intense as the theatre in the later eighteenth century was a place of worship far more potent than the church. The theatres of the time have been likened to the cathedrals of medieval France, such was the energy expended, both in theory and in practice, upon their construction and their urban settings, and the Comédie was no exception. As well as the countless drawings and letters produced by Peyre and de Wailly, and by their rivals and advisers, the two architects composed a long description of their project, dedicated to Marigny, which they apparently intended for publication, together with lengthy quotations from Voltaire, Fréron and the *Encyclopédie*. And though this text of theirs remained unpublished, versions of the accompanying drawings were engraved for the plates illustrating the article 'Théâtre' in the *Encyclopédie*.

The two authors began their treatise by stressing the age and the poor state of repair of the old Comédie *(123)*, which had been built in the late seventeenth century on a site not far from the Hôtel de Condé. The inconvenience of access, the lack of scope for scenery upon its small stage and the domestic appearance of the exterior, they argued, paid little credit to the supremacy of the French drama and the architectural renewal of the capital, as honoured by the king. So unsuitable was the old Comédie that the actors had already moved to Soufflot's new theatre in the Tuileries, and it was there that Voltaire was acclaimed on his triumphant return to France in 1778. As Mrs Thrale had written three years earlier:

The Play House is a Wretched one, Foote's little Theatre is a Palace to it, for size, magnificence and Elegance of Decoration . . . The Queen of France [Marie Antoinette] was at the Play tonight sitting in one [of] the Balcony Boxes like any other Lady, only that she curtsied to the Audience at going out & they applauded her in Return . . . I wished her a better Theatre & handsomer Box to sit in.

Inevitably in all their early projects Peyre and de Wailly chose a circular plan for the auditorium and confined their alterations mainly to the façade of the theatre. At first *(124)* the main façade closely echoed the shape of the auditorium, consisting of a semicircular colonnade of Tuscan columns with curved wings to each side, each containing a café and serving as the main entrances to the theatre. The treatment of the colonnade probably derived from Soufflot's opera design of the early 1760s, but in conjunction with the curving of the side wings the plan unashamedly recalled the architectural methods of seventeenth-century Rome.

In all the later projects the plan is rectangular, like Soufflot's Lyon theatre, and the main façade is equipped with a straight colonnade *(125)*. The front of the theatre and the interior are dramatically presented in two large drawings by de Wailly, probably the ones exhibited by him at the Salon of 1781, which show the building in active use *(127, 128)*. Social convenience, one of the main preoccupations of the two architects, was not overlooked in the design of the exterior, where bridges to each side of the façade lead to cafés incorporated in the buildings flanking the theatre. The whole building is enclosed by an open arcade which, according to the treatise of the architects, would provide shelter for the waiting servants, protecting them from the alternative attractions of the

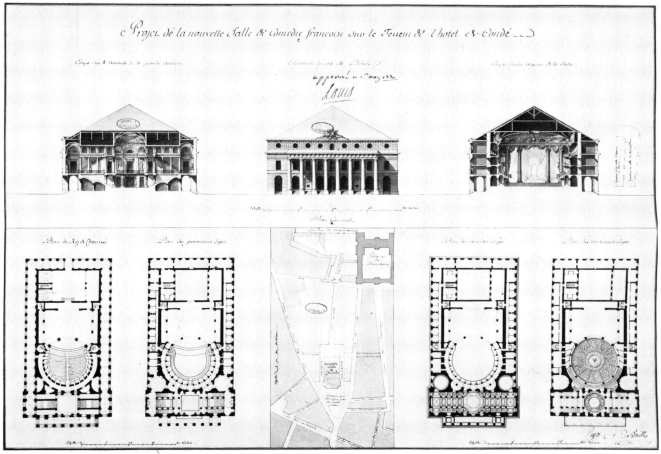

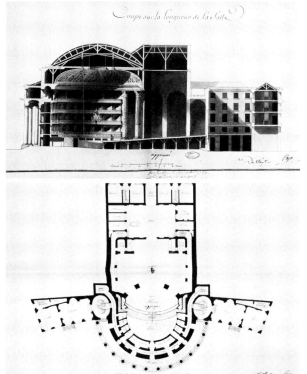

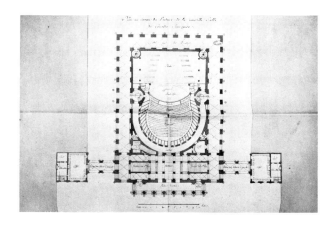

Projects for the Comédie-Française, later known as the Odéon, drawings by de Wailly and Peyre (Archives Nationales, Paris)

124 *Left and below left*: section and plan of the first project, signed by the architects, inscribed 'approuvé' by the king, and dated 31 December 1769 by Marigny

125 *Above*: studies for the second project, showing the site plan (for a rectangular building at the northern end of the Hôtel de Condé site [*108*]), plans at four levels, elevation, and sections of vestibule and auditorium. Approved by the king on 1 May 1770, and signed by him and the architects

126 *Below*: revised plan of 1778 at the level of the stalls, showing the cafés flanking the façade. Marked 'approuvé' by the new king, Louis XVI

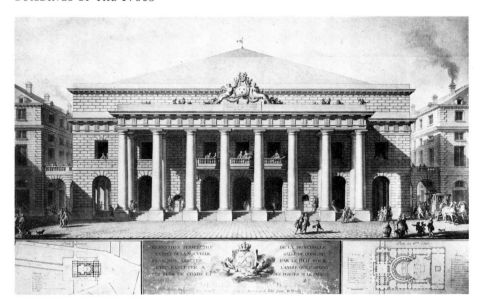

127 The Comédie-Française, perspective view of the main façade, drawing by de Wailly (Musée Carnavalet, Paris). Dated 1770 and corresponding with the second design *(125)*, but probably one of two drawings exhibited at the 1781 Salon

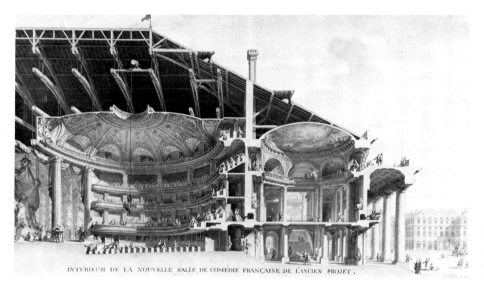

INTÉRIEUR DE LA NOUVELLE SALLE DE COMÉDIE FRANÇAISE DE L'ANCIEN PROJET.

128 The Comédie-Française, long section in perspective, drawing by de Wailly, 1776 (Musée Carnavalet, Paris). A celebrated drawing, probably the second of two exhibited at the 1781 Salon, which exploits the project of 1770 for its visual drama

cabaret and the billiard hall. The Tuscan order of the frontispiece, as their manuscript explains, is the one appropriate to Apollo, the protector of the Arts, and a sculptural group intended for the colonnade, showing the lyre of Apollo flanked by two Muses, proclaimed the deity to whom their temple was dedicated *(127)*. There had been earlier projects for theatres conceived in the guise of classical temples, like the one by Neufforge *(74)*, but the Comédie was the first design for a real theatre conceived in such a form.

Inside the theatre the main vestibule is square *(128)*, with an open gallery above to enhance the social spectacle, and matching colonnaded staircases, like those of a seventeenth-century palace, lead to the upper floors. The interior of the vestibule is recorded in a drawing that was probably de Wailly's reception piece at the Academy of Painting in 1771 *(129)*, an amusing drawing, resembling a

stage set, and not without historical prescience in showing a modern building peopled with figures in Roman dress.

Evidently Peyre and de Wailly felt confident about the exterior of the theatre and its communications, but they were bound to justify themselves at greater length in their treatise when discussing the auditorium, this being the part of a theatre most vehemently debated at the time. The old Comédie, they explained, had too deep an auditorium for the comfort of both the audience and the actors, and they showed themselves sensitive to the naturalism then being introduced on the French stage in considering the close intimacy between audience and actor needed for 'the frank representation of nature'. Though their theatre was not constructed until some years after the dramatic works of Diderot and Rousseau had been staged, it had opened in time for the long-awaited first public performance of *The Marriage of Figaro*. The naturalism of Beaumarchais' play

129 View of the vestibule of the Comédie-Française, drawing by de Wailly (Musée du Louvre, Paris). Probably de Wailly's reception piece at the 1771 Salon

was well appreciated by at least one member of the first-night audience, Mme d'Oberkirch: 'It appears to me that the nobility showed a great want of tact in applauding it, which was nothing less than giving themselves a slap in the face . . . They will repent it yet . . . Their own caricature has been held up before them, and they replied, ''that is it; it is very like.'' What inexplicable blindness.'

Popular as it had become in the later eighteenth century, the circular plan that Peyre and de Wailly favoured for their theatre had its own disadvantages, principally in making the actors hard to see and hear from the sides of the auditorium. In a manuscript prepared in conjunction with his proposals for the Brussels theatre, de Wailly admitted that it was a shape which he preferred for its regularity, but argued that it was also economical with space and one that afforded the spectators, as indeed they then expected, a good view of each other.

The oddest feature of the interior, described at some length by the two authors, was the pair of free-standing columns within the proscenium opening (125). Though the obsession of the age was for free-standing columns, preferably of giant proportions, and these had appeared screening the stage in some earlier theatre designs, Peyre and de Wailly appear to be the only important architects to have adopted this idea. They explained that the columns could be taken down when necessary, but, supported by the evidence of Voltaire, they urged their advantages at some length: as aids to the greater naturalism when eavesdropping was required on the stage, for the design of particular sets, like the throne in Racine's Athalie (as shown in de Wailly's drawing [128]), and for concealing lighting.

The columns were omitted in the final design but they were not without a valuable architectural consequence, for they had come to form part of a coherent design for the articulation of the rest of the auditorium. The two architects had abandoned the old-fashioned division

merely by the presence of tiers of boxes (32, 47), which they had respected in their earliest projects, and introduced an order of square piers, encircling the whole room and rising through the balconies to support the vault.

The interior was designed throughout with greater sympathy for the physical and social comfort of the audience than had been customary hitherto. The architects respected Voltaire's strongly-worded plea, quoted in their treatise, for keeping the audience off the stage, and they also provided seating throughout the stalls. A successful novelty in their design of the interior, based upon advances in techniques of engineering, was the increasing extent to which the balconies projected over the stalls as they descended (128). By giving the boxes only low partitions and providing continuous seating where the first circle projected beyond the boxes, the architects were half way to the more egalitarian seating arrangements that became de rigueur after the Revolution.

Peyre and de Wailly were concerned with the social convenience of their first balcony rather than with social reform, including the protection of the occupants of the boxes from the scrutiny of the stalls, although they also refer to the auditorium as a stage where all may see and be seen without strain. The lighting for this public spectacle was to be provided by a single candelabrum raised and lowered through an opening in the ceiling. The opening may recall nothing so much as the oculus of the Roman Pantheon, but this method of lighting, according to the two authors, was common practice in Italian theatres. The mechanism of the winch for the chandelier is shown in de Wailly's perspective view (128), as are the great wooden beams that support the vault of the auditorium and the roof beyond.

In the project that was finally carried out several small modifications were introduced. The architects lengthened the auditorium a little, giving it a slightly oval shape; the proscenium was narrowed and the columns on the stage

130 The Comédie-Française (since 1797 called the Théâtre de l'Odéon), the main façade. The roof was lowered by Chalgrin after a fire in 1808 and the sculpture planned for the façade *(127)* was never carried out

omitted. The design for the sculpture of the frontispiece was carried out by Caffieri in the interior, over the proscenium arch. Otherwise the architects altered the exterior hardly at all, changing the bridges leading to the cafés from double to single arches, and thereby adding a suggestion of primitive strength in the fashion of the 1780s. Some years after the opening the idea arose of transferring the Opéra to the theatre; de Wailly made proposals for further alterations, and other projects of his for enlarging the building followed after the Revolution. The partitions between the boxes, such as they were, had to be removed at this time as being undemocratic. The building was later gutted by fire (1808) and restored by Chalgrin, who amongst other changes lowered the roof, and further restorations followed in the course of the nineteenth century.

The building as it survives now *(130)* may seem to offer little that is in any way exceptional, but this is to forget that much of its original effect, as shown in the drawings of de Wailly, depended upon the character of the interior and its relation to the shell of the building and its now mutilated setting. Through the efforts of its two architects, each of them apparently curbing the eccentricities of the other, the design of the Comédie was a model for its time,

the austerity of the exterior and the boldness of the structure supporting the elegance and well-organized comfort of the interior.

On its opening in 1782 the building was subjected to the closest public scrutiny, receiving its share of praise and blame. Grimm commented that 'there are many seats where you see badly and where you hear scarcely better'; Mme d'Oberkirch also found the boxes small, while 'the dazzling whiteness of the painting . . . the ladies declared quite eclipsed the most distinguished toilette'. De Croÿ wished for a deeper auditorium, more staircases and better fire precautions, but the shape of the theatre, the seating in the stalls, and much else he found 'à merveille'.

During the 1770s, after the early designs for the Comédie had been produced, de Wailly may have begun to suspect that his particular gifts were becoming unsuited to the changing architectural climate of Paris – if not to the earliest of his foreign clients. Like many architects without official appointments he found his main opportunities in domestic practice, the most ambitious of all his houses being the one that he built for himself and his family, apparently in 1778.

Two of his other houses, little-known buildings, served to bring his work once more to the notice of

131 The *salone* of the Palazzo Spinola, Genoa, long section, drawing by de Wailly, 1773 (Musée des Arts Décoratifs, Paris). De Wailly's most celebrated interior, designed for the Genoese ambassador to Paris and illustrated in the engraved plates which supplemented the *Encyclopédie*

Voltaire. The first was the Hôtel de la Villette, remodelled by de Wailly, where Voltaire was accommodated by his friend, the wife of Charles-Michel de la Villette, Marquis du Plessis, during his visit to Paris, and the second the house that Voltaire's niece, Mme Denis, occupied in the rue de Richelieu after her second marriage. This was one of two adjacent houses, described by Thiéry as being in a 'new style', that de Wailly constructed at the northern end of the road near the boulevard. The house was famous for its ingenious oval staircase, based on a design that de Wailly had developed for the Château of Les Ormes, and one of the last in a long and famous tradition that had begun in the sixteenth century with the staircase designed by Philibert de l'Orme for the Tuileries. A model of the staircase was exhibited at the Salon of 1785, but the house itself must have been completed earlier if it is identical with the one about which Voltaire had asked Chalgrin for a report.

De Wailly's most celebrated work, apart from his collaboration in the Odéon, was the decoration of a room for an Italian patron, the Marchese Cristoforo Spinola, the Genoese ambassador to the French court. The room itself, carried out in the patron's palace in Genoa, has none of its original decoration left, but de Wailly's scheme was the second of his works recorded in the plates of the *Encyclopédie* and it is the subject of his most famous drawings *(131)*. The room condenses much that must have made Versailles so awe-inspiring for the foreign visitor, the mirrors and the carved and fluted columns recalling especially the decoration of the Opéra there.

As at the Hôtel de Voyer the mirrors, much larger here, are set in confrontation with each other and they multiply many times over the super-elaborate room to create a perspective of columns, vaulted arches and smouldering urns that brings to mind reconstructions of antique palaces as they had been pictured in the engravings of Piranesi. Much in the same style de Wailly reconstructed in Paris at this time Servandoni's Chapelle de la Vierge at St-Sulpice, after a fire had damaged the eastern end of the church. 'All the world knows that he is full of genius' was the comment that appeared in the *Journal de Paris* as a consequence of this work.

Yet de Wailly's genius was to bring him few material advantages during the latter part of his career, and his own house – one of the grandest of all the artists' houses that became a feature of the Parisian scene – turned out to be something of a liability to the architect. Originally part of a speculation that apparently involved the construction of five houses on the site, which lay in the north-western

132 The house of de Wailly, Paris, perspective view (engraving by Guyot after Sergent). Built by de Wailly for himself (1776–79), together with a house for Pajou (to the left), the house had a screen of baseless columns (inaccurately shown in the engraving)

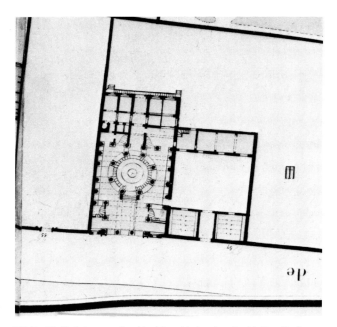

133 De Wailly's house, plan (Archives Nationales, Paris). Detail of a survey plan of the early nineteenth century, showing the circular columned staircase

outskirts of the city (the present rue de la Boétie), it was finally built with stables to one side and a smaller house occupied by Pajou on the other *(132, 133)*.

The house was not an isolated pavilion of the kind that richer proprietors had come increasingly to prefer; it resembled rather a town house of the late seventeenth century with a tall pedimented block at the rear and narrow wings projecting to the street, but where the courtyard might be expected to be de Wailly built a circular colonnade with a fountain at the centre and matching semicircular staircases of the type he had envisaged for Montmusard. The stair chamber was lit from above, where a circular terrace rose above the side wings, and it was visible from the street through a screen of four baseless Tuscan columns. From the main floor of the house a small rectangular staircase led up to the top floor which was equipped with a belvedere affording views across Paris and the neighbouring country.

The very mixed origins of the house are betrayed in its rather freakish appearance. Common to other houses of the period is the exceptional density of the plan, recalling the organization of Roman baths and requiring, like them, an extensive use of top lighting. The classical basis of the plan was underlined by the ring of free-standing columns that make of de Wailly's staircase a species of classical temple. The central fountain was decorated with a group of the Three Graces, based upon designs of the sixteenth-century sculptor, Germain Pilon, and it was replenished from a water-tank on the roof which also supplied the kitchens. Throughout the design the variety of levels and the open vista of the staircases recall the palaces that de Wailly would have learnt to admire in Genoa.

At the time of the construction of his own house de Wailly may have felt confident that success awaited him in Paris, but during the 1780s this failed to materialize. In 1788 de Wailly put up his possessions for sale, with all his paintings and furniture, and the house itself he tried to sell four years later. He continued to contribute ideas for the general improvement of Paris, but his main opportunities lay far afield. Catherine the Great, perhaps at this time, offered him the directorship of the St Petersburg Academy of Fine Arts, which de Wailly declined. He became involved in the construction of a small port in southern France, a scheme whose importance is greatly exaggerated by one early biographer, and then worked for the Landgrave of Hesse on projects for Kassel, and on several designs in Belgium, including the theatre of Brussels.

When the Revolution broke out in Paris nine more years of life remained to de Wailly. Having no sympathies for the court at Versailles, the architect supported the early stages of the Revolution, and one of his tasks at this time was the transformation of the Jesuit church in Brussels into an assembly room for 'Friends of Liberty and Equality'. Remaining despite the Revolution single-minded in his devotion to the arts, as his biographers stress, de Wailly had founded in 1789 the Société des Amis des Arts which was intended to assist young artists through the subscriptions of its two hundred members, and he later became an adviser on the choice of works of art plundered by the French in the Low Countries. He was one of the six architects who become members of the Institut on its foundation in 1795, but this honour was not destined to be his for long. He died in Paris at his rooms in the Louvre on 2 November 1798.

The Revolution brought no more fulfilment to de Wailly's professional hopes than to those of the vast majority of his colleagues. Several further small-scale works by de Wailly are recorded at this time, including his schemes for the alteration of Ste-Geneviève (99), while his major work was to be a great theatre in the heart of Paris that he finished designing in the year of his death. De Wailly had grown disenchanted with the state to which architecture in France had been reduced; his colleague Belanger recorded de Wailly's feelings at this time:

he saw in all the modern salons of Paris, either the tombs of the ancient Romans or the new shops of the streets of London, [and he felt] that soon architecture would be governed in France by the taste of drink sellers or clothes merchants. He was convinced that true architecture of which the Greeks had transmitted the model, cannot support this mean style of decoration . . .

If de Wailly had grown hostile to the architectural developments of the last years of the century, his former friend, Moreau-Desproux, can have liked them still less. After the promise of his early years had passed by, Moreau seems to have grappled only fitfully with the challenges that the classical revival offered in architecture. Famous, like de Wailly, as a designer of temporary decorations, he showed himself less able to understand the distinction of what is appropriate to buildings in stone and what to ephemeral architecture.

Moreau was more fortunately placed at birth than de Wailly, for, like Gabriel, he was one of a famous architectural dynasty that had held the ancient post of Maître des Bâtiments to the city of Paris since the late seventeenth century. He succeeded his uncle, Jean-Baptiste-Augustin Beausire, in this position not long after his return from Italy. He became a member of the first class of the Academy in 1776, and he too was one of the architects of the time ennobled by the king.

As Maître des Bâtiments, 'Moreau de la Ville', as he became known, was provided with a house on the Place Louis XV, and called upon to supervise a wide range of public works, including the maintenance of the roads and quays and even the drainage. Amongst his earliest tasks was a survey of the banks of the Seine that is one of the first of the many projects for the comprehensive improvement of the town characteristic of the later part of the century. At the same time Moreau had responsibility for the decorations for festivals undertaken by the city to commemorate important social and political events, and he was involved in the famous fête organized at the Place Louis XV for the marriage of the Dauphin and Marie Antoinette in 1770, which ended in a stampede and ill-omened tragedy. For a later festival, honouring the birth of a later Dauphin, the first son of Louis XVI, Moreau designed for the quay behind the Hôtel de Ville a Temple

134 Festival decoration in honour of the birth of a Dauphin, 1782, drawing by Moreau-Desproux (Musée Carnavalet, Paris). Designed as a temple to Hymen and one of the several schemes of temporary decoration Moreau undertook as 'Maître des Bâtiments de la Ville'

of Hymen standing on a base of rock with a pedestal supporting fountains and tall triumphal columns at the sides (134). It was a decoration that might almost have been one of the series designed by French architects in Rome nearly thirty years earlier for the festival of the Chinea (71).

Moreau became known as an architect with a small hôtel of the later 1750s constructed in the 'Greek' style of the time (135). Overlooking the boulevard to the north of the city, it was built not for a financier or even an aristocratic amateur, but for a member of the Paris Parlement, a M. de Chavannes, who was a 'Conseiller de Grand' Chambre'. Thiéry praised the planning of the hôtel, and likewise the façade on the boulevard, which was still as famous in the 1780s as it had been twenty years earlier when it had

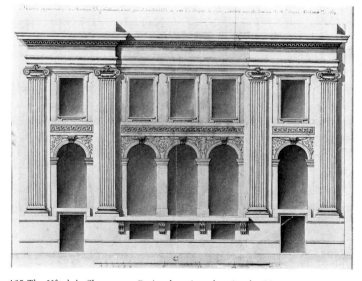

135 The Hôtel de Chavannes, Paris, elevation, drawing by Moreau-Desproux (Musée Carnavalet, Paris). Designed by Moreau in the later 1750s, the house was celebrated as an example of 'Grecian' taste

136 The Palais-Royal, Paris, the main court. Much of the front of the present Palais-Royal was faced by Moreau when in 1763 he reconstructed the Opéra there (199). The Opéra was subsequently destroyed by fire in 1781

emphasized by a running decoration of olive branches threaded through the key-stones. With its central recession of three bays the design seems almost Venetian in inspiration, but the round-headed openings, as Laugier noted, failed to match the severe rectangular frames of the first floor. And despite the presence of its pilasters, the façade indeed seems to owe more to the decorative ebullience of the 'Greek' style, than to a truly architectural talent.

Moreau was entrusted with the design of several other private houses in Paris, but his most extensive surviving work is the front façade of the Palais-Royal (136). This reconstruction was undertaken at the time when the architect was employed at the expense of the city in rebuilding the Opéra on the site of the old Palais-Royal theatre. His Opéra opened in 1763, and was thus the first major theatre of eighteenth-century Paris, but it perished eighteen years later in a famous fire that is depicted in several of the paintings of Robert.

The theatre was generally regarded as a successful building, but very incomplete records of its appearance are known, and there is no reason to think it was a building with much bearing upon the innovations that Peyre and de Wailly created in their rather later design for the Comédie-Française. The theatre was screened from the street by a covered passage, probably an arcade, while a columned vestibule with short flights of steps at each end led to matching square staircases, more domestic in appearance than those of the Comédie, which ascended to the main floor of the theatre.

The adjacent façades of the Palais-Royal, so familiar a sight of the Parisian scene, show many of the peculiarities of Moreau's mature architectural style. His design was in part determined by the existing buildings, the rear façade of the block with its main floor of paired Ionic columns that Contant had recently completed (56), and by the existing fabric of the front court which partly fixed the irregular spacing of Moreau's columns. The architect introduced an order of Tuscan columns for the ground floor and retained the Ionic, the correct sequel, on the main floor, but the smoothness of his elevations and the slender proportions of the order make the architecture of Contant seem almost robust in comparison. Moreau's Ionic order is related to the one used by Soufflot in Lyon, though it appears more ornamental, with its tall base and high neck band, and it was one which Moreau made his own, using it in other domestic buildings.

When, in the following decade, Moreau came to design an alternative project for the Comédie-Française on behalf of the Paris municipality, he avoided a façade decorated with columns, but supplied instead an elegant design redolent of the 'Greek' style of the 1750s (137) which re-calls in its tripartite division and round-headed windows the façade of the Hôtel de Chavannes. In the absence of an order the decoration, which Moreau may have considered to be appropriate to the function of the building, is here largely confined to the sculpture: the six caryatids supporting the central balcony, the long relief showing Apollo and the Muses, and the winged horses at

received a rare commendation from Laugier: 'The architect who has provided the designs for the house of M. de Chavannes at the corner of the Porte du Temple, has shown the public that it is possible in a limited space to do great things.' Laugier faulted the façade on several points of detail, but the presence of an order on a small building clearly delighted him, even though he confessed that columns would have been preferable to pilasters.

The presence of the order and its full entablature indeed put the façade in the vanguard of architectural design, and much of the decoration is equally advanced. Like Soufflot, Moreau rejected the French Ionic order with its hanging garlands and substituted a flattened variation of the order which had been used by Michelangelo for the Capitol palaces, where a single garland hangs between the volutes, a type that was to become popular in the following decade. The Greek key ornament forms a frieze between the two storeys, and consoles, like those favoured by Gabriel, support the balcony beneath the central three windows. The windows themselves are framed to resemble an arcade supported on square piers, their round-headed shape

137 Project for the Comédie-Française, drawing by Moreau-Desproux (Musée Carnavalet, Paris). The elevation of the project, designed by Moreau for the Ville de Paris and illustrated in the engraved plates which supplemented the *Encyclopédie*

roof level. Caryatids were, ironically, a favourite device of de Wailly, and present for example in his drawing of the vestibule of the Comédie *(129)*, but they are never found in his work featured prominently on exteriors.

After the failure of his design for the Comédie, Moreau ended his career disastrously. The post of Maître des Bâtiments was suppressed in 1783, when the Baron de Breteuil became minister with responsibility for Paris, and though Moreau continued as municipal architect, he was forced to resign four years later, and de Breteuil appointed his personal architect, Bernard Poyet, a former pupil of de Wailly, in his place. In 1790 Moreau published a memoir complaining of the treatment he had received, but this was countered by Poyet in a devastating reply which listed instances of administrative incompetence and even corruption on the part of Moreau. The restoration of the

Opéra, according to Poyet, had cost over two million *livres*, whereas the Comédie of Peyre and de Wailly had been constructed in its entirety for several hundred thousand less.

Moreau had retired to the country by the time of the Terror, but he was arrested in 1793. After the death of Peyre his sister had married again and Moreau's new brother-in-law, the poet Jean Ducis, pleaded with the Public Prosecutor Fouquier-Tinville to spare the architect, protesting that he had committed no crime: 'He has always been faithful and submissive to the laws of the country . . . He is a good father to his family, devoted to his wife and daughters'; but Moreau was all the same condemned to death and was one of only two famous architects (the other being Richard Mique) whose life ended upon the Revolutionary scaffold.

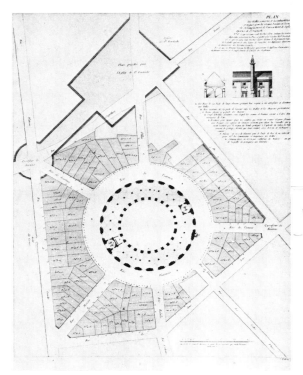

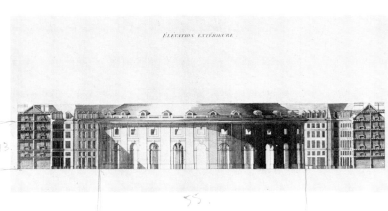

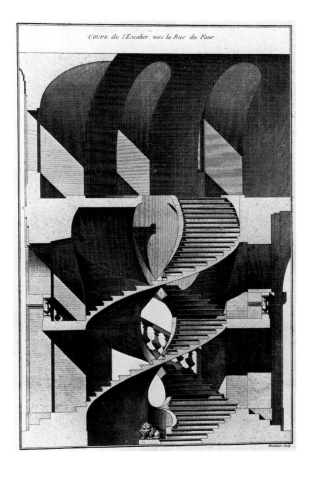

138 The Halle au Blé, Paris, site plan, elevation, section, and section of staircase, engravings from Le Camus' *Recueil*. Designed by Le Camus de Mézières in 1762 and the most celebrated of the many markets of late eighteenth-century Paris

7 Three Paris architects: Le Camus de Mézières, Boullée and Antoine

THE VERY DIFFERENT STYLES of Peyre, de Wailly and Moreau give some indication of the complexity of French architecture in the later part of the eighteenth century. Buildings could range between the extremes of austerity and elaboration depending upon the temperament of the architect, the nature of the commission and the wishes of the patron. The one constant factor was that all were affected in varying degrees by the revolutionary work of the *pensionnaires* of the Academy in Rome – even famous buildings of the 1760s by architects who had not themselves experienced antique architecture at first hand in Rome. The Paris corn market (the Halle au Blé) by Nicolas Le Camus de Mézières, the early town houses of Boullée, and the royal mint (the Hôtel des Monnaies) by Jacques-Denis Antoine, all buildings by architects trained exclusively in Paris, were no less rightly celebrated in their day than the buildings of former students in Rome.

Little is known of the life or the character of Le Camus de Mézières, who practised as 'architecte expert-bourgeois' for over forty years (1751–92), without ever apparently aspiring to join the Academy and become 'Architecte du Roi'. He was the architect attached to the University of Paris, and late in life he published several volumes outlining his views upon architecture and passing on the experience he had gained in its practice. The outstanding opportunity in his own practice came in 1762, when he received the commission for the Halle au Blé *(138)*.

The Halle au Blé was constructed on the site of the sixteenth-century Hôtel de Soissons, which lay not far from the Louvre where the Bourse de Commerce now stands, at the western edge of the area later to become Les Halles. The land was acquired by the municipality and developed on its behalf by a company of financiers as a housing speculation to subsidise the building of the market which lay in the centre of the site. Receiving royal assent late in 1762, the buildings were completed within the space of four years.

The Halle au Blé was one of the first and largest of many new markets constructed in Paris in the later eighteenth century, serving the growing population of the city and reflecting at the same time the increasingly exacting standards of public welfare, where humanitarian motives coincided with political and administrative expediency. Indeed the problem of the circulation of grain – whether it should be unrestricted, as Turgot and the Physiocrats believed, or carefully controlled as Necker maintained – was a crucial political issue throughout the later eighteenth century. But the Paris grain riots of the later eighteenth century were not caused by the lack of a proper market in Paris. Indeed, compared with earlier granaries and other markets in Paris, Le Camus' building must have appeared a veritable palace of Ceres, recalling to many the appearance of a Roman amphitheatre.

Even before it had been completed the building was singled out for praise by Laugier in his *Observations*: 'The merit of this hall is the new shape, and this merit is not negligible. This round building, entirely isolated, open to the daylight throughout, surrounded by houses & roads whose construction will contrast with its own, having in addition the requisite solidity and simplicity, will be in Paris one of our most agreeable landmarks.' The building may later have exhibited weaknesses of structure, but for a market it was indeed a remarkably solid and ingenious fabric, and virtually fireproof, as Le Camus was proud to stress.

The building consisted of a double aisled hall with a flat vault supported on Tuscan columns and a steep upper storey vaulted in brick and stone. The greatest ingenuity was required in the vaulting because of the adoption of a circular plan with narrow bays on the inside and wider bays on the outer perimeter. A variation in the width of the bays was necessary on the east side, where Le Camus, much to the disapproval of Laugier, had been required to retain the sixteenth-century astronomical column of the Hôtel de Soissons, the Colonne de Médicis, which still survives on the site.

Not even in Rome, where the main granaries were housed in the surviving halls of the Baths of Diocletian, had there been a market that consciously referred to the circuses of antiquity; yet as in a circus the circular plan was evidently

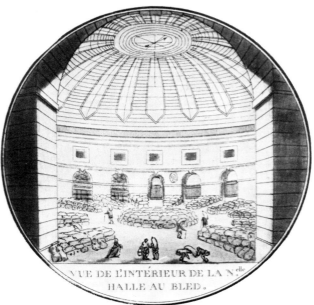

139 The Halle au Blé, views of the exterior and interior after 1783 (engravings after Testard). In 1782–83 Legrand and Molinos covered the court, 150 feet (45·7 metres) in diameter, with a dome of wood and glass, which was replaced by Belanger's iron dome in 1813 *(304)*

well suited for ease of movement in a building that had no particular focus beyond its two staircases. Stairs in granaries, where records of them have survived, seem to have created special problems because of the heavy sacks that had to be carried, and those of Le Camus are amongst the most ingenious. Oval in shape, and thus recalling the greatest masterpieces of the French classical tradition, they had two interweaving flights, one for ascending and one for descending traffic.

Large though it was Le Camus' market soon proved insufficient for the volume of business carried out and there thus arose the idea of covering the central court, where transactions were increasingly conducted, with a dome. Shortly after the building was completed Le Camus himself proposed a low dome supported on giant free-standing columns and buttresses. Since the market had been constructed without foreknowledge of the need for a central covering there was a limit to the weight it could be expected to support. Except for the dome of Ste-Geneviève, which was to a large extent Soufflot's personal responsibility, the covering of the Halle au Blé became the most demanding engineering challenge of the day. Several projects were presented before a design made jointly by the architects Legrand and Molinos was finally carried out *(139)*.

Jacques-Guillaume Legrand (1753–1809), the author of a famous *Description de Paris*, which Landon completed and published after his death, had been trained in engineering by Perronet and he later married the daughter of Clérisseau. At the school of Blondel he formed a partnership with Jacques Molinos, who was ten years his senior. Together they designed the dome of the Halle au Blé and much else besides, including a theatre in the rue de

Richelieu, the Théâtre Feydeau, which they built in the year of the Revolution. For the Halle au Blé the two architects adapted an idea that dated back to the sixteenth century. This was a system of vaulting based upon the use of short wooden planks that had been invented by Philibert de l'Orme. But in addition to wood Legrand and Molinos introduced glazed panels to keep the court clearly lit and iron for the construction of their lantern. By this method they spanned the court of the hall, 150 feet (45·7 metres) in diameter and almost as wide as the Roman Pantheon, without disturbing the existing fabric.

The building became one of the main sights of the city, appealing particularly to Arthur Young, who as a farmer and agriculturalist described how it functioned in the year 1787:

By far the finest thing I have yet seen in Paris is the Halle au Blé, or corn market; it is a vast rotunda, the roof entirely of wood, upon a new principle of carpentry . . . the gallery is 150 yards round, consequently the diameter is as many feet; it is as light as if suspended by the fairies. In the grand area, wheat, pease, beans, lentils, are stored and sold. In the surrounding divisions, flour on wooden stands. You pass by staircases doubly winding within each other to spacious apartments for rye, barley, oats, etc. The whole is so well-planned, and so admirably executed, that I know of no public building that exceeds it in either France or England.

The dome of Legrand and Molinos survived the hazards to which so light a structure was prone for over twenty years, but in 1803 it was finally consumed by fire, and replaced by a dome of even greater significance which belongs amongst the works of Belanger. After the completion of their dome Legrand and Molinos continued to contribute to the development of the Paris markets, a group of buildings, still largely unstudied, that inevitably attracted the most gifted engineers of the time. Their transformation of the cloth market, where they revived the Roman method of supporting the vault on terracotta tubes and used copper for the roof, was almost as celebrated in its day as the dome of the Halle au Blé. Working on his own, Legrand was largely occupied as an author and translator, while Molinos continued to practise as an architect, building the glass conservatory of the Paris botanical gardens and the Napoleonic mortuary.

Another group of vanished buildings, as essential to public welfare as markets and scarcely less experimental in construction, were the many 'Wauxhalls' that appeared all over Paris in the later eighteenth century. These were a type of building, as the name itself implies, that had been imported from England and became fashionable after the peace of 1763. The largest and most famous was the 'Colisée', constructed near the Champs-Elysées by the namesake of Le Camus de Mézières, Louis-Denis Le Camus, the personal architect of the Duc de Choiseul. Built of perishable materials, the Colisée lay somewhere between a palace and a market in its design, according to the rough sketches that record its original appearance, and it survived for less than twenty years *(140)*.

Nearly all who visited the building were enchanted by its appearance, even the sceptical Blaikie, who described the amusements offered there:

. . . the weather being fine there was a great concourse of people; there is little to be seen but the people and the Building which is newly finished and fine, the midle is a large cercular place for dancing suported all round with columns; in the gardens there is some peices of water upon which they exercese different games and in the Evening fire works; in the garden there is a high pole upon the top of which is a dragon fixed full of fire works which is to be set on fire by sky rockets . . .

Some English visitors, however, found French Wauxhalls, like French gardens, mean in scale beside their English equivalents, and Mercier cynically described one difference in their purpose: 'When these Wauxhalls are compared with the charming places in London, it is seen that the French know only one kind of pleasure, that of seeing and being seen.'

Despite the success of his Halle au Blé Le Camus de Mézières built little in his later years, and seems to have been mainly occupied with writing. He published a practical guide to building, a treatise on the strength of wood, and a book, *Le Génie de l'architecture*, in which he formally discussed what is described in the subtitle as 'the analogy of the arts with our sensations'. By the year 1780, when the volume appeared, the expressive use of form to evoke sentiments suitable to the character of a building had long been consciously recognized, but to Le Camus is due the credit for having attempted the first and perhaps the last treatise directly bearing upon the subject. His text, however, is no less ambiguous and intangible than most such verbal prescriptions, as when he rules that beauty 'will only be found in the purity of proportions and in their harmony; Genius alone can lead to it'. More clearly than any words of Le Camus, the drawings of Boullée show how far ideas for buildings could indeed stimulate suitable sensations.

140 The Colisée, Paris, view of the interior, drawing by Gabriel de St-Aubin (The Wallace Collection, London). Built by Louis-Denis Le Camus in 1771–74, the Colisée was the most famous of the many 'Wauxhalls' of pre-Revolutionary Paris

The career of Boullée has something of the same eccentric character as the professional life of Le Camus, as though in both cases interest in the expressive potentialities of architecture diminished the enthusiasm of both men for practice. Boullée has won widespread acclaim less for his real buildings than for the series of inspired drawings which he created in the latter part of his life *(146, 147)*. The legacy of an unfulfilled painter, the drawings occupy an ambiguous position midway between painting and architecture, though they are accompanied by theoretical writings which underline the importance of Boullée as a teacher, in passing on the ideas that are found in so exaggerated a form in his drawings to a younger generation of architects.

Etienne-Louis Boullée was born in Paris in 1728, the son of an architect and destined by his father to follow the same profession. Placed first with Jean-Baptiste Pierre, later Premier Peintre du Roi, he was then compelled, apparently against his will, to attend the school of Blondel. If he was indeed a reluctant architect it is understandable that Legeay should have touched his imagination at this time, as his early biographers suggest. During the 1750s Boullée had already begun to enrol students of his own, including Chalgrin, and had started on some architectural commissions, beginning with the decoration of the Chapelle du Calvaire in St-Roch, which he undertook in association with his former teacher, Pierre.

In the early part of his career Boullée was mainly active in domestic architecture, and he competed unsuccessfully, like Peyre, for the commission to remodel the Palais-Bourbon for the Prince de Condé. Amongst the first of his private commissions was the small Château of Chaville, near Versailles (recorded in drawings by the architect), which he built for the Comte de Tessé, the head of the Créquy family and the husband of Adrienne de Noailles. The Comtesse de Tessé was well known as a 'philosophe',

141 The Hôtel Alexandre, Paris, the court and garden façades. Begun in 1763 and the only surviving building of a group of private houses constructed by Boullée in his early years

'a sceptic except about her own infallibility', according to the Créquy *Souvenirs*, and for her friendship with Thomas Jefferson, who was a frequent visitor to Chaville.

Some impression of the appearance of the château is given by a surviving hôtel built at about the same time by Boullée in Paris *(141)*, one of a small group of town houses that he constructed in the area to the west of the Madeleine (Ville l'Evêque). The most celebrated of this group was one of two houses built for the eccentric M. de Monville *(142)*, a patron famous for the bizarre country estate which he later laid out near Paris (see chapter 14). The surviving hôtel is the Hôtel Alexandre, begun in 1763 for one of the less well-known bankers of the time, André-C.-N. Alexandre. A strangely hybrid building, it suggests something of Boullée's own difficulties as an architect and likewise the stylistic tensions of the time as they affected the traditional design of a Parisian town house.

What is immediately striking about the house is the marked discrepancy between the court and the garden elevations. Whereas the house of de Monville was of one main storey, that of Alexandre, more restricted by the size of the site, has the customary three storeys of the Parisian hôtel. This is frankly admitted on the garden side, where an order of Ionic pilasters rises from a ground-floor podium, but disguised at the front where there is an open portico masked by free-standing columns with an attic storey above, an idea associated rather with a country villa than with the court of a town house *(74)*.

The decoration of the exterior, with its occasional echoes of the work of Gabriel, matches the elegance of Boullée's famous interiors of this date *(143)*. The oval garlanded openings are simplified variants of a familiar French pattern, while smaller garlands throughout create a festive unity between the court and garden façades. Rectangular panels surmount the three attic windows above the main portico and similar panels reappear between the door frames on the garden side. Their garlands are echoed in the capitals chosen for the Ionic order, which is the one used by Moreau at the Hôtel de Chavannes, and one that enjoyed from this time onwards a short vogue in French architecture.

The interior decoration of the hôtel was less lavish than Boullée's other early interiors, with their elaborately carved and gilded pilasters and sculpture *(143)*. The decoration of de Monville's house created as great a sensation as the furniture that his counterpart, La Live de Jully, had provided for himself in the preceding decade. Visitors described its 'Turkish salon decorated with mirrors', and another room designed as 'an arab pavilion with vistas of trees and female nudes'. All this exacerbated the English prudery of Mrs Thale when she and Dr Johnson were taken by Le Roy to see the house. According to the doctor it was 'furnished with effeminate and minute elegance', while Mrs Thrale considered that 'It seems to be contrived merely for the purposes of disgusting Lewdness, & is executed as I conceive on the model of some of the Roman Emperors' Retirements . . .'

The most famous of all the town houses of Boullée was begun some ten years later than his earliest hôtels, in 1774,

and constructed for the Marquise de Brunoy on a site between the rue du Faubourg-St-Honoré and the Champs-Elysées *(144, 145)*. By the time that this hôtel was begun several of the early houses of Ledoux had already been constructed, and the spectacular appearance of the hôtel as it appeared beyond the railings of the Champs-Elysées *(145)* was not without rival. Boullée's hôtel was conceived in almost purely pictorial terms; unremarkable in plan, though lavishly decorated, it sprang to life on the garden side which the architect designed to represent the Temple of Flora. A podium of steps and flower-beds led down to the garden from an arcade of round-headed openings, while raised over the centre of the façade on six Ionic columns there appeared a stepped pyramid with a statue of Flora at the summit, commanding the length of the garden. Though Boullée was no doubt influenced by Soufflot's design of 1764 for the church of Ste-Geneviève, and by the early houses of Ledoux, his was the most radical treatment of the temple theme applied to domestic architecture in a house that truly justified its dedication to a classical deity.

So ostentatious a design, emphasizing the relation between the house and its garden, both physically and thematically, can scarcely have been created without the active participation of the patron, who was not in this case a financier or a liberal aristocrat but a woman living separately from her husband in exceptional circumstances. A member of the aristocratic family of d'Escars, Mme de Brunoy had been married to the only son of Pâris de Montmartel, one of a family of important financiers.

142 The Grand Hôtel de Monville, Paris, view of the garden façade (engraving by Guyot after Sergent). One of two houses built by Boullée (1764) for M. de Monville who later laid out the Désert de Retz *(336–338)*

143 Decoration probably from the Hôtel de Monville (now at 32, rue de Babylone, Paris). Dr Johnson found the decoration of the house 'effeminate', but Boullée's panelling was usually based on the use of the classical orders

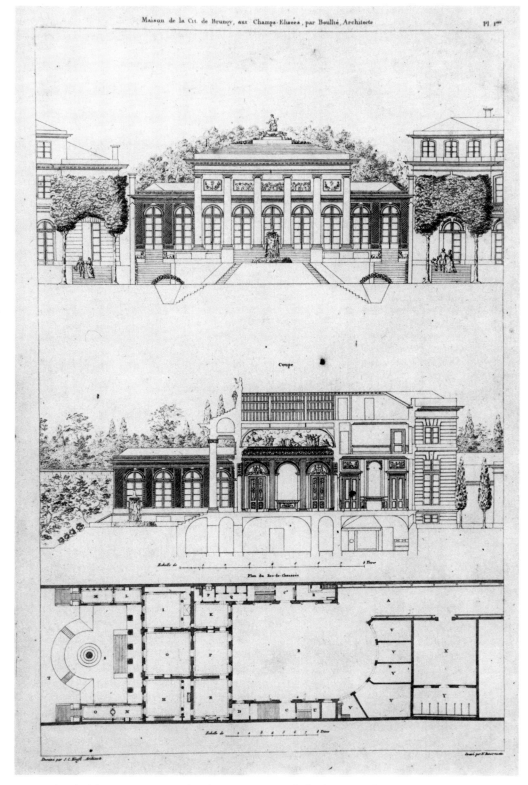

144 The Hôtel de Brunoy, Paris, garden elevation, section and plan (engraving from Krafft and Ransonnette). Boullée's most celebrated house, designed in 1774 for a site overlooking the Champs-Elysées

145 The Hôtel de Brunoy, view of the garden façade (engraving by Janninot after Durand). The house became known as the Temple of Flora from the statue of Flora placed on a podium of steps over the columns of the garden façade

Alliances between finance and aristocracy, with their interesting consequences for patronage, were already a commonplace of social life, but this was a marriage of particular cruelty since the Marquis de Brunoy was well known for fits of overt madness. Shut away from society at Brunoy, he squandered his fortune on bizarre decorations, as when, on the occasion of his father's death, he draped the trees on the estate in black and filled the fountains with ink. These fits continued until he was finally interned by his family in a madhouse. His wife meanwhile led a by no means sheltered life in Paris. Like de Monville she was a close friend of Mme du Barry, and her house in Paris evidently combined the fashionable luxury of Monville's own mansion with the seclusion of a quasi-rural retreat.

Despite the success of the Hôtel de Brunoy Boullée received almost no commissions for private architecture in the latter part of his career. His biographer, Villar, mentions his tenacious honesty as a factor preventing him from winning clients, but at the same time Boullée's exceptional pictorial talents and his gifts as a teacher thereby flourished the more. Having become an Academician in 1762, he was promoted a member of the first class when the death of Soufflot created a vacancy, and he was later to become one of the group of architects who were founder members of the Institut.

Before the outbreak of the Revolution Boullée held several official posts for a short while, first in the household of the Comte d'Artois, and then as Contrôleur at the Invalides and the Ecole Militaire. During his later years Boullée was also responsible for the adaptation of two buildings for the public service, the prison known as 'La Petite Force' and the Bourse, and there were other smaller

commissions for the Finances. Mainly, however, the architect was engaged upon the series of drawings for which he is now best known, referring to public building projects in Paris *(146)* and to purely imaginary sites *(147)*, and later on he composed the *Essai sur l'art*, which is their less imaginative verbal counterpart.

A summary of Boullée's ideas is provided by his biographer, Villar:

The author discourses on the principles of the *beautiful in architecture*. Perrault maintains that, in this art, *beauty* is purely a fantasy. Boullée proves that, in all the arts, *beauty* derives from nature, and nowhere depends on the caprice of men. He discovered new sources in poetry and philosophy, above all *in the architecture of shadows* (*l'architecture des ombres*) of which he declared himself the inventor. He described by this the art of organizing the masses of buildings, in such a way that their projections and the contrast of their forms produced effects of lighting the most calculated to enchant the view. '. . . I have tried', he said, 'to raise art to its full height. It is not sufficiently realized that poetry multiplies our enjoyment by the surest means. Our public buildings should be, in some way, real poems. The images that they offer to our senses, should excite in our hearts sentiments analogous to their functions. In investigating deeply the theory of forms, I have tried to determine their degree of influence on the functioning of man, and the closeness of their *rapport* with him.'

In his *Essai* Boullée stressed the study of geometrical forms as an alternative, based on 'nature', to what he indeed took to be the 'fantasy' of Perrault's rules, and he proceeded to discuss each of his major projects, providing a rationale that nowhere matches their visual daring. 'I too am a painter', he declared on the title page of the treatise, and in Boullée's case this commonplace phrase, also used by Diderot in reference to his novel, *The Nun*, is not a plea for greater artistry in architecture, as exemplified in the work of de Wailly or Ledoux, but evidently the expression of a personal conflict. In so far as his drawings refer to architecture rather than to painting, they clearly represent an extreme of modernity in their use of simple geometric shapes, but their expressive character was by no means unfamiliar in real buildings at this date, and the emotive use of shadows that Boullée claimed as his own invention formed an important part of the Renaissance tradition, which Boullée himself was in the process of destroying.

One of Boullée's projects for the Bibliothèque Nationale, more viable as a building than many of his other designs, shows the crossing of the old and the new in the architect's imagination *(146)*. The atlantes, forming its principal decoration, are figures of the past, which recall especially Bernini's design for the Louvre, where the main entrance was to be guarded by two atlases. Except in the centre the architecture itself is free of all shadows, and decorated only with inscriptions and a frieze of garlands that recalls Soufflot's final design for the walls of Ste-Geneviève. But in the absence of the lower moulding that underlines Soufflot's decoration the design is closer in appearance to the walls of the nearby Bibliothèque Ste-Geneviève built in the following century by Labrouste.

According to Boullée's treatise, 'If there is one subject that should please an architect, and at the same time, inflame his genius, it is a project for a public library. With

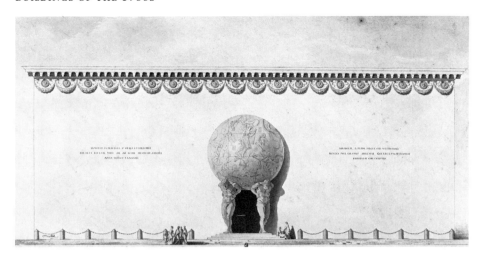

146 Projects for the Bibliothèque du
Roi, rue de Richelieu, Paris, front
elevation (1788) and perspective view of
interior, drawings by Boullée
(Bibliothèque Nationale, Paris). Of the
famous visionary projects of Boullée's
later years, the several designs for the
Royal Library are amongst those
designed for particular sites in Paris

the chance of developing his talents, there is joined the
precious advantage of devoting them to the men who have
honoured their century . . .' One such man who became a
popular hero in the eighteenth century was Newton, and
of all Boullée's imaginary projects the tomb of Newton of
1784 was the one closest to his heart: 'O Newton! if by the
range of your vision and the sublimity of your Genius, you
have determined the shape of the earth, for my part I have
conceived a project to envelop you with your discovery.'
Boullée may have known that one of the discoveries of
Newton was indeed that the earth was originally exactly
spherical in shape, but his wording suggests only a casual
acquaintance with Newton's writings and the cenotaph
itself is more visual than scientific in character; his sphere,
which represents the earth, forms on the inside a
planetarium with the shrine of Newton at its base (147).
Just as Boullée's contemporaries preferred the circle for the
regularity of its shape, so he liked of all forms, the sphere:

'From all these observations, the result is that the sphere,
in every respect, is the image of perfection.'

It has long been customary to group together the
imaginary designs of Boullée with those of Ledoux and
Lequeu, as though these architects were the three heroes –
the Three Musketeers – of the architectural revolution in
France, but three such different artists it would scarcely be
possible to imagine. They have little more in common than
that many fanciful designs by each survive. To the extent
that the ideas underlying his drawings differ greatly from
his early architectural projects and depend upon the
inflation of simple geometrical shapes, it is Boullée who
seems historically the most in advance of his time. It was
his vision that younger architects, especially in their
drawings for the Academy of Architecture, aspired to
emulate, and even to anticipate (264), before Boullée's own
more extreme drawings were produced.

Alive to the values of the young, Boullée himself seems

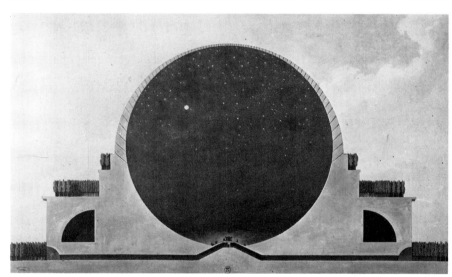

147 Project for a cenotaph for Sir Isaac Newton, elevation and section, drawings by Boullée, 1784 (Bibliothèque Nationale, Paris). Though pictorial in intention, Boullée's later designs, based on the inflation of geometrical shapes, coincided with the ideals of a younger generation of architects *(264)*

to have benefited from their youthful idealism and transformed his own work in response to their imaginings: 'The first part of his benevolence was for talent in distress; he liked to repair the wrongs that fortune had shown them. Deprived of the joys of marriage, he played the part of father to some of his pupils; when they had gone from his hands he drew them into public confidence, and sacrificed to them his personal interest.'

When Boullée died in 1799 his place at the Institut was taken by a younger contemporary, Jacques-Denis Antoine (1733–1801) *(148)*. Like Boullée Antoine had been trained in Paris and the two architects produced rival designs for some of the same buildings in their earlier years. But whereas Boullée has become mainly famous for his visionary architecture, Antoine won the reputation of being the most efficient and practical of all the architects of the time. These qualities of mind are stressed by his two

early biographers, Renou and Lussault, and his buildings even won him a place beside Gabriel and Soufflot in Quatremère's *Vies des architectes*.

The son of a carpenter, Antoine was brought up to be a mason, without receiving any academic training. He might have become, like Le Camus de Mézières, an 'architecte expert-bourgeois', fortunate to receive a single public commission, but his exceptional gifts must have been recognized by the time that he was appointed in 1766 to be the architect of the new royal Mint. Almost nothing is known of his career before this date, or of any buildings he may have designed, with the exception of a precocious project attributed to him for a theatre closely related to Soufflot's Opéra design and destined for the same site, the grounds of the former Hôtel de Conti on the bank of the Seine opposite the Louvre.

This was the site on which the Mint (the Hôtel des Monnaies) was eventually constructed by Antoine in the

148 Portrait of Jacques-Denis Antoine (1733–1801), engraving by Lempereur after Trinquesse

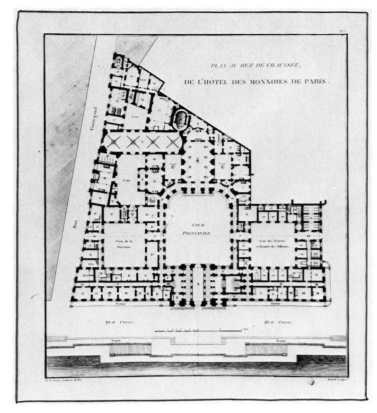

149 The Hôtel des Monnaies, Paris, ground-plan (engraving by Bernard after Antoine). Facing across the Seine to the Louvre, Antoine's masterpiece, the Royal Mint (1768–75), is ingeniously organized on its awkward triangular site

150 The Hôtel des Monnaies, the main façade. Antoine intended to build a new quay on the river bank, providing a base for the façade

years 1768 to 1775, 'one public building that has been constructed with the most speed and the least expense, considering its size . . .', as the *Journal de Paris* described it in 1777. The Monnaie *(149–154)* established for Antoine an international reputation leading to commissions, duly noted by Renou, from Germany, Switzerland, Spain and England (a house for Lord Findlater). He was proposed as a member of the Academy in 1774, though passed over in favour of a younger man (Gondoin), and finally appointed two years later. A journey to Italy followed in 1778, in company with de Wailly, who may indeed have been an early friend of Antoine.

The need for new premises for the royal Mint of France, inadequately housed along the rue de la Monnaie (near the Louvre), had been acknowledged in the earlier part of the century, but it was not until after the peace of 1763, during the ministry of Choiseul, that a serious effort was made to house with appropriate dignity the manufacture and administration of the French coinage. When Antoine became architect of the Monnaie the building was destined for the left-hand block of Gabriel's Place Louis XV *(43)* and the land behind, which had been allocated for the Monnaie as early as 1750. As a small industrial undertaking with a high security risk, the Monnaie was to be disposed around two enclosed courtyards to the rear of the colonnaded building. Antoine must have worked in close association with Gabriel at this time and his final building is influenced by, though by no means subjugated to, the style of Gabriel.

Antoine's original project was halted early in 1767 and the site transferred to the more convenient and central location of the old Hôtel de Conti, a sixteenth-century building that had become a famous landmark in the capital after the addition of the main doorway and other alterations carried out by François Mansart. This was a site that had been considered for some time for the Monnaie, and even before the appointment of Antoine Boullée had prepared a design for the building in this location. It was also a site that afforded far greater scope to the architect, who had above all to consider the river façade of the new building, facing across the Seine towards the Louvre, and flanked by Le Vau's Collège des Quatre-Nations.

Instead of an open courtyard on the lines of a private house, as Boullée had proposed in his designs for the site, Antoine followed the scheme of the Place Louis XV, turning the hôtel back to front so that the main building lay along the river front protectively concealing the workshops beyond *(149, 150)*. The main court lies immediately behind the river wing, with the main foundry ('salle du monnoyage') at the centre of its far side, and the subsidiary courts and workshops are fitted ingeniously within the roughly triangular site of the old hôtel. The service entrance to the building lies to the left in the rue Guénégaud *(152)* where the minting shops ('ateliers des travaux de force') lay. Low and densely rusticated, this wing was admired for its robust and masculine design and it indeed possesses something of the defensive character associated, since the time of Sansovino's Venice Mint, with the architecture of coinage.

151 The Hôtel des Monnaies, the main frontispiece. Though influenced by Gabriel's public architecture *(43)*, Antoine's façade is revolutionary in its horizontal emphasis, with an attic storey in place of a central pediment

152 The Hôtel des Monnaies, the side façade (rue Guénégaud). A suggestion of fortification, customary in architecture associated with coinage, is apparent at the service entrance

153 The Hôtel des Monnaies, project for a statue of Abundance, drawing by Antoine (Bibliothèque Nationale, Paris). Antoine's surviving drawings for the Mint, collected together in six volumes, cover every detail of the planning and design of the building

Antoine's purpose in distinguishing the appearance of the different parts of the building are outlined in one of the more coherent passages of Lussault's loquacious biography.

His intention, which everyone has perhaps not grasped, was to differentiate, in the general disposition, the administrative services from the executive. The first should have over the second a marked pre-eminence; that is to say that the great building on the river should manifest externally and internally a character of grandeur and richness that corresponds with the site and proclaims the idea of the depot being the symbol representing national opulence.

Opulence is perhaps not the precise quality suggested most of all by Antoine's building (150, 151), but rather a subdued and elegant richness that the state of the French finances by no means justified. Of all the later eighteenth-century monuments of the capital Antoine's building shows most clearly that sense of condensation, of being low and narrow in relation to the site, that affected all the arts of the time, in contrast to the frankly opulent grandeur of the earlier part of the century.

The style employed by Antoine in the Monnaie seems neater than Gabriel's, without approaching the aggressive character of Ledoux's public work, but his Mint is a more radical building that its well-mannered appearance might at first suggest. The articulation is approximately in the vernacular manner of Gabriel, as was common at the time with such architects as Boullée, and even Ledoux, who had received their early training in France. The style is not that of the colonnaded buildings of the Place Louis XV, but of the more modest buildings beside them (166) which Gabriel himself had developed at the Ecole Militaire, with a rusticated basement, punctuated by balconies on consoles, discreetly framed windows for the main floor with smaller consoles supporting the upper ledge, and simple eared frames for the upper floor.

What is new in Antoine's Mint, the first major building of its kind in Paris, is the degree of horizontality and evenness of emphasis achieved by the architect. To each side of the central frontispiece the building extends for eleven bays, unbroken save for the presence of three balconies on consoles with formal frames for the main-floor windows above. In an early drawing these frames were to be the only ones with pediments, but even this method of distinction was discarded in the final design. To increase the horizontal emphasis Antoine used a cornice that is disproportionately large for the columns of the frontispiece and even incorrect in design for the Ionic order. And Antoine finally omitted, apparently for the first time in a public building in eighteenth-century France, a pediment over the six columns of the frontispiece, supplying instead a low attic punctuated by six statues presiding directly over the cornice and symbolizing Peace, Commerce, Prudence, Law, Strength and Abundance. The central portico was to receive additional emphasis from the remodelling of the quay, which the architect interpreted as a high podium setting off the bulk of his building and mitigating the weight of the cornice, but this part of the design was never carried out.

To illustrate the exceptionally scrupulous behaviour of Antoine in the construction of the Monnaie Renou described in his life of the architect how the entrepreneurs he had chosen for the work wished to make him a present; so that he should not seem too severe Antoine allowed them to give him a book that was not in his library – the Encyclopédie. When, however, the entrepreneurs accused the inspector of the works of rejecting stone they believed to be perfectly sound, Antoine visited the site and on discovering more than twice as much imperfect stone as his inspector he returned the books he had been given.

The many drawings by Antoine for the building that survive (153), no less than six volumes, tell their own story of his exceptional diligence. There are sheets covering the existing buildings on the site, including a small house at the rear, an early work of Hardouin Mansart, which Antoine preserved with very little alteration, and others illustrating the new Mint and all its processes in the greatest detail. Later sheets refer to the decoration of the interior, the grand staircase and the main salon (154), the Cabinet de l'Ecole des Mines, which was not completed until 1785.

As well as the many projects made by Antoine for foreign patrons after the completion of the Monnaie, he was also active in Paris as the architect of several private houses and some more modest public commissions, notably as one of the architects who participated in the remodelling of the Palais de Justice after a fire in 1776. This

154 The Hôtel des Monnaies, the Cabinet de l'Ecole des Mines. Completed in 1785, the council chamber of the Mint has the architectural inventiveness associated with the interiors of de Wailly (131)

was a work begun by Desmaisons that inspired a typically mordant comment from Sébastien Mercier: 'On rebâtit le palais de la justice, Oh! si l'on pouvoit rebâtir de même l'art de la rendre.'

In his secular buildings Antoine never seriously disturbed conventions of good taste with ideas that were architecturally over-provocative, but the traditions that governed the design of ecclesiastical buildings permitted him greater scope. His circular Eglise Conventuelle at Nancy, mentioned in Thiéry's guide to Paris, was designed with a completely windowless façade, and the famous portico that he built for the hospital of the monastery of the Charité was believed to be the first occasion on which Greek Doric columns without any base mouldings made a public appearance in the French capital *(155)*. 'Antoine wanted to give an idea of the Propylées [of the Acropolis] of which David Le Roy had spoken in his lessons,' according to Legrand and Landon. Though baseless columns had appeared in England as early as 1759 and in France at Ménars some twelve years later *(52)* they were not a common sight in Paris. The date of Antoine's portico is unknown, but it may be a work of the 1760s, completed not very long after the publication of Le Roy's book, and

about the time when Boullée too produced a design for the same portico.

When the Revolution broke out and Necker was briefly reappointed Minister of Finances, Antoine received the unrewarding task of replacing his colleague, Ledoux, as architect of the Paris toll-houses and of bringing order to the chaotic state of their finances. Though he was undoubtedly a more careful administrator than Ledoux, he felt the awkwardness of his position and declared to Renou that 'There was enough in Ledoux's designs to make the reputation of four architects.' According to Renou, Antoine was imprisoned after the Revolution on the charge of having provided a secret hiding-place in the Monnaie so that gold could be smuggled from the country down the river, but he was later allowed to return, under guard, to his house after protests from the personnel involved in the construction of the toll-houses, who were unable to cope without his guidance. Like Ledoux he began to think of having his buildings engraved for publication, and a description of the Monnaie was eventually published after his death. Public acknowledgment of his distinction came with his election to Boullée's seat at the Institut, where he was active for two years before his death in August 1801.

155 The Hôpital de la Charité, Paris, engraved view of portico. Antoine's portico, of uncertain date, was probably the first example of Greek Doric architecture in Paris

8 Early 'basilican' churches and their architects:
Potain, Trouard and Chalgrin

FOLLOWING THE EXAMPLE of Soufflot's Ste-Geneviève and the churches of Contant d'Ivry, the character of ecclesiastical architecture was transformed almost beyond recognition in the later 1750s and 1760s. The earliest church in the new 'basilican' manner was apparently St-Vincent in Soufflot's own town of Lyon, built to the design of a local architect, Léonard Roux, and it was soon followed by designs for three important new churches, one in Paris and two not far from the capital, at St-Germain-en-Laye and at Versailles. As with the construction of Ste-Geneviève itself, the revolutionary intentions of the three architects involved can be the more easily judged since the church was an architectural proposition that had remained relatively unaltered throughout the history of Christendom. Unlike the town house or the château, it was not a building type that had been largely determined, at least during the Renaissance, by social or geographical conditions peculiar to France and her Catholic neighbours in the North.

The defensive role that the Church was forced to assume in France as the eighteenth century advanced cannot have been without its influence upon architects and their ecclesiastical clients, and visitors to Paris were constantly surprised by the growth of atheism in the city. According to Walpole (1765) the Parisians 'are another people from what they were . . . The *savans*—I beg their pardons, the *philosophes* – are insupportable, superficial, overbearing and fanatic: they preach incessantly, and their avowed doctrine is atheism. Voltaire himself does not satisfy them . . .'

Ten years later Mrs Thrale witnessed the consequences:

I went to High Mass at one of the most considerable Churches in the Town, & was astonished at the want of Devotion in the Audience; some were counting their Money, some arguing with the Beggars who interrupt you without ceasing, some receiving Messages and dispatching Answers, some beating Time to the Musick, but scarce any one praying except for one Moment when the Priest elevates the Host.

In their scale, and even in quantity, churches had taken second place to buildings of public utility and amusement, and the very word 'temple' was usurped for private

156 The interior of S. Paolo fuori le Mura, Rome, drawing by Panini (Fitzwilliam Museum, Cambridge). The largest and most famous of the Early Christian churches of Rome surviving into modern times

houses and theatres, centres for communal worship more potent than the Church itself.

In the earlier part of the century churches had borrowed something of the decorative richness associated with domestic architecture, but traditionally they were allowed a severity bordering upon the military that was increasingly welcomed as the century drew towards its close. Not only were the buildings of the earliest Christians spiritually venerable but in also deriving from the basilicas of ancient Rome they provoked no conflict between archaeology and the practice of religion. They had for some while been a subject of popular curiosity, even if the practical difficulty of reviving the basilican form was not seriously

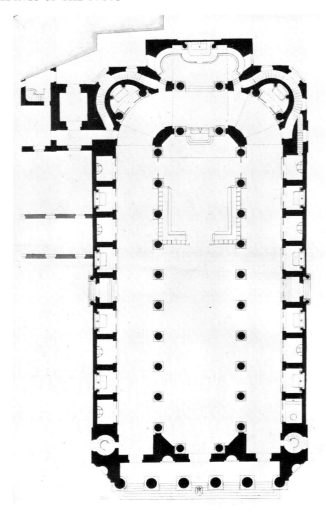

157 The church of St-Louis, St-Germain-en-Laye, ground-plan (Bibliothèque Nationale, Paris). Designed by Potain, probably in 1765, St-Louis was not completed until the early nineteenth century

confronted until after the mid-century. According to Desgodetz, 'To understand well the uses of all parts of a building destined for Divine Service, the first centuries of the Church must be studied, because the Christian religion as the creation of God then enjoyed its perfection.'

Not only had many of the earliest churches been restored in the early eighteenth century, but they had also played their part, however indirectly, in the evolution of Ste-Geneviève, and their general popularity is attested in the paintings of Panini, who produced almost as many representations of the largest of the churches, S. Paolo fuori le Mura, as of the Pantheon and St Peter's (156). It may thus seem inevitable that the smaller churches designed in the aftermath of Ste-Geneviève, including the chapels of Peyre and de Wailly and even Gabriel's chapel at the Ecole Militaire, should all refer in some degree to the basilican form.

The three major basilican churches of the 1760s were by architects who, despite the similarity of their intentions, approached the practical difficulties of their task in very different ways. The church of St-Louis at St-Germain-en-Laye (157, 158) was designed by much the oldest of the three men, Nicolas-Marie Potain. An exact contemporary of Soufflot, Potain had won the Prix de Rome as early as 1738, with a design for a town gate and he was at the Academy in Rome in the same years as Legeay. De Troy reported to Marigny that he spent much of his time there drawing the church of St Peter's, studying the building in greater detail than ever before. He was allowed to remain in Rome until his replacement, Jardin, arrived and was then given a grant to travel on Gabriel's behalf throughout Italy making plans of all the principal theatres.

On his return to France Potain joined the office of Gabriel, where he was active at Versailles and Fontaine-bleau and where he assumed responsibility for the construction of the Place Louis XV. Favoured by Gabriel, Potain was also protected by Marigny, who employed him at Ménars, where he worked in close association with Soufflot and Cochin. He became a member of the Academy in 1755 and was elected to the first class after a wait of only seven years. He outlived Gabriel and Soufflot, dying in 1791, but in the absence of any contemporary records of his life neither the full extent of his work nor the character of the man can be pictured.

All his known independent works were of the decade of the 1760s, including a *Traité des ordres d'architecture* (1767), one of the last of all the books to be written about the classical orders. Potain offers little that is new in his analysis, though the late date of the treatise is occasionally apparent, in his choice of Ionic capital, for example, or when he recommends that columns should not be engaged with the wall surface because they lose all their lightness and grace.

As well as his writing and his activity on Gabriel's behalf, Potain explored the two subjects that had become familiar to him in Italy, the church and the theatre. He made a celebrated design for a small theatre, close to the style of Soufflot in the treatment of the exterior, but oval in plan and with the stage opening from one of the longer sides. His drawings formed the basis for the ideal theatre discussed by Cochin in a book of 1765, but Potain's design was unsuited in scale to offer much guidance in the planning of a major public theatre. Potain's drawings, now at the Ecole des Beaux-Arts, were acquired by the king at Marigny's sale in 1782 for presentation to the Academy.

Potain's first known architectural commission was for work at Rennes, including the restoration of the cathedral and a new episcopal palace. The architect was apparently guided in this work by Soufflot – Ste-Geneviève naturally being a suitable model for the reconstruction of a Gothic cathedral – and Potain intended to replace the medieval piers with giant columns supporting lintels. His projects were shown to the Academy on at least three occasions, beginning in 1762, when members singled out for praise the 'heureuse légèreté' of his design. But 'légèreté' was a quality increasingly under suspicion as the century

VUE JNTERIEURE DE L'EGLISE PAROISSIALE DE S.GERMAIN EN LAYE.

Cette Eglise Composée par le S. Potain Architecte.

158 St-Louis, St-Germain-en-Laye, view of the interior, drawing by Potain (Musée de St-Germain-en-Laye). Unlike the nave at S. Paolo (156), Potain's nave at St-Louis was to have straight lintels over the columns and a barrel vault

advanced, and the reconstruction of Rennes Cathedral was not finally begun until the 1780s, to a design supplied by Boullée's pupil, Mathurin Crucy, and it remained unfinished for over fifty years.

A similar fate was in store for Potain's second major commission, his project for rebuilding the parish church that served the town and the royal Château of St-Germain-en-Laye (157, 158). Drawings for the building were shown to the Academy, together with those for Rennes, in 1765. The foundations and the crypt were then begun, and subsequently discussed and illustrated by Patte as an example of vaulting expertise in his *Monuments sur les objets les plus importants de l'architecture* (1769). This work too, however, was suspended, then restarted in the 1780s, and the present church was built only after the restoration of the monarchy.

Potain's church was much the largest of the basilican churches of the 1760s, intended like the present building for a large congregation and dominating the square in front of the château. The château itself was no longer one of the main residences of the king; it was later assigned by Louis XVI to his youngest brother, the Comte d'Artois, who began, with the assistance of his architect, Belanger, a full-scale development of the bank of the Seine below the castle.

In his plan Potain retained certain features of the Renaissance church formula, including rows of side chapels and buttresses framing the façade – probably bases for the bell-towers – which enclose, as in Contant's Madeleine design (58), the six free-standing columns of the portico. Internally (158) the church was to be of an elegant Doric character with a vista at the end of the nave to a well-lit sanctuary beyond the altar, all of which suggests something of the richness appropriate to a court church

125

dedicated to St Louis. But otherwise the interior retained little of the ecclesiastical conservatism of the plan.

The church marks a departure from the position of Soufflot not in any suggestion of primitive austerity, but rather in the absence of anything that could be described as Gothic 'légèreté'. In this respect the basilican churches, though following the innovations of Soufflot in their use of columns and lintels, began to imply criticism of Soufflot's ideas. The scale and dense grouping of Potain's columns aspire to emulate the robust character of pre-Gothic architecture, and the vault, though not flat and constructed in wood, like the ceiling of a real early Christian church, has a weight and Roman gravity that Soufflot had contrived to avoid. Though Potain's design is no more an archaeological reconstruction than Soufflot's masterpiece, the changes that both architects instigated were to encourage a church architecture more literally derivative than they themselves would have approved of.

The earliest of the three main basilican churches of the 1760s, supposedly designed in 1764, the year before Potain showed his drawings for St-Louis to the Academy, and actually completed some six years later, was the new St-Symphorien, which still stands in Montreuil, a suburb of Versailles (160, 161). Its author was Louis-François Trouard, a much younger man than Potain and a more radical architect, though almost as elusive a personality. An exact contemporary of de Wailly, Trouard was born in 1729 and he journeyed to Rome slightly before de Wailly after winning the Prix de Rome of 1753 with drawings of a gallery.

Trouard was born in comfortable circumstances, his father being a rich marble supplier on the staff of the Bâtiments du Roi, and with the assistance of his family his career in Paris began with the construction of private houses. By the early 1760s the scene of his main activities shifted to Versailles, where he acted as Inspecteur of the exterior of the château and later as municipal architect. He also succeeded to the post of architect of the Economats, a state department then under the direction of the Bishop of Orléans (Louis-Sextus de Jarente de la Bruyère), which dealt with vacant ecclesiastical benefices. Trouard received several ecclesiastical commissions in Versailles through the Economats as well as the task of completing the medieval cathedral, Ste-Croix, at Orléans.

Trouard became a member of the Academy in 1767, having tried for membership two years earlier, but it was not until 1786 that he was placed amongst the sixteen of the first class. Like Potain, he too became involved in the planning of the gardens of Ménars for Marigny, and he also shared the social life that Soufflot and Marigny enjoyed in Paris, with the Abbé Raynal as one of his close friends. Trouard's son also became a successful architect, winning the Prix de Rome in 1780, and Trouard himself has the further distinction of being the architect at whose office Ledoux, not much younger than himself, received his professional training. Like de Wailly, Trouard was a collector and patron of the arts and he is probably the Trouard who is listed as being the owner of a Chardin in the Salon of 1759.

In the midst of all his success, a crisis occurred in Trouard's career, when the Bishop of Orléans resigned the direction of the Economats at the time of the disgrace of Choiseul. Trouard was accused of malpractice in the contracts for the work at Orléans and dismissed, and when the Bâtiments du Roi was reformed at the start of the new reign he also lost his post at Versailles and withdrew to Paris. Next to nothing is known of his life beyond this point up to the time of his death, which occurred probably in the early 1790s.

A recently discovered work of Trouard is one of the earliest town houses in the Grecian style of the 1750s and 1760s (159). It lies at the start of the rue du Faubourg-Poissonnière, the road that is itself a microcosm of the architectural transformation of Paris in the later eighteenth century, where, higher up, Ledoux was to build several houses and, higher still, houses by Lenoir and others still survive. Unlike Moreau's Hôtel de Chavannes of the preceding year (135), Trouard's house is a relatively simple and functional construction, probably always divided into separate apartments and accommodating, though less boisterously than now, a row of shops. It is a type of middle-class apartment house, resembling Servandoni's building on the Place St-Sulpice (24), that proliferated above all with the spread of Paris in the following century.

Trouard's house recalls the Italianate character of Neufforge's designs for large town houses (74), but there is nothing of Neufforge's clumsy detailing in Trouard's façade. The windows are for the most part marked with simple indentations in place of raised mouldings. Eared frames, with austere but intricately hooded ledges, are reserved for the centre and the sides of the main floor,

159 House in the rue du Faubourg-Poissonnière, Paris. Built in 1758 and one of the earliest buildings by Louis-François Trouard, the teacher of Ledoux

160 The church of St-Symphorien, Montreuil,
Versailles, the rear and front façades. Trouard's
church, designed in 1764, was the earliest and the
most austere of the basilican churches of the 1760s in
the neighbourhood of Paris

161 St-Symphorien, view of the interior, painting by
de Machy, 1772 (Musée Carnavalet, Paris). The
primitive austerity of Trouard's interior was spoilt by
nineteenth-century embellishments

while the triads of windows between are contrasted with panels decorated with the Greek key pattern. Inside the house Trouard used the same pattern for the iron balustrade of the staircase. On the exterior the façade rises to a high entablature, with pedimented dormers above that resolve the inequalities of the articulation below. Prominent triangular pediments in groups of three crown the weaker bays of the elevation leaving the softer segmental pediments for the centre and the sides.

A still greater austerity characterizes the buildings that Trouard constructed shortly after at Versailles: the Chapelle des Catéchismes, attached almost reproachfully to the exuberant cathedral, and the church of St-Symphorien (160, 161). Even in its plan Trouard's church is simpler than Potain's, especially in the absence of side chapels, and in this respect it matches more closely the shape of a classical basilica, or even many of the Protestant churches of Northern Europe. Without side chapels the traditional places for the bell-towers, flanking the façade, were denied to Trouard and, like Soufflot at Ste-Geneviève, he transposed the bells to the east end.

In his early drawings the belfry was in the shape of a small circular temple with free-standing columns, but as finally built, presumably to Trouard's design, there is a single heavy tower at the east. This recalls the towers of English parish churches, but avoids by its very bulk any suggestion of Gothic verticality and proclaims from the rear the presence and something of the character of the church. To support the tower Trouard introduced a broad pediment in stucco, supported by plain piers with widely spaced Tuscan columns between, an arrangement that echoes the more overtly classical portico at the front of the church.

Internally the church shows little of the rich harmonies that Potain intended for St-Louis. The order is, like Potain's, a Doric one, succeeding the plainer Tuscan of the exterior, but the columns are of the austere type, with the lower part of the shaft unfluted, which was normally reserved for vestibules (as at the Ecole Militaire) where traffic might too easily damage the flutings. Originally the apse behind the high altar was quite plain, except for the coffering of its semicircular vault, where Trouard introduced a pattern of coffers and rosettes, and the frieze throughout the interior was bare even of the triglyphs that normally accompany the Doric order. The nave vault too is austerely Roman, its plain square coffers undecorated with rosettes, and abruptly punctured by the round-headed clerestory windows. It is an interior that St Symphorien himself, martyred at Autun in the second century, would have recognized as a basilica, a building that others of his faith were subsequently to adapt for their own uses.

The third of the important basilican churches of the 1760s was the work of a far more celebrated architect than either Potain or Trouard. This is the church of St-Philippe-du-Roule (169, 170), designed in 1768 by Jean-François-Thérèse Chalgrin, the architect who was later responsible for the start of the Arc-de-Triomphe at the end of the Champs-Elysées. The busy career of Chalgrin is known in

162 Project for a pavilion, elevation, drawing by Chalgrin (Ecole des Beaux-Arts, Paris). Chalgrin's reduction of the project which won him the Prix de Rome in 1758.

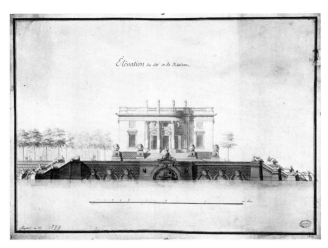

163 Project for a pavilion, elevation, drawing by Mathurin Cherpitel, 1758 (Ecole des Beaux-Arts, Paris). Cherpitel shared the 1758 Prix de Rome with Chalgrin, though he remained a more conservative architect (324, 325)

some detail from two early biographies, from a speech delivered at the Institut by Quatremère de Quincy after the architect's death, and from another read at the Société d'Architecture by a former pupil of Chalgrin, Charles-François Viel, the architect. Trained by Boullée and influenced by Soufflot, Chalgrin was an architect whose work needed little apology in the early years of the nineteenth century: 'M. Chalgrin impressed on all his works a very apparent character of solidity,' is one of Quatremère's comments. Yet Chalgrin never became an obsessive classicist; he was famous as a designer of temporary decorations and even in the latest of his works he retained the sophistication and decorative inventiveness that had distinguished his early achievements.

Chalgrin was born in 1739, the son of poor parents, and his early training was undertaken in Servandoni's office, where he followed in the steps of de Wailly, his senior by nine years. Less in sympathy than de Wailly with the more exuberant side of Servandoni's art, Chalgrin nevertheless showed himself a true disciple both in the elegance of his architectural style and in his technical expertise, and he later had the honour of bringing to completion

Servandoni's façade of St-Sulpice *(171)*. After leaving Servandoni Chalgrin became one of the earliest of Boullée's pupils, and he seems to have known Soufflot well before he went to Rome as the winner of the first prize in the Academy competition for 1758. A small pavilion was the subject of the competition that year and, since no prize had been awarded in the preceding year, Chalgrin was joint winner with another student, Mathurin Cherpitel. The very similar designs of the two architects *(162, 163)* are known in copies made especially for Marigny and acquired for the Academy at the sale of his property. 'At the description of this little building', Viel was later to say to his audience, 'I see some of our present-day students smiling, who, to win prizes in the monthly competitions, compose vast projects and assume their own superiority over the students who competed sixty years ago.'

Natoire had no complaints about Chalgrin's progress in Rome and he was allowed to stay on at the Academy for some months after the term of his scholarship had expired, returning to France in 1763. He and Cherpitel were the two architects who provoked Marigny's observation on the priority of 'our customs' over the temples of the Greeks, and Chalgrin perhaps carried the greater responsibility for this provocation, since Natoire and Marigny admired the drawings of Cherpitel even more than those of Chalgrin.

After his return to France Chalgrin's first recorded position was on the staff of the Ville de Paris under Moreau, who was then engaged on the alteration of the Palais-Royal. But Chalgrin soon established a wider practice thanks to the interest of two patrons, Henri-Léonard Bertin, the minister with responsibility for Paris, and the Comte de St-Florentin, Secretary of State with responsibility for the royal household. Bertin was one of the rare private patrons of Soufflot, and it may have been through Soufflot that Chalgrin was recommended to the minister, for whom he too worked at Chatou. For St-Florentin Chalgrin brought to completion the famous house begun by Gabriel beside the Place Louis XV (later the home of Talleyrand), and to him also Chalgrin apparently owed his appointment as the architect of St-Philippe-du-Roule.

St-Florentin's liking for the young architect who had already disturbed Marigny with the subject-matter of his drawings appears surprising in a courtier of his age and character *(164)*. Born in 1705, he was the last of the La Vrillière family who had served the Crown as Secretaries of State for over a century. He inherited his charge at the age of twenty, and in supervising the Maison du Roi he later worked in close association with Marigny, representing the king, for example, in transactions with the Academy, and St-Florentin also bore the uncomfortable responsibility for the issue of orders of imprisonment *(lettres de cachet)*.

St-Florentin was not a popular figure at court. 'He piqued himself on his expenditure, although the splendour of his apparel could not conceal the meanness of his look' is the opinion attributed to Mme du Barry, and this was by no means an atypical comment. According to Dufort, 'Le *petit saint*, otherwise M. Phélipeaux de Saint

164 Portrait of the Comte de St-Florentin, by Louis-Michel van Loo (Musée de Versailles)

Florentin, lived a debauched life in Paris surrounded by [his?] kind through the weakness of his character ... Having an isolated and particular wife, he dined every evening with his mistress.' The mistress in question was Mme de Langeac and Chalgrin was also employed to build a house for her on the Champs-Elysées, the building which Thomas Jefferson leased during his stay in Paris. St-Florentin's intellectual interests ensured him an honorary membership of the Academy of Sciences, where he supported Lavoisier and served as president in 1775. Having been made Duc de la Vrillière in 1770, St-Florentin was replaced in office by Malesherbes at the start of Louis XVI's reign but he remained officially in favour until his death in 1777 since his sister, 'Phélypeaux in body and spirit', as she is unfavourably described in the Créquy *Souvenirs*, was the wife of Maurepas, the new Premier Ministre.

It is not easy to picture St-Florentin in the setting that Chalgrin created for him in Paris *(165–168)*. His house was the one adjacent to the Place Louis XV on its east side, and Gabriel had established the design of the main elevations to form a transition between the town and his new square. As the eastern colonnaded building was to serve as the repository and show-place for the royal furniture collections (the Garde Meuble), the Secretary of State of the Maison du Roi was well placed in its vicinity. Chalgrin was left with the awkward task of designing the screen for the court and the frontispiece of the house as well as the interior. In August 1768 St-Florentin asked the Academy to report on Chalgrin's drawings, and the house was begun in the following year.

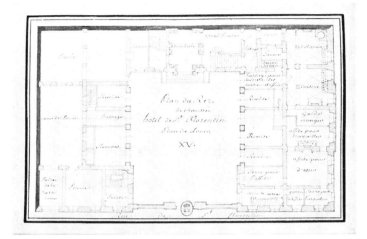

165 The Hôtel de St-Florentin, Paris, ground-plan, drawing by Chalgrin (Bibliothèque Nationale, Paris). Built by Chalgrin in 1767, the house is adjacent to the Place de la Concorde and the street façades (166) were designed by Gabriel

166 The Hôtel de St-Florentin, the side façade. Before the construction of the rue de Rivoli a bridge led from the main floor to the Tuileries Gardens

Chalgrin's contribution is measurably different from anything that Gabriel would have designed. The narrow court is screened by pairs of free-standing Doric columns supporting a plain entablature, aligned as accurately as possible with Gabriel's pre-ordained string-course. A triumphal arch surmounted by the La Vrillière arms occupies the centre of the screen, recalling on a diminutive scale Peyre's earlier project for the Prince de Condé (108). With its Doric columns the gateway is also a direct descendant of a famous doorway that François Mansart had designed well over a hundred years previously for the founder of the La Vrillière fortunes.

The round-headed gateway echoes in perspective the main entrance to the house, designed on the pattern of a Venetian window, with a smaller order of Doric columns flanking a central arched doorway. Looking distinctly foreign in a Parisian setting, it recalls the door of the slightly earlier house designed by Soufflot for Marigny (53). Beyond the door lies a vestibule decorated with columns and then the elegant staircase that leads to the main apartments of the house, grouped together on this shallow site in the broad wing that overlooks the Tuileries gardens. What particularly distinguishes the staircase, apart from the spatial ease of the vaulting, is Chalgrin's treatment of the balusters (168). They are made not of stone but in iron, the material that had especially suited

167 The Hôtel de St-Florentin, the main doorway and entrance screen. Chalgrin's own contribution to the exterior of the house, including the entrance screen with its central triumphal arch, is markedly severer in style than Gabriel's elevations

168 The Hôtel de St-Florentin, the staircase. Though constructed of iron, the balustrade is composed of a series of 'architectural' vase-shaped units

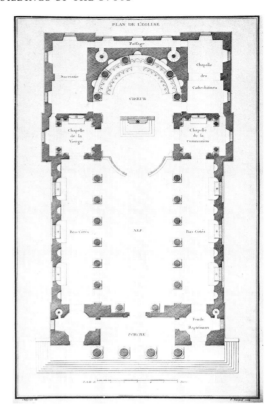

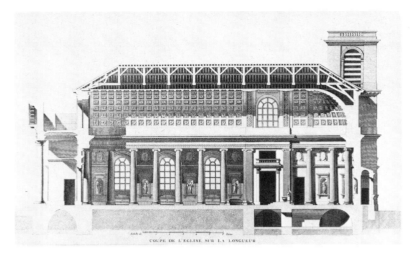

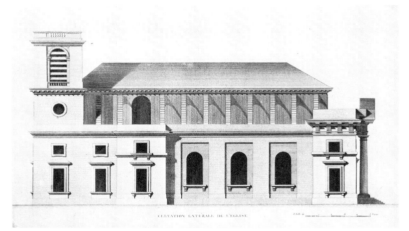

169 The church of St-Philippe-du-Roule, Paris, plan, long section and side elevation (engravings by Taraval after Chalgrin). Designed by Chalgrin in 1768, St-Philippe was the main Paris church in the basilican style of the day

the extravagance of early eighteenth-century design. But like Trouard in his house of ten years earlier, Chalgrin employed the material in a design of great architectural ingenuity, with vases and garlanded capitals which derive from the stone balusters of the seventeenth century.

The new hôtels of the Place Louis XV and its vicinity were to be served by the parish church of the Madeleine, but the area to the west, where so many other new houses were appearing, including those of Marigny and Mme de Langeac, lacked as yet a suitable church, expressing the character of the area. Thanks to the support of St-Florentin it fell to Chalgrin to design the first basilican church to take its place in the long tradition of Parisian ecclesiastical architecture *(169, 170)*. The church was designed, apparently in 1768, and carried out, with important modifications, by 1774. It and the Arc-de-Triomphe were the two buildings of Chalgrin for which the architect himself published the designs. As Quatremère said of the church, echoing the sentiments of Laugier:

At last you see a portico of Doric columns covered by a pediment, to replace those insipid flat façades with several orders one over

the other, of which the least defect is to indicate several floors in a building which has none. The interior, instead of arcades and piers, presents two rows of Ionic columns which define two wings and a nave ended by an apse or circle, in the centre of which the high altar is placed, as was normally the rostrum in a basilica.

Though it recalls in its basic character Trouard's St-Symphorien, Chalgrin's church is an altogether more complex building. Instead of side chapels there are altars in niches beneath the windows, but the building has vestigial transepts (the Chapelle de la Vierge and the Communion chapel) which are expressed on the exterior and the interior, where they interrupt the colonnades of the nave and define the position of the high altar. In Chalgrin's church the columns continue beyond the altar and around the apse where the choir stalls were placed. The vault was to be decorated with plain square coffers, each with a rosette in the middle, and punctuated only above the altar where a single pair of windows cast light from above.

Chalgrin intended the two rows of flying buttresses supporting the vault to be fully visible on the outside, but they were not finally needed, since the vault, as a measure

170 St-Philippe-du-Roule, the main façade. Before its completion in 1775 Chalgrin was forced to move the belfry to the front and to construct a lighter, wooden, vault

of economy, had to be constructed of wood. Chalgrin devised a system of carpentry based upon ideas of Philibert de l'Orme, the source that Legrand and Molinos were later to use for the dome of the Halle au Blé. Chalgrin was also forced to abandon the bell-towers which he had designed, like those of Ste-Geneviève, to flank the choir. A makeshift belfry, much criticized at the time, was added over the roof behind the portico.

As it survives today *(170)*, after much alteration, the church retains very little of the elegance of Chalgrin's original conception and the other churches that Chalgrin designed after St-Philippe progressed much less far. Apart from a surviving chapel of 1769, designed for the Séminaire de St-Esprit in the rue Lhomond, Chalgrin planned the large church of St-Sauveur beside the rue St-Denis in the east of Paris, and the parish church of Gros-Caillou, beyond the Ecole Militaire, where he allegedly built the choir. Speaking of his design for St-Sauveur, of which a model formerly existed, Quatremère summarized Chalgrin's intentions as a church architect: 'You see in this project that M. Chalgrin wished to simplify the system of

Christian churches, and lead them architecturally to a unity of plan and articulation, and to the form of antique temples.'

In the 1770s Chalgrin encountered no difficulty in finding commissions in addition to his ecclesiastical work, even if they were ones that gave less scope to the originality of his art. In 1770 he was involved, like Moreau, with the festivities attendant upon the marriage of the future Louis XVI. He designed for the Austrian ambassador, the Comte de Mercy Argenteau, a temporary hall (beside the embassy at the Hôtel du Petit Luxembourg), which was held to be the first example of a colonnaded assembly room carried out in France, though it followed many years after Lord Burlington's Assembly Rooms at York.

On the marriage of the Dauphin's brother, the Comte de Provence (later Louis XVIII), Chalgrin acquired the position of Premier Architecte in his household (1775), and he was subsequently engaged on several enterprises for his new patron: the transformation of the Château of Brunoy, which the Comte de Provence acquired from the unfortunate Marquis de Brunoy, the enlargement of the stables that Ledoux had constructed for Mme du Barry at Versailles, and the design of a small pavilion at Versailles for the Comtesse de Provence, a building that still survives and which recalls Chalgrin's Prix de Rome design. For a while Chalgrin was also apparently in the employ of the youngest of the three royal brothers, the Comte d'Artois, though nothing is known of any work he carried out for this prince. And in addition to all these private commissions he worked on two public projects in Paris, the alteration of the Collège de France and the completion of St-Sulpice, with Viel acting as his assistant in both undertakings.

In 1769 Chalgrin was beaten by Trouard for a place at the Academy, but in the following year, at the age of thirty-one, he was elected a member, proceeding to the first class only in 1791, when he replaced Potain. His marriage took place in 1776, apparently in the chapel at Brunoy. His wife, later a victim of the Terror and believed to be the subject of a well-known portrait by David, was the daughter of Soufflot's friend, the painter Vernet, and an intimate of Mme Vigée Lebrun. She, but not her husband, was present at the famous Greek supper that Mme Lebrun improvised early in the 1780s for her closest friends.

Of Chalgrin's own private life little is known beyond his association with Voltaire in 1778. His character, as it is described by Viel and Quatremère, had little of the apparent simplicity that distinguished his architecture, though, as Quatremère ingeniously explained, it was a character not unknown in classical times:

Antiquity had several artists, and celebrated ones, proud of their profession and of their talent, who believed that their appearance proclaimed their merit, and that the magnificence of their dress commanded the respect that outward signs usually provoke. Such were, according to Pliny, Parrhasius and Zeuxis. So M. Chalgrin also showed himself in the days of his prosperity. His style of existence had grandeur and magnificence. According to him talent should appear with an opulent exterior . . . For the rest, this manner of existence which would announce vanity, was, with M. Chalgrin, only external. No one was more modest with his equals, patient with his inferiors, gentle in his day-to-day life, zealous for the progress of his pupils.

Chalgrin's work at St-Sulpice, beginning in 1776, is described by Quatremère as an avenging of the memory of his former teacher, Servandoni, who had built the first two storeys of the façade and begun the towers, which he left uncompleted at the time of his death (1766). The existing tower to the right, lacking little but its sculptural decoration, remains as it was left at Servandoni's death *(171)*. Despite the praise it had enjoyed Servandoni's design for the façade was not completely in harmony with the more sophisticated standards of the 1760s; in the year

172 St-Sulpice, details of the baptistery. Chalgrin's baptistery is sited in the base of the north tower

171 The church of St-Sulpice, Paris, the main façade. Chalgrin took over at St-Sulpice in 1776 and reconstructed the north tower (on the left), but the south tower remained as designed by Servandoni *(23)*

after Servandoni's death Soufflot presented to the Academy certain 'projects proposed for St-Sulpice', and he was closely followed by Patte with the submission of a new project of his own. The façade was subsequently put in the charge of a little-known architect, Oudot de Maclaurin, and fate assisted in the transformation of the building when lightning struck the pediment, which had been designed in proportion to the scale of the front elevation but without regard to the size of the upper order that directly supported it. The pediment could conveniently be removed, simplifying the outline of the façade and bringing it into greater conformity with its admired precursor, the east façade of the Louvre (16).

Chalgrin had the unenviable task of completing the towers, survivals of medieval architecture that could not in this case be conveniently relegated to the rear of the building. He simplified the geometry of Servandoni's design in the building of his own north tower and made the decoration more strictly architectural. The lower storey is square, rather than octagonal like Servandoni's, and the pediments are triangular, while the upper storey is designed not as a cylindrical base for a decorated turret supporting a statue, but almost as a circular garden pavilion, a belvedere with eight Composite columns supporting an entablature and balustrade.

Chalgrin was never to have the opportunity of rebuilding the tower of Servandoni to conform with his own, but he provided matching chapels within the church at the base of each tower (172). In the interior he was working side by side with de Wailly, who was then engaged on the reconstruction of the Chapelle de la Vierge at the east end and later on the beautiful pulpit, constructed in 1789. In a style scarcely less elegant and sumptuous than de Wailly's own, if always more restrained, Chalgrin decorated the west-end chapels and with the greatest ingenuity he marshalled within a classical setting the pipes of the great organ above the main doorway of the church.

Chalgrin's work at St-Sulpice was interrupted by the outbreak of the Revolution. As architect to the Comte de Provence, Chalgrin was not well placed, and, according to Quatremère, he was imprisoned during the Terror in the Luxembourg, the palace of his former employer. He was subsequently one of the few architects to receive a share of the meagre patronage available in the 1790s, and his transformation of the palace where he had been imprisoned as the seat of the new government of the Directoire is amongst the last of the architectural achievements still touched with the visual finesse of the Ancien Régime. Chalgrin added a semicircular debating chamber at the back of the palace, which still survives, much altered, as the hall of the French Upper House (the Chambre du Sénat), he introduced a monumental staircase in the right wing in place of the gallery which contained Rubens' cycle of paintings of the life of Marie de Médicis, the original builder of the palace, and he provided a colonnaded vestibule in place of the old staircase in the central pavilion.

On the death of de Wailly in 1798 Chalgrin succeeded to his seat at the Institut, and he was frequently employed at this time, especially for designs of temporary decorations. His career ended with honour, if not without complication, with the building of the Arc-de-Triomphe, begun in 1806 to commemorate the campaign of Austerlitz. Chalgrin was jointly responsible with the architect Raymond for the arch, but it was apparently his design that was finally adopted, and his pupil, Goust, who continued the work after Chalgrin's death, though in a style increasingly unrecognizable as Chalgrin's own. Chalgrin died during the early stages of the building of the arch, in 1811, barely three years before his former patron returned to France as King Louis XVIII.

9 Gondoin and the Ecole de Chirurgie; Victor Louis and the theatre of Bordeaux

THE MOST FAMOUS PARISIAN BUILDING of the later eighteenth century after the church of Ste-Geneviève was not the Odéon, the Halle au Blé, the Monnaie or the church of St-Philippe-du-Roule, but the School of Surgery (the Ecole de Chirurgie), built by Jacques Gondoin *(173)* in the years 1769–74 *(176–183)*. This is a masterpiece that was universally praised at the time of its construction, even if it now looks diminished and a little forlorn in its nineteenth-century setting, just off the boulevard St-Germain, near the Odéon. 'The second monument of the Capital in the purity of its profiles and the regularity of its parts', according to Thiéry, it was described at the Academy in 1780 as a building 'that will make an epoch in architecture', and in the words of Quatremère, the only early biographer of Gondoin, 'Its praise can be voiced in a single word: it is the classic monument of the eighteenth century.'

The author of this remarkable building was himself an exceptional figure, famous in his lifetime as an idealist who remained entirely uncorrupted by professional and social pressures. Except for the Colonne Vendôme, constructed at the end of his life in the reign of Napoleon, the Ecole de Chirurgie is his only known work in architecture. Slightly older than Chalgrin, Gondoin had been born at St-Ouen in 1737. His father, at first a simple gardener, rose to become Jardinier du Roi and, according to Quatremère, a favourite of Louis XV, with responsibility for the gardens of Choisy, itself the favourite château of the king. A dinner-service presented by Louis XV to Gondoin's father in return for a gift of fruit and flowers, as Quatremère records, was the most treasured possession of the son at the time of his death in 1818.

The protection of the king was extended to his gardener's son and Jacques Gondoin entered the school of Blondel and later competed for the Prix de Rome in three successive years. His designs for a riding-school which brought him third place in the first of these competitions (1759) are amongst the surviving Prix de Rome drawings *(174)*, and constitute the only other architectural project of Gondoin's that is known. Here the plan recalls the

173 Portrait of Jacques Gondoin (1737–1818), relief by Houdon (Ecole de Chirurgie, Paris)

disposition of a large town house, while the elevations have a modesty in keeping with the function of the building. But something of the polished and austere elegance of the later Ecole de Chirurgie can also be sensed in Gondoin's treatment of this academic theme.

Gondoin never won first place in the Prix de Rome competitions but the rules were on occasion broken in favour of a protégé of the king, and Gondoin proceeded to the Academy in Rome where he spent four years. What he studied there is unknown, but such was the passion that possessed him for the classical ruins and the landscape of the city that he returned there after his early success in Paris: 'Far from seeming to decrease in him admiration for the objects which had inflamed him in his youth, M. Gondoin was seized anew with a yet greater passion for

174 Project for a riding-school, ground-plan and front elevation, drawings by Gondoin (Ecole des Beaux-Arts, Paris). The project which won Gondoin third place in the 1759 Prix de Rome; though he never won the competition, Gondoin had royal permission to proceed to Rome as the son of a favourite gardener of Louis XV

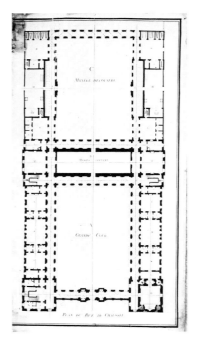

them now that his eyes and mind had no longer to defend themselves against the charms of novelty.' Gondoin conceived the idea of buying up the land of Hadrian's Villa so that he could better explore the site and reconstruct its original appearance, but these plans of his were thwarted and the drawings he had made of the site he presented to his friend, Piranesi.

Natoire had no complaints about the conduct of Gondoin in his years as a *pensionnaire* at the Academy, writing to Marigny that 'This young man promises much, & as much for the good conduct he has shown here as for his talents.' Preceded by this commendation Gondoin returned to Paris in 1764, apparently by way of England and Holland. His first works after his return were supposedly undertaken for the administration of the Postes, and it may also have been at this time that Gondoin

175 Model for an armchair for Queen Marie Antoinette, by Jacques Gondoin (Private Collection). On his return from Rome Gondoin worked as a designer of furniture for the royal household

obtained the appointment (which Quatremère fails to mention) of Inspecteur des Meubles de la Couronne (royal furniture). In this capacity, which he apparently held for some years, Gondoin was responsible for providing designs for the royal cabinet-makers, and some of the wax models he produced for the approval of his royal patrons, including Marie Antoinette, have survived (175).

It was in the years following his return from Rome that Gondoin came in touch with the forceful personality of Germain Pichault de la Martinière, who had been Premier Chirurgien to the king since 1747. 'Normally frank and brutal', in the words of one contemporary, La Martinière had already established a reputation of some notoriety in the annals of medicine after a distinguished patient, Prince Charles of Lorraine, had made him his principal heir. Following a famous lawsuit before the Parlement of Paris, such transactions between doctor and patient were called into question and the family of Prince Charles finally managed to have the will annulled. La Martinière was the only one of the king's doctors – and the story is not hard to believe – who had the temerity to inform the dying monarch that the disease afflicting him was smallpox.

With such a leader it was perhaps inevitable that the status of surgery should be so spectacularly elevated with the building of Gondoin's school. 'Surgeons had for a long time been confused with barbers,' as Mercier explained; 'it was a harmful confusion, it had to end.' Indeed the recognition of surgery was not unlike the struggle that other groups of professionals, not least the architects themselves, were engaged upon as the eighteenth century drew to its close. But surgeons were not amongst the worst placed in the social hierarchy; the study of anatomy not only involved the welfare of the civil and military population, but it was also one of the six sciences admitted by the Academy of Science, and, like the subject of health, the source of enormous popular interest in the later eighteenth century. The traditional grouping of surgery with medicine and pharmacy had ended in 1731 with the establishment (ratified in 1750) of an independent Academy. The surgeons already possessed an impressive anatomy theatre in the rue des Cordeliers *(181)*, near the site of Gondoin's new building, which dated from the early seventeenth century, when interest in anatomy had already become widespread, but the need for a new building was stressed in the act of ratification for the Academy, which also ruled on the training of young surgeons. When Gondoin began work almost twenty years later he may have been guided by earlier projects that had been made for the same site.

Two years after work had begun on the new school Gondoin presented a project for the development of the front of the site *(182)*, and he published a beautifully illustrated description of his designs in 1780, after returning from his second visit to Italy. Inevitably the building came to be known as the Temple of Aesculapius, though Gondoin made no reference to such a dedication in his book, and he omitted to mention the real Temple of Aesculapius on the Isola Tiberiana in Rome. He wrote of the university of Turin and the Collegium Helveticum in Milan as schools 'whose magnificence', based on the use of columns, 'yields to no modern work', and justified his own building as 'a monument of the beneficence of the King', which 'should have the character of magnificence relative to its function; a school whose fame attracts a great concourse of Pupils from all nations should appear open and easy of access. The absolute necessity of columns to

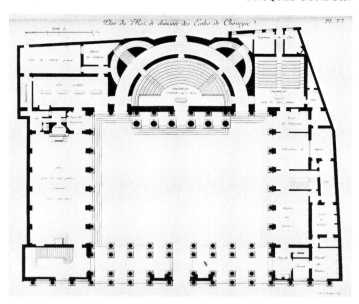

176 The Ecole de Chirurgie, Paris, ground-plan, engraving after Gondoin. Built in the years 1769–74, the Ecole de Chirurgie was the most celebrated building of the day after the church of Ste-Geneviève

177 The Ecole de Chirurgie, the street façade. The streamlined effect of the façade was especially admired by Gondoin's contemporaries

178 The Ecole de Chirurgie, the court frontispiece. The main anatomy theatre lies behind the frontispiece which is decorated on the rear wall with roundels of famous surgeons

fulfil these two objects, is alone sufficient to protect me from the reproach of having multiplied them unduly.'

The plan of Gondoin's school is conceived in the manner of a large town house *(176)*, with three wings around a court and a screen of columns across the front. The focal point of the plan is a huge hemispherical anatomy theatre (seating 1,200) which is announced externally by a projecting portico of giant free-standing Corinthian columns. The effect of openness that Gondoin mentions in his book is achieved, as in earlier designs of Peyre and Chalgrin, by the screen of columns across the front of the court, which are blocked only in the centre to create the illusion of a vestigial triumphal arch *(177)*. Gondoin avoided any harsh break in the articulation by allowing the first floor of the building, determined in height by the Corinthian order of the court, to run across the front of the building supported on the columns of the screen.

The order of the screen is Ionic and it recalls the type of Ionic that Soufflot favoured in the presence of a band below the capital, while also resembling the Greek Ionic order in combining such a moulding with volutes that are parallel to the entablature, instead of projecting diagonally at the corners of the capitals. This is not the only, or indeed ⸱e most conspicuous, of Gondoin's departures from the ⸱ots of classical architecture, for the plain frieze that is

appropriate to the Ionic order is here allowed to rest directly upon the capitals of the columns in opposition to all accepted rules. It may be that Gondoin had studied some primitive classical building, where such omissions can occur, or that a fragment of ruined entablature lacking the mouldings below the frieze suggested to him the effect that such a design could achieve. The absence of mouldings implies, like the Greek Doric order, a direct confrontation of the column with the fabric it supports, and even seems in the context of Gondoin's building to be a conscious act of architectural surgery. The final effect is considerably to increase the streamlining of the front façade, an impression that was not lost on contemporary critics: 'The whole system of French architecture is reversed, the façade is without pavilions, without a central projection.'

Instead of a true frontispiece facing the street Gondoin introduced a long relief panel in the centre of the façade, between the entablature of the Ionic order and the upper cornice. Designed by Berruer, it showed the king (Louis XV), followed by Minerva and surrounded by the sick, ordering the construction of the building, while the Genius of Architecture presents the plan, and Surgery, accompanied by Vigilance and Providence, guide the actions of the king. The main doorway below was decorated with the royal cipher and fleur-de-lis, and the serpents and batons of Aesculapius; the stone reliefs in the bays beside the door, which still survive, show batons, serpents and cornucopias, with a head of Apollo on each relief, alluding to the magnanimity of Louis XV and his successor.

Within the court *(178)* the Ionic order continues on all sides, and capitals with matching adjacent faces are introduced to effect the transitions at the corners *(179)*. The Ionic colonnade also continues below the larger Corinthian order of the main frontispiece, which is chiefly instrumental in suggesting the presence of a temple – the amphitheatre – stretching back within the building. Like other architects of his time Gondoin seems to have looked to the seventeenth century for the inspiration of his court, more precisely to the north portico of the church of the Sorbonne, built by Lemercier, which also lies within a courtyard and announces the presence of a (Christian) temple beyond. To moderate the contrast between the wall and the giant projecting portico the cornice itself is allowed to continue around the court, and large lions' heads mask the junction of the soffit of the entablature and the wall *(179)*. Portrait medallions of five famous French surgeons occupy the spaces between the lions' heads, while the frontispiece itself, recalling the surgeons to their civic responsibilities, showed Theory and Practice swearing upon an altar of Eternal Union.

The amphitheatre behind Gondoin's frontispiece *(180)* is as much an exercise in the practical application of archaeological knowledge as the building itself is un-pedantic as a work of the imagination. In the amphitheatre Gondoin combined the plan of an antique theatre with a vaulted ceiling like that of the Pantheon. The advantages of his design are immediately apparent on comparison with the traditional form of the earlier anatomy theatre *(181)*. The anatomical demonstrations were performed both for the general public and for the students themselves and the plan of an antique theatre allowed a much clearer view to a greater number of spectators than was possible hitherto, while an oculus like that of the Pantheon, but greater in diameter, provided the necessary degree of illumination.

When the students glanced beyond the demonstration taking place in front of them to the semicircular lunette above the main doorway they discovered portraits of famous predecessors including La Martinière (who died in 1783) and above them paintings which developed the theme of the frontispiece. The king was represented encouraging their progress and rewarding their zeal, while the gods were engaged in transmitting the principles of anatomy and staunching the blood spilt in defence of the country. Planned originally for use as an amphitheatre, Gondoin's design was later adapted as the customary plan for debating chambers. It was the form used when the Chambre des Cinq-Cents was installed at the Palais-Bourbon, and the pattern later chosen by Chalgrin for the National Assembly at the Luxembourg.

In addition to the main amphitheatre the ground floor of Gondoin's building housed, to the right, a smaller rectangular theatre for the instruction of midwives, a chemistry laboratory, and a small hospital ward. In the left

179 The Ecole de Chirurgie, details of courtyard. The corner columns of the court have capitals with doubled corner volutes; a lion's head partly masks the junction of the projecting frontispiece and the wall

180 The Ecole de Chirurgie, view of the anatomy theatre, engraving after Gondoin. Gondoin's 'amphitheatre' is a practical adaptation of a classical theatre plan combined with an interior derived from the Pantheon *(7)*

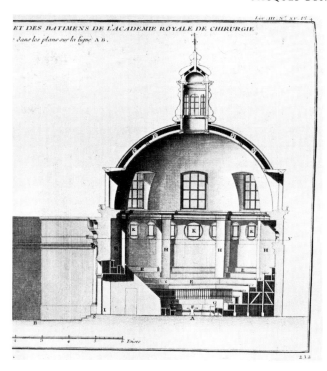

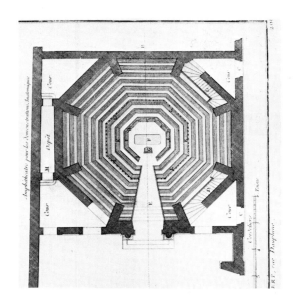

181 The anatomy theatre of the old Academy of Surgery, plan, section and elevation (details of engravings from Blondel, 1752–56). Built during the later seventeenth century the old anatomy theatre in the nearby rue des Cordeliers was inadequate in size and function

wing there was a public hall, and beside the amphitheatre a room for experiments, where the best pupils were allowed to work in training for the army. The first floor of the school (visible in the sections published by Gondoin) contained a library, a room to display collections of instruments, a top-lit lecture room for the instruction of the masters, a council room and the administrative offices; the rooms for the inmates were in the mezzanine, presumably at the back of the building.

Amongst those who wrote appreciatively of Gondoin's building was his colleague Peyre, who pleaded that the architect should not be criticized if his 'monument announced a temple more than many of our churches', and his former teacher, Blondel, whose mouthpiece in *L'Homme du monde*, found 'The articulation new, and of a type of architecture superior to everything I have seen newly constructed in Paris'. Blaikie too came to visit the school in 1775 and he attended a demonstration by La Martinière in the 'Superbe Amphitheatre'. Lodging next to a young surgeon, he also saw a private dissecting-room, where

they told me that there was people brought them as many [Dead Bodys] as they wanted at 6 livres a piece; I thought a horrid practice but certainly this must give great instructions to those students; the smell seemed not to affect them in the least, there was some of them had peaces of Bread lying upon the dead bodies they were desecting.

The only defect that Blondel noticed in the building was the meanness of its approach, but Gondoin's project for the square in front of the Academy, which he later reconsidered when the development of the nearby Odéon site was fixed by Peyre and de Wailly, was never completed.

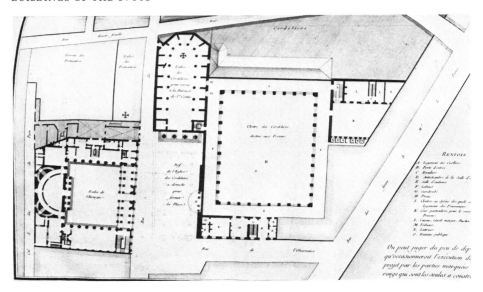

182 The Ecole de Chirurgie, site plan, engraving after Gondoin. Gondoin planned to demolish the nave of the church of St-Côme (St Cosmas) to create a forecourt for his school

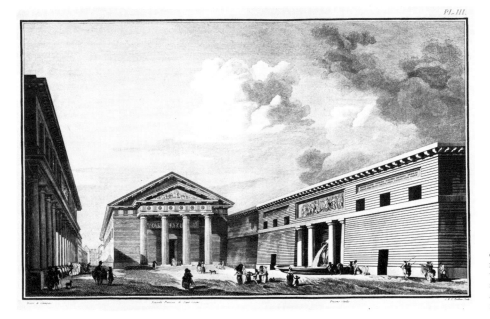

183 The Ecole de Chirurgie, perspective view of forecourt, engraving after Gondoin. The monastery of the Cordeliers (on the right) was to be converted into a prison, while the surviving choir of St-Côme (centre) was to have a new casing that included a giant Doric frontispiece

In Gondoin's project the Ionic courtyard of the school and its Corinthian frontispiece were to be contrasted with an austere Doric and Tuscan court *(182, 183)*. The church of the Cordeliers lay immediately in front of the school and Gondoin proposed demolishing the nave, but leaving the choir as a church dedicated to St Cosmas, the patron of surgeons. The new façade of the church was to dominate the square with its windowless façade – the first such design for a church front – and its projecting frontispiece of four giant Doric columns.

The cloister of the monastery, after the demolition of the nave, was to form the southern border of the square, and this Gondoin proposed adapting as a civil prison, a building that would no doubt have supplied the corpses needed at the school. The prison gave Gondoin the opportunity to design a façade like nothing seen in Paris before. It consists of a bleak rusticated wall surface with a few unframed openings, panels for inscriptions and, in the centre, a fountain decorated with four baseless Tuscan columns with a relief above. 'By a quite different effect in the project for the prisons,' Gondoin explained, 'in leaving only a few openings, I wished to give an impression of solidity, and proclaim public security . . . I placed the frontispiece of the portico [of the church] on an inter-mediate basis, to soften the transition from the rudeness of the prisons to the indispensable richness of a Temple.'

Unfortunately the forecourt was never carried out in this form; the site was later cleared and the architect built a small fountain in the wall opposite the Academy during the reign of Napoleon. Yet Gondoin's purpose in investing a design for real buildings with an intensity of expression such as his friend, Piranesi, had given to the ruins of antiquity, goes beyond anything conceived in the 1760s, and anticipates the greatest of the achievements of Ledoux.

Apart from the Ecole de Chirurgie, Gondoin built almost nothing. Elected to the Academy in 1774, when Antoine was also a candidate, he is recorded as one of the architects who participated in the restoration of the Palais de Justice, but his energies were mainly devoted to the development of his own estate. Thwarted in his project to develop the Villa of Hadrian, Gondoin had later grown to admire the villas of Palladio and with the intention of recreating such models he acquired a site on the banks of the Seine near Melun – Vives-Eaux – where

Retired from the world in the midst of the woods that surrounded him, he spent his whole time in giving his tastes and studies an asylum worthy of the arts, and which became for him in a small scale what the Emperor Hadrian had made on a large scale, the abridged collection of all the memories of his journeys. Already terraces were levelled, ponds and waterfalls had already received their plans; the contours and plantations were established when the Revolution broke out ... Happily for M. Gondoin, the château of his villa was not finished; it still had no roof that could attract fire.

Gondoin took the precaution of pretending to be his own gardener, a ruse which his background must have made the easier, and he escaped the dangers of the Terror, though he suffered financially. He continued work on his estate, where, 'Whether as a memory of his father's profession, or also in gratitude for the happy disguise that had saved him, it was in the clothes of a gardener that he often hid, and enjoyed forbidding the garden to strangers who would have importuned the master.'

Gondoin appears not to have retired entirely from practice after the Revolution. In the years following the Terror he was appointed as one of the Conseil des Bâtiments Civils, and he became a founder member of the Institut in 1795. There followed under Napoleon the commission for the construction of the Colonne Vendôme, pulled down in 1871 and restored at the expense of Courbet. In 1814, at the age of seventy-seven, Gondoin married for the second time, a girl of seventeen, who died shortly after the birth of a son, and Gondoin's own death followed in 1818, three years after the restoration of the monarchy.

The last major architect to affect the course of architectural development in France before the advent of Ledoux was Victor Louis (184). Like de Wailly, Antoine and Chalgrin, Louis was one of the most productive architects of his age, though the centre of his activities became divided between Paris and Bordeaux, where his masterpiece, the Grand-Théâtre, was created. Famous in his lifetime for his touchy and rebellious temperament, Louis can also be singled out as an architect lacking perfect respect for the ideals that his contemporaries cherished. In planning and decoration Louis had few rivals, but his architectural style shows, like Moreau's, a tendency to verticality, which is combined

184 Portrait of Victor Louis (1731–1800), by F. L. Lonsing (Musée des Arts Décoratifs, Bordeaux)

with a tolerance of monotony uncommon before the last years of the century. Louis obtained none of the official posts available in the Bâtiments du Roi, and he was never admitted to the Academy. His main protectors, the Duc de Richelieu and the Duc de Chartres, were, like Louis in his different way, amongst the least conventional figures of the day.

Only a little younger than Peyre and de Wailly, Louis was born in Paris in 1731, the son of a master mason. In the absence of any early accounts of his life, save the list that he compiled of his own works in 1776 when he sought admission to the Academy, little is known of his family background or of his earliest years. He was, however, considered something of a prodigy and was allowed by special permission to compete in the competitions of the Academy from an early age. He finally won first prize in 1755, and was then disqualified because his final drawings were larger than the prescribed limit and differed from his sketches – the first of many conflicts with the architectural establishment during the course of his career.

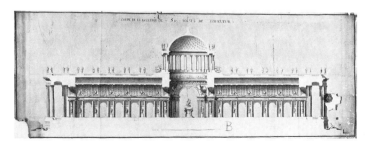

185 Project for a gallery, section, drawing by Louis (Ecole des Beaux-Arts, Paris). One of the drawings that gained Louis the third place in the 1753 Prix de Rome competition, which he finally won in 1755

186 View of the colonnade of St Peter's, drawing by Louis (Archives Municipales, Bordeaux). Sketched by Louis during his years in Rome (1756–59), Bernini's colonnade has the scale and degree of repetition that Louis favoured

Only one of Louis' many drawings for the Academy competitions appears to have survived (185), a section of a gallery, which was the design that won Louis the third place in 1753, when Trouard gained first prize. Though designed for no practical purpose, like all the Prix de Rome drawings, Louis' project clearly shows the changing aesthetic values of the mid-century. In the very year in which Laugier's essay was published, Louis employed free-standing columns both in the articulation of his interior and for the disposition of the dome. Yet he kept to arcades for the main structure of the gallery and allowed the columns to project slightly in pairs with an urn above each break in the entablature.

187 Project for the senate chamber of the Warsaw Parliament, drawing by Louis (Cooper-Hewitt Museum, New York). Part of Louis' project for the restoration of the royal palace in Warsaw (1765–73) undertaken for King Stanislas Poniatowski

Despite his lapses from the rules, Louis was allowed to travel to Rome, where he spent the years from 1756 to 1759 at the Academy. Part of his time he employed in sketching the sights, and several of his attractive drawings, rather in the manner of Robert and Fragonard, who left for Rome in the same year as Louis, have survived, including a sheet at Bordeaux that records in flattering perspective the colonnade of St Peter's (186). Yet however promising he showed himself as an artist, inevitably Louis managed to antagonize Natoire, who wrote of him to Marigny at the time of his return in the same terms he had earlier used of Le Roy: his character was 'peu docile' and he had also left unpaid debts in Rome.

On his return to Paris Louis managed to obtain a number of small commissions. There was his decoration of a chapel in the abbey of Notre-Dame-de-Bonsecours in the eastern outskirts of the city, of which he had a description inserted in the *Année littéraire*, and shortly afterwards a painted chapel decoration in the nearby church of Ste-Marguerite. However unappealing its heavy fake architecture and unconvincing statues may seem, as carried out by Brunetti, the decoration must nevertheless be counted amongst the earliest known basilican designs. The first of many schemes of temporary decoration undertaken by Louis was a colonnaded set on the stage of the old Comédie-Italienne for Favart's celebration of the peace of 1763.

A stroke of fortune in 1765 brought Louis to the attention of Stanislas Auguste Poniatowski, who had been elected in the preceding year to the throne of Poland. A protégé of Mme Geoffrin when he stayed in Paris as a young man in the early 1750s, the new king was anxious to employ French craftsmen and 'avoid the style of splendid richness of a Fermier Général' in the transformations he was planning for the royal palace of Warsaw. According to the Comte de Ségur, Poniatowski even in later life was 'ceaselessly moved by the liveliest affection for the arts, for literature, and above all for poetry . . . His natural and lively spirit was enveloped by simplicity and

188 The Intendance (new Préfecture), Besançon, the garden façade. Louis' first major building, designed in 1770 for Charles-André de la Coré, Intendant of Franche-Comté, and completed in 1776

modesty.' His agent, while keeping in touch with Mme Geoffrin, made the acquaintance of Louis through a goldsmith named Germain. Louis began by making designs for the audience chamber of the palace and in the process he antagonized both Mme Geoffrin and Germain. He was invited to Poland and applied to Marigny for leave, though this was also something of a presumption for an architect who was not 'Architecte du Roi'.

Louis spent some weeks in Warsaw in August and September 1765 on terms of intimacy with the king who wrote of him to Mme Geoffrin as being 'an excellent man. He has the most noble and wisest imagination, and though he really knows more than others, he accepts their ideas when they are happy ones . . . He has corrected my taste in several respects . . .' Louis' proposed improvements to the palace grew enormously in scope to include the provision of a senate hall *(187)*, a chapel and a theatre, as well as alterations to the exterior and the planning of a forecourt based in plan on the Piazza of St Peter's. Mme Geoffrin was left to decide on her own about the paintings by Boucher and Vien that the king had ordered but she became increasingly jealous of Louis. She and the king were reconciled in the summer of 1767, when she paid her famous visit to Poland, the only major expedition she was ever to make. Furniture and decorations for the palace were dispatched from Paris during the late 1760s, but a financial crisis cut short the work in 1773 and except for his beautiful drawings, nothing now survives of Louis' work for Poniatowski.

It was apparently following his return from Poland that Louis adopted in place of his first Christian name, Nicolas, his third name, Victor, by which he has come to be known. The works begun after his return, as listed in his autobiography, include the remodelling of the choir of Chartres Cathedral, and a similar project for Noyen. In 1770 when Chalgrin designed his assembly hall for the residence of the Austrian ambassador, it was Louis who constructed a similar room for the Spanish ambassador, on

189 The Besançon Intendance, detail of garden façade. The building resembles a château in the presence of the curved central projection, where the windows too are arched and the pilasters doubled

a site beside the first of the Parisian Wauxhalls. There followed several projects for Besançon, including the first important building by the architect – the residence of the Intendant *(188, 189)*, which Louis designed in 1770. The patron here was Charles-André de la Coré, one of the most famous of the local administrators of the later eighteenth century. As Intendant of the province of Franche-Comté for twenty-three years (1761–84), La Coré was well known for his enlightened reforms and for his promotion of the arts and literature, and it was he who later commissioned Ledoux for the design of the Besançon theatre. La Coré was evidently also aware of the respect that his own office should command, and his house is the most elegant and imposing Intendance of the time.

The first of Louis' surviving buildings, the Intendance already shows something of the eccentricity of his style. The plan in this case is one associated with the development of the feudal château, a rectangular block, preceded by a court and with an oval salon forming a semicircular projection at the rear. Louis had no scruples about using an order of pilasters for the articulation of the building, with half-columns forming a slight projection for the court frontispiece. The order he chose is Ionic, with continuous fluting and a high base for each pilaster that intensifies its vertical stress. Only where the salon projects on the garden side are the pilasters found in pairs. The ornamentation is confined entirely to the framing of the windows and to the deeply carved beribboned swags of leaves between the two storeys that form an interrupted frieze around the building. A slight variation is introduced in the windows of the garden projection *(189)*: those of the lower storey are arched as though in sympathy with the projection of the plan and pointed triangular panels are inserted in the spandrels.

Louis seems to have been replaced by Ledoux in La Coré's favour after the design of the Intendance, but he had by then been taken under the protection of the Duc de Richelieu. Louis-François Armand du Plessis, the great-nephew of the famous cardinal, was a soldier and courtier who, like the Comte de St-Florentin, had already served the king for most of his long reign. Richelieu had become acquainted with Louis at least since 1771 when he tried to get Mme du Barry to approve a project that the architect had made in rivalry with Peyre and de Wailly for the Comédie-Française, and probably at about this time Louis was working on Richelieu's town house in Paris, which lay in the rue Louis-le-Grand, near St-Roch. A building of the earlier eighteenth century, it had already been altered by Chevotet who built there the famous 'pavillon d'Hanovre', named after the military exploits of Richelieu during the Seven Years' War. Louis' task was to modernise the building by the alteration of the courtyard and the provision of a new main entrance.

Even more than Louis, the Duc de Richelieu was celebrated for the excesses of his behaviour – particularly for his exploits in the bedroom. He was already over seventy when Louis became his architect and in a position of considerable power at the court, as an ally of Mme du Barry and the most senior of the Premiers Gentilshommes

of the (king's) bedchamber. An amusing description of him at this time by Horace Walpole reveals something of Richelieu's character and the rejuvenating possibilities he may have associated with fashionable taste: 'The other [Richelieu] is an old piece of tawdry, worn out, but endeavouring to brush itself up; and put one in mind of Lord Chesterfield, for they laugh before they know what he has said – and are in the right, for I think they would not laugh afterwards.' Richelieu was nevertheless known for his success as a military commander, for an intellectual curiosity that extended to ecclesiastical history and astronomy, and for his uneasy patronage of Voltaire in defiance of the king's wishes. It was even said that Richelieu 'owed a considerable portion of the reputation he enjoyed as a general to the brilliant verses in which Voltaire had celebrated his exploits'.

Since 1758 Richelieu had been Governor of the province of Guyenne, with his residence at Bordeaux, the wealthiest of all the French ports. The old town, protected at the north by a large medieval castle, the Château de la Trompette, had already been considerably developed earlier in the century, notably by the building of the Place Royale (Place de la Bourse) by the father of Gabriel *(21)*. In 1755 a fire had destroyed the Hôtel de Ville, and with it the municipal theatre, and in the following year the house of the Intendant was also damaged by fire. Projects for replacing the buildings were made by several architects, including Soufflot, who showed his designs to the Academy in 1758, and two local architects, Bonfin and Lhote, who supplied a theatre design based on Soufflot's own work at Lyon. But beyond the construction of a temporary theatre and the restoration of the Intendance for Boutin to the designs of Barreau little immediate action was taken.

Early in the 1770s it was decided that Lhote should build the new theatre on a site forming part of the southern escarpment of the Château de la Trompette. Richelieu obtained the permission of the Minister of War and informed Bertin, who was then acting as Contrôleur-Général. At this moment Louis entered the proceedings. He prepared drawings in Paris in the later half of 1772 and travelled to Bordeaux early in the following year, taking up residence in the governor's house. His plans were approved by Richelieu and the town council and work began in the winter of 1773. An altered plan was approved early in the following year and work continued for five months until funds ran short.

Shortage of money was to be a continual difficulty throughout the history of the construction, as was the antagonism of the town council to the tyranny of Richelieu and to the interference of the Intendant, added to which there was also the resentment of the local architects towards their Parisian rival. Louis' theatre was to be built on the site chosen for Lhote's design, funds being made available in anticipation of the development of the escarpment of the château, and from the shops that were to be incorporated in the building. Louis had taken the additional precaution of appointing Bonfin clerk of the works. The architect also hoped to divert funds designated for the new Hôtel de Ville and for a Palais de Justice which an engineer of the Ponts et Chaussées, St-André, was in the process of building.

The situation became so complex that a Parisian architect, Pierre-Adrien Pâris, was sent to Bordeaux to report, but as with the Comédie-Française, the death of Louis XV and the appointment of a new administration brought the project to a standstill. Louis returned to Paris and discussed the situation with Turgot, who finally agreed that the building should continue, on condition that the town council relinquished its hold on the administration of the theatre. Louis forfeited the sympathy of the council and he also lost the protection of Richelieu, when his nephew, the Duc de Mouchy, succeeded as Governor of Guyenne and turned Louis out of the governor's residence. In 1776 the Duc de Chartres visited Bordeaux and laid the foundation-stone of the building, by that time well advanced, and later in the same year Louis gained the support of a new Intendant, Nicolas Dupré de St-Maux. The theatre had already become a famous building and later visitors who were taken there included the king's two brothers and the Emperor Joseph II of Austria, who paid an unofficial visit to France in 1777. By this time the over-liberal administration of Necker had begun, and the council was once again made responsible for the theatre, which finally opened on 7 August 1780, leaving the town of Bordeaux in possession of the largest and grandest of all eighteenth-century theatres *(190–195)*.

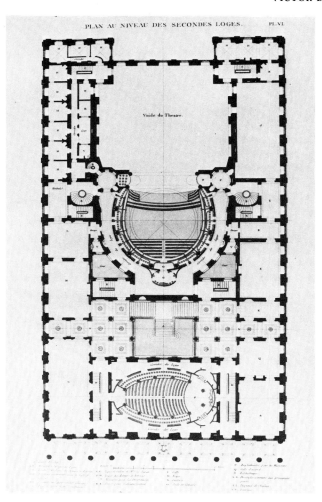

190 The Grand-Théâtre, Bordeaux, main-floor plan and long section, engravings by Berthault after Louis. The largest of the theatres of pre-Revolutionary France, designed in 1772–73 and opened in 1780, the building contains an oval concert hall in addition to the main auditorium

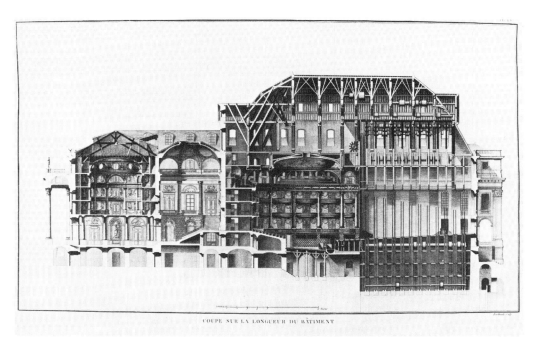

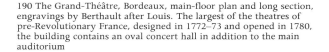

191 The Bordeaux theatre, the main façade. Corinthian columns on high bases extend across the whole width of the front; the steps are later in date

192 The Bordeaux theatre, detail of main façade. Since the cleaning of the façade the complex joining of the masonry at the corners has become visible

Louis approached his task not entirely as an outsider, for he had a personal involvement with the theatre and with music through his wife, Marie Bayon, who was a well-known pianist and singer. It was she who played and sang at Diderot's house in the rue Taranne on the occasion of his birthday in 1770. Louis himself later became a friend of the composer, Grétry, and it is recorded that he composed a play that was performed at the theatre of the Duc d'Orléans (see chapter 13). Yet even in his social dealings Louis' behaviour was notorious. Diderot mentions a discussion about his difficult character which took place at a dinner party given by Pigalle in 1781 and the *Mémoires secrets*, referring to an example of his arrogance at the Opéra in 1783, described him as being 'steeped in pride' ('pétri d'amour-propre') and 'most imprudent'.

Louis' own theatre *(190)* is more complex than those designed by Moreau, and Peyre and de Wailly, incorporating over the vestibule an oval concert hall in addition to the theatre itself. The disposition recalls the plan of a town house, the staircase occupying the position of the forecourt, the theatre that of the house itself. The auditorium, compared with the extent of the building, may seem relatively small; as indicated on the architect's plan the arcades at the sides were lined with shops, while the

193 The Bordeaux theatre, the main vestibule. A prominent feature of the theatre, showing Louis' genius for interiors, the staircase was adapted by Charles Garnier for the Paris Opéra in the following century

194 The Bordeaux theatre, detail of stairchamber. A square umbrella vault of stone, decorated with rosettes and asymmetrical swags, covers the stairchamber

public and private rooms needed for the theatre – foyers, a café and dressing-rooms – were on the first floor above.

Designed for a relatively open setting, the theatre required no special manipulation in its siting (191). It stands isolated between two broad roads with a shallow rectangular square in front of the portico. The exterior is recognizably in the style of the Besançon Intendance, with its repetition of pilasters on high bases, but in following the shape of a classical temple the articulation seems almost as relentlessly regular as the monuments of Napoleonic Paris, and by no means a true expression of the magic of the interior. Even the columns of the portico lack the modest element of dramatic contrast that Peyre and de Wailly had introduced at the Comédie-Française (130). Standing on their high bases (and originally without the flight of steps which is a modern addition), they stretch from end to end of the façade and they imposed upon the architect the structural problem of stabilizing the corner columns against the pressure of the building. Louis apparently used, or invented, a metal brace, the famous 'clou' of which there is apparently no visual record. However, now that the stonework of the theatre has been cleaned the ingenuity of the masonry at the sides of the portico can at least be appreciated, with the stones on both sides of the keystone sloping in the same direction diagonally inwards (192).

Little in the treatment of the exterior gives warning of the splendours of the interior and of its staircase (193, 194), a type of structure with an open colonnaded first floor that had originated in France in the previous century, undergoing further development in the palaces of Germany. Such staircases were less suited to vernacular buildings than to the needs of a princely court, or – as Louis discovered, and Garnier after him at the Paris Opéra – to the public spectacle created by a theatre audience. The

immediate precedent for the Bordeaux staircase may have been a design of Gabriel's for the Louvre; its remote ancestry includes the Escalier des Ambassadeurs at Versailles, built by Le Vau for Louis XIV but demolished in 1752, where painted architecture decorated the walls of the principal floor and painted figures looked over the balustrade towards the stairs below.

The magic of Louis' design resides ultimately in the union of the new style of decoration which he employs with one of the grandest architectural forms of the past. In placing the stairs on the central axis the symmetry of the plan remains undisturbed, and the architectural integrity of the design is likewise enhanced by the stony handling. The order is Ionic, the columns resting this time on pedestals of conventional height, and decorated with garlanded capitals that match the fitful exuberance of the walls and vault. The vault itself is square with twelve curving panels divided by ribs of diminishing coffers and decorated at the base by swags twisted asymmetrically through single eyes. The ground floor is plainer in character and treated almost as an exterior, with rusticated walls interrupted by the flights of stairs.

Interior rustication, though common in Palladian buildings in England, is rare in France, where it cannot have been considered in good taste ('convenable'). Louis clearly thought it appropriate in the public context of his theatre, and the same consideration must have guided him in the choice of balustrade for the staircase. This follows no conventional type, and is indeed more like a wall than a true balustrade, decorated with a key pattern that sweeps down in a continuous band from the moulding of the wall.

Louis was fortunate in his choice of staircase plan in that the first landing had a real importance commensurate with the visual dominance it would in any case have assumed. The landing leads, or gives the impression of leading, to the principal box of the theatre, allocated to the Jurats of the city, and the entrance is designed with suitable effusiveness as the focal point of the stairchamber. The Muses of Tragedy and Comedy, sculpted by Berruer, are transformed into caryatids on each side of the doorway; the attributes of music and drama form the unusual subject of the pediment relief, and the arms of Bordeaux surmount the inscription above the doorway.

In the interior of the theatre (195), unsympathetically refurbished in the nineteenth century, the Corinthian order of the exterior reappears. Like Peyre and de Wailly, Louis too preferred a circular plan for the auditorium but in place of continuous rows of boxes with square piers visible beyond, Louis' columns are uninterrupted and the boxes project between them. There are also boxes in his design facing across the proscenium arch and these were apparently for the Governor of Guyenne and the Intendant, and the subject of one of the last of Richelieu's quarrels with the municipality. The theatre was particularly celebrated for the spaciousness of the interior and for the height of the stage, and no less structural ingenuity was required for the cantilevering of the boxes and the expanse of vaulted ceiling than in the handling of the portico.

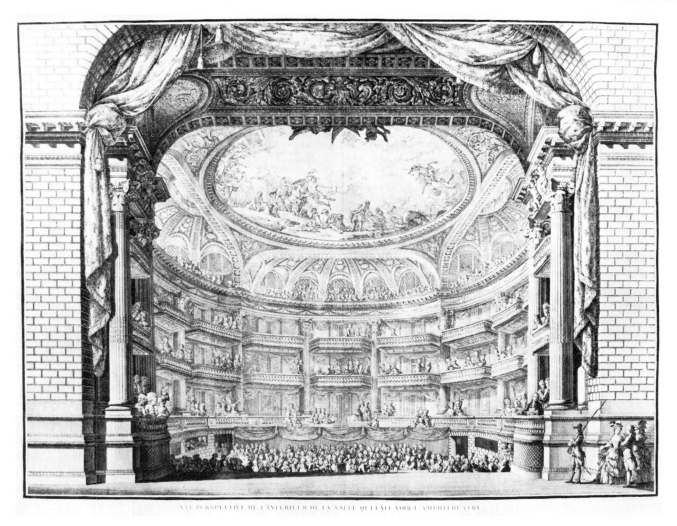

195 The Bordeaux theatre, view of the interior, engraving by Berthault after Louis. The circular interior has giant columns separating the tiers of boxes; the original decoration was altered in the nineteenth century

The ceiling of the auditorium is circular while the entablature consists of four arcs which meet at projecting angles. Four arches, as wide as they are low, spring from the angles, one enclosing the proscenium and the others framing the three galleries of the theatre, each of which is vaulted according to the pattern established for the staircase. The whole was originally painted in veined white, with blue draperies and ornaments of gold. In his treatise upon the theatre Patte readily conceded that Louis had created 'The most magnificent of all modern theatres. The aim of the architect has evidently been to avoid the usual monotony of this kind of building and to make a magnificent assembly hall.' All visitors to Bordeaux have since then endorsed this opinion, including Arthur Young, who confessed to having 'seen nothing that approaches it . . . This theatre, which does so much honour to the pleasures of Bordeaux, was raised at the expense of the town, and cost £270,000.'

In addition to the theatre of Bordeaux Louis was responsible for many private houses in its vicinity, beginning with the Hôtel Saige, which lies immediately behind the building, and he later conceived the idea of a great public square occupying the whole site of the Château de la Trompette, a semicircular Place opening from the river and dwarfing even the adjacent Place Louis XV. And indirectly too Louis participated in the transformation of Bordeaux into the grandest town of late eighteenth-century France, as its most distinguished younger architects, Combes and Dufart, were formed in his shadow. As well as his town buildings Louis was also involved in the design of several châteaux in Guyenne and the neighbouring provinces, and for one such commission he produced what might well have been considered his second masterpiece, the Château of Le Bouilh, which was designed on the eve of the Revolution for a henchman of the Duc de Chartres, the Marquis de la Tour du Pin.

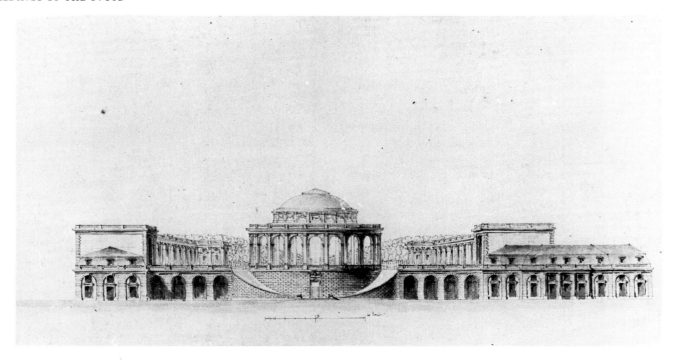

196 Project for the Château of Le Bouilh, near Bordeaux, elevation, drawing by Louis (Archives Municipales, Bordeaux). The most ambitious of Louis' private commissions in the Bordeaux region, the château, of which only part was built before 1789, is still a centre of wine production

197 The Château of Le Bouilh, the main *corps de logis*. The central temple *(196)* and matching *corps de logis* were never carried out, and the decoration (capitals, etc.) remained unfinished

As it now survives the Château of Le Bouilh consists of a single tall block *(197)* attached to a semicircular range of much lower buildings, with a chapel in the centre and rooms to either side used for the production of wine on which the economy of the estate is still based. The unfinished capitals to the side of the main building and its irregular articulation betray the unfortunate timing of the commission, which coincided with the outbreak of the Revolution, the situation being described in the memoirs of the owner's daughter-in-law, the Marquise de la Tour du Pin.

In Louis' drawings for the château a building extraordinary in both scale and conception is revealed *(196)*, and one that is not easily reconciled with the building now existing on the site. There were to be two matching wings according to the original designs and between them a giant circular temple raised on a terrace and approached by curving ramps or flights of steps. Though clearly taking its inspiration from de Wailly's projects for Montmusard *(122)*, Louis' original scheme, catering for the extensive planning needed for a wine-producing château, marks a new stage in the dissolution of the traditional château form towards a visionary ideal based upon classical precedent.

During the 1780s and until his death in 1800, the main centre of Louis' activities was transferred to Paris, and his chief patron became the Duc de Chartres (Philippe-Egalité), who succeeded his father in 1785 as Duc d'Orléans, and thus first prince of the blood. Louis built for Chartres the galleries of the Palais-Royal and the theatre there, a private enclave within the city of Paris that had its own important part to play during the early years of the Revolution *(199, 200)*. During the years that Louis worked for him Chartres was the unlovable figurehead of liberal opposition to the

Crown. His family, like that of the Prince de Condé, had traditionally preserved a certain independence from the court: 'They tended to keep a distance from Versailles, where they felt themselves in tutelage to the King and the Ministers whom they avoided, when favours were refused them, and to make their own court where they reigned and where nothing and no one crossed them.'

Such was the family into which Chartres had been born in 1747. He lost his mother, an aunt of the Prince de Condé, at an early age and was married to the daughter of the Duc de Penthièvre in 1769. At the same time he witnessed his father's infatuation, and later his clandestine marriage to a commoner, Mme de Montesson. The Duc d'Orléans forsook the Palais-Royal to live less publicly in Paris with his wife, leaving his son to do the honours of the house. Chartres opposed more bitterly than his father the Parlement Maupeou and he later became the grand master of freemasonry in France. With a view to his father-in-law's post of Grand Admiral he persuaded the new king, Louis XVI, to appoint him to the navy, but showing cowardice in the face of battle he brought disgrace upon himself.

Contrary to the wishes of the king, Chartres was the most persistent champion of Anglomania, with his English park at Monceau and the passion he shared with the Comte d'Artois for betting and horse racing. Much to the embarrassment of Louis XVI Chartres paid several visits to England after the peace of 1783, visiting Newmarket and having his portrait painted by Reynolds *(198)*. George III was impressed by the simple manners of the prince, which he compared favourably to the extravagance of his own son, the Prince Regent. But simplicity was a greater advantage for a prince in England than in France and public ridicule pursued Chartres in Paris when he placed all his children, sons (including the future Louis-Philippe) as well as daughters, in charge of a female governess, Mme de Genlis, who brought them up according to the fashionable educational principles of Rousseau.

Constantly in need of money, the Duc de Chartres decided apparently on the suggestion of one of his gentlemen, the Marquis Ducrest, the brother of Mme de Genlis, upon the development of the Palais-Royal for gain. The palace was given to him in December 1780 by his father on condition that the important paintings and furniture it contained, which he reserved as his own property, should be properly housed in the new buildings. A public outcry followed upon the rumoured development of the gardens, the most frequented park within the walls of the city, and the duke's neighbours, including the Marquis de Voyer, made public protests. In consultation with Ducrest, however, Louis continued to work on his plans for the palace, which were approved in July 1781, just four days after the fire that destroyed Moreau's Opéra.

In Louis' project, an inversion of the system he had used at Bordeaux, the garden was to be enclosed by a continuous arcaded building that could be let for shops, restaurants and cafés with private dwellings above them *(200)*. The buildings were begun late in 1781 and finished two years later, although the interiors took two further

198 Portrait of the Duc de Chartres, by Sir Joshua Reynolds (Royal Collection, Buckingham Palace). Reynolds' now much damaged portrait of the anglophile owner of the Palais-Royal

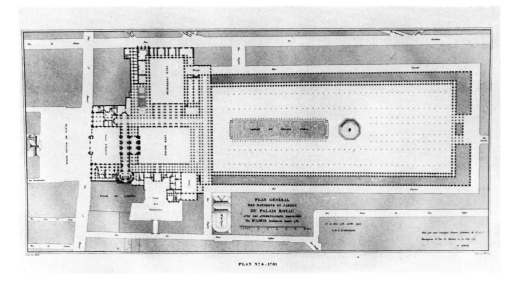

199 The Palais-Royal, Paris, plan (engraving from Percier and Fontaine). The plan shows Louis' scheme (1781) for the development of the garden (Moreau's Opéra, burnt in 1781, is below the main staircase, and the Hôtel de Voyer *(117)* just left of the title)

200 The Palais-Royal, detail of garden façade. The most popular pleasure resort of pre-Revolutionary Paris after its re-opening in 1783, the garden is suitably decorative in its architectural patterning but otherwise shows Louis at his most repetitive

years to complete. The garden itself was excavated for the creation of an underground circus and planted with mature trees to satisfy public criticism. The architect intended to construct a fourth wing, enclosing the near end of the garden and serving as an extension to the palace with rooms for the duke and a gallery for the collections of the Palais-Royal. This was to have a passageway at ground level supported on rows of Doric columns, and a columned façade matching the order of pilasters on the other sides of the garden. Begun in 1783, only the passageway was constructed before funds ran short, and a temporary wooden structure was added at main floor level.

Despite early opposition the transformation of the palace was a great popular success, providing a pleasure-ground for the evening as well as during the day, and all were admitted except porters and the poorest classes whose presence was allowed on only three days in the year. According to Mme d'Oberkirch, 'of all the public walks the new garden of the Palais Royal is the most frequented by the court and the citizens . . . I heard the other day that the Place St. Marc, at Venice, was to serve as a model for the buildings.' One of the many visitors to the garden was Mrs Thrale:

In the Evening [12 September 1784] my Husband showed me the new Square called the Palais Royal, whence the Duc de Chartres took away all the fine high Trees, which having stood for Centuries, it was a Shame to touch with an Ax, and accordingly the people were as angry as Frenchmen can be, when the Folly was first committed. The Court had however Wit enough to convert the place into a sort of Vauxhall, with Tents, Fountains & a Colonade of Shops and Coffeehouses surrounding it on every Side; and now they are all happy & contented and *Vive le Duc de Chartres.*

Chartres' confidence in Louis was not therefore misplaced, and the architect continued in favour with his patron. The two had probably first met in Bordeaux in 1776, when Louis designed the decorations for Chartres' triumphal entry to the town; he had then proceeded belatedly to lay the foundation-stone of the theatre, a ceremony apparently attended by a large masonic contingent. Louis himself was almost certainly a mason and therefore in touch with Chartres as grand master, although this was a function he performed without enthusiasm. A further asset was no doubt the acquaintance of Mme Louis, the architect's wife, with Mme de Genlis. In 1780 the duke already had an architect attached to his house, Henri Piètre, who had worked there with Contant d'Ivry, but he had employed at least one outsider, Poyet, on the construction of the pavilion of Bellechasse, where his children were brought up by Mme de Genlis, and on his huge stables, near the Tuileries.

Of Louis' work at the Palais-Royal the most intelligent account is given by Thiéry, who had evidently spoken to the architect about his designs. Thiéry explains Louis'

difficulties in having to match the existing, rather narrow, arcades of the palace and the main levels of the old building. The architect's extensive façades with the order repeated over two hundred times he justified with reference to the enclosed plan and the precedent of classical architecture:

The fine effect of the thoroughfares of the ancients proves that great façades on straight lines, and uniformity in details, gives architecture a character of grandeur that can never be achieved with variety of masses and decoration in a small enclosed space as this is . . . In one word it is the vast enclosure of a Palace of a Prince of the House of France that this artist has wished to convey to all those who will enter the gardens.

The order chosen by Louis is the most elaborate of all, the Composite, with an entablature of consoles continuously interrupted by a decoration of threaded swags and by the windows of the mezzanine. Laurel sprays decorate the spandrels of the arcades and between the capitals there are reliefs of different patterns over the main-floor windows. At the Palais-Royal this decoration seems appropriate to the garden setting, where its monotony is in any case mitigated by the outlines of the trees, and suitably festive for a place of public entertainment. Despite the degree of repetition which Thiéry for one took to be in the most advanced classical taste, the pilasters on their high bases seem decidedly of the past, and only in the richness of the decoration is the architecture noticeably different from Louis' earlier works.

The two important buildings that closed the career of Louis were both theatres, and both variations upon the theatre of Bordeaux. Much to the dismay of the Duc de Chartres the Opéra, after it had been burnt in 1781, was not reconstructed on its old site beside the Palais-Royal, and Louis undertook to build a new theatre (the present Comédie-Française) on the opposite side of the palace. Begun in 1786, the theatre opened four years later. Structurally it was more complex than the Bordeaux theatre, with a foyer placed beneath the auditorium and a yet more elaborate vault, supported by extensive iron girders which were rediscovered during the most recent reconstruction of the building, carried out after a fire in 1900.

Louis' final theatre followed some years later, the Théâtre des Arts, or Théâtre-National, which was built on a site further along the rue de Richelieu. Despite the extent of his practice Louis' contribution to the architecture of his age was principally in his theatre designs, where the importance of the interiors allowed the widest scope for his real skill, in the manipulation of space and in decoration. As an architect he seems to have profited little from the lessons of his older contemporaries, Peyre and de Wailly, and he showed little of the inventive genius that distinguishes all the productions of Ledoux.

201 Portrait of Claude-Nicolas Ledoux, with his elder daughter Adélaïde, attributed to Vestier (Musée Carnavalet, Paris). Of the later 1770s and formerly attributed to Fragonard, the portrait shows Ledoux with the plan of the entrance to the saltworks of Arc and Senans *(238)*

Part Three
CLAUDE-NICOLAS LEDOUX
(1735–1806)

10 Introduction: training and early works

THE HALF-CENTURY OF TRANSITION between the earlier eighteenth century and the era of Napoleon witnessed some of the greatest achievements of French architecture, but the period was dominated by no single artist. Its main monuments are the works of different authors each with a single masterpiece to his credit: Soufflot's church of Ste-Geneviève, the Odéon by Peyre and de Wailly, the Halle au Blé by Le Camus, Antoine's Monnaie, the Ecole de Chirurgie by Gondoin, and Louis' theatre of Bordeaux. What distinguishes Ledoux from his contemporaries, however talented, is the extraordinary range of his competence which resulted in major works in every conceivable genre: the many private houses, the saltworks of Arc and Senans, the theatre of Besançon, the Parlement and prison of Aix, the town gates of Paris, and the designs for the imaginary town of Chaux. As Ledoux's first biographer, Jacques Cellerier, stressed, the architect 'had that force of character, that active perseverance, which triumphs over the greatest obstacles' *(201)*.

The work of Ledoux is mainly known through his own book, *L'Architecture considérée sous le rapport de l'art, des moeurs et de la législation'*, of which the first volume appeared in 1804, two years before the architect's death *(202)*. This volume shows for the most part projects for the imaginary town that Ledoux was engaged in designing, and represents Ledoux as he wished to be known to posterity. The second volume, appearing as late as 1847, contains engravings of buildings that had been commissioned or built during the earlier part of his life.

The ponderous title of the *Architecture* was not uncharacteristic of its date. It recalls especially Mme de Staël's *De la littérature considérée dans ses rapports avec les institutions sociales* of four years earlier, but there is little other similarity between the two works, since Ledoux adopted for the press a style of writing so pretentious as to be virtually unintelligible. He defended the text with typical allusiveness, claiming that 'the artist writes as he makes; always inspired, the offices of clerks become, under his hand, magnificent propylaea; the house of a famous dancer presents the temple of Terpsichore; the

202 The frontispiece of Ledoux's *Architecture*, 1804 (engraving by Varin). The first edition of the *Architecture* contains engravings of Ledoux's projects for the imaginary town of Chaux; the posthumous edition of 1847 includes many of his other works

warehouse of a merchant develops the gardens of Zephyr and Flora, and fields produce factories, and cities where columns spring up beside nettles', and more to the same effect.

The book seems totally at variance with the character of the man, for, however ambitious his architectural projects may have been, Ledoux was amongst the most practical and rational architects of his age. As his letters show, he also remained in full possession of his mental faculties right up to the time of his death, despite his imprisonment during the Terror and the domestic grief which clouded the last years of his life. Cellerier, who was himself an architect and one of the friends chosen by Ledoux to edit the second volume of the *Architecture*, speaks of the architect as 'Gifted with an agreeable exterior, with a fine spirit, [and] that tone of assurance that seduces and inspires confidence', and he mentions his liking for the company of men of letters and especially of fellow-artists and women.

Though Ledoux was evidently unable to express his creative inspiration in the medium of words, adopting the allegorical and hysterical tone of the literature of the Revolution, the almost mystic nature of the *Architecture* must also be related to the character of the town that he illustrates, which is evidently the one major project of the time directly inspired by masonic, or crypto-masonic, ideas. This hidden side of Ledoux's life, the interest he shared with so many of his contemporaries in secret societies and the occult, is vividly illustrated in a letter of William Beckford, who describes a visit paid in the company of Ledoux in 1784 to an occult meeting of some kind at a house where the architect had worked, within an hour's drive of Paris. A 'very suspicious place of bewilderment and mystery' was Beckford's opinion of the house, which he left with the greatest relief. Ledoux himself Beckford otherwise describes as a 'singularly high-flown personage', with his 'courtly blandishments', and he also implies that the architect was something of a dandy, wearing a 'magnificent full powdered aile de Pigeon coiffure'.

Quite apart from an unintelligible text, the two volumes of the *Architecture* – as has only recently been realized – are positively misleading in the impression they give of Ledoux's career and in their visual presentation of his works. Ledoux improved the appearance of his buildings in the engravings he prepared for the press, altering the earlier works in accordance with his late style. The designs for the town of Chaux, formerly dated within the lifetime of Louis XV, and assumed, even by Cellerier, to have been intended for a real town, have in the past been studied almost to the exclusion of his real buildings, and Ledoux has been bracketed with Boullée and even Lequeu as one of the three visionary architects of 'Romantic classicism'. Without questioning the very real interest of Ledoux's imaginary designs and their relation to suburban and garden-city planning, which ensured their popularity in the early years of the present century, or indeed their affiliation with the late works of other artists of genius, they must be regarded as only a small part of the total production of an architect of much greater practical ability than is generally allowed.

As a consequence of the many discoveries that have recently been made about the work of Ledoux, the true extent of his achievement can now the more easily be appreciated. If the distortions which the architect practised in the publication of his work have been exposed, the course of his early career is also much better known, partly through the publication of Ledoux's own memoir informing the Academy about his earliest commissions. There remains to be investigated the character of his private clients, amongst whom were numbered many of the most distinguished families of the kingdom, and likewise the social and political implications of his public buildings, scarcely less varied in character than the architect's domestic work.

Like Gondoin, Ledoux was one of the few architects of his generation not to have been born in Paris, but in the country – at Dormans in Champagne. This is not without significance considering the real importance that the effects of nature assumed in the imagination of the architect; moreover, circumstances conspired to force him at the start of his career to return to the countryside around the place of his birth. It was not until the early 1770s that Ledoux's work began to be appreciated, but he had been born in 1735, and he was thus a little older than Chalgrin and Gondoin. His parents, according to Cellerier, were poor, but with a grant he entered the Collège de Beauvais in Paris. The college had been founded by a fellow-citizen of Dormans and was then under the administration of a Jansenist, Père Coffin, who subsequently became famous as one of the most eminent of his faith to be denied the sacraments on his death in 1749. Ledoux stayed at the college until the age of fifteen (1750) and on leaving supported himself as an engraver, making plates of battles which are so far untraced.

Like Boullée Ledoux received a grounding in the figurative arts, but he turned spontaneously, it appears, to architecture, attending the classes of Blondel and then joining the office of Trouard. He was not, therefore, subjected to the training of the Academy and Cellerier denies categorically that he ever visited Italy, although it seems that he made a journey to England. It must have been through prints and drawings that antiquity and Italian architecture were revealed to Ledoux, and his own approach to the classical past was never fettered by considerations of archaeological accuracy, recalling always in its imaginative force and in its reliance upon nature the intensity of Piranesi's vision.

Ledoux's move to the office of Trouard was presumably in the later 1750s, and he must have been at the school of Blondel earlier in the decade when Chalgrin and Gondoin were also pupils there. In 1762 he came briefly to the attention of the public with a scheme of decoration carried out at the Café Godot, where he ingeniously used spears and helmets for the articulation of the walls, the form of decoration that de Wailly employed slightly later for the bed of the Marquis de Voyer. For much of the 1760s Ledoux was active as the architect attached to the department known as the Eaux et Forêts de France, a post which took him frequently beyond his birthplace to the forests of eastern France. Like the engineers of the Ponts et Chaussées, the architects of the Eaux et Forêts took responsibility for local architectural projects, and the participation of Ledoux has recently been discovered in about twelve, mainly ecclesiastical, works in Burgundy and its vicinity. At this time two more important commissions in this part of France also fell to Ledoux, the redecoration of the choir of Auxerre Cathedral and work on the cathedral of Sens, including the chapter house. These two projects are included in the list of works that Ledoux prepared, probably about 1768, to facilitate his admission to the Academy.

Ledoux's list radically alters accepted views of his early work and of the patrons he had attracted at the start of his career. The Château of Maupertuis is listed as his first work, though whether first in date or in importance is unclear (203). Ledoux claims that this was a large château, decorated with an Ionic order, with wings and outbuildings in a park. He describes in detail the method of access:

the entrance in the middle had seemed almost impracticable because of the enormous rocks in the earth and up to the level of the ground rising to the front floor of the château. I made a horseshoe 150 *toises* [959 feet: 292·3 metres] in circumference crowned with balustrades, pierced with square and round niches, arriving at a gentle incline at the door of the vestibule; and since the rock of the country by its random forms and its colour contributed to the decoration, I used it as it was in ending the horseshoe with a river god and naiads mounted on pedestals and distributing the water for the whole château. There was formerly a Pavilion of about ten *toises* [64 feet: 19·6 metres] without form which was subjected to the new ensemble.

The owner of Maupertuis was one of the most celebrated of the liberal noblemen of the time, and one of the most pretentious in his claims to a lineage grander than that of the royal house. He was Anne-Pierre de Montesquiou-Fezenzac, junior to Ledoux by three years and described by the architect as Premier Gentilhomme to the Dauphin, though he later joined the household of the Comte de Provence, the patron of Chalgrin. A Maréchal de Camp, as well as being a member of the Académie des Lettres, Montesquiou aligned himself with the Third Estate in 1789 and later became a general in the Revolutionary army. In 1760 he married the daughter of Président Hocquart, of a well-known family of tax farmers, and it may have been as a consequence of this alliance that Maupertuis was reconstructed.

Laid out by Ledoux at this early date, Maupertuis was further embellished right up until the time of the Revolution, for Brongniart too worked there (see chapter 13), creating one of the most famous gardens of the time. Nothing now remains of Ledoux's work at Maupertuis, but his description of the site shows something of the priority that he gave to the natural setting of a building even at the very start of his career. The engravings in his book that show the Château of Maupertuis with a giant Doric order (203), and the famous spherical house of the 'gardes agricoles', must be a much later fantasy based on this early work of his.

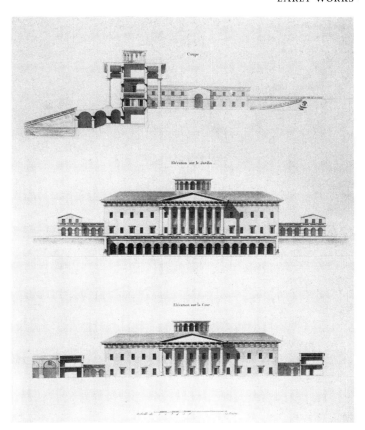

203 The Château of Maupertuis, section and elevations, engraving from Ledoux. The reconstruction of Maupertuis for the Marquis de Montesquiou-Fezenzac was one of Ledoux's first works (early 1760s); his engraving shows a later variant of the design

The second two works on the list which Ledoux prepared for the Academy were carried out for Président Hocquart, the father of Mme de Montesquiou and the respected Premier Président of the Parlement of Metz. The two buildings in question are the Château of Montfermeil, near Paris, of which little is known, and a town house, described by Ledoux as a 'Pavillon', 'isolated and amidst gardens'. This last may have been largely a work of reconstruction as the architect explains that the external sculpture and the entrance gate were not of his design, and that for the interior he was asked to reuse the woodwork of a demolished château, that of Gagny. Again the engravings of the house in the *Architecture* appear to be a fantasy based upon his work, though he correctly shows the order as Ionic. As well as Hocquart and Montesquiou Ledoux's patrons at this date included the Marquise de Foucault, the Cardinal de Luynes and the Baron de Thiers, for all of whom he was engaged on small projects.

The fourth item on Ledoux's list is the Hôtel d'Hallwyl, a building that, according to Cellerier, attracted new patrons to the architect and the acclaim both of the general public and of fellow-artists. The Hôtel d'Hallwyl is one of the very few surviving works of Ledoux (though one that is badly in need of restoration) and it provides the earliest

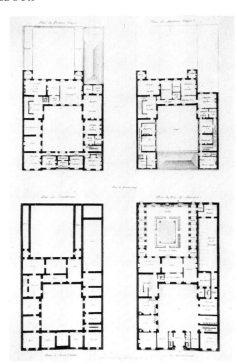

204 The Hôtel d'Hallwyl, Paris, plans, engraving from Ledoux. The alteration of the Hôtel de Bouligneux in eastern Paris for the Comte d'Hallwyl was begun by Ledoux in 1766

205 The Hôtel d'Hallwyl, the street façade. The doorway combines the traditional arched shape of the Paris *porte cochère* with an articulation of columns and a lintel

206 The Hôtel d'Hallwyl, street elevation and section through rear court, engraving from Ledoux. The street façade is made more regular in the engraving; the section shows the Ionic colonnade that was to be painted on the wall facing the end of the garden

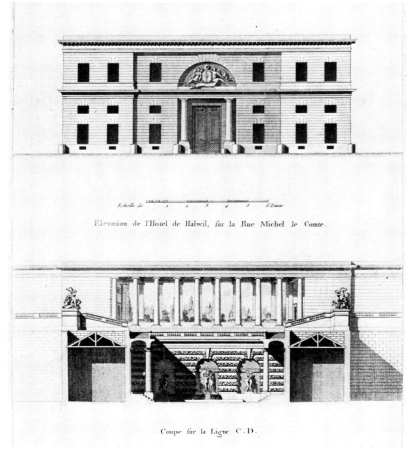

Elevation de l'Hotel de Halwil, sur la Rue Michel le Comte.

Coupe sur la Ligne C.D.

point of reference showing the improvements made by the architect in his engravings *(205, 206)*. The building also marks the start of Ledoux's fruitful association with the fraternity of Swiss bankers and soldiers who had taken up residence in Paris. François-Joseph d'Hallwyl had been the colonel of the Swiss regiment that bore his name, and later a Maréchal de Camp. He is occasionally mentioned as a figure at court in the memoirs of the period and on one occasion he is recorded as Marigny's host at a dinner.

His Paris house, transformed for him by Ledoux, was the former Hôtel de Bouligneux, in the rue Michel-le-Comte, in the eastern part of the city. It had recently been the house of the Swiss banker, Isaac Thélusson, and was let to the Comte d'Hallwyl in 1764 by Jacques Necker, then a partner in the Thélusson bank, which had its office in an adjacent building. The hôtel follows the traditional tall shape that houses had assumed for over a century in this part of Paris; Ledoux used part of the existing fabric but transformed the character of the old building almost beyond recognition.

The architect employed rustication with narrow horizontal bands to impose his own will upon the shape of the house and especially to reduce its sense of verticality. The main doorway *(205)* recalls the normal form of the Parisian *porte cochère* in its round-headed shape, but it too is transformed by Ledoux into a more modern composition by the insertion of columns at the sides supporting a straight lintel. The lintel effectively obscures the structural importance of the main arch in a design, later much used by Ledoux and his contemporaries, that reconciles the French vernacular tradition with recent prescriptions for classical purity.

Because of the presence of columns beside the doorway the façade has two entablatures, the upper one breaking back once in the centre and the lower one twice. This too refers to the traditional complexity of French architectural practice, no less than the dropped keystones above the windows, which recall de Wailly's slightly earlier use of rustication at Montmusard. When Ledoux came to engrave the façade for publication *(206)* he could not radically transform such a street elevation, but he straightened the cornices and simplified the keystones, producing a more streamlined design, reminiscent of the street façade of the Ecole de Chirurgie *(177)*. Yet here, as in all his engravings, Ledoux's acute sense of spacing is not greatly affected by the simplifications he introduced and the contrasts of light and shade are even intensified, much against the prevailing taste of post-Revolutionary art.

The forecourt *(207)* is designed with a greater sense of contrast than the street façade, the rustication breaking off in the centre of the main façade to provide a plain frontispiece with pedimented windows and stone balustrades in the newest fashion, but the most unusual feature of the house is the garden, where the order of the main doorway reappears to form straight Tuscan colonnades at each side *(208)*. Colonnaded gardens were not unknown in Paris, where the forecourt of the Hôtel de Soubise is a notable example, but in its severity and density of scale the garden of the Hôtel d'Hallwyl is unique in its resemblance

207 The Hôtel d'Hallwyl, the court frontispiece. The channelled rustication, which reduces the vertical emphasis of the court, is omitted on the three central window bays

208 The Hôtel d'Hallwyl, garden colonnade, detail. In so enclosed a space the colonnades resemble those of a Roman atrium

209 The Hôtel d'Hallwyl, the decoration of the rear garden wall. Sculpted decoration serves in place of real fountains in the garden

210 Detail of the Fontaine de Médicis, Palais du Luxembourg, Paris, early seventeenth century. Much of Ledoux's decorative imagery, including sculpted water, was inspired by French Renaissance architecture

to the atrium of a Roman house, and like an atrium, it is to all appearances copiously supplied with water (209).

On the rear wall two sculpted urns spill water over ledges and down the rusticated wall, while in the centre – spoiling the illusion – is a frame that also seems composed of water, enclosing a niche. Paris, unlike Rome, was never well supplied with aqueducts, and water was for the most part carried from the Seine by porters and sold from door to door. Ledoux's illusionistic fountains seem to have been inspired by no very obvious classical precedent, but rather by decorative sculpture of the early Renaissance in France, particularly the Fontaine de Médicis in the Luxembourg gardens (210). Indeed the revival of interest in the sculpture of the sixteenth century, already encountered in the work of Soufflot and de Wailly, was to provide the source of many of Ledoux's wittiest effects. The illusionism of the garden of the Hôtel d'Hallwyl was to be completed by a mural painted on the wall beyond the street behind the hôtel (206). It is not unusual to find painted architecture in the courtyards of houses in eastern Paris, but rarely is it as spectacular as in Ledoux's scheme, which shows an Ionic colonnade with shrubs in vases and a park beyond.

After the Hôtel d'Hallwyl Ledoux's next major commission (not included in his list) seems to have been the restoration of the town house of the Duc d'Uzès, which was apparently completed in 1769 (211–215). It lay at the northern extremity of the city within the seventeenth-century walls and was recorded in photographs before its demolition in the later nineteenth century. The house was one of the examples of modern architecture mentioned by Blondel in his *Homme du monde*, where the daring of the frontispiece is condemned and the beauty of the interior praised:

We then passed on to a town house that a young architect has just built for a great nobleman. To judge the talents of this artist by the exterior he can certainly be ranked amongst the class of his emulators, who, still novices, seek only to astonish and often mistake delirium for imagination. The gateway is in a good style but the façades [of the house] are in bad taste: the scale is colossal, and the proportions defective. But I can't pretend to dissimulate: the interior is heavenly. Never have I seen forms so agreeable, so appropriate, and architecture so perfectly related to sculpture [215].

For the reconstruction of his hôtel the Duc d'Uzès apparently asked several architects to submit drawings before the work was entrusted to Ledoux. François-Emmanuel de Crussol, Duc d'Uzès, was the most senior of the non-royal dukes. Born in 1728, he had married in 1753 the daughter of the Duc d'Antin, the bastard son of Louis XIV who had served as Surintendant des Bâtiments du Roi. He pursued an active military career and was promoted to the rank of brigadier at the start of the Seven Years' War. With the peace of 1763 he, like the Marquis de Voyer and other officers, was able to pursue an active interest in intellectual matters; as early as 1751 he had corresponded with Voltaire on the subject of Rousseau's *Essai*. Though entitled by his rank to duties at court he is rarely mentioned in the memoirs of the period. A representative of the nobles in 1789, he later joined the army of the exiled princes in

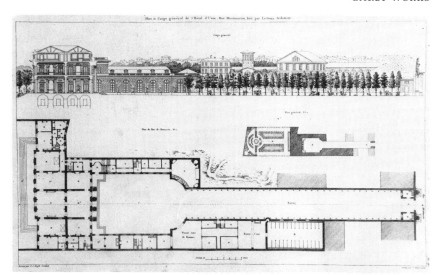

211 The Hôtel d'Uzès, Paris, section and plan (engraving from Krafft and Ransonnette). The reconstruction of the now destroyed Hotel d'Uzès in eastern Paris was completed by Ledoux for the Duc d'Uzès in 1769

212 The Hôtel d'Uzès,, the main frontispiece before demolition. Though the Duc d'Uzès was Premier Duc, the frontispiece of his house was considered pretentious

213 The Hôtel d'Uzès, the garden façade before demolition. Giant Ionic pilasters with statues above decorated the garden façade of the house

214 The Hôtel d'Uzès, the main gateway, elevation, engraving from Ledoux. Separated by a long avenue from the house *(211)*, the main door was conceived in the form of an arch with two triumphal columns before it, proclaiming the military prowess of the owner

Germany, and after a short visit to England he returned to Paris, where he died in 1802. The duke was an active patron at Uzès and he possessed another château (Bonnelles), not far from Paris, which was laid out with a garden in the 'English' style.

Like the Hôtel d'Hallwyl the house of the Duc d'Uzès had the characteristically tall shape of a seventeenth-century mansion, and it also resembled a château in having a long drive from the street to the main courtyard *(212)*. Both of these peculiarities may have encouraged the architect and his patron to experiment more boldly than was customary, but the columned façade added to the front of the building was also not without its social implications. It gave an impression of almost royal or civic consequence to the building, thus disturbing the rules of *convenance* as Blondel understood them. What Peyre in fact had proposed for the Prince de Condé *(108)*, Ledoux carried out for the Duc d'Uzès, and architecturally the frontispiece must have seemed all the more provocative in the absence of a pediment.

The garden side of the building was also decorated with a giant order *(213)*, though here it consisted of pilasters

and of the garlanded Ionic that Boullée and Moreau liked to use. The entablature continued without alteration around the building and appears to have been a compromise between the design appropriate for the Ionic and for the more elaborate Corinthian order.

As in many other town houses of the period it was the decoration of the interior, often costing more than the masonry, that most delighted the owners and their visitors *(215)*. Many of the panels designed by Ledoux for his early interiors have survived and though the architect gave no prominence to such decorations in his books, they were no less inventive than his buildings, and are indeed amongst the most elegant and magical of all the interiors of the time. While Gabriel had introduced greater severity in the design of panelling, and Boullée had invented interiors of great architectural richness *(143)*, Ledoux was a master of fanciful ornamental design that recalled the achievements of the earlier eighteenth century, but which remained always more disciplined in character. The panels of the Grand Salon of the Hôtel d'Uzès were designed as a series of trees rooted in the floor and bearing on their branches trophies of war.

166

215 The Hôtel d'Uzès, the salon (Musée Carnavalet, Paris). Described by Blondel as 'heavenly', the interiors of the hôtel were largely sculpted by Joseph Métivier to Ledoux's designs

The military exploits of the patron likewise inspired the most inventive architectural feature of the house, the main gateway *(214)*. Instead of a conventional door like those suggested by Ledoux's competitors, Ledoux provided not only a free-standing triumphal arch, but one with two columns in front of the gate each decorated with military trophies. Like the triumphal columns of Imperial Rome they proclaim to all who pass the nature of the duke's achievements and the status of his family.

Just how far the Hôtel d'Uzès approximated to a château rather than a town house is shown by its virtual twin, the surviving Château of Bénouville, near Caen in Normandy, which Ledoux remodelled for Hippolyte-François Sauguin, Marquis de Livry, beginning in 1768 *(216–220)*. Like the Hôtel d'Uzès this too was apparently an existing building and one that remains typical of a Normandy château in its height and relative isolation. In this case Ledoux employed the Ionic order for both façades and a simplified Ionic entablature. The order is garlanded but more sculptural in its effect – with the garlands interrupting, on the rear façade, the channelling of the pilasters – and on the main frontispiece the four central columns

project well forwards crowned with a panel of arms. Yet despite these differences the resemblance is so close to the Hôtel d'Uzès as to suggest a deliberate connection between the two buildings, though no direct relationship between their respective patrons is known.

The Marquis de Livry was a little older than the Duc d'Uzès, and he had served in the navy where he had become an admiral (Chef d'Escadre) and visited Italy and Greece. The estate of Bénouville came to him on the death of his father-in-law, Antoine Gillain, Marquis de Bénouville, in 1768. Livry is rarely mentioned in the memoirs of the time, though both his parents were intimates of Louis XV, his father being Premier Maître d'Hôtel to the king when he died in 1758. As at the Hôtel d'Uzès the military exploits of the owner are recorded in the decoration of the exterior, in the trophies sculpted above the entablature of the rear façade.

Bénouville was one of the buildings that Ledoux altered most of all in his engravings *(216, 219)*. As finally envisaged, the design incorporated projecting frontispieces of six columns on both façades, a simple Ionic order and a severe attic entirely bare of windows. The plan,

216 The Château of Bénouville, near Caen, Normandy, front elevation, engraving from Ledoux. Redesigned for the Marquis de Livry in 1768, Bénouville was extensively revised in Ledoux's engravings

217 The Château of Bénouville, the front façade. Falsely shown in the engraving (216), the château has a windowed attic storey and a frontispiece of four garlanded Ionic columns with two set back at the sides

218 The Château of Bénouville, the garden façade. The pilasters of the garden façade match the Ionic columns of the front, though the elevation otherwise resembles the garden of the Hôtel d'Uzès (213)

however, apparently remained relatively unaltered and while it is not one of the most inventive of Ledoux's plans, it is of particular interest for the placing of the main staircase *(219, 220)*. Without, presumably, altering the existing fabric of the building, Ledoux created his staircase at the centre of the garden façade in the position normally reserved for the principal salon. Like Peyre at the Hôtel de Condé Ledoux thus ensured an absolute symmetry for the main rooms of the château in accordance with the latest fashion. At Bénouville, however, the plan of the staircase is more traditional than Peyre's *(108)*, being a simpler variant of the type later used by Louis at the Bordeaux theatre *(193)*, and the presence of a central flight of steps prevents direct access to the garden on the main axis of the house.

As at the theatre of Bordeaux, the staircase at Bénouville also recalls the seventeenth century in its stony appearance, which depends not only on the extensive low vaults that support the flights and the landing, but also on the balusters themselves, which are composed of stone piers. In the decoration of the main floor Ledoux used the motif he had invented for the doorway of the Hôtel d'Hallwyl *(205)*, with a series of arches surmounting pairs of columns and pilasters, though in the absence of an upper cornice the arches are diminished in importance. A coffered vault with an open rectangular gallery again recalls the open domes of seventeenth-century architecture, like Mansart's staircase at Maisons, which Ledoux would have visited in Blondel's company *(39)*.

For real ingenuity in planning Ledoux's early masterpiece was his next Parisian town house, the Hôtel de Montmorency, designed apparently in 1769 and contracted for building in January of the following year *(221)*. The house was built on the northern boulevard of the city, at the west corner of the newly developing rue de la Chaussée-d'Antin. Given an irregular rectangular site Ledoux placed the hôtel not discreetly at the rear but prominently at the street corner, with the court and the stables behind. The exterior had two matching façades, each with a projecting frontispiece of four engaged Ionic columns with partial fluting like those used by Ledoux's teacher, Trouard, in St-Symphorien at Versailles *(161)*. The presence of the giant order lent the house something of the grandeur of a public building, but the effect must have been less overtly provocative than at the Hôtel d'Uzès since an engaged giant order was a commonplace of civic architecture in Paris. The design indeed closely resembles the corner pavilions of Gabriel's Place Louis XV *(43)*, which Ledoux mentions with apparent approval in his book, although he uses no pediments at the Hôtel de Montmorency and no proper frames for any of the windows. Architecturally the house was well received, the Prince de Croÿ describing it as a 'charming *maison du boulevard* where there are new ideas', but the statues over the frontispieces, where the pretensions of the owners became explicit, were not so readily tolerated. Like Soufflot's statues at Lyon *(27)*, they represented medieval heroes, in this case the ancestors of the occupants.

The prolific house of Montmorency, which had produced six constables of France in the Middle Ages, had

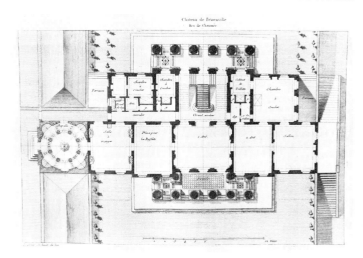

219 The Château of Bénouville, ground-plan, engraving from Ledoux. The staircase is placed on the central axis of the plan in place of the salon; the engraving falsely shows projecting frontispieces of six columns on both façades

220 The Château of Bénouville, the stairchamber. The 'architectural' character of the stairchamber recalls French staircases of the seventeenth century *(39)*

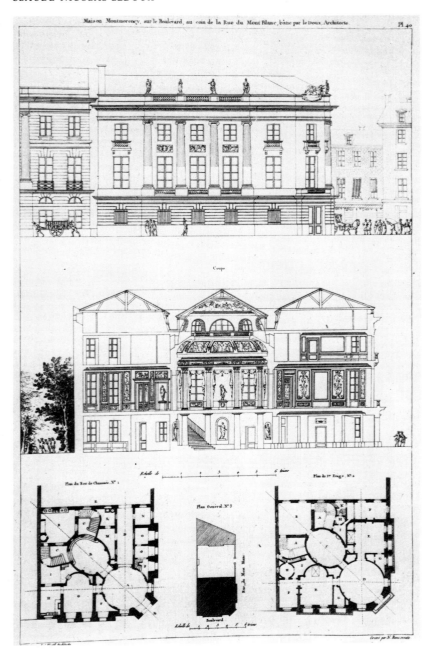

221 The Hôtel de Montmorency, Paris, elevation, section and plans (engraving from Krafft and Ransonnette). Designed by Ledoux in 1769 for the Prince and Princesse de Montmorency (Logny) on the corner of the rue de la Chaussée-d'Antin, the hôtel was the masterpiece amongst Ledoux's early houses for ingenuity of planning

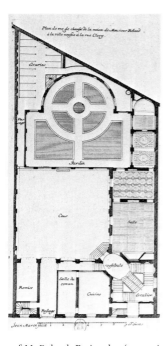

222 The house of M. Roland, Paris, plan (engraving by Marot). Designed by the mathematician and engineer, Gérard Desargues (1593–1661), and recalling the Hôtel de Montmorency (221) in the diagonally planned staircase

subsequently suffered disgrace and exile in Flanders. Gradually the members of the different branches of the family had returned to France; several had served with distinction in the French army, and by the later eighteenth century they had become the most vociferous pretenders to the oldest lineage in the country, with a five-volume book on their ancestry published in 1764. These claims were generally (and perhaps rightly) accepted, though not in the Créquy *Souvenirs*, where they are attributed to the scheming of Mme de Luxembourg, the wife of the Duc de Montmorency-Luxembourg. The Luxembourgs were famous for the protection they had given to Rousseau, and the duchess more especially as an arbiter in social and intellectual matters. Well known through the reputation of Mme de Luxembourg, the Montmorency were also celebrated for their support of the masonic movement in France, and the lodge of Montmorency-Luxembourg formed the nucleus of the Grand-Orient.

The patron of Ledoux was one of the less famous members of the clan, Louis-François-Joseph, Comte de Logny, who was known from his Belgian title as the Prince de Montmorency. Little is known of his life, though he was closely related to several other branches of the family. One year younger than Ledoux, he had pursued a career in the army during the Seven Years' War, like most other aristocrats of his generation, and he became a brigadier in 1762. Two years later came an alliance with the Luxembourg branch of the family on his marriage to Mme de Luxembourg's widowed daughter-in-law. His new wife, Louise-Françoise-Pauline de Montmorency-Luxembourg, was three times over a Montmorency: allied by marriage to the Luxembourg and Logny branches, she was also the only surviving child of the Prince de Tingry-Montmorency. The memoirs of the time, especially those of de Croÿ, suggest that she was more active and ambitious than her new husband. She created at Boulogne-sur-Seine one of the earliest of the 'English' gardens and had the single-mindedness to seek the friendship of Mme du Barry, apparently in the interests of her husband's career.

Certainly she took an active part in the planning of her new hôtel, witnessing with her husband the contract of January 1770, which she signed 'Montmorency Montmorency'. Shortly before the house was built the Comte de Logny had become the chief of his branch of the family on the death of an elder brother, and about the same time his step-daughter married into the senior branch of the family (Fosseux), bringing to her husband the title of Duc de Montmorency. The Fosseux house was an early eighteenth-century mansion, not far from the Hôtel d'Uzès, where a special building was constructed shortly before the Revolution for the genealogical papers of the Montmorency family.

Exactly how the talents of Ledoux came to serve the social ambitions of his Montmorency patrons is not clear. The land on which Ledoux's building was constructed was owned by the financier Joseph-Florent Le Normand de Mézières, who had also acquired land at Eaubonne, near the estate of Mme de Luxembourg, and it may have been through de Mézières that Ledoux was chosen. Either way,

223 The Hôtel de Montmorency, panel from the salon (Museum of Fine Arts, Boston). As at the Hôtel d'Uzès *(215)*, the decoration was carried out to Ledoux's designs by Métivier

the Prince and Princesse de Montmorency, thanks to the skill of the architect, had the distinction of owning one of the most elegant houses of the capital, a prominently sited stronghold, or so it must have appeared, of uncompromising symmetry, its matching frontispieces, guarded by the ancestors of the family, clearly referring to the dynastic liaison within.

The main entrance was not obtrusive. It lay at the corner, announced by an inscription and by the presence

224 Portrait of Marie Ledoux with her younger daughter Alexandrine (Private Collection). The recently discovered pair to the portrait of Ledoux *(201)*

above the cornice of a winged figure against a background of flags. From a circular lobby inside the entrance a passage led to the right where carriages passed underneath the house to the court at the back. An oval vestibule in the very centre of the block gave access to matching staircases in the rear corner, hiding the kitchen and ascending to the first antechamber. Re-crossing the house diagonally on the first floor there followed a second antechamber, an oval room two storeys in height surmounted, like the staircase at Bénouville, by a gallery and a shallow dome, and finally the main circular salon over the entrance vestibule. The private rooms of the house led from the salon, with the bedroom of the princess behind the frontispiece over the boulevard and that of the prince behind the frontispiece at the side. The decoration throughout was as lavish as the architecture seemed to demand; nine panels from the walls of the salon, which Métivier sculpted in the style of Goujon, survive at Boston *(223)*.

The plan itself has all the ingenuity traditionally associated with French house design, with its sequence of rooms of varied shapes interlocked in harmony on the site, but there is a perceptible change of emphasis in the absolute symmetry and density of the planning, centred upon the top-lit oval antechamber. Houses based upon a square divided into nine sections, recalling the villas of Palladio and the dense regularity of Roman baths, were to become a commonplace of planning later in the century,

though they were never again to be treated with the artistry commanded by Ledoux.

Ledoux's sympathy for tradition is revealed, for example, in the choice of an oval form at the centre of the house to give direction to the plan, and this he seems to have combined in the ground-floor vestibule with an order of baseless Tuscan columns, apparently the first of their kind to appear in Paris, though in a suitably subterranean context. In his contract drawings Ledoux had envisaged conventional Tuscan columns for the vestibule but it seems likely that the change to a baseless order, a favourite device of the architect, was introduced during the course of construction and not at a later date, especially as the building seems not to have been altered in other ways in the years immediately following its construction.

If the vestibule is a reinterpretation of a classic of French architectural practice, so too is the staircase. Whereas Roman bath plans and Palladian villas had only one main floor and, when necessary, outside stairs, houses in the centre of Paris required stairs within their walls that suggested something of the luxury and social prestige of the main living rooms. Like Peyre at the Hôtel de Condé *(108)* Ledoux designed matching staircases rising symmetrically from the sides of the vestibule but in his case the plan appears to have been inspired by an ingenious idea devised by the seventeenth-century architect and geometrician, Gérard Desargues, for the house of a M. Roland *(222)*.

Beyond the contacts that his illustrious patrons provided little is known of Ledoux's personal life in the 1760s. Cellerier claims as a positive fact that Ledoux never visited Italy, but there is evidence of one or more journeys to England, possibly in his youth. Ledoux himself speaks of works of his carried out in England, as well as in Germany, Holland and Russia, though this may indicate no more than the commission of projects by foreign clients. Yet there are references in the *Architecture* that have been taken to indicate a journey to England, while Beckford mentions projects designed by Ledoux for Villa Pitt and Cellerier work undertaken for Lord Clive (Cliwes). Clive of India, who died in 1774, was in England in the earlier 1760s and from 1767, developing his estate at Styche in Shropshire. Whatever the relations between Clive and Ledoux, it is certainly curious that so famous an enemy of France may have been the patron of a French architect.

Ledoux's marriage probably took place in the late 1760s, as the first of his daughters, Adélaïde, was born about 1770 *(201)*, and the second, Alexandrine, five years later *(224)*. His wife, Marie Bureau, was the daughter of a musician, formerly in the King's Musketeers, who lived at Corbeil, not far from Paris. Marie Bureau may have brought property to her husband, or the means for its acquisition, for the couple later owned jointly six houses in Paris, including the house they themselves inhabited. This looked south over the northern boulevard of the city between the Porte St-Martin and the Porte St-Denis, with its entrance in the rue Neuve-d'Orléans, and it was described by Beckford as 'one of the strangest mock palaces you ever saw'.

11 The 1770s: the patronage of Mlle Guimard and Mme du Barry; the saltworks of Arc and Senans; the theatre of Besançon; the Hôtel de Thélusson

THE DECADE OF THE 1770S, opening for Ledoux with the signing of the contract for the Hôtel de Montmorency, marked the peak of his early success. The patronage of Mme du Barry began at the start of the decade, ensuring the success of the architect at court. His most famous houses in Paris were also designed in the 1770s, as well as the saltworks at Arc and Senans and the theatre of Besançon. And the promise of work at Kassel and at Aix opened up for the architect in the middle of the decade.

The most celebrated of all the smaller houses of Ledoux was the hôtel he constructed for Mlle Guimard, Première Danseuse of the Opéra *(225)*, the house that became famous as the 'Temple de Terpsichore' *(226, 227)*. The site lay a little beyond the Hôtel de Montmorency, on the same side of the rue de la Chaussée-d'Antin, and just beyond the avenue that led to a house later constructed by Necker. The design was apparently approved in 1770 and the house completed in the following year, but little is known of the negotiations that led to its construction or to the choice of Ledoux as its architect. The site, it seems, belonged to one of the dancer's many lovers, Jean-Benjamin de La Borde, a financier and celebrated amateur musician, who was also a favourite of the king and his Premier Valet de Chambre.

Funds are also said to have been provided by another lover of Mlle Guimard, the Prince de Soubise, a member of the distinguished Rohan family, which in the person of the Cardinal de Rohan was later to bring dishonour to Queen Marie Antoinette over the affair of the diamond necklace. Soubise was a courtier cast in the same mould as his friend, the Duc de Richelieu:

His frenetic taste for women [whom] his age placed him beyond the ability to please had thrown him into a scandalous way of life. The girls of the opera formed his court, and, on the other hand, there was a Madame de l'Hôpital, his official mistress, [who was] deeply engaged in gambling. But nevertheless everyone had a kind of deference for him, inspired by his birth, and his status, and also the position he held in the [royal] Council.

Not only Soubise, but also his son-in-law, the Prince de Guéménée, supported the dancer, and when Guéménée's

225 Portrait of Mlle Guimard, by Fragonard, 1771 (Musée du Louvre, Paris). The owner of the most famous of Ledoux's smaller houses *(226)*, Mlle Guimard was Première Danseuse of the Académie Royale de Musique (the Opéra)

famous bankruptcy occurred in 1786 she was forced to sell the house, which she put on the market in a characteristically piquant way, as a lottery.

However Ledoux came to be appointed its architect, this house too, in its very different way from the nearby Hôtel de Montmorency, was ingeniously keyed to the personality of its owner and to the nature of the hospitality offered there. It was a house of one main storey, with a small courtyard in front, hidden from the street by an entrance wing that also accommodated a small theatre on

Maison de Melle Guimard située à la chaussée d'Antin.

226 The Hôtel Guimard, Paris, front elevation, engraving from Ledoux. Designed by Ledoux in 1770 on a site near to that of the Hôtel de Montmorency *(221)*, the hôtel (here falsely shown in a park setting) was known as the Temple de Terpsichore from the Muse of dancing, who is shown over the columns of the frontispiece

the main floor. The owner had formerly lived on the outskirts of Paris, where she had enjoyed the use of a theatre, and Ledoux's house is cast rather in the form of a villa than a true town house.

The frontispiece, dominating the courtyard, sets the tone of the dwelling no less effectively than the gateway of the Hôtel d'Uzès or the frontispieces of the Montmorency house. It recalls in its shape the arched and trabeated door of the Hôtel d'Hallwyl *(205)*, but as a concave variant of the design it is also rooted in the long French tradition whereby a true niche acted as the principal entrance. At the Hôtel Guimard, however, the upper part of the niche has a pattern of coffering that very appropriately recalls the ruins of the temple which Venus shared with Rome in the Forum, an interior made visible by the process of decay *(228)*. Columns span the whole width of the niche at the Hôtel Guimard and in the opening above the screen Ledoux designed a sculptural group, carried out by Félix Lecomte, of the Crowning of Terpsichore, the Muse of dancing. A triumph of Terpsichore was the subject of the long relief, by the same sculptor, that decorated the rear of the niche behind the entablature of the screen.

Openings screened by columns had appeared in the 1760s, notably in Boullée's Hôtel Alexandre *(141)*, and in conjunction with an arch they had been introduced in interiors, as in Adam's work at Syon. The secret of Ledoux's design resides in the effect he achieved by using such a columned niche externally to give a mood of positive intimacy to the house, with the space of the open courtyard passing beyond the screen of columns to penetrate the wall of the façade. The boldness of Ledoux's design was not entirely lost on contemporaries and Grimm described the house in flattering terms to his foreign readers: 'if love bore the cost [of the house], pleasure itself drew the plan, and that divinity never had in Greece a temple worthier of her cult'.

The Hôtel Guimard was an immediate success and set other actresses (Mlles Dervieux and Arnould) dreaming of such houses for themselves. Distinguished visitors to the capital, the Emperor Joseph II and the Tsarevitch Paul, were taken to see the building, and it was one of the two works that Ledoux illustrated beneath the portrait bust that forms the frontispiece of his *Architecture (202)*. When he came to engrave the house for his book, Ledoux made

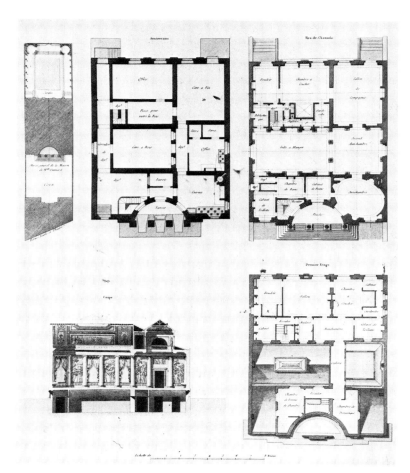

227 The Hôtel Guimard, plans, and section of the dining-room, engraving from Ledoux. As in many of Ledoux's houses the density of the planning made top-lighting necessary for the central rooms

very few alterations: inevitably he sited the building in a park and he tidied up the windows and the rustication, omitting the two openings in the front façade that gave light to the kitchens in the basement.

After the main façade the interior of the house was not a disappointment: an oval vestibule, with a series of niches subtly masking the diverted axis of the plan, led to an antechamber screened by columns from the dining-room, the main salon and the principal bedroom on the garden side. The dining-room itself and the bathrooms at the front of the house required the greatest ingenuity in their planning: 'I have heard no instance of luxury but in Mademoiselle Guimard, a favourite dancer, who is building a palace,' wrote Walpole in August 1771; 'round the *salle à manger* there are windows that open on hot-houses, that are to produce flowers all winter.' Even Blondel admitted that the house justified its celebrity:

It couldn't be better done or excelled . . . The rooms . . . gallant without indecorousness, suggest the interior of the Palace of Love, embellished by the Graces . . . and (I mustn't forget) the execution of all these different marvels seems to be the work of a single hand; delicious harmony, which puts the finish to the

228 View of the Roman Forum with the Temple of Venus and Rome, etching by Piranesi, 1759, from the *Vedute di Roma*. The interior of the temple, exposed by decay, recalls the portico of the Hôtel Guimard

and function the two buildings had much in common, not least the publicity they conferred on the owners with their similar ways of life. In the person of Mme du Barry Ledoux gained not merely an influential client, but a loyal and powerful protectress:

Good-natured, easy-going, with charm and charity she won many hearts, including the king's, and became *maîtresse en titre*, an office unoccupied since Mme de Pompadour had died. The du Barry had no political interests and Choiseul's bitter hostility to her, unless it is accounted for by the story that he had aspired to place his sister in the vacant office of titular mistress, is difficult to explain.

Mme du Barry had been given the estate of Louveciennes, with its beautiful site on a cliff overlooking the Seine to the west of Paris, in 1769. Its former owner, the Prince de Lamballe, the only brother of the Duc de Chartres' future wife, had died there in the preceding year. The château was altered for Mme du Barry by Gabriel, but she subsequently adopted Ledoux as her architect. He began by constructing for her the pavilion in the park at Louveciennes, he nearly completed her large – and partly surviving – stables in Versailles *(234)*, he began a new château at Louveciennes *(232)* and made projects for a large town house in Paris *(233)*. In 1774, after the death of Louis XV, he continued to work for her in exile, first apparently at the Convent of Pont-aux-Dames, and then at the Château of St-Vrain, not far from Arpajon, where she stayed for several months before the new king allowed her to return to Louveciennes. Architect and royal mistress evidently established a mutual affection and William Beckford, examining drawings of Louveciennes in 1784, refers to the architect speaking 'most rapturously in praise of their still lovely and once all powerful proprietress, the charming Comtesse Du Barri'.

The countess, however limited her interest in politics may have been, was inevitably a source of enormous power at court and the focus of many intrigues, as the various memoirs attributed to her indicate. Even the most respectable of these may be all or in part by another hand, but its author nevertheless knew her well and understood her tastes. Supported by Richelieu and Soubise and opposed by Choiseul and his sister, she formed an alliance with Maupeou, the Chancellor, and with the Abbé Terray, the Contrôleur des Finances and Marigny's successor as director of the Bâtiments du Roi. Anxious to maintain his own power, Terray was apparently the source of the unlimited money that was forthcoming for Mme du Barry's patronage of the arts, and, according to Ledoux himself, he had promised to procure the *cordon noir* for the architect.

The new royal mistress, confronted as a commoner of the humblest birth with even greater antagonism than her predecessor, Mme de Pompadour, had inspired, seems positively to have welcomed the most recent artistic developments of Paris as a means of self-assertion, and one that was no doubt pleasing enough for her lover, the old king. Apparently she had little time for the 'philosophes', though she admired Voltaire and Rousseau, while the painters she preferred were Vernet, Greuze and Drouais, whose portrait of her *en déshabillé* shocked the more

229 Portrait of Mme du Barry as a Muse, by François-Hubert Drouais (Chambre de Commerce, Versailles). Drouais' portrait of Ledoux's patroness, the last mistress of Louis XV, shocked public opinion at the 1771 Salon and was later altered

praise of the architect, because it proves that he understands the importance of the choice of artist and the need to inspire them with his ideas.

After the house of Mlle Guimard Ledoux created many further houses in the capital, for a great variety of clients and speculators, becoming one of the most prolific architects in the city. The house of M. Tabary, apparently the earliest of these, was Palladian in the treatment of its gateway, and the first of four houses by Ledoux that appeared on the rue du Faubourg-Poissonnière, where Trouard had earlier worked *(159)*. Most of Ledoux's town houses were on the approximate lines of the Hôtels de Montmorency and Guimard, roughly square in plan and set within a small garden or raised above the street, and varied in the treatment of the frontispieces and the method of access. Other houses Ledoux constructed further to the west, where he had earlier worked for Président Hocquart, and where he built the most ambitious of all his houses, carried out in the later 1770s for Mme de Thélusson.

The house of Mlle Guimard was rivalled in fame not by any of Ledoux's smaller town houses, but by the country pavilion that he constructed at approximately the same time for Mme du Barry in her park just outside Paris at Louveciennes *(230, 231)*. Despite the differences in setting

respectable visitors to the Salon of 1771 *(229)*. For her pavilion Mme du Barry also employed Fragonard who produced the famous series of canvases (now in the Frick Collection) of 'Le progrès de l'amour'; for reasons unknown these were never installed but replaced by classicizing paintings by Vien. Even before Mme du Barry's alliance with the king began her taste for novelty had been remarked, especially a carriage 'à la grecque' which she owned. 'Her toilette', according to the Créquy *Souvenirs*, 'was outside fashion, pretending to lead or to advance it, which is always a sign of bad taste. We shall find her twenty-four years later at Saint-Pélagie, the unfortunate woman, and you will see that her toilettes in prison were scarcely less *recherchées* than her toilettes at court.'

There is apparently no record of how or when Ledoux first made the acquaintance of Mme du Barry. Possibly it was through the Princesse de Montmorency or through Mlle Guimard and her lovers, though even if Mme du Barry admired the Hôtel Guimard she seems to have disapproved of the character of its owner. The pavilion at Louveciennes must have been largely built by September 1771, when the *Mémoires secrets* reported that Ledoux had been rewarded with the posts of 'Commissaire du Roi' and inspector of saltworks in Franche-Comté (with an income of 8,000 *livres*) as a reward for the speedy completion of the building. But the interior may not have been finished until two years later, when the king, according to Ledoux himself, paid his first visit there and spoke in person to the architect.

Like Gabriel's Petit Trianon *(46)*, begun little more than ten years previously for Mme de Pompadour, the pavilion of Louveciennes appears, at this distance in time, to have that apparent directness and simplicity that marks the well-bred courtier, but whereas Gabriel's house is a perfected version of a traditional villa, decorated with an order and set formally upon a rusticated base, Ledoux's pavilion implies a fundamentally different attitude of mind, based upon a new intimacy between man and nature. The building was not intended to be lived in but as a house for entertaining, and the first room after the curved peristyle, in almost medieval fashion, was the dining-room. The salon beyond, marked by an order of unfluted Ionic columns, afforded a view of the terrace behind the pavilion and of the countryside to the north of the Seine, while doors at the sides of the house gave access to the garden. Two temples in the garden, considered to be the earliest circular pavilions in France, have been claimed as the work of Ledoux, but it is rather in the treatment of the pavilion itself that the architect's sensitivity to the aesthetic potentialities of the setting was more subtly expressed.

The pavilion is small in relation to its site, a formal building which rises directly from the garden and is of only one main storey. The density of the design was achieved at some cost to the service rooms in the basement, lit only from small apertures on the garden side and notorious for their unhealthy conditions. The front of the building with its deeply curved portico is more sculptural than that of

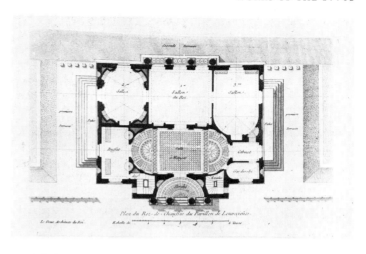

230 The pavilion of the Château of Louveciennes, plan and elevation, engraving from Ledoux. The famous pavilion built by Ledoux for Mme du Barry was largely completed by 1771

231 The pavilion of the Château of Louveciennes, the front façade. The house is now altered and largely remodelled

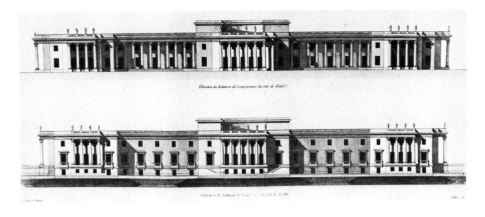

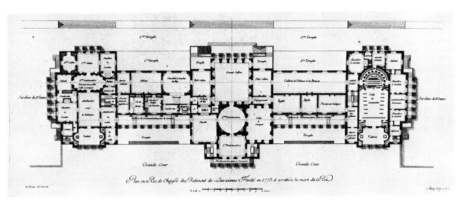

232 Project for the Château of Louveciennes, elevations and plan, engravings from Ledoux. The reconstruction of the château was halted by the death of Louis XV in 1774

Gabriel's Petit Trianon and relies, especially as engraved by Ledoux, upon the shadows made by the passage of the sun on the façade. The use of light and shade, unfashionable as it was to become, harmonizes in this work of Ledoux with the emphasis given by the architect to the natural advantages of the site.

The château that Ledoux began to construct at Louveciennes in 1773 extended the principles of the pavilion to a more conventional building type (232). Since all the main rooms were on the ground floor, the building would have covered an unusually wide area. Loosely symmetrical and densely organized, the plan has a sequence of rooms on the central axis like that of the Hôtel de Montmorency, with a rectangular antechamber, a top-lit circular second antechamber, and a rectangular salon. The right wing was to contain a large theatre with a bell-shaped colonnaded auditorium, and the left wing private apartments and bedrooms for the king and his mistress.

The plain walls of the exterior are juxtaposed with recessed or projecting colonnades, forming frontispieces without pediments, and only the end pavilions, recalling the design of the Hôtel de Montmorency (221), seem recognizably French in origin. For all its formality and its occasional echoes of town mansions, the building is accessible on the garden side for the whole of its considerable extent directly from the park, where it appears as a series of temples projecting and receding with

the wall. This effect is emphasized in Ledoux's engravings which omit altogether the roofing that appears in his drawings of the design.

Mme du Barry's Paris house was designed for a large site, leased from the banker Jean-Joseph de Laborde, on the rue d'Artois, a turning from the northern boulevard a little to the east of the rue de la Chaussée-d'Antin (233). The design was a variant of the Château of Louveciennes, organized around a large central court, but the use of the order would here have been even more pronounced, especially in the entrance passage with its sixteen pairs of free-standing columns, and inside the court, which remained plain in articulation except for an unusually long frontispiece of sixteen further columns, masking the whole of the front of the hôtel. Within the limits of the city such a plan would indeed have marked its creator, after Peyre, as the most radical and imaginative classicist of the time.

Of the town house of Mme du Barry and the Château of Louveciennes almost nothing was built, and the pavilion at Louveciennes is no more than a poor reconstruction, though usefully complementing the setting. The only building created for Mme du Barry by Ledoux that still gives some impression of the force of his style is the now much darkened stables which he built in the avenue de Paris at Versailles (234). The huge frontispiece, dominating the avenue as it emerges into the open in front of the château, is the last in the great tradition of giant arched

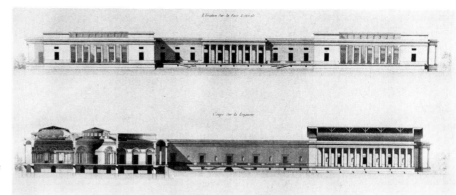

233 Project for the Hôtel du Barry, rue d'Artois, Paris, side elevation, long section and plan, engravings from Ledoux. Ledoux's design for Mme du Barry's Paris house on the road to the east of the rue de la Chaussée-d'Antin is distinguished by its extensive use of colonnades

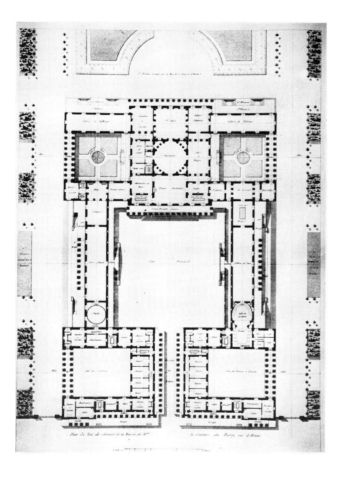

openings that had flourished in France since the sixteenth century. The design is that of the doorway of the Hôtel d'Hallwyl *(205)* transposed to a much larger scale and into an independent composition. Here the cornice is allowed to break backwards over the columns and the composition is a shade more Venetian in appearance. The lower cornice is diminished in relation to the upper one, with its decoration of metopes and triglyphs circumscribing the whole building. In this instance the design may have been carried out more simply than Ledoux intended; in his engravings the building is enriched with continuous rustication and a pattern of dropped keystones like those of the Hôtel d'Hallwyl.

234 The stables of Mme du Barry, avenue de Paris, Versailles, the main doorway. The doorway of the stables, which passed to the Comte de Provence after the death of Louis XV, is a large-scale variant of the door of the Hôtel d'Hallwyl *(205)*

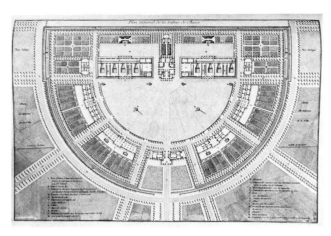

235 The saltworks of Arc and Senans, near Besançon, plan, engraving from Ledoux. Ledoux's famous salt factory, approved in 1773 and built in 1775–79, is semicircular in plan, with the house of the director and the salt-extracting buildings on the straight side

VUE DE LA CHAUDIERE

236 Salt-extracting in the factory of Lons-le-Saunier, near Besançon (engraving by Née after Lallemand, from La Borde). The salty spring-water, found largely in eastern France (the Pays des Salines), was evaporated by heating to extract the salt

In the years when he was employed by Mme du Barry Ledoux built little for other patrons outside Paris, though he apparently continued to work for Le Normand de Mézières, the owner of the Hôtel de Montmorency site. It is usually supposed that he was engaged by Le Normand on the development of the village of Eaubonne near Montmorency, and it would indeed be appropriate had he been active there in the years following the departure of Rousseau from the 'Hermitage' that the Duc and Duchesse de Luxembourg had provided for Rousseau on their estate. But Ledoux says nothing of such work in the list of his own early commissions, and the buildings themselves seem unworthy of him.

The so-called 'Petit Château', built a few years later at Eaubonne, is a better authenticated work, and one of symbolic importance in being constructed for the poet St-Lambert, the author of 'Les Saisons' and Rousseau's rival in the affections of Mme d'Houdetot. Uninspired though it is generally held to be, the work of St-Lambert is not without relevance to the architectural style of Ledoux, the influence of the classical pastoral poetry of Horace and Virgil inspiring, in the case of the poet, an intenser appreciation of nature, as St-Lambert himself explained:

In the centuries of discussion and reason . . . when the pleasures of luxury were reduced to their just value, the virtue of country life was felt to advantage; what was owed to agriculture was better known; its occupations were honoured; the peace, the innocence which accompanied them were regretted. Sybarites, bored with their vices and their intrigues, enjoyed seeing the simple man, without artifice, discovering his manner of feeling and thinking.

It was not, however, with St-Lambert that Ledoux formed a personal friendship, but with the more talented Abbé Delille, who was later to flatter the architect in his poems 'Les Jardins' and 'L'Imagination'.

The particular genius of Ledoux for architectural metaphor, employed up till now largely on behalf of private clients, was one that promised much in the public domain. Thanks to the influence of Mme du Barry Ledoux

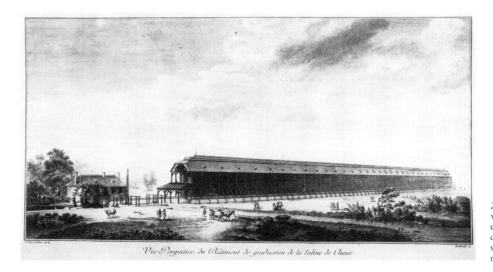

Vue Perspective du Bâtiment de graduation de la Saline de Chaux.

237 The saltworks of Arc and Senans, view of the 'bâtiment de graduation', engraving from Ledoux. A spring was conducted from Salins to Ledoux's saltworks, and the water content was reduced in the 'bâtiment de graduation'

238 The saltworks of Arc and Senans, the main entrance. The production of salt was a monopoly of the Ferme Générale, which severely punished illicit extraction – hence the severity of Ledoux's design, with its heavy baseless Tuscan columns

had been appointed inspector of saltworks in Franche-Comté and chosen in 1773 for the Academy, becoming 'Architecte du Roi'. The first of his major public buildings is the famous saltworks that he constructed between the villages of Arc and Senans, near the forest of Chaux, not far from Besançon *(235–242)*. This is the project that also formed the nucleus of the ideal town, engraved in the first volume of Ledoux's *Architecture*, and confused in date by the architect and by his early biographers with the saltworks. Clearly the factory, however ambitious in design, could not have supported all the other structures that Ledoux planned for its environs, and the town itself must also be an 'improvement', indeed the most ambitious one of all, that the architect later imposed upon his executed work. But quite apart from the ideal town which Ledoux designed to accompany them, the saltworks are in themselves a remarkable achievement.

Most of the salt produced in eighteenth-century France came from the springs of Franche-Comté in the north east of the country (the Pays des Salines). The saltworks in the area were the responsibility of the Ponts et Chaussées, under the Trudaines (father and son), and the post of inspector of saltworks had belonged nominally to Perronet before it fell to Ledoux as a result of the influence of Mme du Barry. The distribution of salt, however, was a monopoly of the tax farmers, under the control of a subcommittee of the Ferme Générale, with Lavoisier as a member, which levied the tax known as the *gabelle*.

Ledoux's factory was one of several such buildings in Franche-Comté, utilitarian buildings now destroyed that are largely unrecorded on paper. The common method of producing salt at the time was by heating saline spring water in vats until the water evaporated leaving its precious deposit of salt – a seemingly infernal process that is recorded in an engraving of the factory at Lons-le-Saunier *(236)*. If a spring ran low in salt a means had been devised to reduce the water content before it reached the factory in a long building known as a 'bâtiment de graduation' *(237)*, but a plentiful supply of wood to heat the water was

239 The saltworks of Arc and Senans, the interior of the portico. The rusticated archway contains a grotto of natural rock

240 The saltworks of Arc and Senans, details of decoration. The windows of the entrance portico are framed as urns spilling forth petrified water, and the entrance grotto *(239)* has imitation springs to each side

always essential. Ledoux's saltworks were designed to replace those at Salins, where the neighbouring woods had become depleted. A new site was chosen near the forest of Chaux, sufficiently open for a 'bâtiment de graduation' to be constructed, and the spring water was diverted through a wooden conduit from its source at Salins.

Ledoux's project for the new works, which had won the approval of Trudaine de Montigny, was agreed by the king in 1773. The buildings were begun in 1775 and finished four years later. The funds for the construction were provided by a speculator who was in return to have a monopoly of the profits for twenty-four years, but

unfortunately the salt content in the spring declined and more economical methods of extracting salt were meanwhile discovered. Ledoux's first idea was apparently to arrange the buildings around an open square courtyard, with lawns and gardens on the outside, enclosed by a wall. This may have been the customary plan of such works, though Ledoux says in his book that they were built 'au hazard'.

The plan as built *(235)* is more modest in scale and semicircular, with the buildings for each different process separated from the others, but still protected by an enclosing wall *(238)*. The forest of Chaux lies to the north, while the 'bâtiment de graduation' and a reservoir were constructed on the opposite bank of the river Loue to the south east. Inside the walls of the saltworks the house of the director *(242)* lies on the diameter of the plan with the buildings for the evaporation of the water to each side. The circumference is occupied by the storage halls, with the main entrance in the centre, directly below the house of the director. A sovereign state in miniature, the factory recalls the plans of palace buildings, remotely resembling the forecourt of Versailles and more closely the palace of Nymphenburg at Munich. But Ledoux himself referred to the plan not in traditional terms, but as a form which is 'pure like that which the sun describes in its course'.

Now that salt can be bought for little at any tobacconist in France it might seem that Ledoux in designing a factory so expressive of austere primitive strength had been led astray by irrational dreams of a lost classical world. Though he was undoubtedly an extravagant architect, influenced, perhaps to a greater degree than any of his contemporaries, by the emotional resonance of antique architecture and its relation to nature, he nevertheless remained even here supremely rational in the control of his imagination. The salt trade was amongst the grimmest aspects of life in eighteenth-century France, the forcible imposition of the *gabelle* giving rise to widespread

241 The saltworks of Arc and Senans, one of the salt-extracting buildings. The architecture recalls French and Italian buildings of the sixteenth century

242 The saltworks of Arc and Senans, the house of the director. The remoteness of the site and the authority of the director of the factory are emphasized by the heavy banded columns

smuggling and robbery, and illicit distillation was punishable by death or the galleys. The security of the saltworks was essential, as was the role of the director who had jurisdiction even beyond the walls of his small kingdom, and this is underlined by Ledoux in his design.

The entrance wing, containing guard rooms and a small prison, is marked by a dense peristyle of six baseless Tuscan columns with a squat attic above destined for an inscription *(238)*. Though this was not the first time that baseless columns had made their appearance in France, they are employed here more conspicuously, and indeed more purposefully, than in the more domestic contexts where they had been seen hitherto. The function of the building is more precisely underlined by the urns that punctuate the walls to each side of the portico *(240)*. They resemble the urns designed for the garden of the Hôtel d'Hallwyl *(209)*, but appear here in a more imaginative context, acting as portholes for the guard rooms, and suggesting not merely the flow of water, but water congealed by the density of salt it would contain. For Ledoux they enhanced the sculptural effect of the building: 'What are those overturned urns which appear before my eyes? these torrents of water that congeal . . . to prolong the shadows that the sun casts at the will of art.'

The metaphor of the urns is developed further inside the portico where a low rusticated arch is disrupted by a cavern of natural rock with sculpted springs to each side bubbling forth their water (239, 240). The grotto is not discordant within the context of the classical architecture that encloses it, although its ancestry in art is much more recent, an example of the beneficial persistence – by means of garden architecture – of Bernini's influence in the later eighteenth century.

The buildings within the courtyard (241, 242), the evaporation halls, the offices of the clerks, and the warehouses, are marginally less aggressive than the portico. The variety of patterns employed in their façades is greater than in any earlier work of Ledoux's and greater than was customary in French architecture after the start of the seventeenth century. The elevations recall the early Renaissance in France and its sources in northern Italy, in the work of Serlio and even Giulio Romano. Though Ledoux may have imitated the ideas of such architects, and some precise quotations have been noticed, his purpose was clearly the conscious one of expressing thereby the unusual character of the buildings of the saltworks, and the same is true of the principal building of the ensemble, the house of the director (242). This too is treated more as a public building than as a country villa, with its temple portico of giant banded Tuscan columns. Banded columns, which Ledoux also used in his later designs for some of the Paris toll-houses, are a rare sight in France though common in Italy in sixteenth-century buildings. At the saltworks they clearly enhance the strength and authority of the director, while the presence of the pediment within a precinct such as this seems expressive of a degree, at least, of civilized administration.

The middle years of the 1770s, while the saltworks were under construction, marked one of the most physically active periods of Ledoux's career, with the promise of important commissions awaiting him in Paris, in the provinces and in Germany. In the year 1775 he was commissioned to build the theatre of Besançon and later travelled to Kassel, while in the following year there occurred the first of his visits to Aix-en-Provence in connection with the rebuilding of the local Parlement and the prison, and the start of work on the most ambitious of all his Paris town houses, the Hôtel de Thélusson.

Ledoux's host at Kassel was the Landgrave, Frederick of Hesse-Kassel, who was a brother-in-law of the Prince de Soubise. One of the many francophile princes of eighteenth-century Germany, he had the discrimination to summon first Ledoux and later de Wailly to work at Kassel. Ledoux's visit is recorded in two amusing letters written by the court architect, Simon-Louis du Ry, to his sister in December 1775 and in February of the following year. According to du Ry the Landgrave had become acquainted with Ledoux in the previous summer in Paris, where he had admired the house of Mlle Guimard (a house well known to his French brother-in-law). Du Ry had been a contemporary of Ledoux at the school of Blondel and he received from Ledoux the latest news of the friends they had both made there. Du Ry was shown projects for the saltworks, which, he said, Ledoux had designed with four possible sites in mind. In du Ry's opinion Ledoux was

very sensible, according to the views he expresses, a man of honour, who offends no one . . . He is an architect of great vision who speaks of an outlay of 3 or 4 million Thalers as we would of 3 or 4 thousand; he also expresses himself very well and the Landgrave likes him very much and at Court he is admitted to the degree of Marshal and allowed to attend the concerts and finally so fêted that all the Nobility are beside themselves.

At Kassel Ledoux was consulted about the design of a triumphal arch, and at the same time, presumably, he conceived the projects for a library and a town palace for the Landgrave that are also engraved in the second edition of the Architecture (243). But he left Kassel in disgrace, dissatisfied with his fee and maintaining that he could earn as much as 48,000 livres a year in Paris. Du Ry was impressed by the elegance of his travelling carriage and by the well-dressed appearance of his servant, but the architect himself he described as stingy, borrowing clothes and appearing in the morning in a 'coat with both elbows . . . so worn through that you could have put your fist through'. The picture is not the same as that suggested by Beckford eight years later.

In his architectural projects at Kassel Ledoux proposed more extravagant buildings than were required. Du Ry was daunted by the cost and the size of the triumphal arch, which he assured his sister would not be carried out. To du Ry the arch resembled the Porte St-Denis, but it was really an extended reworking of the gate of the Hôtel d'Uzès. The library comprised a building decorated with an Ionic order of columns, with alternating closed and open bays across the façade. Over the portico Ledoux designed a circular Corinthian temple, perhaps an observatory, and he provided a staircase modelled upon that of Bénouville for access to the upper floors of the building. The project that seems the most bizarre in character, at least in the design supplied by Ledoux to the engraver, is the palace (243), a project that appears the closest of all his works to the inflated

243 Project for the palace of Kassel, Germany, elevation, engraving from Ledoux. Ledoux travelled to Kassel in 1775, where he designed a triumphal arch, a library and a palace for the reigning Landgrave, none of which were carried out

manner of Boullée, with its colossal Corinthian order, its huge sculptured pediment over a completely plain entablature and its even rows of Serlian windows visible in the shadows of the portico. If the Landgrave had expected anything like the house of Mlle Guimard, he had seriously miscalculated the mind of his architect, and Ledoux too seems to have misread the character of the Landgrave, who was evidently not the tyrant who might be expected to inhabit such a palace, but a notably cultivated and enlightened ruler.

Ledoux had greater success in Besançon, where his protector was the Intendant, La Coré, for whom Louis had already worked. The architect must have become a familiar figure in the neighbourhood of Besançon during the early stages of the building of the saltworks, and he sent his project for the theatre and a short letter explaining his intentions to La Coré in August 1775. After a delay of two years a royal subsidy of just over 80,000 *livres* became available for the construction, a local architect, C.-J.-A. Bertrand, was put in charge of the work and the theatre opened in August 1784 *(244–246)*. The inauguration of the building was announced in the *Mercure de France* and likewise in the *Mémoires secrets* 'to the designs of the famous Le Doux, whose name alone means its praise'. The modesty of the budget (about twice the sum originally agreed) was duly stressed as well as the new type of plan that Ledoux had devised. And in Besançon itself the building was a source of great civic pride, La Coré's successor as Intendant, M. de Caumartin, regarding the theatre 'despite the criticism of some detractors' as 'the finest building in the province'.

By 1775, when the designs were made, Gabriel's Opéra was already well known and Peyre and de Wailly, as well as Louis, had established their respective projects for Paris and Bordeaux. But Ledoux's theatre, closely resembling the design he had made for the Château of Louveciennes, owes little to its immediate precursors. What was most remarkable in his project, partly no doubt for reasons of economy but also in accordance with the architect's own wishes and with the acquiescence of the Intendant, is the virtual absence of boxes. In this respect his was the theatre that approximated most closely to a classical amphitheatre – the form that Gondoin had recently revived at the Ecole de Chirurgie *(180)* – and which also anticipated the more egalitarian seating arrangements that became *de rigueur* after the Revolution. As in an amphitheatre, the plan too was semicircular for most of its extent, but it fanned out at each side of the orchestra in the shape of a bell.

Like Palladio's Vicenza theatre and the Opéra of Gabriel a row of free-standing columns appeared above the rows of seats at gallery level, columns of the Greek Doric order that the architect used to support the ceiling of the auditorium *(245)*. The baseless Doric was not an order otherwise frequently encountered in the upper registers of any building, and in the Besançon theatre it clearly emphasized the primitive ancestry of the design, matching the character of the very architectural proscenium – decorated in the spandrels with reliefs of charioteers – which resembled a sunken triumphal arch.

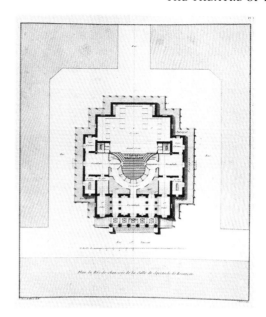

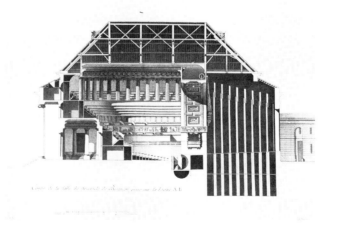

244 The theatre of Besançon, plan and sections, engravings from Ledoux. The small theatre designed by Ledoux for Besançon in 1775 recalls classical amphitheatres in the absence of tiers of boxes

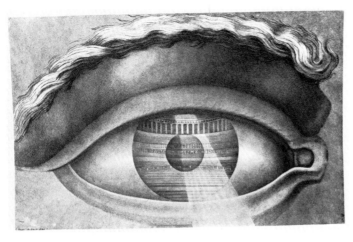

245 The interior of the Besançon theatre reflected in the pupil of an eye, engraving from Ledoux. A view of the interior probably inspired by the architect's mystical and masonic ideas

246 The theatre of Besançon, the front façade. The economically designed façade recalls Ledoux's engraving of Bénouville (216); the interior is now greatly altered

Such a proscenium may have seemed to the audience suitable only for the more austere dramas of the French classical theatre, and Arthur Young for one, passing through Besançon on the eve of the Revolution in a mood of depression, found 'the arch that parts the stage front the house . . . like the entrance of a cavern, and the line of the amphitheatre that of a wounded eel'. Yet however spartan the theatre may have looked, the architect was also conscious of the physical comfort of the audience. As he stressed to La Coré, he was anxious (like Peyre and de Wailly) that the spectators in the stalls should have seats provided, and he too carefully considered the problem of access to the auditorium. Being one of the smaller theatres of the time, the interior could be approached from vestibules to the sides of the auditorium, adjacent to staircases that lead at right angles from the main vestibule.

The exterior, which is the only part of the theatre that survives as Ledoux intended, was contrived with the greatest economy (246). The plain wall surfaces and unframed windows are relieved only by the projections and recessions that the plan imposes. In Ledoux's engravings a full entablature is shown on all sides of the building, projecting forwards over the six Ionic columns that form the simple portico of the theatre. As the theatre was built only the upper mouldings of the entablature continue around the building and the junction of portico and wall is all the more frankly exposed, without the transitional ornaments that even Gondoin had employed at the Ecole de Chirurgie (179).

Ledoux himself appears to have been well pleased with his theatre, later describing it as 'a Republican Theatre built during the Despotism'. He provided engravings of the building to accompany the illustrations of the ideal town that formed the first volume of the *Architecture* and produced a larger variant of the same design when he was asked in 1785 for projects for the theatre of Marseille. In the *Architecture* he illustrated an arresting plate (245) showing the interior of the theatre reflected in the eye of a beholder, possibly the architect himself or his Maker, and illuminated by a ray of light from the brain. By the end of his life Ledoux had developed a decidedly moral, if unchristian, attitude towards the theatre:

It must not be forgotten that theatrical performances, for the ancients, formed part of religion. It was there that the favour of the gods was earned, it was there that their anger was appeased. If our theatres are not part of religious cult, it is at least to be desired that their organization ensures the purity of [our] morals; it is easier to correct man through the attraction of pleasure than by religious ceremonies, practices accredited by superstition.

Designed shortly after the Besançon theatre and built in the same years was the most remarkable of Ledoux's town houses, a building that overtook in fame the Hôtel Guimard. This was the Hôtel de Thélusson (247, 248, 250) which stood formerly in the rue de Provence, at the end of the rue d'Artois, where the house of Mme du Barry was destined to be built. The patron was Mme de Thélusson, who had inherited in 1776, at the age of forty, a fortune upon the death of her husband, Georges-Tobie, the head of the banking firm of Thélusson and Necker. According to

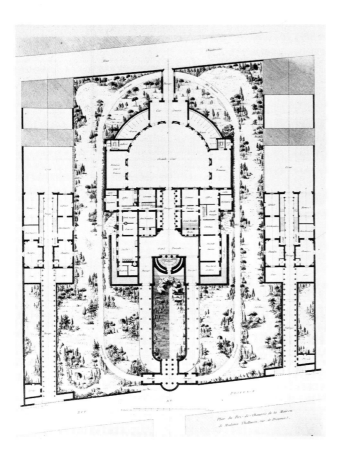

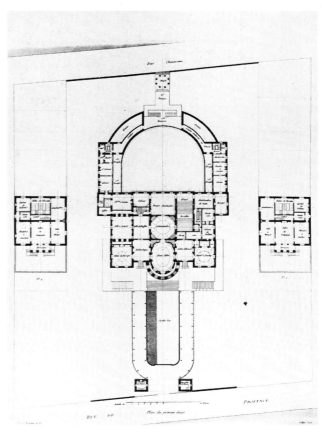

247 The Hôtel de Thélusson, rue de Provence, Paris, plans and section, engravings from Ledoux. Built by Ledoux in the late 1770s near the rue de la Chaussée-d'Antin for a Swiss banker's widow; the large central and the two smaller houses at the sides (for the widow's sons) were closely integrated in their landscape setting

the Créquy *Souvenirs* Mme de Thélusson was 'a little mad', and 'in a state of continual fright and mental anxiety about bad air and skin diseases'. This indeed seems to have been the indirect cause of her death, for she was one of the relatively few casualties of the widespread mania of the time for inoculation against smallpox. She died in 1781 before her house was entirely finished, leaving her sons to complete the building, which they then leased three years later to a new occupant.

The social prestige that attached to the possession of such a house, not because of its expense alone, but also, by this date, on the grounds of its originality, is suggested in the Créquy *Souvenirs* in a perhaps apocryphal story inspired by the author's hatred of the Neckers. Necker, who had succeeded Turgot in 1776, and his wife conceived the idea of building a hospital for scrofulous

diseases beside the house 'of which the magnificence and originality eclipsed them all the more because every one was talking of it and . . . you were naturally led on from the Hôtel to the proprietor and from the old woman to the former clerk [Necker] of her husband, who was excluded from her beautiful salon'. In this story Mme de Thélusson was finally forced to buy the land destined for the hospital and add it to her own property.

The kind of building that the patron required was apparently 'a house, convenient and pretty, half urban, half rustic, but rather with the air of a retreat than the appearance of a rich hôtel'. Ledoux is said to have been recommended to her by a friend, a M. Haudry de Soucy, but Mme de Thélusson must also have known Ledoux as a native of Dormans, where her family held estates, and as the designer of the Hôtel d'Hallwyl, created some ten years

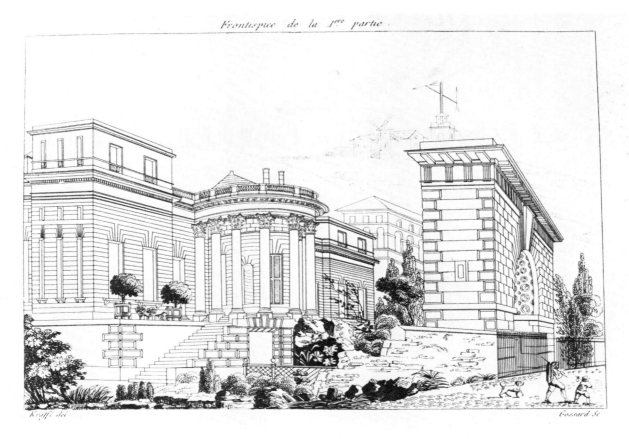

Frontispice de la 1ère partie.

248 The Hôtel de Thélusson, perspective view of gateway and salon (engraving from Krafft, 1838). Carriages drove through the gateway and the garden to a passage beneath the salon leading to the stable court at the rear

previously on former premises of her father-in-law; Ledoux may also have been brought to her notice as an architect involved in the speculations of the banker Laborde in the rue de Provence.

The site occupied a large plot of land that extended from the rue des Postes, or rue Chantereine, at the north and the rue de Provence at the south, and the architect constructed in addition to the main hôtel, two smaller houses at the sides, probably destined for two of the three sons of the owner *(247)*. The three houses shared an informal garden laid out as a park and planted with groups of trees in the fashion of an 'English' garden, of which several examples had been laid out in Paris itself by the late 1770s. What was new, however, in Ledoux's design, given the scale and the relatively central position of the site, was the close juxtaposition between the buildings and the garden into which the houses seemed indeed to intrude. The idea, likely in any case to have been urged by Ledoux, cannot have been unconnected with the curious disposition of the owner and the nature of her apprehensions.

Ledoux admitted in the planning almost no distinction between the garden and the houses. He contrived that the main entrance led through the park to the south of the buildings and passed beneath the houses, instead of leading directly into the courtyard from the street at the

north, which would have been the normal method of access. The main house was exceptionally dense in plan, five rooms across and three deep, with a square and an octagonal antechamber on the central axis leading to a deep oval salon in the centre of the south side, articulated on the exterior with a semicircle of Corinthian columns. As at the Hôtel de Montmorency the vestibule was below the salon and a broad flight of steps, marked by columns, led upwards to the principal floor.

There were two carriageways leading to the house and between them Ledoux designed as part of his park setting a sunken garden with a mound of natural rock forming a base for the colonnaded façade of the salon *(248)*. The projecting salon, a traditional feature of a French domestic building, appeared as a result to reside, like an antique temple, upon a bed of natural rock in a landscape. Perhaps the Temple of Vesta at Tivoli, known in Piranesi's etchings *(249)* and from many other views, was the immediate source of Ledoux's idea, but at the Hôtel de Thélusson he created not an image on paper but a work of real stone and rock, part of a living landscape. The design embodies a considerable extension of the idea behind the grotto of the entrance wing of the saltworks *(239)* and, quite apart from its aesthetic impact, such a design, blending architecture and nature in overlapping layers,

249 The Temple of Vesta at Tivoli, etching by Piranesi, 1761, from the *Vedute di Roma*. With its columns set over a bed of rock, the Hôtel de Thélusson resembled a circular classical temple in a landscape

was extremely costly to carry out in the eighteenth century. Some famous structures embodying these ideas were later to appear in garden settings, but in domestic architecture they remained a speciality of the later eighteenth century confined largely to Ledoux and scarcely attempted again before the present century.

In the context of the house as a whole the famous gateway is less eccentric than it seemed to Ledoux's contemporaries or indeed has appeared to modern critics *(250)*. It was in the form of a monolithic Doric triumphal arch, its squat proportions emphasized by the treatment of the rustication, and it recalls the arches of antiquity half-buried by the earth and rubble which had accumulated for centuries at their bases *(79)*. The arch may indeed have been an extravagance upon the part of the architect, but it is in no way inconsistent with his treatment of the site. It was constructed over a grotto with passages leading into the garden and contained guard rooms and the main water tank for the house. A structure of great apparent strength, it marked the entrance to the central hôtel, serving in place of a wall to provide the necessary sense of security, while also forming a free-standing building within the context of the park. In Ledoux's engraving the garden extends into the rue de Provence where a shepherd delays the passage of a carriage. In essence the doorway sets off the elegance

of the main hôtel and is seen to derive, not inappropriately, from the same imaginative world.

There is little doubt that Ledoux, in pursuing his ideas, abused the confidence of Mme de Thélusson, as her lawyers later complained. Though he could, as at Besançon, keep within reasonable limits of expenditure, he appears, like other famous architects, to have found this increasingly irksome as his ideas grew bolder in conception. In 1781 the *Mémoires secrets* recorded that Ledoux had no head for reconciling the ideas and the financial resources of his patrons; it was also alleged that Mme de Thélusson had wished to spend 400,000 *livres*, but that the house had already cost two million (just less than the cost of the Bordeaux theatre).

The house was by then a famous building and one much criticized for breaking the rules of *convenance*: 'For a long time a bizarre house has been spoken of, erected in the form of a temple or a palace at the end of the rue d'Artois . . . He [Ledoux] has built a hôtel that requires the presence of a prince.' Mme d'Oberkirch gave the evidently very exaggerated sum of seven million *livres* as the total cost, and added that 'It was one of the greatest attractions of Paris', requiring the issue of tickets to procure admission. She went on to criticize 'The arcade which looked upon the street' (presumably the main doorway), which she alleged 'spoilt the perspective and was universally condemned'. The actress Sophie Arnould described the doorway as a 'giant mouth open to say nothing', and Landon later compared the house unaccountably to a Bastille. Ledoux's intentions seem to have gone largely unappreciated, though no one was left unmoved by the building. Its demolition in 1824 for the piercing of the rue Laffitte was certainly one of the worst of the many tragedies in the history of the development of Paris; a small part remained standing as late as 1929, but a pair of doors are the only souvenir that now remains of the palace of Mme de Thélusson.

250 The Hôtel de Thélusson, the main gateway, engraving from Ledoux. The gateway, serving also as a garden structure and a watertank, resembled a half-buried classical triumphal arch *(79)*

12 The later works: the barrières of Paris; projects for Aix; the ideal town of Chaux

AFTER THE RETIREMENT OF GABRIEL in 1775 and the death of Soufflot five years later, Ledoux, his reputation established by the buildings he had constructed in the previous decade, was unquestionably the reigning genius amongst the architects of his age, even if the public honours that Soufflot and Gabriel had enjoyed were never offered to him. Beginning with the Landgrave of Kassel, most visiting rulers to Paris had been taken to see his buildings, especially the house of Mlle Guimard. The Emperor Joseph II, travelling incognito in France as the Comte de Falkenstein, was shown his work and likewise the Tsarevitch Paul, the son of Catherine the Great, who was in Paris under the name of 'Comte du Nord' in 1782. Paul even visited Ledoux at his house and agreed to accept the dedication of the book that Ledoux was then apparently preparing or considering; the architect later sent to Russia two volumes of his drawings – presumably duplicates or sheets that he had already recorded in engravings – which have now disappeared.

During the 1780s Ledoux began his rewarding but unpopular works on behalf of the Ferme Générale. It was probably through his saltworks project, requiring mediation between the office of Contrôleur-Général des Finances and the tax farmers, that this opening was offered to him, though nothing definite is known of his relations at this date with Turgot or Necker, whose first term as Directeur des Finances lasted from 1776 to 1781. Ledoux's protectors in the finance department were Trudaine de Montigny, who died in 1777, and in the 1780s Calonne. It was, however, following the reforms of Turgot and Necker that several of Ledoux's projects came into existence. The foundation of a national savings bank, the Caisse d'Escompte, the precursor of the Banque de France, had been one of the last of Turgot's proposals before his dismissal, and a design for the bank was created by Ledoux apparently in 1778. The architect was then engaged in the construction of the Hôtel de Thélusson, which would not have recommended his work to Necker, if the Créquy *Souvenirs* are to be believed, but Ledoux was soon able to show his ability in the new role of fiscal architect.

The Ferme Générale was reorganized by Necker when the time came, in 1780, for the renewal of its six-year lease. The number of tax farmers was reduced to forty and their profits were for the first time to be shared with the state. This new measure inevitably involved the enlargement of the staff and administration, and the new buildings designed and started by Ledoux for the offices of the Ferme must have been a direct result of Necker's initiative *(251)*.

The main departments of the Ferme, dealing with general administration, customs, the tobacco monopoly and the salt tax, were housed separately in old buildings in different parts of the capital. There had been earlier projects to centralize their premises, and Soufflot, as Contrôleur des Bâtiments du Roi in Paris, had made designs for their accommodation in the buildings of the Bibliothèque Royale in the rue de Richelieu when the library itself was due to be moved to the Louvre. Ledoux's project involved the development of the site of the old Hôtel Séguier, near the Halle au Blé, which had belonged to the Ferme since the late seventeenth century. By 1787 one wing of his building had been constructed, and Thiéry mentioned its cornice and the masculine character of the block, which he judged 'will present an imposing mass'.

With its central spine running from side to side across the site and its three wings projecting at the back and front, Ledoux's building is perhaps one of the earliest designs that is recognizably an office-block. Its four courts and central staircase recall in plan the largest royal palaces of the earlier eighteenth century – Caserta, for example, or de Cotte's design for Madrid – but in this case the courtyards are not entirely enclosed but masked on one side by screening walls which leave the central core of the building open to the air and to a measure of public scrutiny.

The left half of the building was destined for the administrative offices of the Ferme and the right half, with its open passages and warehouses, for the traffic to be impounded or searched by the customs. The main offices of the Ferme were apparently on the ground floor of the left wing, accessible from a corridor flanking the court,

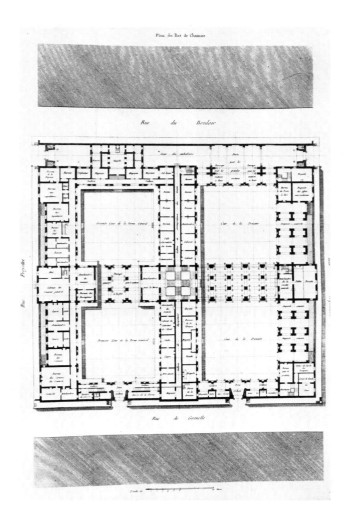

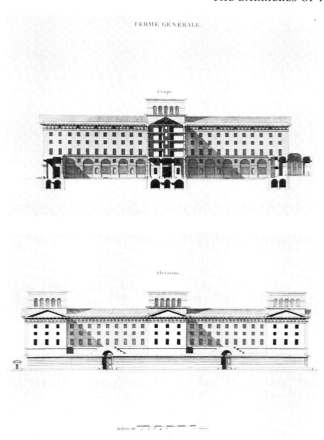

251 The Hôtel des Fermes, Paris, plan, section and elevation, engravings from Ledoux. After the 1780 reconstitution of the Ferme Générale (the Tax Farm) a new centralized office-block was started to Ledoux's designs

with the 'Cabinet du Receveur Général' in the central pavilion. Above the ground floor was a mezzanine and then four upper storeys, all of equal height, though differing in the sizes of their windows. A small chapel, shown on the right of Ledoux's section *(251)*, was centrally placed at the top of the second courtyard, with the salt department occupying the rooms to the right.

The staircase at the very centre of the plan, a large square chamber, which linked the customs with the administrative offices, was amongst the most ingenious of Ledoux's essays in a famous French tradition. Flights rising from opposite directions apparently met on a common landing and led at right angles to the corridors serving the main-floor offices, with further flights rising along the sides of the cage to the upper floors.

The functional character of the building is stressed in the treatment of the exterior, and, as in the design of the saltworks, there is more than a suggestion of a fortress in the unpierced wall of the ground floor and in the two heavy doorways marking the front entrances. The first of their kind in Ledoux's work, the doorways are based upon traditional patterns for rusticated doorways, but have no effective frames of their own. The presence of the doors is aggressively acknowledged by the rustication to each side of the arch, forming a stepped truncated triangle. The upper walls are articulated with the Doric cornice noted by Thiéry and with three curious squat towers which give to the building a suggestion of active surveillance. Functional in their design, the towers incorporate the form of the arcade, which here makes the first of its appearances in the later work of Ledoux.

The second of Ledoux's commissions for the Ferme was the building of the *barrières* of Paris, the most extensive and costly of all his projects, and one that involved him directly with Lavoisier in his role as tax farmer. After he had worked on the committee that supervised the salt tax, Lavoisier turned his attention to the customs regulations of the city of Paris, and to the revenue lost to the Ferme through smuggling, which had become widespread partly as a consequence of the expansion of the city during the later eighteenth century. Lavoisier proposed the construction of a new wall around the capital, an idea that was

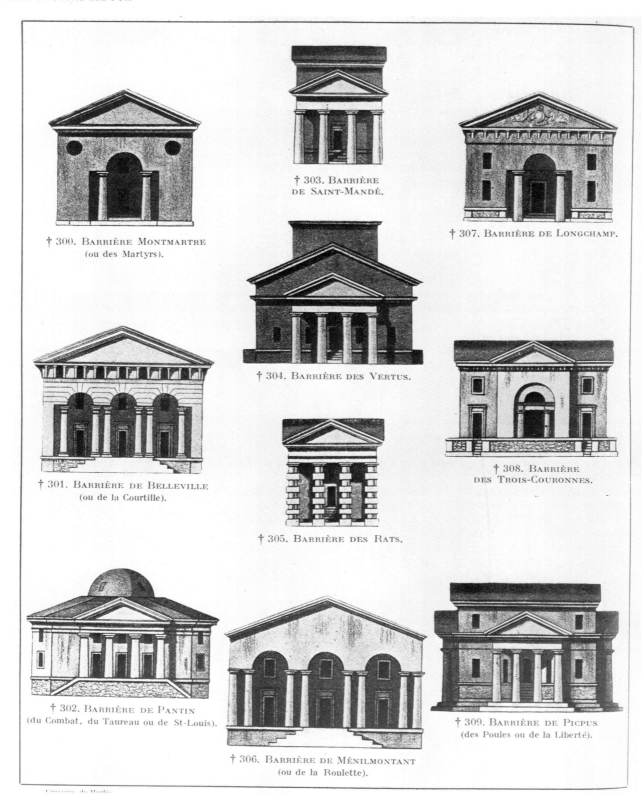

† 300. Barrière Montmartre
(ou des Martyrs).

† 303. Barrière
de Saint-Mandé.

† 307. Barrière de Longchamp.

† 301. Barrière de Belleville
(ou de la Courtille).

† 304. Barrière des Vertus.

† 308. Barrière
des Trois-Couronnes.

† 305. Barrière des Rats.

† 302. Barrière de Pantin
(du Combat, du Taureau ou de St-Louis).

† 306. Barrière de Ménilmontant
(ou de la Roulette).

† 309. Barrière de Picpus
(des Poules ou de la Liberté).

252 The Barrières of Paris, elevations of ten now destroyed customs posts (after Marlès). A new wall around the city of Paris with over fifty customs posts was proposed by the Ferme Générale in 1783 and carried out by Ledoux from 1784 to 1787

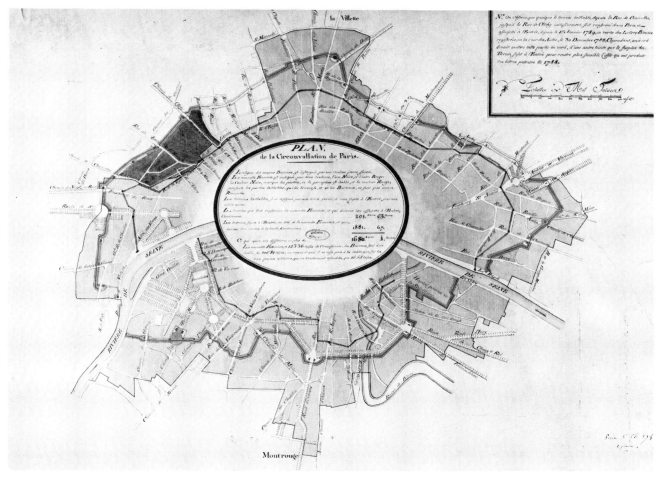

253 Plan of Paris showing the old and new walls of the Ferme Générale (Archives Nationales, Paris). The new (outer) wall caused consternation in Paris and Ledoux was dismissed because of the cost of the enterprise, though this was less than the revenue lost to the Ferme from smuggling

taken up by Calonne after his appointment as Contrôleur des Finances in 1783. The project was submitted in February of the following year to the Baron de Breteuil, recently appointed Secretary of State with responsibility for Paris. Breteuil consulted with Calonne and the municipal authorities, who asked Moreau-Desproux for a detailed report (Breteuil had not yet replaced Moreau with Poyet). The project finally received the approval of the king in January 1785, though work had already begun in the previous September, Ledoux having presumably considered and established his plans at the request of the Ferme and in consultation with Lavoisier, at least in the later months of 1783 and perhaps earlier.

The wall was to encircle the whole of the city on approximately the lines now marked by the outer boulevards, enclosing the new quarters that had grown up outside the earlier walls (253). From the Salpêtrière at the east the wall was to extend southwards and across to the west, embracing the southern outskirts of the city. It passed outside the Ecole Militaire and resumed on the north bank of the river at Chaillot. Continuing northwards from there it joined the Place de l'Etoile (Place de l'Arc-de-

Triomphe) and skirted the park of the Duc de Chartres at Monceau. It incorporated the new quarters of Roule, the Chaussée-d'Antin and Montmartre, and stretched across through Ménilmontant and Montreuil, turning down finally to the river beyond the Arsenal opposite its point of departure.

The wall was to be punctuated by a series of over fifty pavilions, guarding all the roads leading into the capital, single pavilions for the smaller roads and pairs of matching pavilions for the main thoroughfares. Ledoux also designed several inns, which remained unexecuted, in connection with the barrières, where those who arrived after the closing of the gates could spend the night. Inevitably in the 1780s the barrières caused consternation in Paris, as they might have done at any date, though the extent of their unpopularity was in its own way a measure of Ledoux's success. According to Beckford in 1784 Ledoux would be marked as 'the very prince of pomposity and ponderosity' for 'the whole string of custom-house palaces he has been erecting all around Paris, and which from their massive, sepulchral character look more like the entrances of a necropolis, a city of the dead, than of a city

254 The Barrière de l'Etoile, before demolition. One of a pair of customs posts near the present Arc-de-Triomphe, demolished in the 1860s, and recalling the director's house at Arc and Senans (242)

255 The Barrière des Bonshommes, before demolition. A single pavilion on the western perimeter, north of the Seine, modelled on the house of Mlle Guimard (226)

so damnably alive as this confounded capital'. Many were attacked at the outset of the Revolution, but the majority survived until the 1860s when they were officially suppressed. Several had meanwhile been recorded in photographs and four of them, two single pavilions and two double, have survived to the present day (256–260).

The commission could clearly have become a monotonous affair in the hands of any architect who had not the imaginative resources of Ledoux, but, like Wren before him in the design of the London city churches, Ledoux turned this opportunity into one of the most exciting of all his commissions. Indeed so varied and forceful are the *barrières* as a sequence of buildings that Ledoux is commonly believed to have imposed upon the Ferme the megalomania of his own fevered imagination. This, however, is very much an over-simplification, for there are

obvious practical reasons for the *barrières* to be widely varied in character, and both monolithic and deeply-sculpted in appearance (252).

Their fortress-like style is in keeping with the function they were to serve. As Thiéry noted in 1787, 'These entrance bureaux have a simple and masculine character which has seemed to us to correspond with the purpose for which they are destined.' And their varied shapes, easily visible at a distance, allowed them to function as landmarks, distinguishing the different entrances and exits of the capital from each other. (Visitors nowadays, trying to enter Paris from the outer motorway, would indeed be thankful if a similar system was still in operation.) It was Ledoux's intention to incorporate in the sculptural decoration of the *barrières* personifications of the main provincial towns that lay ahead of the traveller on his chosen road, but the architect was forced to economize and the sculpture remained for the most part unexecuted.

The question of antique precedent was also in the architect's mind in the design of his *barrières*, which he described as 'Propylées', in allusion to the Propylaea of Athens (79). None of the buildings greatly resembles the Propylaea, as reconstructed by Le Roy, but in guarding the entrances to Paris – enclosing the new quarters of the city and mediating between the capital and the roads and bridges leading to the other cities of the realm – Ledoux can scarcely be blamed if he claimed for the *barrières* an aesthetic and functional importance equivalent to that of their distinguished Athenian precursor.

The *barrières* are so different in character that it seems misguided to attempt to fit them into categories; they resemble temples and pavilions of all shapes, with decoration and rustication disproportionate in scale and derived from French and Italian art of the sixteenth century, and many are based upon patterns that had already made their appearance in earlier works of Ledoux. The *barrières* of the Place de l'Etoile, for example, were variants of the director's house at Arc and Senans with banded columns on all four sides giving them the appearance of being fortified temples (254). The Barrière des Bonshommes, on the north bank of the Seine above the Ecole Militaire, recalled the house of Mlle Guimard, but with a niche of squatter proportions and a colonnade masking the whole width of the front elevation (255).

Of the four surviving *barrières* that of La Villette was one of the largest of the single pavilions, a square surmounted by a cylindrical drum (256). Its open colonnade was intended to facilitate the surveillance of the Ourcq canal which ended at the harbour just behind the *barrière*. The design is related to that of the watchtowers of the Hôtel des Fermes, with arched openings, here divided by pairs of baseless Tuscan columns which justify the heavy Doric cornice, crowning the composition. The Barrière de Monceau is one of the smallest of the toll-houses, placed on the outer boundary of the Parc de Monceau (257). It has something of the character of a garden pavilion, and the upper storey was reserved as a belvedere for the use of the owner of the garden, the Duc de Chartres. With its baseless columns and heavy lower

256 The Barrière de la Villette, after restoration. One of the four surviving *barrières,* a large circular building that commanded the harbour of the Ourcq canal in north-eastern Paris

257 The Barrière de Monceau. A circular Doric 'temple' sited on the outer wall of the Duc de Chartres' Parc de Monceau in western Paris

258 The Barrière d'Orléans (Barrière d'Enfer), the western pavilion.
Two of the four surviving *barrières* are pairs of matching
pavilions, which Ledoux reserved for the major roads into Paris,
like the road to Orléans and the south.

259 The Barrière du Trône, the northern
pavilion. The authority of the Ferme Générale
was underlined by the bold shapes of the
barrières, which also allowed them to function
as landmarks

cornice the building also has the robust character required
for a customs post, but it is even so recognizable as a late
descendant of the Tempietto of Bramante at S. Pietro in
Montorio, and one informed by a sense of proportion and
interval no less perfectly judged.

The two surviving double pavilions are the Barrière
d'Orléans *(258)*, guarding the main road to the south of Paris,
and the Barrière du Trône at the north east, one of the
grandest of all the *barrière* designs, with free-standing
columns in addition to its square pavilions and guichettes
(259, 260). The pavilions themselves are designed with
their front façades bare of all windows; they are
articulated with a heavy cornice and a lunette of keystones
threaded on a moulding. Their cavernous entrances,
decorated with heavy square piers, give an entirely false
sense of the depth of the outer walls. The columns between
the pavilions were originally undecorated, though Ledoux
later wished to transform them into a monument to the
victories of Napoleon; the present decoration was added in
the 1860s.

No sooner had the *barrières* begun to make their
appearance than Ledoux and Lavoisier were publicly
reviled. The *Mémoires secrets* in October 1785 described
the *barrières* as 'a monument of slavery and despotism',
dwelling upon the proliferation of columns and 'the
injustice, the folly and the horror of this wall'. A brochure
of 1787 complained of the expense of the wall and
suggested that it was a health hazard, preventing fresh air
circulating in the city. Ledoux continued to enjoy the
support of Calonne, but after the minister's dismissal in
1787 the work was suspended and the accounts examined.
Ledoux at this critical time was sacrificed to placate public
opinion, and he was forced to hand over his plans to a
commission headed by Antoine and Raymond. In 1789 they
reported that the cost had so far mounted to seventeen
million *livres*, considerably in excess of the original
estimate, and Necker, reappointed Minister of Finances,

260 The Barrière du Trône, engraving
by Mercier after Courvoisier
(Bibliothèque Nationale, Paris). The
main road to the east had giant
columns in addition to a pair of large
pavilions

dismissed Ledoux and appointed Antoine to complete the work.

Ledoux protested in vain at his dismissal, writing to Necker 'You, Mons. Necker, whose fortunes and principles are pure, how can it be said that your name should be placed beneath an injustice? After public affronts not merited [by me], public consolations are necessary.' But it seems that Ledoux had indeed exceeded, *barrière* by *barrière*, the estimated cost, though presumably not altogether on his own responsibility, and the total expenditure was just over a third of the 48 million *livres* at which the Ferme had estimated its losses from the absence of an effective customs system. Ledoux himself put the cost at 12 million but against this, he argued, the annual income reclaimed was 1·2 million.

Not everyone felt violently antagonistic towards the *barrières*. Antoine himself praised the work of Ledoux (see above), and Thiéry was sympathetic to the purpose of the customs houses and impressed by their design. Marmontel too has left an amusing description of how exaggerated was the fury inspired by Ledoux's work in 1789:

there was nothing in which some mark of tyranny was not evident . . . Of this I will cite but one example.
The subject was the wall and the gates of Paris, which were denounced as calculated only to confine beasts, and as most offensive to men.
'I have seen,' said one of the orators, 'yes, citizens, I have seen at the gate St Victor, on one of the pillars, in sculpture, will you believe it? I have seen the enormous head of a lion, open jawed, and vomiting chains, with which he threatens the passengers. Is it possible to imagine a more fearful emblem of despotism and slavery?' The orator himself imitated the lion's roar. The whole audience was moved; and I, who so often pass by the gate St Victor, was astonished that this horrible image should never have struck me. On that day therefore I paid particular attention to it; and on the pilaster I saw, as an ornament, a shield suspended by a small chain, which the sculptor had fixed to a little lion's muzzle, such as we see on the knocker of a door, or on the cock of a fountain.

In June 1790 by a decree of the Constituent Assembly the *barrières* were put into service, but in the following year all customs dues at the entry to towns were abolished and Antoine was ordered to stop further work on the *barrières*. Fortunately they and their wall were not destroyed, for they were regarded as a public monument which might furthermore prove of military advantage in time of war. Social and financial chaos in any case resulted from the lifting of the customs dues, and finally in 1798 these were imposed once again, as a municipal tax. It is in some measure a vindication of Ledoux that the *barrières* remained in useful service for over sixty years, until the dawn of the railway age.

At least by the time of Napoleon the toll-houses had come to be accepted as a worthy addition to the Parisian townscape. Landon campaigned in their favour, writing a sympathetic account of several of them. The banded columns ('en bossage') of the Barrière de l'Etoile were, he noted, rare in France though more common in Italy and intended, as he realized, to make the site recognizable from afar. The Barrière d'Orléans reminded him a little of the style of Inigo Jones, while the Barrière d'Italie had 'an elegant aspect, and the play of its colonnaded portico recalls the gracious compositions with which Palladio had peopled the neighbourhood of Vicenza'. The *barrières*, he finally argued, were indeed sufficiently imposing to be 'appropriate as the entries to the city of Paris'.

During the early stages of the construction of the *barrières* Ledoux began work on the largest single building of his entire career, the new Palais du Parlement for the Etats de Provence at Aix *(261, 262)*, to which a prison was to be attached. The Parlement of Provence was one of the twelve regional Parlements of pre-Revolutionary France, administered by a hereditary local magistracy and organized approximately on the lines of the Paris Parlement. It had been founded in the fifteenth century with three main departments, a Grande Chambre, a Cour des Aides and a Cour des Requêtes, and it shared accommodation with the Governor of Provence in one of the oldest and most venerable of French castles, the Palais d'Aix. It was not one of the more outrageously obstructive of the French Parlements in the eighteenth century, and had caused no scandal comparable to the ones initiated by the Etats de Languedoc through the prosecution of the Calas family, or by the Etats de Bretagne in its dispute with the Governor of Brittany, the Duc d'Aiguillon. But it was not without a local reputation for corruption, and it had suffered in the skirmish between Crown and Parlement that marked the last years of the reign of Louis XV.

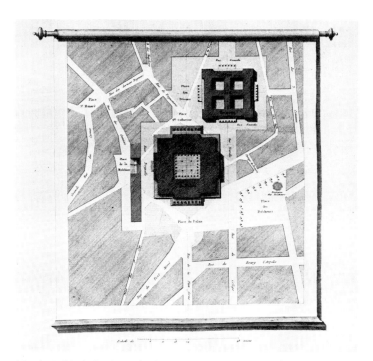

261 The Palais de Justice and prison, Aix-en-Provence, site plan, engraving from Ledoux. Ledoux's designs for the rebuilding of the Parlement building at Aix, the medieval Palais d'Aix, and for the provision of a new prison, were made under the auspices of Calonne, the Minister of Finances, in 1784

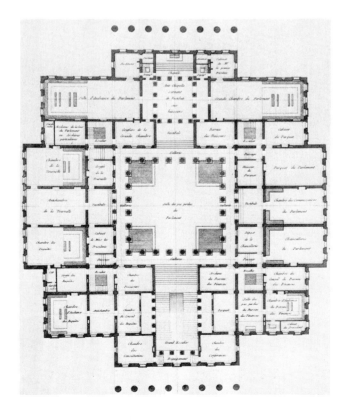

262 The Palais de Justice, Aix, section, elevation and plan, engravings from Ledoux. Resembling a large villa, Ledoux's new Parlement building, like the prison, was begun in 1786 but suspended in 1790 and completed more modestly after 1815

Shortly after Louis XVI had recalled the Parlements, which had been exiled by his grandfather, it was discovered that the Palais d'Aix was no longer sound enough structurally for the accommodation of the Parlement de Provence. After it had been examined by a local architect, Lebrun, Ledoux was sent to Aix by the Contrôleur-Général, presumably Turgot, and apparently on the recommendation of Trudaine de Montigny, who as Intendant des Finances had supported Ledoux's saltworks project. The architect apparently travelled to Provence upon the pretext that a visit there was necessary for his health, and this was presumably to counteract any feelings of resentment that would have arisen in the province in consequence of his interference. Ledoux confirmed the opinion of Lebrun, not perhaps with perfect disinterest, and he made a plan for a new palace outside the town, while Lebrun on the orders of the Premier Président of the Parlement proposed a new building on the site of the existing palace.

Nothing, however, was resolved until 1784, by which time a third competitor for the commission had made an appearance, a local sculptor, Gilles-Pierre Cauvet. The Parlement had meanwhile attracted to itself public interest through the case brought by Mirabeau for a legal separation from his troublesome wife. The proceedings, witnessed by the younger brother of Marie Antoinette, the Archduke Ferdinand, and his wife, who were travelling

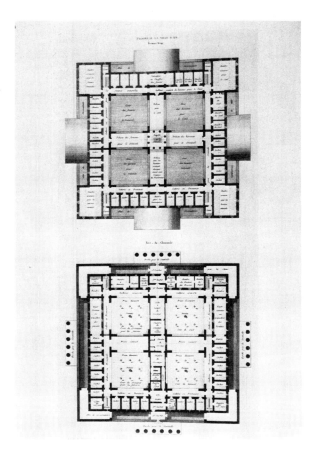 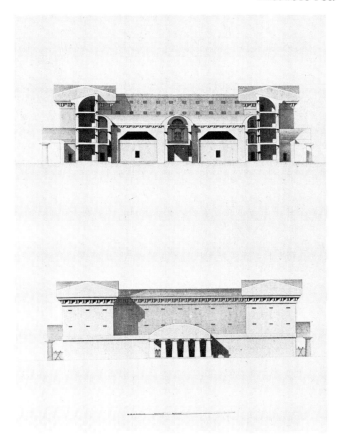

263 The prison, Aix, plans, section and elevation, engravings from Ledoux. Despite its expressive fortified appearance, Ledoux's design takes account internally of the reforms in prison design recommended by Lavoisier and other 'enlightened' administrators

incognito in France, had exposed the corruption of the hereditary magistrates, many of whom were related to the local landowners and entirely prejudiced in their favour.

By 1784 Ledoux's protector, Calonne, had been appointed Contrôleur des Finances, and the royal exchequer, as was reported in Aix in December, had committed itself to bear two-thirds of the cost of the reconstruction (estimated apparently at 1·2 million *livres*). The Premier Président approached Ledoux, whose plans were ready in the same month of December. They provided for a new building on the site of the old palace, with a separate prison to the side, and also a design for a new palace for the governor (the Prince de Beauveau). The reconstruction of the Parlement building was authorized by the king in 1786, the work to be under the supervision of the Intendant, assisted by a committee of the Parlement, and the chief local engineer of the Ponts et Chaussées. Demolition and reconstruction proceeded side by side, but the work was suspended in 1790, when the walls were only two metres high and the estimated cost had already been exceeded.

An interesting series of letters about the construction of the Parlement, including many by Ledoux himself, shows that the prison had also been started. Evidently Ledoux was conscious of his reputation for financial irresponsi-

bility: 'As it cannot be said of me that I am ignorant, or a dishonest man, people will not fail to say that I am expensive', and he stressed the successful economies at the theatre of Besançon. Ledoux saw with increasing desperation during the early years of the Revolution that his project for Aix was unlikely to be completed, and it was this work, together with the house of Mlle Guimard, that he chose to display beneath the portrait bust that appears on the title-page of the *Architecture (202)*.

His pride in the project was fully understandable, for the Parlement building and the prison, designed to be seen in juxtaposition with one another, show the imaginative and practical aspects of his genius at their most inventive. Scattered in the different provinces of the kingdom and of widely varying dates and scale, the existing Parlement buildings offered little guidance to an architect attempting a new design. Traditionally, the larger Parlements, as at Rennes, had been designed either with a central square court, or they conformed to the plan of a large town house with three wings around a court, as at Dijon, or in Paris itself, where the Parlement buildings had recently been restored by Desmaisons and Antoine (see above). Ledoux preferred a more compact plan for his palace, which gave it something of the appearance of a large villa, recalling in its dense massing the character of the medieval castle it was due to replace (262).

The front entrance led directly to the main staircase, an 'objet principal', in Ledoux's words, which ascended to a large waiting-room at the centre of the plan, the 'Salle des Pas Perdus', named after the corresponding room in the Paris Parlement. Lit from above, the room resembled the courtyard of a Renaissance palace with its decoration of free-standing Corinthian columns. Smaller staircases were positioned in the corners of the plan, and on the central axis, opposite the entrance, Ledoux placed a chapel, as at the Hôtel des Fermes; it was to be preceded by a vestibule articulated, like the main floor of the principal staircase, with small Ionic columns. The vestibule served as part of the chapel and as the antechamber to the large Salle d'Audience (left) and the Grande Chambre (right) of the Parlement.

Elsewhere on the first floor were smaller audience rooms attached to the two main courts and the rooms of their dependent departments, the 'Chambre de la Tournelle', the 'Enquêtes', the 'Requêtes', the 'Bureau des Finances', the 'Commissariat' and the Chancellery of the Parlement. The ground floor was similar to the principal floor in plan, with the Cour des Comptes occupying the rooms immediately below the Parlement. This had its own entrance in the right side of the building, its own Salle des Pas Perdus in the centre, with baseless Doric columns supporting the Corinthian order above, and its own chapel between the two principal audience rooms at the rear. Otherwise the ground floor was occupied by the department of the Maréchaussée, responsible for the security of the public highways.

Writing of the exterior of the palace, Ledoux explained that the elevations 'must be so simple, that they could never disturb the Palace. The regularity of the decoration will make for grandeur, without the need of accessories.' Ledoux seems to have made the design even more regular in his engravings than it was in reality by adding, as in his plates of Bénouville, a full portico at the rear matching the one at the front.

Apart from the portico, the façades are indeed relatively simple, surmounted by a deep Doric cornice that projects over the giant columns of the front portico and encircles the whole perimeter. But the exterior is not without its imaginative surprises. As in the design of the saltworks, an irregular sculptured pattern is visible behind the columns of the portico, in this case a relief of figures emerging abruptly from the surface of the wall to surmount the main doorway. Repeated with no screening columns over the other three entrances, these reliefs are an extreme example of Ledoux's architectural libertarianism, while the broad pediment of the main façade, the accepted field for sculpture in relief, appears in Ledoux's engravings entirely bare of decoration.

The windows too are designed with little regard for the methods of Renaissance practice. Those of the principal floor are entirely without frames, while on the floor above similar unmarked windows alternate with others that are equipped with ostentatiously heavy frames. The principle recalls the alternation of straight and segmental pediments, as practised throughout the Renaissance, which Ledoux and others had revived in the 1760s. For some of the barrières Ledoux had already adopted this more extreme form of alternation, though not with frames as heavy as those suggested for Aix. Seen in relation to the nearby prison the fenestration of the Parlement seems not merely a free and economical variant of traditional methods of articulation, but at the same time deliberately to mirror the hopes and fears of those who waited within to hear the outcome of the trials.

Similarly the attic storey of the building has its own symbolic resonance, suggesting, like the towers of the Hôtel des Fermes (251), watchfulness and authority. The whole structure was far more modest in extent than it appears to be in true elevation (262). The stepped walls at the corners are set considerably forward from the central square tower, which is supported on the columns of the Salle des Pas Perdus. The steps of the projecting corners, however, are aligned with the rustication of the walls of the tower so that the whole attic, rising from the body of the palace and topped by its heavy Doric lantern in the guise of a temple, seems more substantial, more authoritative, than was really the case.

Compared with the prison and its massive frontispiece (263), centred on the road to the right, the palace stands for civilization tempered, like the director's house at Arc and Senans, with strength and dominion. The prison itself expressed from the outside an extreme of oppression and force, a purposeful negation of all the familiar principles of Renaissance design. It resembles a medieval castle with its narrow windows, its projecting corner towers and its almost machicolated cornice. In Ledoux's engravings the block has four matching frontispieces though only two are required by the plan. Each has a colonnade of Tuscan columns, like those employed for the barrières, but even more exaggerated in their proportions and almost impeding entrance into the prison, or indeed departure.

Though Ledoux's prison is an extreme example of the expressive use of form, he was by no means the only architect, motivated by concern for justice and humanity, to discover that a prison justified experiments in the most primitive forms of architecture. While many artists, from Piranesi to Beethoven, discovered in the idea of prison life moving analogies to the oppression of the human spirit, reformers, like Beccaria, were at the same time attempting to improve the physical conditions of the prisons and to reform the injustices of the penal code. Some of the main abuses in France were eradicated after the succession of Louis XVI. The use of torture to extract confessions was forbidden, the issue of lettres de cachet restricted, and the power of families to imprison their children, as in the case of Mirabeau, was finally curtailed.

The physical conditions of prisons became a matter of public concern and a source of embarrassment to the government. The Neckers took a special interest in the problem and Lavoisier was asked in 1780 to report on the Paris prisons. He stressed their overcrowding and recommended the reconstruction of existing buildings and the provision of new prisons on more humane principles, with yards for exercise, training facilities for the prisoners, and in general more air, water and space. Presenting his report to Mme Necker, Lavoisier complained of the hostility to reform that he had encountered on the part of the magistrates and the prison officers.

Germany and Holland were apparently the countries that then had the best record for the treatment of prisoners, though Lavoisier was also impressed with the work of John Howard in England. The first humane prison, however, seems to have been the one devised by Pope Clement XI at the turn of the eighteenth century and carried out by Carlo Fontana in Rome. Designed for sixty young criminals, it had separate cells for each inmate, all visible from a large central hall which also acted as a chapel, and facilities for training in the profession of wool dying. Externally the building had a relatively domestic appearance, despite its rows of small windows, but later prisons are far more austere in character, like Dance's Newgate Prison, or Gondoin's design for the prison facing the Ecole de Chirurgie *(183)*. Few prisons were actually built in France in the later eighteenth century, but there is an abundance of drawings for prison buildings, amongst them the designs for the Grand Prix of 1778, which was won by a pupil of Boullée, Jacques-Pierre Gisors *(264)*. Though handicapped, like most such drawings, by the academic aimlessness of the subject, Gisors' design has very much the same feudal and military appearance as Ledoux's prison for Aix.

The weight of justice may be stressed externally in Ledoux's design but internally the prison has the appearance of being remarkably humane in character. Similar in plan to the Hôtel des Fermes, it has four courtyards with trees and fountains, and small cells for the prisoners at the sides together with larger communal workrooms. The apartment of the jailer occupies the central spine of the building at ground level, with the chapel on the floor above. The prison is directly connected to the Palais de Justice by two underground corridors that meet at the staircase leading down beside the Grande Chambre of the Parlement.

The *barrières* and the designs for Aix were the major commissions that Ledoux was engaged upon in the 1780s, but he continued at the same time to receive smaller commissions from private clients, even if many of the more modest works recorded in his engravings may be later elaborations of quite tentative ideas. He appears to have been replaced by Brongniart as architect at Maupertuis at least by 1780, but designs for three other estates, La Roche Bernard, Bourneville and Meilland, are recorded in the engravings. The house of M. de Witt of 1781 is one of several radical experiments with the circular plan that was in fashion in Paris in the 1780s. The amusing design for the Château of Eguière, a villa of markedly Palladian appearance but with a canal flowing through the basement, may date from the same years as the Parlement at Aix, if Eguière is the town of that name in Provence. The design for the theatre of Marseille, a large-scale version of the Besançon theatre, also dates from the mid-1780s, and that for the archiepiscopal palace of Sisteron, where the incumbent

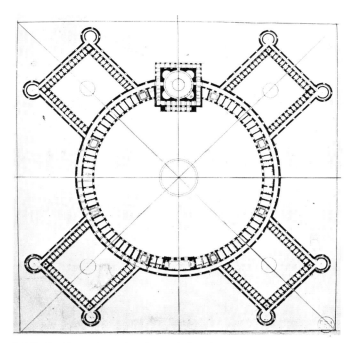

264 Project for a prison, elevation and plan, drawing by Jacques-Pierre Gisors (Ecole des Beaux-Arts, Paris). The winning design for the 1778 Prix de Rome, the project recalls Ledoux's prison in its fortified appearance, and the work of Boullée in its scale

was the celebrated Suffren de St-Tropez, was probably likewise supplied by Ledoux while he was at Aix. The other public commission that Ledoux received at this time was for the town hall of Neuchâtel, a Prussian state in Switzerland which was famous in the later eighteenth century as a haven for the uncensored printing of subversive French books. Ledoux's designs are of 1784, but the commission finally devolved upon Pierre-Adrien Pâris.

The two main commissions that Ledoux carried out in Paris in the later 1780s and early 1790s were for groups of houses built on speculation and forming part of a new type of urban development. Grouped houses, like tenement buildings, became an increasingly frequent sight in pre-Revolutionary Paris. Perhaps influenced by the buildings of eighteenth-century London, but quite different in character, they were often planned in groups of three or five, like several of the designs of Belanger, or de Wailly's houses in the rue de la Pépinière *(132)*. Where larger plots of land were owned by a single proprietor, as was often the case in London, such developments were more ambitious in scope, like the Palais-Royal or the planning of 'Nouvelle Londres' and 'Nouvelle Amérique' for the Comte d'Artois (see chapter 13), but little evidence has survived of the

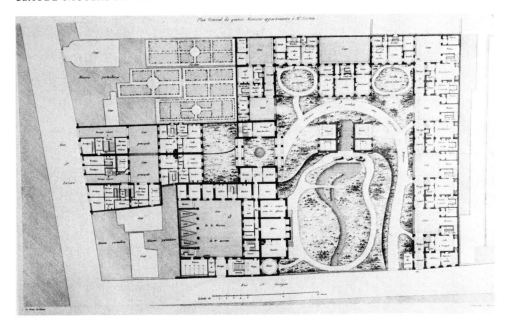

265 The houses of M. Hosten, Paris, plan, engraving by Ledoux. An estate of houses, just to the north of the Hôtel de Thélusson *(247)*, carried out to designs made by Ledoux in 1792

266 The houses of M. Hosten, the house of the landlord, elevations, engraving from Ledoux. M. Hosten's own house was the largest on the estate, with its entrance from the rue St-Georges and the garden façade facing south across the garden

appearance of these larger speculations. Ledoux himself had already supplied a development of three related houses for Mme de Thélusson. In the year before the Revolution he planned and built a group of eight houses on a rectangular site on the opposite bank of the Seine to the Tuileries for a M. Saiseval, while in 1792 he undertook a larger development of the same kind for a rich American speculator, M. Hosten, just to the north of the Hôtel de Thélusson.

The houses are recorded in drawings and in the closely similar engravings in the *Architecture* of Ledoux, showing the whole of what was originally planned *(265–267)*. The development incorporated at the north three shops fronting the rue des Porcherons and a courtyard behind overlooked by two matching houses. The largest building on the site was the house of the owner himself, facing southwards, with its entrance from the rue St-Georges to the west and an irregular garden behind. The garden was open to the rue St-Georges and lined on the other three sides with houses, rather on the principle of the Palais-Royal, though each was a clearly separate building, which contributed to a lively, even picturesque, design clearly visible from the road. The three houses at the east were the smallest and shared a common court, while the larger buildings to the south *(266)* were joined together by a long passage, leading from the rue St-Georges, which stretched from court to court beneath the houses.

What united the development architecturally was the use of the arch motif, which had made its first appearance in Ledoux's work at the Hôtel des Fermes *(251)*. As architects began to care less for the letter of antique law, the architecture of the early Renaissance slowly returned to fashion and arcading was welcomed for its economic advantages. By the time that the Hosten houses were

MAISON DE M. HOSTEN.

Elevation sur la Cour

Elevation sur la Rue

Elevation sur le Jardin

designed columns and arches had already made their appearance in the domestic architecture of Paris, especially in the work of Belanger *(302)*. Ledoux, however, with characteristic boldness uses them more extensively and consistently than any of his contemporaries, allowing them to project and recede across the whole site high up on the garden façades of the buildings. Only the house of the proprietor is excepted from this uniform decoration *(266)*. The arches and columns present on the façade of his house form part of three Venetian windows that distinguished the ground floor of the owner's establishment.

By 1792 architectural opportunities in Paris were becoming increasingly rare, and Ledoux, though he was promoted to the first class of the Academy in that very year, received no further major commissions in the fourteen years that ensued before his death in 1806. Like most professional men of the time he appears to have favoured the Revolution in its early stages, though a note of frustration can perhaps be discerned in a letter of November 1789 by the architect in which he describes the Revolutionary activities of the contractor responsible for the building of the Aix Parlement: 'One can only applaud all these patriotic views, but, while he looks for supplies from others, he is deprived of his own: he cannot think except in [terms of] summonses [and] proceedings; one degrades with the times the men who are the object [of the summonses?] as one distorts the most human business, undertaken for the wisest reasons.' At the same time, too, Ledoux apparently kept in touch with some of his former protectors who had fled the country, and there had been talk of him designing a house in London for the *émigré*, Calonne.

The later years of the Revolution were a time of great personal distress to the architect, beginning with the death of his wife at the end of August 1792. She died not at their house in Paris, but in the nearby village of Chaillot, where she was buried in the church of St-Pierre. She left her property jointly to her two daughters, and Ledoux went to law to have himself appointed guardian of the younger girl. Then, acting in concert with his elder daughter, he raised the substantial loan of 114,000 *livres* on the six houses that he and his wife owned. The legal complexities in which Ledoux became involved suggest some degree of alienation between the architect and his wife at the time of her death. But this was not the last of his troubles for he was shortly thereafter denounced to the Committee of Public Safety and removed in 1793 (9 Brumaire, An II) to the prison of La Force, where he remained for almost a year during the Terror.

Following upon his denunciation Ledoux was taken some weeks after his imprisonment to witness the search of his own house and the removal of some of his papers. He is

267 The houses of M. Hosten, perspective view (Musée Carnavalet, Paris). The houses around the garden were distinguished by continuous arcading at main-floor level

mentioned on his charge sheet as the architect of the pavilion of Louveciennes, as living on an income of five to six thousand *livres* and as claiming over a million *livres* from the state in unpaid fees, including those for the *barrières*. He was accused of being in contact with ex-nobles and financiers, of applying for the *cordon noir* and of possessing the almanac of a royalist club (the Club de Valois). And to this was also added the charge of being the architect of the *barrières*. A royalist before the death of the 'Tyrant', he was accused of now trying to show his patriotism by conversing with patriots, though he had not appeared at the assemblies of his section after the first six months of the Revolution.

Replying to some of these charges, Ledoux's young daughters maintained that the club had been flattered to have distinguished artists in its ranks, including Vernet, and that in designing the *barrières* their father was acting under orders. Ledoux himself stressed that the club was social and not political in character and that his application to the king for the *cordon noir* was a draft of a letter and not even signed. Writing of himself in the third person he added that 'he is busy with a substantial work for the public instruction of young architects . . . which breathes throughout liberty and humanitarian views. You see there Republican theatres built during the Despotism [Besançon].' The architect wished, he said, to decorate the *barrières* with reference to the victories of the Republic, and he stressed the works of public utility on which he had worked, including farms and granaries.

Amongst the papers confiscated from his house are two long memoirs on the *barrières*, documents connected with the pension of his father-in-law, and Ledoux's own letter (dated 1789) applying for the *cordon noir*. Promised him during the reign of Louis XV, the honour, he claimed, was all the more appropriate now that he had built over one hundred useful monuments, including buildings in Russia, Germany, Holland, England, and in nearly all the provinces of France, and had engraved one hundred and fifty plates of his works. Saddest of all amongst the papers are the letters of Ledoux's daughters pleading for the architect's release. In Thermidor, An II, he had been imprisoned for eight months and the children wrote of being 'left as a desolate family, deprived of the society of a tender father, who is dearest in the world to them'. During the same months Lavoisier was attacked for his part in devising the *barrières* and finally guillotined as a Fermier Général, and Mme du Barry too went to the guillotine after her imprisonment at St-Pélagie.

Prison seems to have left Ledoux yet more determined to finish his *Architecture*, and it no doubt intensified the egalitarian character that the first volume finally assumed, in the choice of buildings illustrated and discussed, but in other ways his mind was apparently unaffected. He continued to enjoy the company of his pupils and friends, including Cellerier, and his letters remain perfectly coherent in tone. Yet his troubles were still not ended. About the time of his release his elder daughter died, and some years later the architect was again denounced to the government as one who was in correspondence with the enemies of the Republic. In 1800 (An VIII) his younger daughter married a violinist, Jean-Nicolas Chol, who had been for some years a friend of the family, but the couple were separated at the time of Ledoux's death on 19 November 1806. One week earlier 'in a salon on the first floor of [his] house with a view over the Boulevard, sitting on a sofa near the window, ill in body but sound in mind', Ledoux signed an act that disinherited his daughter of half of his goods in favour of his pupil, Pierre Vignon, the architect of the Madeleine.

As a result of this codicil an inventory of his possessions was drawn up in the months after his death. It lists briefly his furniture and ornaments (including an ivory bust of Voltaire), his pictures (including one by Robert) and some of his books. But nothing of any great value is mentioned in the inventory, which closes with a list of his papers and a reference to thirty volumes of the *Architecture* found in a chest together with Blondel's *Cours*. Cellerier explained the sad state of his fortune and his health: 'Domestic troubles, and the rapid diminution of his fortune acquired by fifty years of work, had for long altered his natural gaiety. An attack of paralysis took him to the grave before the age to which a robust constitution should have entitled him.' Yet Ledoux was not forsaken by his friends and fellow-artists, and according to one obituary

Nearly all the savants and artists of Paris attended [his funeral]. Twenty carriages were not sufficient to take them to the church and cemetery of Mont-Martre . . . M. Luce de Lanceval delivered a very short but very expressive oration to which he joined the verses that M. Delille composed on the subject of the famous man that the arts had just lost, and placed a crown of laurel upon his grave.

During the years of the Revolution Ledoux had not been appointed to any of the official posts then available to architects and he apparently fretted that his talents were not in use. According to Cellerier he 'complained privately of staying inactive and not being able to dedicate to Napoleon the last fires of his talent. He took, thus, a favourable opportunity to show to His Excellency, the Minister of the Interior, a project to restore and finish the two triumphal columns, which form one of the most magnificent entries to Paris, at the Barrière du Trône.' But nothing came of his efforts and it was the *Architecture* that absorbed most of his time. Vignon, who had helped to bring out the first volume, undertook, with Cellerier and Damesne, to ensure that the second volume should also appear.

The publication of Ledoux's work, first mentioned in 1782 when the Tsarevitch visited the architect, was also noted five years later in Thiéry's guide to Paris. Cellerier describes how Ledoux worked on the project during his imprisonment, when 'amidst his companions in misfortune, he meditated, traced, drew the gayest of his projects with which he embellished his work . . . "They can assassinate me," he would sometimes exclaim, "but they cannot take from me the distinction of having honoured my country with my productions."' In 1794 the Abbé Delille had completed his poem 'L'Imagination', and he devoted a disproportionately large section of its ninth part, dealing with the whole of the arts, to praising parts of the imaginary town of Ledoux, whose gift for friendship he particularly stressed.

A long prospectus appeared, probably in 1802, promising the first volume at the beginning of the following year. Even the prospectus is written in the self-conscious style that mars the book itself: 'I wake up, like Epimenides, after a sleep of twelve years, my arms tired of their chains, withered by misery, raising the slab of my tomb.' Writing to Aix in March 1803 Ledoux spoke with complete detachment of the prospectus, which he claimed was written 'with energy and in a good tone'; the *Architecture* itself, he explained, would be 'of a greater luxury. I believe that it will have a great effect.'

But the first volume when it appeared caused evident embarrassment to Ledoux's supporters: 'It must be agreed', wrote Landon, 'that the style is diffuse and inflated. The simplest diction is the only [kind] that suits works of this type.' The book dealt not with the familiar masterpieces that the architect had actually constructed, though two of these appear in the frontispiece *(202)*, but almost exclusively with the imaginary town of Chaux. The book is dedicated to the son and successor of Paul II of Russia who had visited Ledoux in 1782, the Tsar Alexander, who was still an ally of Napoleon in 1804.

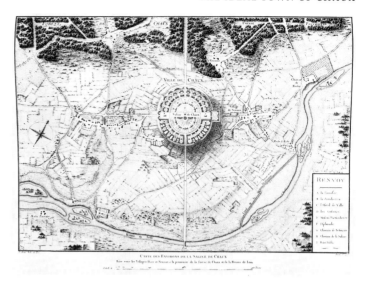

268 Arc and Senans, the imaginary town of Chaux, site plan, engraving from Ledoux. The saltworks *(235)* forms the lower half of the oval nucleus of the town, lying between the forest of Chaux and the river Loue

269 Chaux, perspective view, engraving from Ledoux. New buildings, not shown on the plan *(268)*, surround the centre and extend into the forest above; the church *(274, 275)* is on the left

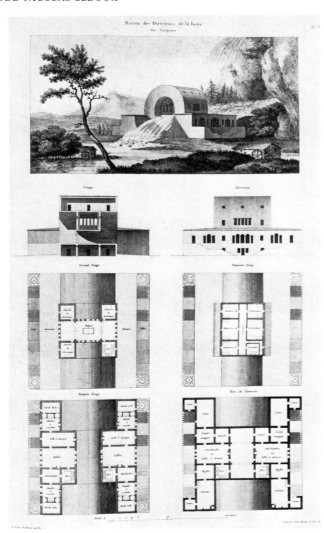

270 Chaux, the house of the directors of the river Loue, perspective view, section, elevation and plans, engraving from Ledoux. Even the most imaginative of the designs are equipped with detailed plans.

As it finally emerged Ledoux's town is a peculiar and highly personal mixture of new and old ideas, both social and architectural. The nucleus of the town remains the saltworks but the authority of its director extends over a whole range of new buildings that were to fill the landscape. Though the town has no customs barriers, its conception is evidently linked, in the extent and variety of its component buildings, with Ledoux's master plan for the *barrières* of Paris, where he had been forced to consider for the first time the implications of large-scale urban development. And as the project became more extensive, accommodating buildings that derive in design from the *barrières*, it came to include the river Loue, with its bridge and its own director's house *(270)*, just as the *barrières* themselves had enclosed the Seine as it passed through Paris. Even the aspect of the town that appears so modern in conception today, the setting of the buildings within the surrounding landscape, depends upon the original character of the saltworks, and was not in any case foreign to the architect of the Hôtel de Thélusson and the Hosten houses.

At the same time the town is without precedent in being a translation into visual and social terms of many of the deepest preoccupations of the later eighteenth century, preoccupations that had for the most part been confined to the written and the spoken word, and perhaps only an architect of Ledoux's imaginative fecundity, pondering throughout his life the social needs of his fellow men, could have visualized the physical embodiment of this spiritual inheritance.

Ledoux's well-adjusted character set him apart from the insecure personality of Rousseau, but the concept of his town is deeply touched by the scope of Rousseau's thought, even to the extent of being largely introspective in the character of its principal monuments. It is a curious fact that the town lacks many of the buildings of public convenience that had become so conspicuous a phenomenon of the pre-Revolutionary years. There are, for example, no hospitals, no fountains or public squares, and no theatre, even though plates of the Besançon theatre are

The idea of creating at Chaux a model country town may have occurred to Ledoux while work was progressing at the saltworks. It was accepted, even when the book appeared, that Ledoux's town had been conceived at the same time as the saltworks, and that it had even won the approval of Louis XV, but it seems most probable that the majority of the designs for the town itself are the product of Ledoux's last fifteen years. Ledoux's idea was to double the extent of the saltworks *(235)*, making a complete circle enclosed by a boulevard, with public and private buildings extending on all sides into the surrounding countryside *(269)*. The church appears on the left, and a circular amphitheatre on the right, but there is otherwise little correspondence between the buildings shown in the general view and those engraved separately in the plates of the book *(270–275)*.

271 Chaux, 'The shelter of the poor man' ('L'abri du pauvre'), engraving from Ledoux. Several of the engravings are allegorical and political in character, and here the gods of antiquity appear in the sky

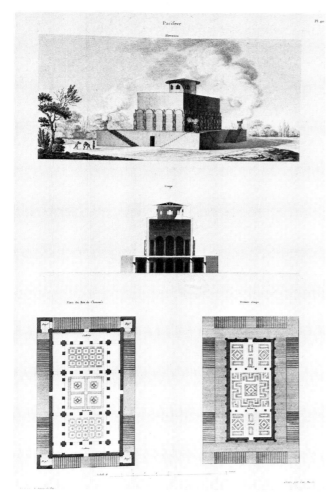

272 Chaux, the 'Pacifère', perspective view, section and plans, engraving from Ledoux. In the Pacifère quarrels (like the one shown in the foreground, top) were to be settled peaceably

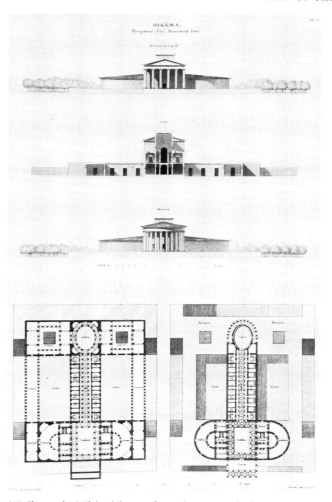

273 Chaux, the 'Oïkéma' (house of sexual instruction), elevations, section and plans, engraving from Ledoux. An extreme example of Ledoux's use of visual metaphor

included in the volume. And as if to underline the direct relation with Rousseau, and the idealistic character of Ledoux's conception, the copy of the *Architecture* that was supplied to the Institut (presumably by the architect himself) was entered with the title 'Architecture Sentimentale'.

For Ledoux himself the spiritual aims, unrecorded in print, that he had inherited from freemasonry were probably the direct source of much of his inspiration. A general concern for the spiritual rather than the narrowly physical welfare of mankind is conveyed in the plates that stand out as being not strictly architectural, 'The shelter of the poor man' *(271)*, and the cosmic vision poignantly labelled 'Cemetery of Chaux'. In the private dwellings of the town even the poorest inhabitant is well sheltered, and though social distinctions are maintained in the design and size of the houses, they are apparently levelled in the shared communal buildings like the Maison d'Union, the

Pacifère, where quarrels were to be settled peacefully *(272)*, and the Oïkéma (the house of sexual instruction), designed to resemble in plan an erect phallus, and one of the most extreme instances of Ledoux's gift for architectural metaphor *(273)*. This chilling, if well-intentioned, institution may seem to recall Rousseau's description of his own sad sexual affairs, and it also evokes Mozart's late masonic masterpiece, *The Magic Flute*, and the benevolent but authoritarian trials that Pamina and Tamino undergo before they are finally reunited.

For the architectural presentation of the buildings Ledoux uses a shorthand that omits all but the essential structure and decoration. This is one reason why many of the buildings appear so modern in character, in addition to the priority given to their landscape settings. The essential role of light and shade in the sculptural articulation of the buildings, is not, however, overlooked even if this treatment gives the projects a visual complexity that must

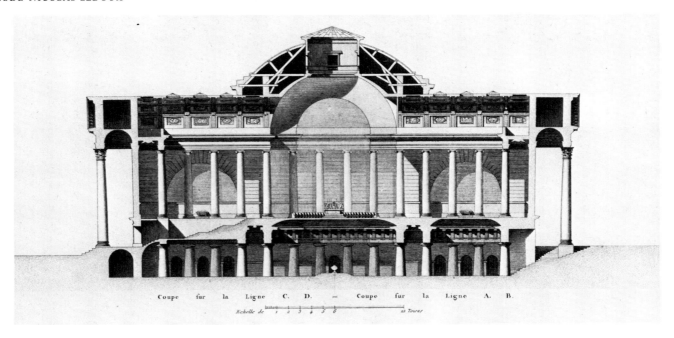

Coupe fur la Ligne C. D. — Coupe fur la Ligne A. B.

Echelle de 1 2 3 4 5 6   12 Toises

274 Chaux, the church, section and plan, engraving from Ledoux. A Greek cross church, closely related to Ledoux's projects for the Parlement at Aix *(262)*

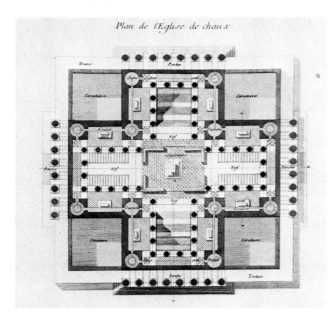

Plan de l'Eglise de chaux

have seemed old-fashioned by the year 1804. All the buildings are presented in plan, section and elevation, and they seem viable as practical architectural projects, though many of them – especially the house of the Loue directors and the Oïkéma – express their function more frankly than any of the earlier buildings of the architect.

Amongst the most ambitious of the institutions of the town is Ledoux's only known project for a church *(274, 275)*, a scheme that can be compared with Boullée's cathedral design as an experiment in a familiar idiom *(276)*. Ledoux's project recalls his design for the Parlement of Aix with its crypt of baseless Tuscan columns and an Ionic 'Salle des Pas Perdus' above. Like the church of Ste-Geneviève as modified in the 1790s *(100)* the exterior is bare of all windows, the light concentrated upon the altar from a central oculus. The design may seem extreme for Ledoux in its regularity and austerity, but compared with the simple inflation of scale on which Boullée depends for his effects, Ledoux's design is as feasible an architectural proposition and as adroit in its sense of interval and dramatic contrast as any of his earlier works.

What is less certain is the deity to whom this temple is dedicated, and Ledoux's text seems to offer no guidance on this important issue beyond the mystical inflections of its wording. Though there are candlesticks and a cross upon the altar, and the people outside kneel as a priest passes with incense burners and what appears to be the Host in front, the building itself seems more suited to the secrecy of a masonic meeting. The Supreme Being may here be the Christian deity, but in the plate showing the shelter of the poor man *(271)* the gods who preside over the empty landscape are those of Olympus, though whether it is they to whom the poor may apply for help is not made clear.

One important aspect of the town which has passed

208

largely unremarked, perhaps as a consequence of the all-too-serious tone of the text, is the visual wit of Ledoux's designs, a virtue of the book that remained still very much within the eighteenth-century tradition. In this respect the *Architecture* seems closer in style not to the architecture of its own day, but to the spirited memoirs composed after the fall of the Ancien Régime. As Marmontel wrote towards the end of his own memoirs:

When my imagination could be diverted by amusing reveries, I made new tales, less gay than those which I had written in the sunshine of my life, and the smiling leisure of prosperity; but a little more philosophical, and in a tone that suited better with my age and the circumstances of the times . . .

These recollections were a real comfort and alleviation to me, inasmuch as they effaced, at least for moments, the sad images of the present, by the gentle dreams of the past.

275 Chaux, the church, perspective view, engraving from Ledoux. The Host is shown to the people in the foreground; the building itself is entirely symmetrical and without windows

276 Project for a metropolitan church, drawing by Boullée, 1781–82 (Bibliothèque Nationale, Paris). Unlike Ledoux, Boullée depends largely upon inflation of scale in the design of his own metropolitan church

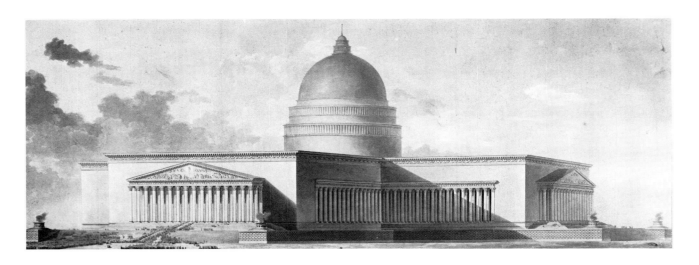

Part Four

ARCHITECTURE BEFORE AND AFTER THE REVOLUTION

13 Two Paris architects: Brongniart and Belanger

BY THE TIME Ledoux's *Architecture* appeared in 1804, the development of Paris, postponed during the years of the Revolution, was once again resumed on the orders of Napoleon, who had declared early in life: 'If I were the master of France, I would make Paris, not only the most beautiful town which existed, but the most beautiful town that could exist.' Yet the major buildings of the Napoleonic era, the Arc-de-Triomphe, the Madeleine *(345)*, the Bourse, the portico of the Chambre des Députés *(346)* and the Colonne Vendôme, so far from truly beautifying the city, are amongst the most derivative and monotonous monuments of European architecture. How far this was due to Napoleon himself numbing the imagination of his architects through his megalomania, just as he undoubtedly enslaved the painters who served him at this time, or to an absence of new talent, seems impossible to determine.

The style of architectural design had certainly changed, as exemplified in the work of Napoleon's personal architects, Charles Percier and Pierre Fontaine *(347–350)*. Partly no doubt as a consequence of new methods of engineering and new techniques of cutting stone, buildings were conceived in a more precise and linear fashion than hitherto, simpler in shape and sharper in the definition of their forms. Indeed the same developments affected all the visual arts and not least methods of architectural drawing. When Krafft surveyed the buildings of pre-Revolutionary Paris in his many books, he used a form of shorthand that highlights the aesthetic priorities of the architecture of his own day *(221)*. He was able to record in great quantities the buildings of the later eighteenth century, reducing masterpieces to the level of being mere diagrams, but showing thereby in what ways they had contributed to the formulation of post-Revolutionary architecture. The works of Ledoux are perhaps those which suffer the most in Krafft's engravings since the play of light and shade, blurring the outlines of Ledoux's forms and setting in relief his ingenious decoration, is as essential to the character of his buildings as it had been throughout the Renaissance.

277 The former customs house, rue Chauchat, Paris. A building, designed by Lusson, that is influenced by Ledoux in the shape but more precise in handling

By the turn of the nineteenth century the visual standards of Ledoux, no longer of much consequence in his own country, persisted beneficially abroad, and particularly in Russia, a country that lacked adequate supplies of stone that could be cut with the accuracy that Napoleon's architects required. French buildings of the nineteenth century that derive from Ledoux in their shaping, like the former customs house of the rue Chauchat *(277)*, or the buildings by Ledoux himself that have been recently reconstructed *(256)*, seem too precise in their detailing to match the daring of their spatial conception, and the same is true even when Schinkel, Hansen, or occasionally Soane employ forms in stone which are as structurally dramatic as those of Ledoux. In Leningrad, however, it was not until the advent of Von Klenze and Bryullov in the 1840s that the influence of Percier and Fontaine prevailed, and the buildings meanwhile constructed in brick and stucco, by architects like Stasov, Zakharov (278) and Rossi, combine the forms of Ledoux with an appropriately sculptural treatment. Even so the rational basis of Ledoux's work was often overlooked by many of those whom he influenced, and Stasov, for example, designed houses based not on the hôtels of Ledoux, but upon the barrières which had never been intended by their architect as private dwellings.

The development towards the simplified architecture of Napoleon's Paris followed rather from the style of Boullée and the related work of the students at the Academy, where both Percier and Fontaine were successful beginners, than from the more varied and humane achievements of Ledoux. This change of aesthetic priorities involved many architects no less talented than those who witnessed the dawn of the antique revival in the middle years of the eighteenth century.

The two most accomplished and prolific of Ledoux's younger contemporaries were Alexandre-Théodore Brongniart (279) and François-Joseph Belanger (291), architects famous for their town houses and garden designs, both of whom were still active in the Paris of Napoleon. Though they differed in their approach to architecture they were alike to the extent that neither of them had visited Italy. They became close friends, sharing in the social pleasures of Parisian society, and when Brongniart died in 1813 it was Belanger who delivered the oration at his funeral.

Four years younger than Ledoux, Brongniart was born in Paris in 1739 and educated, like Ledoux, at the Collège de Beauvais. His family was distinguished rather in the sciences than in the arts, his father being a professor at the Collège de Pharmacie, his mother a relation of the celebrated chemist, the Comte de Fourcroy, who married de Wailly's widow, and his younger brother, Antoine-Louis, the Premier Apothicaire du Roi. Brongniart's teachers in architecture were Blondel and Boullée, with whom he studied shortly after Chalgrin, presumably about 1760. He competed unsuccessfully for several of the prizes of the Academy (1762–65) and thereafter probably began work as an assistant to Boullée, whose influence is very apparent in his early buildings.

Brongniart's independent career is mainly associated with the patronage of the Orléans and the Condé families and with the development of two areas of Paris: the northern part of the Chaussée-d'Antin quarter and the neighbourhood of the Invalides. In 1769 he allied himself with the entrepreneur Jean-François Le Tellier, who had acquired a large plot of land to the east of the rue de la Chaussée-d'Antin, and this they resold to the Marquise de Montesson, who commissioned Brongniart to build a house for her on the site. The opportunity could scarcely have been more fortunate for not only had Mme de Montesson come into a fortune on the death of her husband in 1769, but she was also the mistress and later the

278 The Admiralty, Leningrad (1806–15), detail of river façade. A Russian monument – of typical brick and stucco – by Chalgrin's pupil, Zakharov, which recalls the public architecture of Ledoux

wife of the Duc d'Orléans, Louis 'Le Gros', the father of Philippe-Egalité – an irregular alliance with important architectural consequences that involved both Brongniart and Victor Louis.

The house of Mme de Montesson was comparatively modest in scale (280). The design, recorded in one of Brongniart's many accomplished drawings, recalls the early houses of Boullée, especially the Hôtel de Monville (142), while being slightly less rigid in appearance. A central frontispiece of pilasters on the garden side took under its protection the round-headed doorways in the centre and one of each pair of rectangular windows which closed the composition at the sides. No accurate plan of the house appears to be known, but the organization of the building was probably fairly simple, since the main rooms were on the ground floor and only service staircases would have been required. Within the house was the small chapel where the owner and the Duc d'Orléans were secretly married on 23 April 1773.

As a member of the lesser nobility Mme de Montesson was disqualified from enjoying the title and the privileges

279 Portrait of Alexandre-Théodore Brongniart (1739–1813), lithograph by Béranger after Gérard and Arnoult (Bibliothèque Nationale, Paris). A late portrait showing Brongniart's design for the Paris Bourse (1808) at the base

280 The Hôtel de Montesson, Paris, elevation of the garden façade, drawing by Brongniart (Musée Carnavalet, Paris). Designed by Brongniart in 1769 for Mme de Montesson, the mistress and later wife of the Duc d'Orléans, the house is influenced by the style of Brongniart's teacher, Boullée (142)

due to her upon her ambitious marriage to the first prince of the blood. She was not received at court and to be with her the Duc d'Orléans preferred to give up the Palais-Royal to his son and live in relative retirement; 'Unable to make her Duchesse d'Orléans, he made himself M. de Montesson', was how Grimm summarized the situation. With their own circle of close friends the duke and duchess passed their time in Paris and at Ste-Assise or Le Raincy, enjoying above all hunting and private theatricals, where the talents of Mme de Montesson as actress and aspiring author could be exercised.

In the year of their marriage Brongniart designed for the corner site adjacent to the Hôtel de Montesson, a large house for the Duc d'Orléans (281, 282), which was carried out, with drastic modifications, by the Orléans family architect, Henri Piètre. The two establishments had separate entrances but enjoyed a communal garden and interconnecting passages: 'All the inside dividing walls had been pulled down and the two gardens made into one. However, the Duc d'Orléans had his own entrance in the rue de Provence, with a porter in his livery, and Mme de Montesson had hers with a porter in grey livery.' Brongniart's design for the Duc d'Orléans was far from being a conventional town house, but it expressed the unusual character of the commission, arising from the exalted status of his client, forced to live in comparative retirement. The building, with its extensive plan, has something of the character of a country palace. The architect planned a large oval courtyard with a substantial theatre to one side, a low house opposite, and an irregular garden, less prominent than Ledoux's later garden at the Hôtel de Thélusson, filling the awkward spaces beyond the walls of the court. The house itself is freely designed in plan – a pavilion in a landscape – with curved galleries overlooking a formal garden at the back. A circular salon forms the nucleus of the house, preceded by two antechambers, and breaking the inward curve of the garden galleries with a gentle convex projection.

The variety of the room shapes, fitted into their semicircular shell, and the curved outline of the garden façade may suggest something of the princely elegance of the earlier part of the century, but in elevation the house appeared far more severe than its plan indicated. In Krafft's engraving (281) the garden façade had an

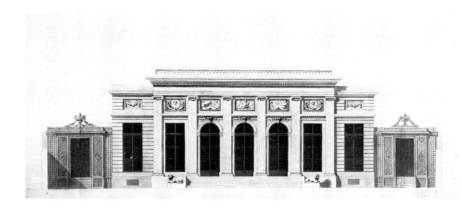

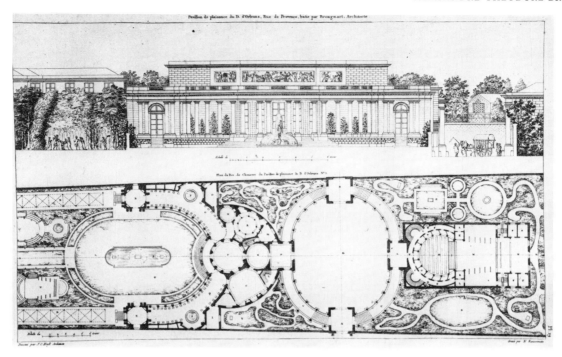

281 The house and theatre of the Duc d'Orléans, Paris, garden elevation of house, and plan (engraving from Krafft and Ransonnette). Designed in 1773 on the site adjacent to the house of the Duc d'Orléans' wife, Mme de Montesson, the house has the appearance of a large semi-rural retreat

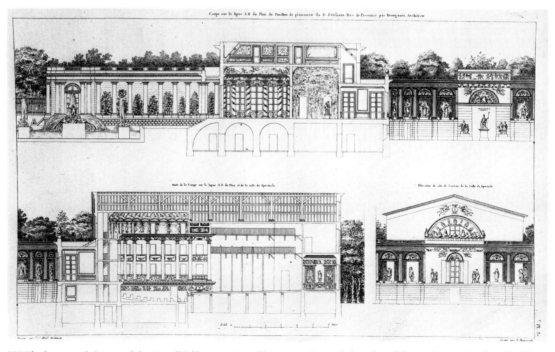

282 The house and theatre of the Duc d'Orléans, section of house, section and elevation of theatre (engraving from Krafft and Ransonnette). Brongniart's design was greatly modified in execution by the Orléans family architect, Henri Piètre

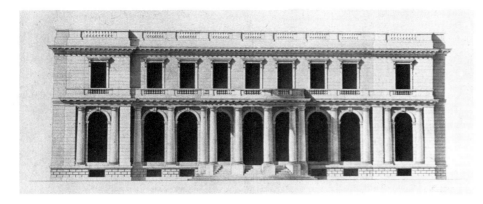

283 The Hôtel de Monaco, rue St-Dominique, Paris, elevation of court façade, drawing by Brongniart (Musée Carnavalet, Paris). Built by Brongniart in 1774–77 on a site near the Palais-Bourbon, for the Princesse de Monaco, the mistress of the Prince de Condé (109)

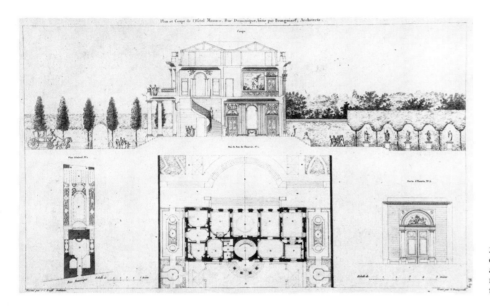

284 The Hôtel de Monaco, section, plans, and elevation of gateway (engraving from Krafft and Ransonnette). The house survives but is now much altered; the staircase is at the rear of the main (circular) vestibule

articulation of Tuscan columns, doubled at the centre and sides, and a plain attic, probably also curved in shape, that acted as a frame for three classical reliefs. The central relief in Krafft's engraving appears to show a goddess in triumph, alluding, as would be touchingly appropriate, to the power of love. Also included in the engraving is a family group at play in the garden of Mme de Montesson's house and a cart on the right turning to enter the courtyard of the larger hôtel.

A theatre was built at the house, apparently in the later 1770s, but in a quite different design, and on a different site, to the one proposed by Brongniart (282). In the original design, if Krafft is to be believed, the theatre shared the countrified character of the house itself, with trees in tubs arranged over the cornice of the portico. Simple in design the building seems as linear as any post-Revolutionary work, with its small reliefs attached without frames to the wide expanse of bare wall. The main feature of the portico, a single small window with crowning lunette, was a motif much favoured by both Brongniart and Belanger in the design of their buildings, and one which contributes not a little to the severity of the theatre façade. Internally the building follows the designs of Peyre and de Wailly, and of Victor Louis in its nearly circular plan and in the presence of giant columns encircling the auditorium.

Brongniart's work for the Duc d'Orléans appears to have continued in the later 1770s when he designed a large stables facing the entrance to the duke's house, and at the same time he was engaged upon the building of several other houses in the north-eastern quarter of the capital, starting with a house at the top of the rue de Richelieu for the Receveur des Finances for Auch, Taillepied de Bondy. In 1775 he began the famous hôtel, two doors away from Ledoux's Hôtel de Montmorency, that was owned by the notoriously corrupt agent of the Comte d'Artois, Claude-Pierre-Maximilien Radix de Ste-Foix, and other houses by the architect in this area that are recorded in early engravings include the Hôtel de Massais, in the rue de la Chaussée-d'Antin, and the house of a Mlle de Charlotte. The actress and singer, Mlle Dervieux, who later became the wife of Belanger, followed Mlle Guimard in ordering her own sumptuous hôtel, which Brongniart constructed for her in the rue Chantereine. Later extended for her by

Belanger, it was a house of two main storeys and more conventional in appearance than Ledoux's 'Temple de Terpsichore' *(226)*.

Unlike his hôtels in the north of Paris, Brongniart's later houses to the south of the Seine, beginning with the hôtel of the Princesse de Monaco, have nearly all survived. From being architect to the Duc d'Orléans in the north of the city, Brongniart had the unusual distinction of working in the south for the rival house of Condé and in circumstances similar to those that governed his work for the Duc d'Orléans and Mme de Montesson. After the Prince de Condé had moved into the Palais-Bourbon and remodelled the palace, he bought up most of the adjacent properties to form an estate not unlike the small kingdom that the Duc d'Orléans was to create near the Chaussée-d'Antin. After the death of his wife in 1760 the Prince de Condé formed an alliance with the Princesse de Monaco, the only daughter of a Genoese nobleman, the Marchese di Brignole Sale. The princess left her husband in 1769 and moved into the Hôtel de Lassay, a dependence of the Palais-Bourbon. No less accomplished than Mme de Montesson, she too suffered contempt at the court, where Queen Marie Antoinette managed to alienate the Prince de Condé by her self-righteous attitude towards his mistress. Subsequently Mme de Monaco devoted her life to Condé; she followed him to Germany in 1789, inspiring in exile a flattering description by Goethe of her grace and gaiety, and the two were finally married in London.

From the Hôtel de Lassay the Princesse de Monaco moved into a new house that Brongniart built for her on a neighbouring site in the rue St-Dominique, a surviving but altered building, which was begun probably in 1774 and completed three years later *(283, 284)*. How Brongniart came to be chosen as architect is unclear. There had been an alliance between the Orléans and the Condé families in 1770 with the marriage of Condé's son to the daughter of the Duc d'Orléans (the parents of the Duc d'Enghien), but it seems unlikely that Mme de Montesson would have recommended the tact and skill of her architect to the Prince de Condé. It may rather have been through the owner of the site, which formed yet another of the

286 The Hôtel de Bourbon-Condé, the salon. Brongniart followed his teacher, Boullée, in his use of the classical orders internally *(143)*

287 The Château of Maupertuis, the pyramid, *c.* 1780 (engraving by Mme Massard after Bourgeois). After Ledoux had remodelled the château *(203)*, Brongniart was employed on the layout of the gardens at Maupertuis where he constructed the famous ruined pyramid, which still survives

speculations of Jean-Joseph de Laborde, that the architect came directly to his attention.

Despite its two storeys and simple rectangular plan, the house is distinctly reminiscent of the pavilion of the Duc d'Orléans in the treatment of its front façade *(283)*. There is the same low Tuscan colonnade and a curved projection in the centre, acting here as the main portico of the building. The garden elevation is in contrast decorated with an order of giant Corinthian pilasters, an alternative articulation that Brongniart also frequently employed. The plan itself, presumably reflecting the unusual character of the household, is especially interesting for the treatment of its staircase. It swept in a single curved flight, attached to the rear wall of the entrance vestibule, directly to the principal floor landing, where openings with pairs of baseless columns gave access to the upper rooms. Following the experiments of Peyre and de Wailly in the 1760s the installation of the staircase in the central vestibule became common practice in Paris in the following decade, especially as a measure of economy in smaller houses. Even if there was no room in such houses for one of the more elaborate symmetrical staircases, at least the staircase itself was sited in the main axis of the plan. At the Hôtel de Monaco, where space was not greatly restricted, the staircase seems deliberately to impose social informality on the plan. With the main bedroom on the ground floor to its left, the principal salon lay directly behind the stairchamber and was accessible only from the two antechambers to the right.

The majority of Brongniart's work to the south of the Seine was concentrated in the area to the east and south of the Invalides, where the architect later succeeded his teacher, Boullée, as Contrôleur. In concert with the Marquis de Montesquiou, an intimate of the Orléans family and Ledoux's former client at Maupertuis, Brongniart obtained permission in 1778 to open the rue Monsieur,

where he built a stables for the marquis and a hôtel, which survives in part, and also a small building for the archives of the Order of St-Lazare. Next door is the hôtel that the Prince de Condé charged Brongniart to build for his saintly unmarried daughter, Louise de Condé *(285, 286)*. The hôtel resembles in plan the house of Mme de Monaco, but the staircase lies in this case to the left of the building. The elevations, enlivened only by rustication, are exceptional in their simplicity, and as unpretentious as the occupant would no doubt have wished.

In these same years Brongniart was also employed by the Marquis de Montesquiou at Maupertuis and he designed what is perhaps his most celebrated building, the Capuchin monastery of the rue des Capucins. At Maupertuis he assisted in the shaping of the gardens, 'one of the most beautiful spots in France', according to Alexandre de Laborde, and designed the valley on the estate known as the 'Elysée', which Montesquiou himself had sketched in outline, possibly with a view to holding masonic meetings there. As well as the famous pyramid, the only surviving feature of the garden *(287)*, the owner also constructed a monument to the sixteenth-century Protestant hero, Admiral Coligny, which, according to Blaikie, 'Shows the Marquis not to be a friend of those catholick persicutions which is looked upon by most reasonable people as a disgrace to France. Here about this part of the country are a great Many protestant familly allthough not tolerated in France yet they are much respected.'

As the possessor of this curious monument, of the Elysée and its remarkable pyramid, and of the extensive château that Ledoux had built for him, the Marquis de Montesquiou may have felt the more confident in the elevated position he claimed for himself in society: 'The Marquis was descended from a very ancient family . . . [and he] made no difficulty in affirming seriously, that he belonged to the Merovingian race, in a direct line from Clovis . . . M. de Montesquiou was overwhelmed with jokes upon the subject of his birth.' According to Mme Vigée Lebrun the independent spirit of the marquis matched that of his master, the Comte de Provence: 'The King's brother was then what is called a Liberal (in the moderate sense of the word, of course). He and his followers formed a party at the Court quite distinct from that of the King. So I was by no means surprised during the Revolution to see the Marquis de Montesquiou appointed General-in-Chief of the Republican Army of Savoy.'

An accomplished designer of elegant hôtels and amusing gardens, Brongniart also commanded, like Ledoux, a style of supreme severity when the occasion was appropriate. His Capuchin monastery *(288–290)* was designed in 1779 to provide a new parish church for the Chaussée-d'Antin, and was completed four years later when the Capuchins of the rue St-Honoré were installed in the new building. The monastery came into existence through the piety of a celebrated parishioner, Mme de Montesson herself, and though several architects submitted designs for the building, including many by the Orléans family architect, Piètre, it was Brongniart's ideas which fortunately prevailed.

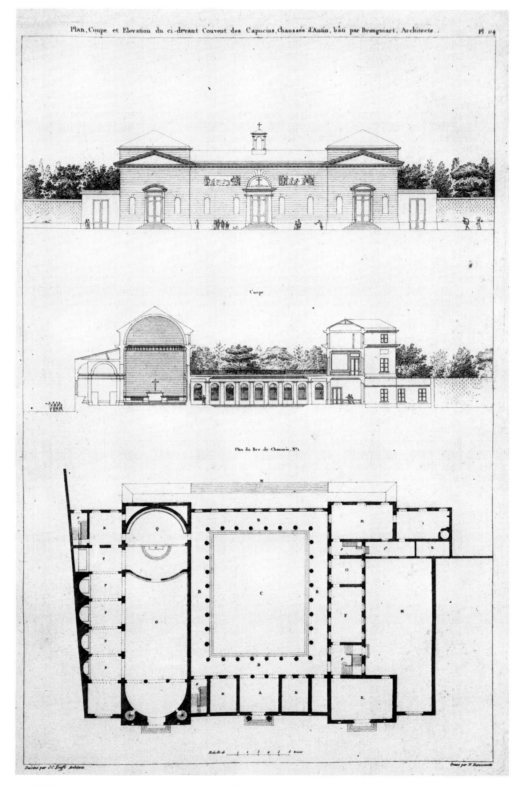

Plan, Coupe et Elevation du ci-devant Couvent des Capucins, Chaussée d'Antin, bâti par Brongniart, Architecte.

Coupe

Plan du Rez-de-Chaussée, N°1.

288 The Capuchin monastery of the Chaussée-d'Antin (Lycée Condorcet), Paris, elevation, section and plan (engraving from Krafft and Ransonnette). Created by Brongniart in 1779 through the initiative of Mme de Montesson in order to house the Capuchins of the rue St-Honoré in the developing Chaussée-d'Antin

The building, now forming part of the Lycée Condorcet, is centred upon its celebrated courtyard *(290)*, articulated with an order of baseless Tuscan columns, which are believed to have inspired the architecture of David's painting of 'The Victors bringing Brutus the Bodies of his Sons' (1789). The entrance to the courtyard occupies the centre of the main façade *(289)*, a portico flanked by free-standing columns of the same Tuscan order as within the courtyard and surmounted by an entablature projecting from the rusticated wall and a squat semicircular window embrasure. The monastic buildings were to the right of the court, and in addition to their spiritual duties the Capuchins apparently acted as the municipal fire brigade, so that a fire station was incorporated in the building behind the courtyard together with a small garden.

The parish church of St-Louis-d'Antin is placed to the left of the court, matched by a hall for public meetings to the right, where the monks also had their quarters. Both church and hall form projections at the ends of the main façade, entered by doorways of more conventional type than that of the monastery, which mitigated for the parishioners the extreme austerity inflicted by the Capuchins upon themselves. According to Brongniart's biographer in the *Journal de l'Empire*, 'it was pleasant to see these good fathers, who prided themselves for having kept the costume of the philosophers "du Portique", come and go beneath a portico very similar in effect to those of Athens'. The same writer claims that the monks wanted windows in the façade but that the architect resisted their

demands. He proposed instead two long reliefs which were carried out by the sculptor, Claude-Michel Clodion, but not finally installed.

The monks may have hoped for a less bleak monastery, but the severity of the Capuchin order was a byword even at the end of the eighteenth century, and in the amusing account of the construction of the governor's palace at Metz in the Créquy *Souvenirs* the Duc de Broglie is ridiculed precisely because he insisted on a building that came to resemble a 'Capucinière'. Hence it is that Brongniart's monastery recalls some of the more extreme works of Ledoux, particularly the *barrières*; and Brongniart being the younger architect, it depends for its effect more than any building by Ledoux upon the decoration, such as it is, remaining extraneous to the cubic structure of the building, especially in the treatment of the central doorway with its free-standing columns, its projecting entablature and the shrunken lunette above.

After the design of the Capuchin monastery Brongniart pursued a successful career that was only temporarily muffled during the years of the Revolution. In 1781 after several attempts he finally joined the Academy, although he remained a relatively inactive member. He moved with his family in the same year to a house that he built for himself on the boulevard des Invalides, but it was also then that he succeeded Boullée as architect at the Ecole Militaire and at the Invalides. Living at the Invalides thereafter, Brongniart brought to completion the outbuildings of the Ecole Militaire and laid out the roads before the Invalides. He continued to be involved in speculative projects and constructed two of his latest houses to the south of the Invalides, the Hôtel Masseran, owned by a Piedmontese in the service of Spain (who later became Spanish am-

289 The Capuchin monastery (Lycée Condorcet), the main façade. The central doorway leads to the courtyard, and the side doors to the monastery (right) and to the parish church of St-Louis-d'Antin (left)

290 The Capuchin monastery (Lycée Condorcet). The court, like the façade, reflects the extreme austerity of the Capuchin order

bassador), which is one of the least altered of his surviving buildings, and the nearby Maison Chamblin. Outside Paris he worked on the estate of the Maréchal de Ségur at Romainville, and reconstructed the church there, which still survives.

Like Ledoux, Brongniart pursued an active social life and enjoyed the company and friendship of artists and writers, including the Abbé Delille, Hubert Robert, and Mme Vigée Lebrun, who stayed with him at the Invalides before escaping to Italy at the time of the Revolution. She, like Houdon and Gérard, was commissioned to make portraits of Brongniart's children, while David and Chaudet gave lessons in drawing to his younger daughter, Emilie. Brongniart's wealth and his Orléans connections endangered his position after the outbreak of the Revolution; he lost his posts at the Ecole Militaire and the Invalides, and in 1792 he sold his extensive private collection, which was remarkable for its many sculptures by Clodion. His one major commission in the early part of the 1790s was the Théâtre Louvois in the rue de Richelieu, a late successor of the theatre designed for the Hôtel d'Orléans. After a prolonged stay in Bordeaux he returned to Paris in 1795, exhibiting at the Salon in that year and joining with Chalgrin and Rondelet to supervise the reorganized Conseil des Bâtiments Civils (see chapter 15).

In 1800 Brongniart took employment with his son at the Sèvres porcelain factory, which had been revived in the service of Napoleon, and the architect turned to the design of china and furniture, including the 'Table des Maréchaux', now at Buckingham Palace, which was made for Napoleon in 1808. Brongniart continued to work for Mme de Montesson, who was engaged by Napoleon to teach his own courtiers the manners of the Ancien Régime, and his architectural career reopened with his appointment as Inspecteur des Travaux Publics in 1801.

The last two important commissions of Brongniart's career were the lay-out of the Père Lachaise cemetery and the design of the Bourse, which became yet another of the vast Corinthian temples of Napoleon's capital. The Bourse, which is now much altered, was originally to have been an Ionic 'Temple de l'Argent', and a building that retained something of the imaginative spirit of the eighteenth century in its decoration, where Brongniart intended to represent the coinage of the realm. His designs, having been sent to the emperor at Tilsit in 1807, were gradually modified in conformity with the pedantry of the age. Brongniart aspired to become a member of the Institut, but he was overtaken by Napoleon's architects, Percier and Fontaine. He died in 1813, shortly before the restoration of the monarchy and was buried in the cemetery that he had himself created.

Brongniart's friend and colleague, François ger (291), pursued a career of even grea variety, for Belanger's achievement centre

291 Portrait of François-Joseph Belanger (1744–1818), medallion on Belanger's tomb, cemetery of Père Lachaise, Paris

series of strictly architectural projects than upon a gift for invention extending through the applied arts and landscape gardening to engineering. Belanger's life is also better documented than Brongniart's, with a host of surviving manuscripts and drawings (largely unpublished), a short autobiography, an accurate *éloge* by his assistant, Mlle Loiseau, and a thorough modern biography. He was born in 1744, one of the nineteen children of a haberdasher, and, like Ledoux and Brongniart, he too was educated at the Collège de Beauvais. According to Mlle Loiseau he specialized in physics, under the Abbé Nollet, and then trained as an architect with David Le Roy, who had been appointed Blondel's assistant at the Academy in 1764. He was also apparently a protégé of the Comte de Caylus, and he spent some time with Contant d'Ivry, no doubt perfecting there the draughtsman's skills which he added to his knowledge of antiquity and physics.

Belanger is first mentioned in 1764, at the age of twenty, in the minutes of the Academy of Architecture, when he competed for one of the monthly prizes, the Prix d'Emulation, which Marigny had recently introduced in addition to the annual Prix de Rome, and again in the following year when Brongniart too was a contestant. He continued to submit designs for the approval of the

292 The bath-house of the Hôtel de Brancas, rue de l'Université, Paris, front elevation, drawing by Belanger (Musée des Arts Décoratifs, Paris). Built in the early 1770s for the Comte de Lauraguais and modelled externally upon a small classical temple

293 The bath-house of the Hôtel de Brancas, section of vestibule, drawing by Belanger (Musée des Arts Décoratifs, Paris). The interior was chiefly famous for the revival of the 'grotesque' decoration of classical antiquity, presumably in the bathing chamber itself, of which no visual record is known

Academy, including the earliest of the projects made for his most important patron, the Comte d'Artois, and he applied unsuccessfully for membership in 1774, submitting then a note on his works.

Belanger's professional career had opened seven years earlier with his appointment as draughtsman to the Menus-Plaisirs du Roi, where he designed a jewel cabinet for the Dauphine, Marie Antoinette, and worked with Arnoult on the construction of the stage of the Versailles Opéra. Belanger also drafted for the Duc d'Aumont, one of the four Premiers Gentilshommes de la Chambre, a scheme for the exhibition of his collection of precious stones, and he prepared a comprehensive treatise on the quarrying of stones in antiquity and modern times. This was a few years after the mineralogical research of Guettard, in which Lavoisier collaborated.

The architect's lively character won the affection of the celebrated *prima donna* of the Paris Opéra, Sophie Arnould, whose short theatrical career, then nearing its end, was to include the title role in the first performance of Gluck's *Iphigénie en Aulide* in 1774. The singer introduced Belanger to her amusing circle of friends, the Prince de Ligne, the 'friend of all the Philosophes' for whom Belanger worked on the design of the gardens of the Château of Beloeil in Belgium, and the Comte de Lauraguais, who commissioned a famous bath-house in the garden of his Paris hôtel, near the Palais-Bourbon, in the rue de l'Université *(292, 293)*.

The nature of this unusual commission expresses something of the patron's own originality, for Louis-Léon-Félicité, Comte de Lauraguais and later Duc de Brancas, was singled out by his contemporaries for the eccentricity of his character, for 'loving to excess the excitement and the pleasures of life', and for uniting 'qualities and defects of which the least part would have sufficed to mark any one with the seal of great originality'. Eleven years older than Belanger, and of a distinguished aristocratic family, he was known as a dabbler in literature and in science, making ruinous tests in dissolving diamonds, as an advocate of inoculation, as one of the earliest devotees of the turf in France and, later in life, as one of the most libertarian aristocrats, affecting in his dress 'the simplicity of a peasant of the Danube'. Another claim widely made on Lauraguais' behalf was that of having campaigned for

294 View of Hagley Hall, Worcestershire, leaf from Belanger's English sketchbook (Ecole des Beaux-Arts, Paris). The sketchbook is almost the only surviving visual record of the visit of a French architect to England in the later eighteenth century

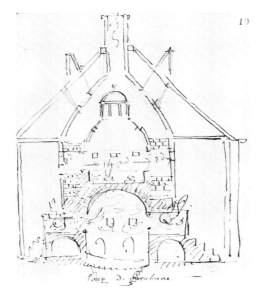

295 Section of a porcelain kiln, leaf from Belanger's English sketchbook (Ecole des Beaux-Arts, Paris). Belanger was interested in manufacturing in England as well as in English landscape and landscape gardens

greater naturalism in the theatre by banishing the audience from the stage and introducing authentic costumes, especially for plays on classical themes, in place of modern dress.

Though baths were not themselves rare in eighteenth-century France (they had become common in the earlier part of the century), a free-standing temple serving as a bath-house, a modest successor to the public *thermae* of classical Rome, seems an idea fully in character with the whims of the patron. The building is described by Belanger as 'a little monument for the use of a bath in the manner of the Orientals, ornamented with four Ionic and free-standing columns . . . it recalls in its appearance one of those temples, Systyle or Prostyle, such as that of Fortuna Virilis or one of those which Palladio described & which existed at Pola in Istria'. Evidently Belanger's intentions

were not strictly archaeological, yet his pavilion, limited in scale and function, was perhaps the closest approximation to a small classical temple to be seen at the time in a town rather than a park.

The building was chiefly famous less for its architecture than for its decoration, since Belanger, with the help of Clérisseau, encouraged the sculptor, Lhuillier, to return from Rome and to recreate for the first time in Paris the 'grotesque' style of antique decoration which had remained largely unexplored since the sixteenth century. Seemingly ignoring Soufflot's design for the shrine of Ste-Geneviève, Belanger claimed that 'no production of this kind had been carried out in Paris since the sublime works of Jean Goujon and Germain Pilon'. The style became so popular in Paris later in the century, as Belanger mentions, that printed wallpapers were manufactured to the same patterns.

Inevitably Lauraguais was one of the pioneers of the 'English' garden in France. A frequent visitor to England, he had his own stables at Newmarket; he had bought the famous horse 'Gimcrack', and it was he who organized the first horse race to take place in France (1766). He and a cousin were known as two of the very few Frenchmen of distinction to have travelled extensively, and in 1768 he was said to have sold to the Prince de Condé a garden he had just finished, 'where he had begun a volcano to great effect'. Later on Lauraguais became the first French patron of Blaikie, who subsequently worked uneasily with Belanger.

Belanger was scarcely old enough to have promoted the importation of the 'English' garden into France, but he was famous for encouraging the development of the style, principally at four noted sites, Beloeil, Bagatelle, Neuilly

296 Portrait of the Comte d'Artois in hunting dress, gouache by Alexandre Moitte (Musée de Picardie, Amiens). Belanger's principal patron, the anglophile youngest brother of King Louis XVI, is shown with the Château of Bagatelle *(297)* in the background

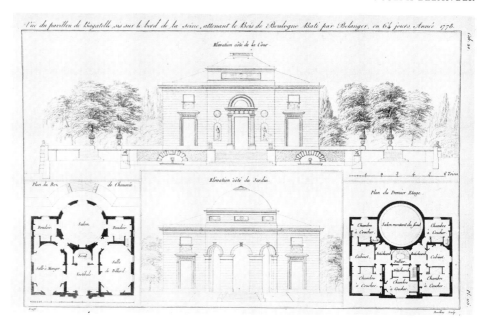

297 The Château of Bagatelle, Bois de Boulogne, Paris, elevations and plans (engraving by Boullay after Krafft, 1812). Built for the Comte d'Artois in sixty-four days in 1777 as a result of a bet with the queen, Marie Antoinette, the château survives but has been greatly modified

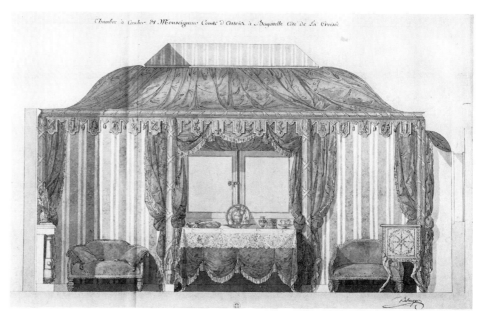

298 The Château of Bagatelle, section of the main bedroom, drawing by Belanger (Bibliothèque Nationale, Paris). Decorated by Belanger as an exercise in military metaphor in the form of a tent supported by bundles of spears; the fireplace with its cannon piers is on the left

and finally at Méréville. He visited England on at least one occasion and it is possible that he had already crossed the Channel at the time of his association with Lauraguais, for he may by then have met William Chambers, to whom his drawings of the bath-temple are dedicated. A sketchbook by Belanger is almost the only surviving visual record of the visit of a French architect to England in the eighteenth century, showing the many sites that he visited (294) and also his lively interest in manufacturing processes (295) in which England had far outdistanced his native country. The architect also produced coloured watercolours of English scenes, which were shown by Mme de Genlis to

the children of the Duc d'Orléans, though she later discovered that they had been copied from engravings and were misleading in colour.

The most famous of the many works commissioned from Belanger by the Comte d'Artois (296), after he had become firmly established in his service on buying the post of Premier Architecte to the king's youngest brother in 1777, were the Château and park of Bagatelle, in the Bois de Boulogne (297–299). Patron and architect were evidently well matched in the liveliness of their characters: 'The Count of Artois', according to a typical opinion of the time, 'is a most amiab[l]e man, and very clever, not like his

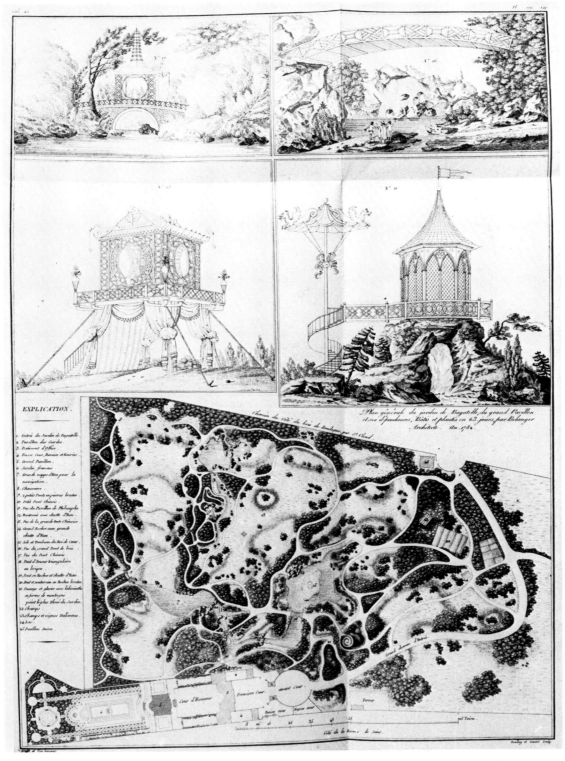

299 The Château of Bagatelle, views of the garden buildings and plan of the park (engraving by Boullay after Krafft, 1812). Belanger's project for the park was described by the Scottish gardener, Thomas Blaikie, as a 'ridiculus affaire'

brother, the Count of Provence, serious and grave, but possessing the true French genius for raillery and repartee.' Indeed the origin of Bagatelle was one of the best known instances of Artois' extravagant wit, being constructed in just sixty-four days (21 September to 26 November 1777), following a bet with his sister-in-law, Marie Antoinette.

Like the bath-temple of Lauraguais the completed building was mainly celebrated for its interior, particularly for the main bedroom, which Belanger carried out as an exercise in military metaphor *(298)*. The room itself was conceived as a tent and all its details were devised accordingly: 'The chimney piece was supported on cannon raised on end, the stoves were constructed of a heap of cannon balls and grenades.' In keeping with the social disorientation of the times visitors found the house too mean in size for the rank of its owner, just as Mme de Thélusson's hôtel was considered more appropriate in scale for a prince. In the words attributed to Mme du Barry, 'its diminutive proportions [were not] calculated to impress the mind of the beholder with any great or vast idea of the state and majesty of him who inhabited it', yet its beauty suggested 'the idea of its being precisely what, in the days of heathenish superstitions, any one would have supposed a god might have selected for his abode whenever he had chosen to assume the mortal, and visit this terrestrial sphere'.

The building itself is less consistently radical than Mme du Barry's own pavilion at Louveciennes. Resembling in scale a hôtel rather than a château, the plan is strictly symmetrical, with a small staircase as the central pivot. The house seems at its most conventional on the garden side, where there was a projecting circular salon with round-headed windows overlooking a small formal garden. At the front, however, the columned doorway with its semicircular lunette above, emphasizing the projecting wall of the front façade, shows the new priorities of the time.

The main route of access to Bagatelle was originally a winding road that crossed the south of the park to reach the circular *avant-cour*. Following the example of his friend, the Duc de Chartres, the king's brother intended to have an 'English' garden of his own, and while the house itself was being constructed he engaged the services of Blaikie, who was then in the employ of Lauraguais. Blaikie apparently designed a plan for the gardens which Belanger then altered to suit French taste, much to the Scotsman's irritation. At the end of 1778 the two men paid a visit together to the site and Blaikie recorded in his diary: 'examined the grounds which is only wood and very indifferant unless a Road cut at great expense; this ridiculus affaire was the plan of Mr Belanger which had cost at least 30,000 [*livres*]'.

Blaikie remained Artois' gardener and lived at Bagatelle until the time of the Revolution, but the park as it is recorded in early plans has all the complexity and artificiality of the French rather than the English style *(299)*. The main buildings of the park were constructed of wood and comparatively modest in scale: a grotto with a

300 The Hôtel de St-James, Bois de Boulogne, Paris, *c.* 1780. The financier Claude Baudard de St-James commissioned Belanger to develop a yet more extravagant garden on a neighbouring site to Bagatelle

Gothic kiosk above, a stone bridge with a pagoda, a Japanese bridge, and a second pagoda forming the superstructure of a tent. Once the work was completed the Comte d'Artois transferred his interest to other building projects: 'the Parisians and foreigners', according to Mme d'Oberkirch, 'profited more by it than its illustrious proprietors, who rarely walked in it'.

The gardens of Bagatelle were quickly eclipsed in interest by a rival park on a neighbouring estate which Belanger created for a very different patron, Claude Baudard de St-James, the son of a rich financier (Receveur-Général des Tailles at Angers) and himself treasurer of the American Colonies and one of the two navy treasurers. From 1780 he shared this last post with Charles-Robert Boutin, the instigator and owner of 'Tivoli', and though they shared a common interest in gardens, St-James apparently lacked Boutin's intellectual refinement. The receptions at his house in the Place Vendôme were 'more hearty than elegant', according to Mme Vigée Lebrun, who compared his circle of friends unfavourably with Boutin's (which included herself and Brongniart). Belanger built a small brick house for St-James *(300)*, embellished with stone dressings and an almost Renaissance garden portico, and he had laid out a large park that extended to the bank of the Seine, passing beneath the road that led from Neuilly

301 The 'Grand Rocher' in the park of the St-James estate, detail showing Doric portico. The artificial rock, known as the 'Eighth Wonder of the World', accommodated a bathroom, a reservoir, a grotto and a gallery

down to Bagatelle. In addition to the pavilions and kiosks, the grottoes and the swings that made up the furniture of these smaller urban parks, the garden contained what was perhaps the most expensive and certainly the most famous 'fabrique' of the time, the so-called 'Grand Rocher', known as the 'Eighth Wonder of the World'; the rock still survives but looks considerably less imposing today (301).

The owner himself was popularly known as 'l'homme du rocher', a name supposedly given him by the young Louis XVI, who had encountered, when hunting one day in the forest of Fontainebleau, a team of forty horses transporting one of the rocks needed for the Grand Rocher. The rock itself accommodated a substantial bathroom and a reservoir, a grotto and a gallery, and this alliance of civilization and nature is expressed by the presence beneath the arch of a portico of baseless Doric columns. Metaphorically nature may seem to overwhelm architecture, a reversal of the effect that Ledoux had achieved at the Hôtel de Thélusson, but the idea was presumably not symbolic but rather an amusing conceit on the part of the patron and his architect.

Blaikie who had declined to interfere in the execution of the garden, inevitably despised the Rocher:

Mr. Belanger has carryed every thing to the Greatest pitch of extravagance; there is a Rock formed before the house or rather an arch of prodigeous large Stones where the water seems to arrive, but this although at a great expence has nothing of nature or natural beauty being entermixed with hewen Stone and a litle temple in the midle in the Corinthian [sic] order and every thing equally ridiculous as there is neither elevation nor mountain to form this huge pile of rocks . . . And endeed all this extravagance was the desire of the Compte Dartois who I heard say to Mr. Belanger 'I hope you will ruin St James' as endeed that soon happened.

St-James was declared a bankrupt in 1783, one of several famous cases of bankruptcy which shook public confidence in the 1780s, and he died soon after.

At the time when the Folie St-James was being laid out Belanger was engaged on two ambitious schemes for his royal patron. Artois had acquired the land of a large nursery garden, the Pépinière du Roi, in western Paris near the village of Roule, and here Belanger built stables to house the racehorses of the count and countess, and he began to develop an estate that was called 'Nouvelle Amérique', centred upon its 'Place Franklin'. The houses, in conformity with the taste of the owner, and with his depleted purse too no doubt, were designed in the English style 'denuded of all types of ornaments, well-aired, and commodiously planned', as Thiéry defined the type. How far this experiment in English living was successful is unknown, but architecturally it conformed with the emphasis upon functionalism that became increasingly evident in the architecture of Paris. The second of Artois' costly projects was no less than the development of the Château of St-Germain-en-Laye and the river bank of the Seine below the castle, which the king had given to his brother. In Blaikie's opinion it was a 'Palais which according to Mr. Belanger's project would cost many millions even in terrace walls, and his project was to have all the front from the River to the top of the hill where the Chateau was to be Built and the Road up was from terrace to terrace from the Pont du Pique'.

Following Bagatelle and the Folie St-James Belanger's supremacy as a garden designer was widely acknowledged, and it was he, no less well matched in this case with the lively intelligence of his client than with the Comte d'Artois, who laid out the garden of the ambitious house that Beaumarchais built for himself in the shadow of the Bastille (see chapter 14). Belanger also participated with the painter, Robert, in the design of the most lavish and most famous of all pre-Revolutionary gardens, the park at Méréville, which belonged to the court banker Jean-Joseph de Laborde, whose fortune had also been derived from extensive speculations in land. The last of Belanger's gardens was the one that he created for himself some years after the Revolution at Santeny. On the estate there he and his wife also built a house, one of the first of its kind in France, designed by Belanger in a curious Gothic revival style.

The town houses that Belanger constructed in Paris in the years immediately before the Revolution show the dissolution of the Renaissance style in French architecture at its clearest. Six schemes are known in early engravings,

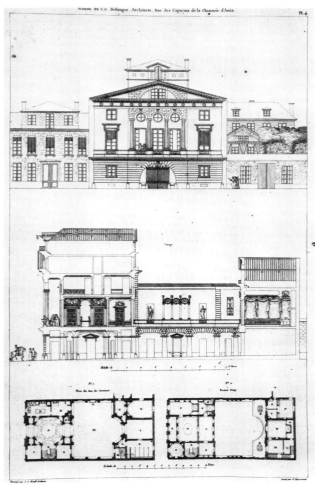

302 House by Belanger in the rue des Capucins de la Chaussée-d'Antin (rue Joubert), Paris, elevation, long section and plans (engraving from Krafft and Ransonnette). Probably of 1787 and showing the disparate character of Belanger's late architectural style

but exact symmetry is sacrificed to economy in the placing of the staircase.

In elevation the pedimented mass of the house supports a system of decoration not far removed in principle from the architect's picturesque gardens, the ornaments being both widely dispersed and of very mixed origin. The general effect of the main façade, with its central three-bay loggia overlooking the street, is perhaps Venetian, but the Ionic order of the centre is separated from the cornice by rusticated arcading resting on the capitals. The entablature is a free invention, patterned with widely spaced roundels, and the rustication continues above, forming a low arch within the pediment. In the court there are no straight lintels *(303)*. Low rusticated arches span the intervals between the baseless columns, and the side walls are patterned at main-floor level with three-bay arcades. It may have been through such designs of Belanger that Ledoux became reconciled to the use of arcading in a domestic context, but when he himself later employed arcades in the nearby houses of M. Hosten *(266)*, he imposed a degree of consistency and logic that Belanger evidently felt no obligation to observe.

In 1789 Belanger was elected to the States General for the St-Joseph district of Paris. A moderate Revolutionary, he was imprisoned during the Terror on suspicion of collaborating with the *émigrés*. In 1796 he joined the staff of the newly-formed Monuments Publics and became for a while architect of the Bibliothèque Nationale, but he was less successful than some of his colleagues in obtaining commissions. In 1804 he produced for Brussels the last of several projects for theatres that he had been designing since the start of his career. The two major works of Belanger's last years, both begun in 1808, were quite different in character from the type of work on which he had been engaged in his youth. The slaughterhouse of

while others, including the house that the architect drew up for Talleyrand in 1792, are recorded in the architect's drawings. St-James and Artois were both involved in these speculations of Belanger, as was Mlle Dervieux, the actress who succeeded Sophie Arnould in the affections of the architect, and who became his wife in 1794. She was then comfortably installed in the house which Brongniart had built for her, and Belanger later added for her a room at the side of the house, which was, like Lauraguais' bath-house, celebrated for its grotesque decoration.

The most elaborate of the hôtels that Belanger constructed was the one in the rue des Capucins de la Chaussée-d'Antin, near Brongniart's monastery, which still survives today though in a largely reconstructed form *(302, 303)*. Here as in many of his other houses the building fronts directly on the street, and carriages passed through a vestibule with a staircase beside it to the court at the rear of the site. The plan is as dense as Ledoux's house plans,

303 Belanger's house (rue Joubert), detail of courtyard. Less altered than the rest of the house, the court has squat Doric columns supporting low arches

304 The Halle au Blé, Paris, view of the interior showing dome (engraving by Guiguet after Courvoisier) (Bibliothèque Nationale, Paris). The first iron dome, completed by Belanger in 1813 to replace the wooden dome of Legrand and Molinos *(139)*

Rochechouart, which is paradoxically recorded in some of the most attractive of Belanger's drawings, was one of a series of abattoirs built under Napoleon in the outskirts of Paris as part of a long overdue campaign to halt the slaughter of animals within the city. The second work, the dome of the Halle au Blé, was the masterpiece of Belanger in his capacity as engineer, the first iron and glass dome in the history of architecture *(304)*.

The dome follows several smaller achievements in engineering by Belanger: the roof of a house in the rue Chantereine, made partly of copper, the roofing of the Château of Buzancy where deal boards were used, and the pump of the Perrier brothers at Chaillot that brought water for consumption in Paris from the Seine. The dome of the Halle au Blé shows a knowledge of the use of iron in architecture that Belanger had discovered in England, where 'iron serves them in the absence of stone' as the architect himself explained. But if the English had constructed bridges of iron, it was in France that the material had been extensively used in conjunction with stone to reproduce the long colonnades and great vaults of antique architecture, and Belanger was to this extent following in the steps of Soufflot and Victor Louis. His dome was designed to replace the wooden covering of Legrand and Molinos which had finally burnt down in 1802, and it served until the Halle au Blé was transformed into the Bourse de Commerce in 1885. The architect

encountered great hostility to the idea of a dome of iron, but its economy was an unanswerable advantage and on the completion of the dome in 1813 Belanger wrote with pride to Jacques-Louis David, describing his creation: 'a new conception for the first time, in this genre, which gives Europe the idea'. Sadly too he had to note in one of his amusing letters to Fontaine that 'the monument is without precedent, but the architect is without a post'. Later he published anonymously a booklet that bitterly attacked the administration of public buildings at this time, naming several architects who, like himself, had suffered from the ignorant administration of La Bruyère.

Belanger had to wait only a short time before the Bourbon dynasty was restored, and it was he who designed the decorations for the entry to Paris of Louis XVIII in 1814. Later he was admitted to the Légion d'Honneur and reappointed architect to the Menus-Plaisirs as well as to the household of his former patron, the new king's brother. Having assisted in the decoration of Reims Cathedral for the coronation of Louis XVI in 1775, Belanger organized several schemes of decoration there on behalf of his successor, Louis XVIII, but he died in 1818 without witnessing the accession to the throne of the Comte d'Artois as Charles X. He was buried in the Père Lachaise cemetery, his epitaph recording that he was 'superior to Kent in the gardens of Méréville/worthy follower of Michelangelo in the cupola of the Halle au Blé'.

14 Paris, the country and the court

BRONGNIART AND BELANGER were only two of countless architects active in Paris on the eve of the Revolution, contributing in their different ways to the extraordinary variety of architecture in the city. Changing priorities in social and intellectual life, and the example in architecture of so many recent masterpieces, seem to have enlivened, almost to the pitch of madness, the development of the capital before the Revolution marked a partial halt and a new turning. With an appropriately architectural metaphor the Comte de Ségur likened life in Paris to the fate of 'one placed at the summit of a tower, for whom the vertigo induced by the sight of an immense horizon came a little before the most terrible fall'.

Several of the larger town houses bordering the northern circuit of the city and on the south bank of the Seine escaped the nineteenth-century redevelopment of Paris, notably the Hôtel de Salm (now the Palace of the Légion d'Honneur), which was built by Pierre Rousseau for Prince Frederick of Salm-Kyrberg in the early 1780s *(305–307)*. Born in 1745 and educated in Paris, Prince Frederick was not content, like many of his fellow German rulers, with enjoying the pleasures of France at a distance. He had taken up residence in the French capital and had tried, according to the Créquy *Souvenirs*, to have himself created a French duke in order to enjoy the same privileges at court as the French aristocracy, but having failed in this he had to remain a simple gentleman despite his supremacy in his own principality. A liberal in politics, he willingly conceded liberties to his subjects at the time of the Revolution; the guillotine finally brought him the equality he sought with the French peerage.

The building of his ambitious hôtel in Paris, along the river from the Prince de Condé's Palais-Bourbon, brought the prince prestige of a kind, but it soon turned to mockery when it became apparent how far he had ruined himself financially for the sake of his hôtel. He employed as his architect a man six years younger than himself, Pierre Rousseau, who had been born at Nantes in 1751. Rousseau had been a *pensionnaire* in Rome after winning only the second prize in the Academy competition of 1773. He

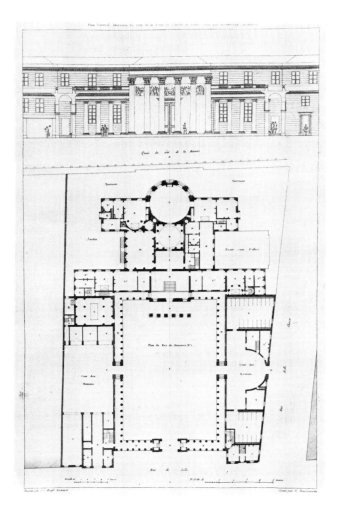

305 The Hôtel de Salm, Paris, cross-section of court and plan (engraving from Krafft and Ransonnette). Designed by Pierre Rousseau for a German prince living in Paris, Frederick of Salm-Kyrberg

306 The Hôtel de Salm, the river façade. One of the largest and one of the few surviving houses of pre-Revolutionary Paris, the building later became the headquarters of the Légion d'Honneur

307 The Hôtel de Salm, the court frontispiece. The court recalls Peyre's design for the Hôtel de Condé (108) and Gondoin's Ecole de Chirurgie (178)

became Potain's son-in-law and his successor at the church of St-Louis at St-Germain-en-Laye. As well as the Hôtel de Salm, he is the author of a much smaller surviving hôtel in the north of Paris (rue de la Rochefoucauld) and it was also he who designed the muniment room at the Hôtel de Montmorency which contained the genealogical papers of the family, together with a Chinese pavilion for the garden of the same house.

For the Hôtel de Salm Rousseau looked to several distinguished prototypes for his design, using Peyre's project for the Prince de Condé (108) for the entrance screen, Gondoin's Ecole de Chirurgie (178) for the courtyard, and the Hôtel de Thélusson for the plan of the house (247), though he reversed Ledoux's inverted design so that the projecting salon lies at the back, on the garden side, overlooking the river (306). Rousseau's plan is even denser than Ledoux's, with a series of four rooms on the central axis, two of them top lit. Derivative as the hôtel may seem to be, it is touched with a severity, not to say monotony, that is foreign to the work of Rousseau's older contemporaries. The main frontispiece (307), consisting of six Corinthian columns against a bare wall with only a frieze of garlands and a rectangular relief for its decoration, has an austerity until then associated rather with religious or public architecture than with the pleasures of domestic existence in the later eighteenth century. When in 1804 the palace became the headquarters of the Légion d'Honneur it required only slight alterations, and must have seemed to offer little that was in any way discordant with the public architecture of Napoleon's own reign.

Indeed the public character of domestic architecture, reflecting the pretensions of clients more rich than they were socially important, is the most striking characteristic of much Parisian building in the years preceding the Revolution. Imposing colonnades, which made the frontispiece of the Hôtel d'Uzès *(212)* seem modest in comparison, invaded many of the larger houses of the time. The Hôtel de Montholon *(308)*, sited not far from the Duc d'Uzès' house on the southern side of the boulevard Poissonnière, was constructed not for a duke or prince but for a wealthy magistrate, M.de Montholon, who, like other magistrates before him, notably M. de Chavannes, had chosen the northern boulevard of the city for his home. Thiéry, describing the house in 1787, mentions that it accommodated six apartments, suggesting that it may have been constructed partly as a speculation. 'The exterior façade,' he continued, 'in the Ionic order, unites with a noble and grave manner that expresses the status of the magistrate who is the owner, the severe and pure style of antiquity, of which this young artist seems to have made a profound study.'

The young artist in question was Soufflot's nephew, François Soufflot, who was indeed known as 'le Romain'. Due presumably to the influence of his uncle he had, without winning the Grand Prix, been sent to Rome, where he is recorded in 1761, at the same time as Gondoin. He joined Soufflot's studio on his return to Paris, later becoming Inspecteur des Travaux at Ste-Geneviève, and in 1789 he married a niece of Antoine. The Hôtel de Montholon is the most substantial of the few independent works he is known to have built and here he worked with another young architect who had also been in the studio of his uncle, Jean-Jacques Lequeu.

308 The Hôtel de Montholon, Paris, the street façade. Designed in 1785 by Soufflot's nephew, François Soufflot 'le Romain', for a wealthy magistrate

309 The Hôtel de Montholon, section of lavatory and bathroom, drawing by Jean-Jacques Lequeu (Bibliothèque Nationale, Paris). Lequeu, who was a pupil of Soufflot, collaborated with François Soufflot on the building

310 'A cowshed in a cool meadow' ('L'Etable, Vache tournèe au midi, est sur la fraîche prairie'), drawing by Jean-Jacques Lequeu (Bibliothèque Nationale, Paris). One of the many fanciful and bizarre drawings produced by Lequeu later in life

Lequeu's participation in the design of the Hôtel de Montholon and his authorship of drawings in an album of sketches for the interior decoration of the house *(309)* are almost the only certain facts known about his career. Most of the other projects for which he is now so famous have been shown to be the fantasies of an increasingly deranged mind *(310, 311)*. However obscure their aesthetic merits, this may not affect the importance of the designs in so far as they embody and indeed exaggerate topical ideas, but it distinguishes them from the imaginative but less literary projects of Boullée and Ledoux. The Temple of Silence, for example *(311)*, supposedly built for a Comte de Bouville at Boulogne-sur-Seine, near Paris, and engraved by Krafft, was probably designed in part for masonic functions. With its two porticos and colonnaded side elevations the house represents an extreme of dedication to antiquity in a domestic context, yet such houses indeed appeared in the English landscape in the early years of the nineteenth century.

The grandest of all the surviving colonnaded Parisian houses of the late eighteenth century is the Hôtel de Gallifet, which lies in the aristocratic neighbourhood between the rue de Grenelle and the rue de Varenne on the south of the Seine *(313, 314)*. The patron here was Baron

311 The Temple of Silence, elevation, drawing by Lequeu (Bibliothèque Nationale, Paris). A country house in the form of a classical temple, dated by Lequeu 1788

312 The Temple of Silence, plan, drawing by Lequeu (Bibliothèque Nationale, Paris). The plan may have been designed particularly for masonic meetings

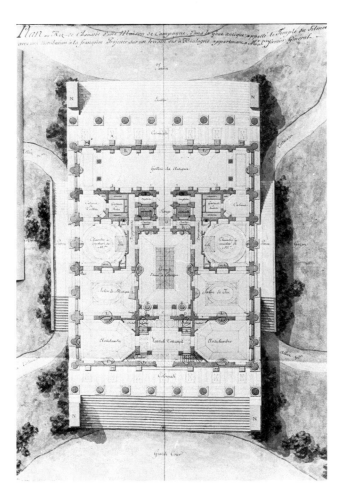

313 The Hôtel de Gallifet, Paris, the court frontispiece. Designed about 1775 by Etienne-François Legrand, and possessing one of the most extensive of the many colonnades that made their appearance in private buildings at this time

Louis-François de Gallifet, a member of a Marseille family which derived its enormous wealth from plantations in Santo Domingo, and a cousin of the Marquis de Gallifet who had gained notoriety in France at the time of Mirabeau's divorce as the undeclared lover of Mme de Mirabeau.

At the Baron de Gallifet's house the colonnade forms a frontispiece which conceals the whole of the front façade, rather in the manner of a country house in the tropics. The deeply sculpted Ionic order with its pronounced volutes was a favourite motif of the architect responsible, Etienne-François Legrand. One of several architects of the period bearing the same surname, of whom Jacques-Guillaume, the partner of Molinos, was the foremost, Etienne-François began his career under the patronage of de Jarente's follower as Director of the Economats, Feydeau de Marville, who engineered his succession as architect to the Economats at the time of Trouard's dismissal. He was the son of Etienne Legrand, an 'architecte expert-bourgeois', who had worked for the Paris police. The Hôtel de Gallifet is one of two surviving houses by Legrand in Paris, the

other being the Hôtel de Jarnac, which lies beside the house that Brongniart built for Louise de Condé in the rue Monsieur. Both the houses by Legrand are informal in plan, with circular staircases adjacent to the main vestibules, and the internal decoration is carried out in the rich if slightly eccentric architectural style that characterizes the treatment of the exteriors *(314)*.

Just as the larger Parisian town houses mirror the social confusion of the last years of the eighteenth century, so too the more interesting of the smaller houses are infinitely varied in their social and architectural ramifications. Many are recorded in the popular collections of views of Parisian monuments, in coloured engravings, which themselves follow architectural fashion in their predominantly circular format, and in the engravings of Krafft and Ransonnette, which exaggerate the geometrical basis of their designs. Krafft records *(315)* the first circular town house, built for a M. Vassale in the rue Pigalle by an architect of the name of Henry, who is probably the Henry 'Trou' responsible for several smaller buildings of the 1770s and 1780s. The house derives from the ideas of

314 The Hôtel de Gallifet, the staircase. Circular stairchambers became common in Paris in the 1770s and 1780s together with semicircular flights of stairs

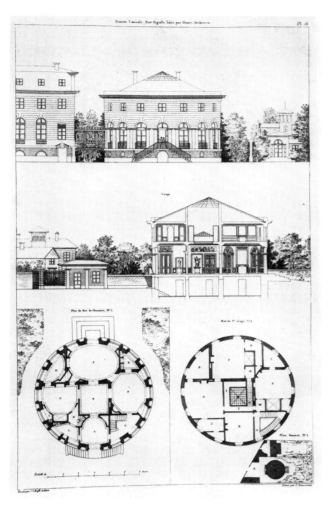

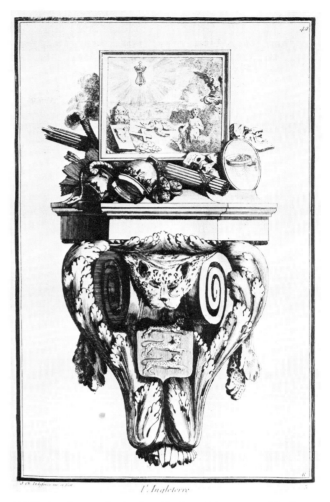

315 The house of M. Vassale, Paris, elevation, section and plans (engraving from Krafft and Ransonnette). An experiment in circular planning designed by Henry in 1788

316 'England', engraving by Jean-Charles Delafosse. One of the designs for decorations from Delafosse's *Nouvelle Iconologie historique*, 1768

Ledoux, especially his design for the country house of M. Witt, and the Barrière de la Villette *(256)*.

Designing a house rather than a customs post, Henry divided the plan on a nine-part grid, with the staircase occupying the triangular wedge to the right of the main vestibule. An oval salon overlooks the garden, while the central, rectangular, space, instead of being two storeys in height and lit directly from roof level, has a small laylight at main-floor level, which must considerably have impeded circulation around the upper storey. In choosing a geometrical shape that Ledoux had used for a customs post overlooking a harbour Henry encountered difficulties that would not have arisen had he been content with a more traditional plan.

A more ornamental approach to domestic architecture is encountered in two houses designed by the engraver Jean-Charles Delafosse. Delafosse is the author of a collection of elegant ornamental designs, the *Nouvelle Iconologie*

historique (1768), that forms the more amusing counterpart to the architectural plates of Neufforge. In the plate representing England *(316)*, for example, leopards decorate the centre of a corbel where the volutes of the Ionic order and the acanthus leaves of the Corinthian merge into leopard skins. England is associated above the corbel with a collection of emblems, not all of them equally intelligible. There are the masks of Tragedy and Comedy, a crown with medallions of monarchs actually chained beside it, military equipment, including an arrow and a smoking rope, and a picture showing the crown triumphant over the papal tiara and the cross.

The inventions of Delafosse are at their most piquant when he included figures in his designs to give a grossly inflated scale to his compositions *(317)*, and in his two houses *(318)*, both designed for neighbouring sites in the rue du Faubourg-Poissonnière, decoration plays a major part, as prolific and crisp as in the engravings, but more

235

317 Project for a prison, engraving from Delafosse, 1768. An ornamental design given spurious architectural validity by the incorporation of figures

318 The Hôtel de Titon, Paris, the court façade. One of two adjacent hôtels in the rue du Faubourg-Poissonnière designed by Delafosse in the late 1770s

inhibited in its allusiveness. Little is known about the proprietors of either of the two houses.

A better-known architectural client is Beaumarchais, whose house was also in the eastern part of the city, built on a long narrow site facing the Bastille (319, 320). In this case the owner, like M. Hosten, set aside the land facing the main street (the rue St-Antoine) as a development for shops and apartments, and himself occupied the part of the building facing the garden, which was laid out for him by Belanger. The buildings were commissioned from Paul-Guillaume Lemoine, known like Soufflot's nephew as 'le Romain', who had won the Prix de Rome in 1775.

Though he had mocked the habits of the aristocracy in his plays Beaumarchais planned to live in some style, supported by the rents of his own tenants. His part of the building was designed on a curved plan that, in addition to its attraction as a shape associated with classical architecture, provided a longer suite of rooms than a straight plan would have permitted. The design lost in compactness what it gained in spaciousness, but several other examples of the type are known, including the house built for Mme Vigée Lebrun and her picture-dealer husband by Jean-Arnaud Raymond, who later collaborated with Chalgrin in the design of the Arc-de-Triomphe.

Lemoine's plan relies heavily upon the circle for both exterior and interior. A vestibule at the side of the house led to a large circular staircase, which gave access at principal floor level via a rectangular antechamber to the round salon in the centre of the plan, and it must have been here that Beaumarchais gave his famous receptions where he would read to his guests, standing upon a stool in the centre of the room. The space below the central salon was also occupied by a flight of steps leading down to the garden, while other stairways around the salon, forced upon the architect by the extended plan, gave access to the top storey of the house. Below the garden façade a large circular court was provided by the architect, covered by a roof that also acted as a terrace leading to the embankments that flanked the garden. The design recalls de Wailly's Château of Montmusard (119), though in scale and in its loose relation to the house it seems not a little theatrical in its effect and related to the kind of scenery that might have been provided for the plays of the owner.

In their different ways the houses of Beaumarchais and Montholon recall the principle of the apartment house, which was to become the most popular of all Parisian house types in the following century. Such houses had appeared in Paris from the early years of the reign of Louis XV, though at the start they seem to have been largely anonymous in character – the style of the time, in its tendency to centralization, being more suited to express the wealth and rank of a single owner. Following the example of Servandoni's designs for the Place St-Sulpice (24) and the house of Trouard at the beginning of the rue du Faubourg-Poissonnière (159), lavish but neatly articulated apartment houses, sometimes of substantial size, became a common feature of urban life in France, and many contain hidden riches in the treatment of the communal vestibules and staircases.

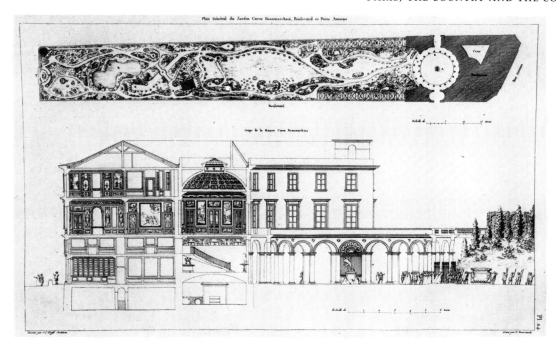

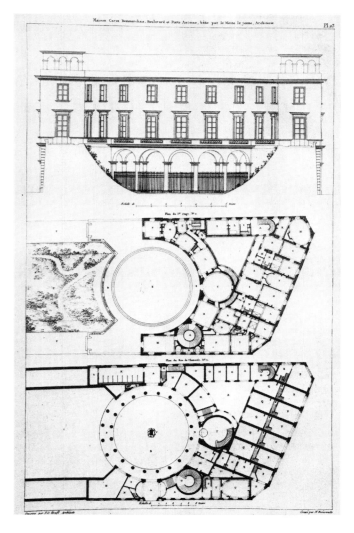

319 The house of Beaumarchais, Paris, site plan and section (engraving from Krafft and Ransonnette). Built near the Bastille for the playwright Beaumarchais by Paul-Guillaume Lemoine 'le Romain' in 1790, and with an 'English' garden planned by Belanger

320 The house of Beaumarchais, garden elevation and plans (engraving from Krafft and Ransonnette). The main house, with its circular staircase, salon and court, faced the garden, concealed from the main street by a row of shops

321 Apartment house in the rue de Tournon, Paris. Apartment houses in Paris became larger and more lavish in the 1770s and 1780s

The most extensive group of such houses in Paris dating from the later years of the eighteenth century is probably that in the rue de Tournon, the road opening to the north from the Palais du Luxembourg, where the Duc de Nivernais lived in the house which Peyre had remodelled for him. The larger of these houses (321) loosely resemble Italian palaces of the sixteenth century in their rectangular appearance, their deep cornices and in the gentle emphasis allowed to central windows. But the more striking of them have in their articulation the broken rhythms and subtle variety that still persisted beneficially in France. The side bays may be set back, a secondary cornice may be introduced, the balconies may vary in elaboration from the more expensive lower apartments to the floors nearer the roof, and the window frames too may follow an intricate counterpoint from floor to floor across the façade.

If the richer classes were comfortably housed in the new buildings of the capital, the same was undeniably true of their horses. As Paris increasingly eclipsed Versailles in the attractions which it offered to noblemen of the court, and as horse racing became ever more popular, monumental stables began to make their appearance on the streets of the city. The ground floor of the Grande Galerie of the Louvre continued to serve as the royal stables, but new buildings had been constructed for the Orléans horses by Brongniart in the rue de Provence, for those of the Comte d'Artois by Belanger in the rue de Bourbon and for those of the Duc de Chartres in the rue St-Thomas-du-Louvre. And following the example of the royal family the wealthier inhabitants of Paris began to construct ambitiously for their own horses.

The most inventive of all such buildings is probably the one which Cellerier carried out for a Spanish nobleman, the Duc de l'Infantado, on a site beside the Hôtel de St-Florentin, which Infantado's wife had acquired in 1784 (322). To the north of the house Cellerier constructed a circular building with a covered court in the centre surmounted by a broad lantern. Twenty-four horses could be stabled in the front part of the building and staircases on the diameter led to the quarters of the grooms on the first floor, accessible from a corridor illuminated by circular windows which circumscribed the plan. The model for the building was presumably the Halle au Blé and its dome by Legrand and Molinos. The author of the Infantado stables, Jacques Cellerier, had been born in Dijon in 1742, and without having any affiliation with the Academy of Architecture, had already established himself as a fashionable architect in Paris with a range of clients that included Mme d'Epinay and the Prince de Soubise. A friend and later biographer of Ledoux, Cellerier was also the architect of the triumphal arch of the Champ de Mars designed for the celebrations that marked the first anniversary of the Revolution and later on of the theatre in his native Dijon.

Relatively few theatres were constructed in Paris before the Revolution, though the theatre was by far the most popular social amusement of the day. It remained under royal patronage, the actors being servants of the Crown and under the supervision of the Premiers Gentilshommes de la Chambre, and only in the 1790s could public demand for new theatres be adequately satisfied. Several small establishments were licensed by the king during the 1780s, the most substantial being the new building that Victor Louis constructed at the Palais-Royal, but the major companies of actors, singers and dancers continued to be employed by the Académie Royale de Musique (the Opéra), the Comédie-Italienne and the Comédie-Française. All three companies were rehoused in the 1780s, the Comédie-Française in the new theatre that Peyre and de Wailly had built, the Comédie-Italienne in a theatre by Jean-François Heurtier, later altered by de Wailly, on a site between the northern boulevard and the rue de Richelieu which had formed part of the Duc de Choiseul's property (now the Théâtre-Lyrique), and finally the Opéra, which moved in to a celebrated temporary theatre built by Samson-Nicolas Lenoir 'le Romain'. Also sited on the northern boulevard of the city, near the Porte St-Martin, Lenoir's building replaced Moreau's Opéra at the Palais-Royal, which had burnt to the ground after only eighteen years of existence (1781).

Lenoir was the brother-in-law of Cellerier, though older

by some years, and he too enjoyed an active and distinguished career in Paris, despite being barred, like Cellerier, from the Academy for his extensive speculations. After studying in Rome under Marigny's protection, and working at Dijon *(118)* and Ferney, his first commission in Paris was at the Abbey of St-Antoine (now part of the Hôpital St-Antoine). Later he specialized in the building of tenements, markets and vauxhalls, as well as private houses. The construction of the Opéra, though its design may have been unremarkable, illustrates the sound practical efficiency of Lenoir. The commission itself was one that attracted many competitors, who hoped to build a permanent theatre in place of Moreau's building. Lenoir's was a provisional opera house, completed in the space of a few months (August to October 1781) and constructed largely of wood, though with vaults of brick *(323)*.

The plan seems to have derived from the Comédie of Peyre and de Wailly, with a circular auditorium, and tiers of boxes with low partitions that receded in plan as they ascended above the stalls, while the ceiling was rectangular and chamfered at the corners. The main façade, however, showed little if any of the commitment to antiquity that had inspired Peyre and de Wailly. More domestic in appearance than the grander hôtels of the 1770s and 1780s, the theatre resembled in particular some of the smaller private houses of Belanger. The cubic mass of the building was expressed in the projecting sides of the façade and in its deep Doric cornice, while the central section was loosely patterned with three arcaded windows and a long relief. Busts of Quinault, Lully, Rameau and Gluck were placed in the intervals between the windows, and eight caryatids originally supported a central balcony. It was a design shaped partly in the interests of economy, which marked the general acceptance, in so public a building, of a much looser relation between function and decoration that was becoming increasingly the rule.

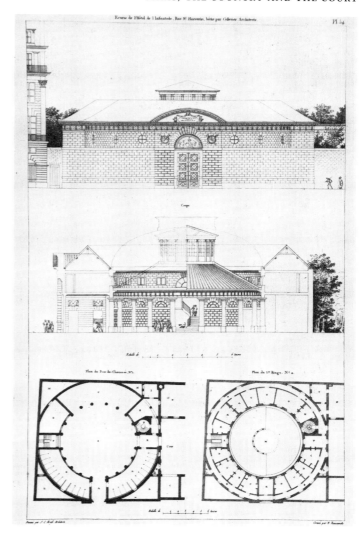

322 The stables of the Duc de l' Infantado, Paris, elevation, section and plans (engraving from Krafft and Ransonnette). Built by Jacques Cellerier on the adjacent site to the Hôtel de St-Florentin *(166)* in 1786, and one of the many famous stables of pre-Revolutionary Paris

323 The Opéra of the boulevard St-Martin, Paris (engraving by Née after Lallemand). The long-lived temporary theatre built by Samson-Nicolas Lenoir 'le Romain' to replace Moreau's Opéra after the Palais-Royal fire of 1781

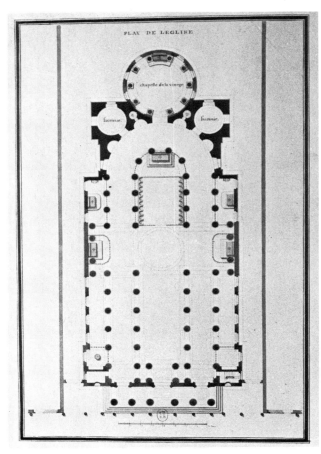

324 Project for the church of Gros-Caillou, Paris, plan, drawing by Mathurin Cherpitel (Bibliothèque Nationale, Paris). The basilican church of Gros-Caillou (not far from the Ecole Militaire) was begun by Cherpitel in the mid-1770s, a chapel by Chalgrin forming its choir

325 Project for the church of Gros-Caillou, Paris, front elevation, drawing by Mathurin Cherpitel (Bibliothèque Nationale, Paris). The Greek Doric columns of the frontispiece are equipped with plain bases

As places of public amusement increased in numbers so ecclesiastical building dwindled in Paris. Though the size of the city and its population had increased rapidly in the later eighteenth century, little money was available for the construction of new churches or for the rehabilitation of those in decay. The church of Ste-Geneviève may have dominated the architectural revolution of the mid-century, but few of the architects who admired Soufflot's building were able to carry out churches of their own. The new western quarter of the city beyond St-Roch was to be served by the Madeleine and by St-Philippe-du-Roule (completed with crippling economy), while to the north there was the church of St-Louis-d'Antin incorporated in Brongniart's Capuchin monastery. South of the river Chalgrin had begun beyond the Invalides a parish church at Gros-Caillou, which his fellow student in Rome, Mathurin Cherpitel, took over (324, 325). A larger building than St-Philippe the church as developed by Cherpitel closely resembled a medieval cathedral in its plan with a double row of columns to each side of the nave and an ambulatory around the choir leading to the circular chapel at the north begun by Chalgrin. A Doric order with a residual base moulding, not unlike the type originally chosen by Soufflot for the crypt of Ste-Geneviève (90), was to be used for the interior and for the façade, where it formed a projecting portico five bays wide with a broad central opening leading to the main doorway.

Evidently Cherpitel was less at ease than Chalgrin with the degree of simplification that was increasingly expected in architectural design. He had worked mainly in domestic architecture, submitting drawings at the same time as Ledoux for the Hôtel d'Uzès, and he later built the Hôtel de Châtelet and the house that Necker owned off the Chaussée-d'Antin. A second ecclesiastical commission of his was for the transformation of St-Barthélemy-en-la-Cité, a small

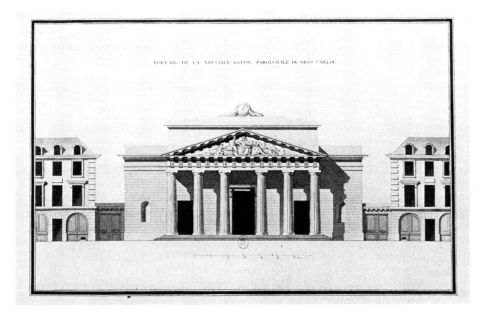

326 The Destruction of the Houses on the Pont Notre-Dame, by Hubert Robert (Musée du Louvre, Paris)

medieval church that faced the court of the Palais de Justice. This was one of several medieval churches of the city whose appearance was radically changed in the later eighteenth century. Some were equipped with new chapels, like de Wailly's crypt chapel at St-Leu-St-Gilles, while others were altered in the decoration of their choirs, following the precedent of St-Germain-l'Auxerrois, where Baccarit and Vassé had recut the Gothic piers to make columns of a more acceptable type. The largest reconstruction projected was that of the church of St-Sauveur in the rue St-Denis, also started by Chalgrin and continued by one of the most talented of the younger generation, Bernard Poyet.

Poyet is best known as the architect of the portico of the Chambre des Députés (346), which faces across the Seine towards the Madeleine, and as the author of a pioneering design for a circular hospital for the Ile-aux-Cygnes in the Seine. A pupil of de Wailly, he came second in the Prix de Rome competition of 1768, and began his varied and active career in the service of the Duc de Chartres. It was Poyet who constructed the simple house in the rue de Belle-chasse where Mme de Genlis lived with Chartres' children, and likewise the stables of the duke, near the Louvre, as well as those of the Archbishop of Paris, near Notre-Dame. He collaborated with Cellerier on the design of a theatre, and for Antoine Callet, the painter, he constructed one of the many artists' houses making their appearance on the streets of the capital. After succeeding Moreau as Maître des Bâtiments de la Ville Poyet supervised the demolition of the houses on the medieval bridges of the city, an act of destruction which was symbolically to be one of the very

last architectural events that preceded the downfall of the monarchy (326).

Such projects of social utility had occupied public consciousness and the minds of architects increasingly as the century advanced but, despite the many proposals that exist on paper, scarcely any of them were actually built. It was not until the régime of Napoleon that public facilities showed a marked improvement, with the construction of new prisons, slaughterhouses, fountains and cemeteries. In prison architecture, for example, which deeply concerned the Necker administration, despite the example of Newgate in London and the prison that Ledoux was to plan in Aix, improvements in Paris were limited to the rehabilitation of the inadequate buildings already in existence, and no one could then foresee the demands that would be made during the Terror.

Private charity, widespread as it was, could rarely rise to the foundation of a new institution, and the school created by Nicolas Beaujon for the poor children of the district of Roule (327) remained without any obvious rivals. Beaujon himself, 'One of the curiosities of the century', had been born in 1718, and he became Receveur des Finances for La Rochelle and later one of the court bankers. It was he who bought the Elysée palace after the death of Mme de Pompadour and had the interior refurbished by Boullée. Later on he built for himself the so-called 'Pavillon de la Chartreuse', constructed in the style of a Dutch farmhouse, further along the rue du Faubourg-St-Honoré near the village of Roule.

There he dwelt in the greatest luxury, although he was himself unable to enjoy the fruits of his wealth, living on

327 The Hospice Beaujon, Paris, c. 1784, the main façade. Built by Nicolas-Claude Girardin, a pupil of Boullée, for the financier Nicolas Beaujon, for the fostering of poor children

spinach and lulled to sleep at night by girls he employed simply as 'cradle-rockers'. Beaujon's architect at this time was Nicolas-Claude Girardin, a pupil of Boullée, who is recorded as a competitor at the Academy in 1772. He had worked at the Elysée with Boullée and then designed the Pavillon de la Chartreuse. For Beaujon Girardin also built on a circular plan the nearby Chapelle de St-Nicolas, which combined the functions of a private chapel and a local church for the inhabitants of the area who were unwilling or unable to cover the distance to St-Philippe-du-Roule.

Finally the architect constructed the Hospice on the opposite (north) side of the rue du Faubourg-St-Honoré, the only building of the three to survive (327). It was intended for the fostering and education of twenty-four poor local children, who were cared for between the ages of six and twelve, and then sent out into the world with a gift of 400 *livres*. On four sides of a central court the Hospice contained classrooms on the ground floor and on the floor above rooms for the priests in charge. In such a context Girardin evidently felt at liberty to discard the mask of antiquity and work in a more strictly functional manner, introducing a round-headed doorway and windows of the same shape, banked in two storeys in the courtyard. Only the simplified Doric cornice, used for both the exterior and the interior of the court, directly acknowledges the authority of antiquity.

Educational institutions and hospitals in the years preceding the Revolution were still largely served and controlled by the church but the Crown was not inactive in seeking to improve the facilities offered in the capital. Indeed the Ecole Militaire (fathered by the financier Pâris

de Montmartel and Mme de Pompadour), Soufflot's Ecole de Droit, Gondoin's Ecole de Chirurgie and Chalgrin's reconstruction of the Collège de France were amongst the most notable architectural creations of the later eighteenth century. The hospitals of Paris, especially the largest, the old Hôtel-Dieu, were notorious for their squalor and for their appallingly high death rate. When most of the Hôtel-Dieu was destroyed by fire (1772), the government asked the Academy of Sciences to report on the problem. A committee, which included Lavoisier, considered the solution of moving the hospital to a healthier site outside the city boundaries, and prepared reports that recommended the building of four new hospitals. Several projects were supplied, including Poyet's design for a circular hospital, but time was by then already running short.

The central administration for hospitals (the Hôpital-Général) had nevertheless acquired by then an able architect who specialized in hospital design. This was Charles-François Viel, the pupil, assistant and biographer of Chalgrin. Viel's extensive practice was concerned almost entirely with hospitals and related buildings, and his most famous building is the Hôpital de St-Jacques-du-Haut-Pas, or Hôpital Cochin, which was begun on the initiative of the curé of the parish in 1780 and opened in 1782 (328). An appropriately functional building, it recalls Brongniart's Capuchin monastery in the treatment of its doorway, though it is otherwise light and airy in appearance with its tall round-headed and rectangular windows.

In addition to his architectural practice Viel was also a prolific author, especially in the years after the Revolution,

328 The Hôpital Cochin (Hôpital de St-Jacques-du-Haut-Pas), the main façade (engraving by Guyot after Testard). Built in 1780–82 by Charles-François Viel, the architect to the Hôpital-Général

who maintained in his theoretical writings (notably in the *Décadence de l'architecture à la fin du XVIII siècle*) an approach of unusual conservatism towards the excesses of his contemporaries. His instinct, clearly apparent in his life of Chalgrin, was to oppose all tendencies, including 'functionalism', which led away from the inspiration of antiquity that had guided the work of his former teacher. Until recently Viel has also been credited with one of the most famous statements of the 'revolutionary' position in architecture, the *Lettres sur l'architecture des anciens, et celle des modernes*, published in 1787, which is now known to be from the pen of Viel's brother, Jean-Louis Viel de St-Maux. For Viel de St-Maux the drawings of Boullée clearly fulfilled his feelings of what architecture should be. Blondel he dismissed as the 'charlatan' of architecture and the church of the Invalides as inappropriate for a 'hospital of old soldiers'. The primitive origins of society should furnish the inspiration for modern architecture in buildings expressive of their real functions.

While Paris witnessed the burgeoning of such theoretical debates and the social and architectural pressures from which they derived, the other major towns of the kingdom were in a state of transformation scarcely less remarkable. As Grimm reported as early as 1760, 'Great buildings of all kinds are being multiplied in France on all sides. There is scarcely a large town which does not want to have a square, a statue in bronze, a town hall, a fountain.' In several such towns the great figures of Parisian architecture had been active, Soufflot in Lyon, Ledoux at Besançon, Marseille and Aix, Louis at Besançon and Bordeaux, and Blondel and Clérisseau at Metz, yet the development of

regional architecture at this time in France is a study still in its infancy. As in the capital, however, social amenities – the provision of squares, fountains and decent streets, of prisons, hospitals and theatres – were a priority throughout the land and in many cases the results were by no means inferior to the best that Paris itself could offer: for example the Place Peyrou at Montpellier amongst squares, or amongst theatres that of Nantes, begun in the later 1780s by Boullée's pupil, Mathurin Crucy *(329)*.

329 The Grand-Théâtre, Nantes, the main façade. The theatre of Nantes was begun in 1784 by Boullée's pupil, Mathurin Crucy, together with the development of the Place Graslin

330 Project for the renovation of the Château of Versailles, perspective view, drawing by Boullée (Bibliothèque Nationale, Paris). One of many grandiose designs of about 1780 for the renovation of Versailles, for which funds never became available

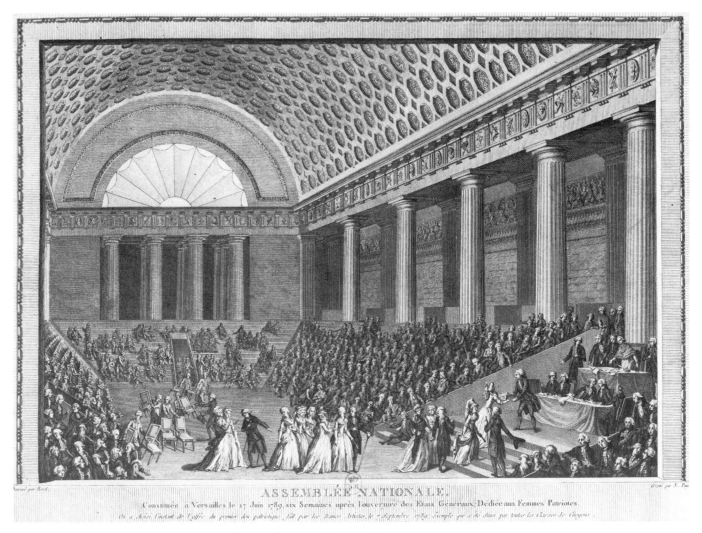

ASSEMBLÉE NATIONALE.
Constituée a Versailles le 17 Juin 1789, six Semaines après l'ouverture des Etats Généraux; Dediée aux Femmes Patriotes.

331 The Hall of the Assemblée Nationale, Versailles, 1789 (engraving by Ponce after Bord). The hall was designed by the chief architect of the Menus-Plaisirs du Roi, Pierre-Adrien Pâris; the engraving shows the first gift of money by women artists (7 September 1789)

Compared with the main regional towns or with the capital itself the architecture of the court in the years before the Revolution offers comparatively little of interest. For all the extravagance of his brothers Louis XVI was ruled by an intelligent sense of economy, which even Marie Antoinette largely respected. Apart from the completion of work already in hand on the royal palaces, especially at Compiègne, little building was undertaken. The need for change, for the king to be seen as a leader of taste, expressed itself in a series of projects of the early 1780s for the completion of the Château of Versailles *(330)*. The architectural character of Versailles, evoking the despotism of Louis XV and his grandfather, corresponded by this time in little more than its oppressive scale with the fashion of the age. Though the Bâtiments du Roi was constantly at work there creating new rooms and apartments, the possibility of a radical change to the exterior involved an expense that cannot have been to the liking of the king, and nothing finally emerged from the many projects supplied.

The alteration of the château had been outlined by Gabriel in the various 'grands projets' designed for Louis XV, and these formed the approximate basis for the schemes of the 1780s. Amongst those who submitted drawings then were several of the younger generation of architects, notably Antoine Peyre, the nephew of Marie-Joseph, Pierre-Adrien Pâris, the architect of the Menus-Plaisirs, and Heurtier, the architect of the Comédie-Italienne, who was also Contrôleur of Versailles. Older architects included Richard Mique, Gabriel's successor as Premier Architecte, Boullée and Gondoin. In Boullée's project *(330)*, one of the few that is known not just in plan, a new forecourt with triumphal columns and buildings for the ministries to each side precedes the palace itself, which is transformed beyond recognition by a new façade entirely enclosing the Cour Royale.

Though permanent architecture almost ceased to exist at Versailles, temporary decoration was in the very capable hands of Pâris, who had joined the Menus-Plaisirs in 1783. A native of Besançon and, like Ledoux, a pupil of Trouard, Pâris left to his native town at his death an extensive collection of drawings which show the range of interests that a gifted young architect could then be expected to cultivate. Many record buildings that Pâris had seen in Italy, where he was a *pensionnaire* in the early 1770s, including Renaissance monuments like the Farnese palace at Caprarola. Others show the decorations Pâris carried out for the court, especially settings for funerals and stage scenery, as well as the actual buildings that the architect constructed. It was Pâris who designed the Hôtel de Ville of Neuchâtel, for which Ledoux had also prepared a project, and he who later modelled the room where the National Assembly met in 1789 *(331)*.

The two principal buildings of the king's Premier Architecte, Richard Mique, are not domestic buildings, but convents which he constructed for the wife of Louis XV, Queen Maria Leczinska, and for one of his three unmarried daughters, the first at Versailles *(332)* and the second at St-Denis. Born at Nancy in 1728, Mique had been

332 The Couvent de la Reine (Lycée Hoche), Versailles, portico of the church. Commissioned in 1767 by the wife of Louis XV, Queen Maria Leczinska, as a memorial to her father, King Stanislas of Lorraine, and designed by Richard Mique who later succeeded Gabriel as Premier Architecte du Roi

court architect to Maria Leczinska's father, King Stanislas of Lorraine, and when the king died in 1766 his daughter determined to found a convent in his memory in Versailles, the Couvent de la Reine, which she commissioned Mique to design. When the queen in turn died in 1768 Mique became architect to the daughters of Louis XV and then architect to Marie Antoinette. It was thus that he gained ground over Soufflot and became Premier Architecte on the retirement of Gabriel in 1775.

Mique was essentially a safe architect, rather as Maurepas may have appeared a safe Premier Ministre, and he was almost unique in the competent conservatism of his style, which perpetuated the memory of Gabriel right up until the time of the Revolution, despite the innovations in the town of Versailles of Trouard and of younger architects, like Charles-François d'Arnaudin, who were active there. For Marie Antoinette Mique was chiefly engaged upon the transformation of the park of the Petit Trianon. Discouraged from interfering in politics, the queen had cultivated a group of close personal friends, notably the Polignacs, and she was regarded, like Mme de Pompadour and Mme du Barry before her, as a leader of fashion at the court. Yet it was rather in her personal adornment that she had the greatest success, impressing the public by the 'simplicity' of her appearance. As in architecture, the borderline between what was natural and what artificial was difficult to distinguish, and the subject of an amusing satire in the Créquy *Souvenirs*: 'Ask my niece de Matignon if it isn't true that she had her hair dressed, in the year 1785, *à la jardinière* . . . "I want to wear only vegetables! It has an air of such *simplicity*, vegetables! It's more *natural* than flowers!"'

The queen's interest in architecture was confined mainly to garden buildings, carried out for her at Rambouillet, which the king acquired in 1784, as well as at the Petit Trianon. In the Laiterie at Rambouillet *(333)*, constructed to the designs of Hubert Robert and Jacques-Jean Thévenin near the model farm that was laid out in the park, Marie Antoinette could engage in the fashionable and healthy pastime of drinking milk. At the Petit Trianon most of the park was transformed into an 'English' garden, including the famous model village and farm *(334)*, which was designed by Mique in collaboration with the gardener Antoine Richard and with the advice of the queen and her

333 The Château of Rambouillet, the dairy. Designed for Queen Marie Antoinette by Hubert Robert and Jacques-Jean Thévenin (1778)

334 The model village of the Petit Trianon, Versailles, begun 1783. The transformation of the grounds of the Petit Trianon *(46)* with buildings designed by Mique was the most extensive architectural enterprise of Queen Marie Antoinette

friend, the Comte de Caraman. Blaikie saw the early stages of the work in 1777 and recorded his dismay at the destruction of the old garden:

here is a great Alterations going on but upon another plan, this is eregular; here we met with Monsr. Richard who showed us very cevilly the gardins which formerly was one of the first Botanick gardens of Europe; there is stil a great many rare and curiousss plants but, as this belongs to the Queen who is not fond of plants, they are turning it all into a sort of English garden – what a pity such a valuable colection should be destroyed!

The garden was not one of the most expensive transformations of the time, as Mme d'Oberkirch noted, but, designed for the queen, it gave impetus to the growing fashion for informal landscaping. Blaikie records a great many such transformations that he was consulted about, including several on behalf of friends of the queen, the Princesse de Lamballe (at Passy) and the Duc de Polignac (at Clay). As the century progressed, the design of gardens in France gradually became less artificial, moving towards a closer approximation of the English park. 'The art of gardening', according to Laborde in 1808, 'may be divided into two equal epochs or periods. All these gardens of the first epoch are loaden with useless and incoherent ornaments; and it is only in those of the second period that sense and utility are found combined with elegance.' 'Useless ornaments' continued to play an essential part in many French gardens, however, especially in the more urban estates that encircled Paris itself. The most famous of them have inevitably been destroyed or altered beyond recognition, like Méréville, where Belanger worked, but there are at least two surviving monuments of exceptional architectural interest: the Pavillon Chinois of Cassan and the house of M. de Monville in the Désert de Retz.

The park of Cassan, near the estate of the Prince de Conti at l'Isle-Adam, was owned by Fragonard's friend, the financier, Pierre-Jacques Bergeret de Grandcourt, and it was he who commissioned the bath-house and Chinese pavilion as part of the improvement of the park which he had acquired in 1778. Recently restored, the pavilion is one of the very few surviving examples in France of the Chinese kiosks and pavilions that were once so common a feature of the gardens of the time (335). Though built of wood, like most such structures, Bergeret's pavilion was more substantial than many, its yellow panelled walls and red eaves rising over a stone bath-house where baseless Tuscan columns support a flattened vault. The pavilion itself, though in principle a belvedere that stems from the 'frivolous' taste in Chinoiserie of the earlier part of the century, has a simplicity common to the last examples of the style, including the designs for Marigny's own Chinese pavilion which Soufflot had disdained to consider.

The park of M. de Monville also had its Chinese pavilion, a rectangular house that has fallen tragically to the ground within the last twenty years (336). With its bamboo columns and Chinese inscriptions it was a wittier and seemingly more authentic building than Bergeret's pavilion. And so too was the main focus of the park, the famous house that the owner constructed for himself, a building of four storeys in the shape of a gigantic broken

335 The Chinese pavilion of Cassan, l'Isle-Adam, near Paris. Built for the financier Pierre-Jacques Bergeret de Grandcourt after 1778 and one of the few surviving garden buildings in the Chinese taste

column *(337)* with its base largely embedded in the ground and its shattered top planted with vegetation. Like the salon of Mme de Thélusson the house emerges directly from the landscape with no formal garden as a barrier, and it marks an eccentric extreme in the process of rebuilding in France the ruins of antiquity.

The patron himself was as famous a 'character' in his own country as William Beckford in England, who later attempted to equip his house at Fonthill with a spire taller than that of Salisbury cathedral. Nicolas-Henri de Racine de Monville was the son of the Receveur des Finances of Alençon, and he numbered the post of Grand Maître des Eaux et Forêts of Normandy among his own official appointments. The house he had earlier built for himself in Paris, to the designs of Boullée *(142)*, was celebrated for the lavish eccentricity of its decoration, which had so shocked Mrs Thrale on her visit there. His accomplishments were described by his friend Dufort de Cheverny: 'He danced admirably, he succeeded in astonishing in all exercises, mounting horses, playing tennis, playing instruments, shooting arrows with a bow better than a savage.' Mme Vigée Lebrun encountered him as a frequent visitor at

336 The Chinese pavilion of the 'Désert de Retz', near Marly. The house was the country residence of Nicolas-Henri de Monville, whose Paris houses Boullée had designed *(142)*; the pavilion was mainly of wood and has now disappeared

337 The tower house of the 'Désert de Retz'. The guest house of de Monville, carried out for him by François Barbier in the 1780s, and now being restored

338 The entrance to the 'Désert de Retz', view of the inside of the gateway (engraving from Le Rouge). Rocks of stucco, here peopled by satyrs, formed the inside of the main entrance

Louveciennes after the disgrace of Mme du Barry: 'He was pleasant and very elegant, and took us to see his estate called Le Désert, the house of which is only a tower.'

Blaikie, however, who met de Monville in the company of Philippe-Egalité, expressed some contempt for the man and his garden:

The Duke had many of those pretended Connisseurs about him; he had frequently M.de Monville who was frequently one of his party and a Pretended Connisseur in everything; he had formed a garden and Path according to his own designs adjacent to the forest de Marly where he had made his chateau in the form of an Old round tower with a Staire in the Midle surrounded with flower pots which made a tolerable agreable effect; the Appartements was small all arround the tower from the staircase; the tope of the tower seemed to have been ruined – I cannot think but he meant to emitate the tower of Babel. He had some good Hotthouses and by them a little Chinese building where he generally lodged [336]. The whole of the park was a Laberynth of rather narrow crooked walks without forming many agreable Landscapes, the Entry was rather an Arch of Tryumph of Gothic building, and to the left upon the rising ground stood a Smal temple in the Doric taste, the tower formed another but too confined. However he was tolerable admired by the Duke and Many others for his address, he was the best Archer in France and Perhaps in Europe.

If Blaikie is to be believed, the column house was mainly for show, de Monville preferring to inhabit the Chinese pavilion, and the motives that inspired the creation of the house in the guise of a column remain unexplained. Though many of the ruins of Rome had subsequently become palaces and houses, the triumphal columns of the city had never, for obvious reasons, been inhabited. Only in the design of lighthouses can any analogy be discovered for a house remotely resembling the form of a column, and in Italy there was at least one other circular house, resembling the stump of a lighthouse, perched on an island in the midst of a lake. Circular plans, on the other hand, had been widely adapted for domestic architecture in France, and the column house is a variant of these designs, with its central top-lit circular staircase giving access to rooms of ingeniously varied shape. Blaikie mentions the small scale of the rooms as a disadvantage; many must also have been dark, with only a single narrow window fitted into the channelling of the column, and the servants' quarters on the top floor were illuminated only from the roof. There were no kitchens in the tower itself, and food was brought through an underground passage from an outhouse kitchen to the dining-room.

Originally the park was more densely furnished with follies, but of the larger structures only the Temple of Pan, the ice-house in the form of a pyramid, and the ruins of a real medieval church now remain. The principal entrance was in keeping with the rest of the park, for here nature had completely assumed the responsibilities of architecture (338). The inside of the gate was designed as an outcrop of rock fashioned of stucco. In a contemporary engraving that shows the inner side of the entrance two satyrs, emanating no doubt from the Temple of Pan, spring from the rocks to light the path for an innocent family of visitors.

339 The old Hermitage, Leningrad (1764–67), the street façade. Built for Catherine the Great by Jean-Baptiste Vallin de la Mothe

340 The Exchange, Leningrad, the main façade. The principal surviving building constructed in Leningrad (1801) by Thomas de Thomon, a pupil of Ledoux

15 Architectural theory and practice after the Revolution

THE ARCHITECTURAL CHANGES that became apparent in the years after the Revolution formed part of a gradual process of development to which individual architects had contributed throughout the later years of the eighteenth century. If Soufflot and Ledoux had responded to the wit and visual sophistication of the Renaissance tradition in buildings that otherwise undermined accepted principles of design, there were other architects, like Boullée, who aimed to substitute simple geometrical shapes as the basis of a more expressive architecture, and others again, like Belanger, who united simplification of form with inexhaustible patterning based largely, but not exclusively, upon the classical repertoire.

Even so the Revolution marked a decisive break in architecture by temporarily disrupting both practice and teaching, and with the exception of small houses, theatres and temporary decorations, little was constructed in France. Many French architects found greater opportunities abroad than in their native country, where promising students were increasingly encouraged to enter the army as military engineers. The production of drawings and the publication of books took the place of architectural commissions, now in short supply. The experience of the later eighteenth century was codified and transmitted to posterity in the influential writings of Rondelet and Durand, and embodied in the buildings of Napoleon's chief architects, Percier and Fontaine.

Throughout the eighteenth century French architects had been in demand in foreign countries, especially at the princely courts of Germany, and Paris itself had – in its modern architecture – replaced Rome as the magnet that attracted architects from abroad. In the later years of the century Soane, following Chambers, was deeply influenced by brief acquaintance with the French capital, and Jefferson studied at greater leisure the architecture of Paris during the course of his diplomatic visit to France. Friedrich Gilly was in Paris in the mid-1790s and Schinkel not long after. And as well as trained architects, students, especially from Russia, came to Paris for their training – Bajenev with de Wailly and Zakharov with Chalgrin.

Amongst French architects who had travelled in northern Europe, Gondoin, Belanger, de Wailly and Ledoux had all apparently been in England, and the last two were also active in Germany. De Wailly and Belanger both worked in Belgium where Nicolas Barré also practised, while Jardin had worked for the Danish Crown and Louis-Jean Desprez, a collaborator of de Wailly's, served the court in Stockholm. Ennemond Petitot became court architect at Parma, and Léon Dufourny practised as far south as Sicily. French architects were likewise active in both Russia and America, where Pierre-Charles l'Enfant and Maximilien Godefroy had extensive practices in the early nineteenth century.

The patronage of Catherine the Great had attracted to St Petersburg both Diderot and the sculptor Falconet, but the empress had been less successful with French architects. Le Lorrain had died shortly after arriving in her capital, and de Wailly had declined to serve as President of the Academy there. French architecture was represented in the Russian capital by Jean-Baptiste Vallin de la Mothe, the designer of the Academy buildings and of Catherine's Hermitage *(339)*. It was not until the arrival of Thomas de Thomon in 1798 that Russia acquired a French architect as able as the Italian, Giacomo Quarenghi, or any of her own younger architects *(340)*.

In France, meanwhile, the years after 1789 were chiefly remarkable in architecture for administrative reforms that effected the transition between the institutions of the Ancien Régime and the organization of architecture in the nineteenth century. The Surintendant des Bâtiments du Roi, the Comte d'Angiviller, before his flight from France, was one of the first to suggest (1790) that changes should be instigated in the organization of the Academy of Architecture, and the students too demanded modest reforms. The abolition of the Academy in 1793 came about through the efforts of the painter, David, to suppress the Academy of Painting and Sculpture. Motivated by resentment against the Academy, which had belatedly awarded him the Prix de Rome in 1774, and against the Premier Peintre du Roi, Jean-Baptiste Pierre, David created in 1790 the Commune des Arts, which demanded the suppression of the Academy. But it was not until two years later, when he had become a Député in the National Convention, that David could move further. He then contrived to have the directorship of the Academy in Rome, which was due to go to his enemy, Joseph-Benoit Suvée, abolished and all nominations and replacements of personnel in the Academies halted. In August 1793 the Convention finally suppressed the Academies, 'the last refuge of all the aristocracies', as David described them in his tirade.

The school of the Academy of Architecture, headed by David Le Roy, was however too useful to be allowed to disappear and it continued to function with Antoine-Léon Vaudoyer assisting Le Roy, and Percier and Fontaine acting as chairmen in judging the work of the students. Evidently a teacher whom even David respected, Le Roy was appointed one of the fifty-five eminent men, including seven architects, who replaced the Commune des Arts in the judging of artistic competitions, including the Prix de Rome. Later Le Roy also became one of the committee of ten appointed to supervise the newly created Musée des Arts, of which de Wailly was the architect, the forerunner of the Musée du Louvre.

In April 1791 a Conseil des Bâtiments Civils, with nine architects, had been created in place of the existing administration and in 1794 a Commission des Travaux Publics was formed. In the constitution of August 1795, which founded the Directoire, the Conseil was placed under the Minister of the Interior. In December Chalgrin, Brongniart and Rondelet were appointed the architectural advisers of its six departments – government, justice, education, 'approvisionnements', hospitals and public amenities – each of which was headed by an inspector. Faced with the threat of military invasion in 1794, the Convention charged the Commission des Travaux Publics with the founding of a school for the training of civil and military engineers. The Ecole Centrale des Travaux Publics, renamed Ecole Polytechnique in 1795 and enlarged in the scope of its syllabus, prepared students for more specialized training with the Ponts et Chaussées, the Ecole des Mines, and the other civil and military engineering schools. It became celebrated architecturally through the teaching of Jean-Louis Durand, its professor of architecture.

In September 1795 the Convention ruled on the reorganization of education in France and founded the Institut in succession to the Academies of the Ancien Régime. Architecture was represented by six of the 144 members, and formed part of the third class of the Institut, which covered literature and the fine arts. All six architects, Gondoin, de Wailly, Raymond, Pâris, Antoine-François Peyre and Boullée, had been amongst the sixteen of the first class of the old Academy, and its former professor Le Roy was also a founder member of the Institut, one of the six who represented 'Antiquities and Monuments'. The same decree on education also acknowledged Le Roy's school, renamed the Ecole Speciale d'Architecture, as the principal school of architecture.

Some years later, in 1803, the school of architecture moved with the other special schools to Le Vau's Collège des Quatre-Nations, leaving the Louvre free for the creation of the Musée du Louvre, and they were joined four years later by the Institut, which still occupies Le Vau's building.

About the time of the move of the Institut across the river Napoleon reorganized its constitution, creating four classes instead of three and dividing the section of 'Literature and Fine Arts' into two. After the restoration of the monarchy the separate classes of the Institut resumed their old titles of 'Academy', and the membership of the Académie des Beaux-Arts was increased from 28 to 40 allowing two further places for architects. Final changes in 1832 introduced a fifth Academy, and raised the total membership to 206. The Ecole Speciale d'Architecture was finally incorporated in the Ecole des Beaux-Arts on its foundation in 1807.

As building activity dwindled after the Revolution so the number of drawings and books produced increased and the years from 1789 to 1815 are indeed remarkable for the scope of their publications, in which the achievements of the later eighteenth century were codified, and almost all periods of the architecture of the past and most aspects of building technique covered. For the later eighteenth century there were the various collections of Krafft, beginning with the town houses of Paris, engraved by Ransonnette, which appeared in 1802, and continuing with volumes on gardens (1809) and country houses (1812). Guides to Paris, following in a long tradition, included the *Description* by Legrand and Landon; and in the many volumes of Landon's *Annales du Musée* architecture is extensively discussed. Amongst the many periodicals to which architects frequently contributed was one, probably the first of its kind, dealing largely with architecture, the *Annales de l'architecture et des arts*, where Ledoux is frequently mentioned.

The *Mémoires* of the Institut, appearing first in 1798, included obituaries of deceased members, notably Boullée and de Wailly, and later on the orations that Quatremère pronounced on Chalgrin, Gondoin, and many others, who are thus better recorded in print than their predecessors, Gabriel and Soufflot. Books which dealt with relatively unexplored subjects included the influential *Architecture toscane*, the first detailed account of Quattrocento architecture, by Famin and Grandjean de Montigny, of which the earliest parts appeared in 1806. As examples of less celebrated works there were the many structural treatises by François Cointeraux and a treatise on the use of precious stones in the ornamentation of buildings (the *Traité des pierres précieuses* of 1808 by Prosper Brard).

The two most influential contributors to this growing body of literature were Rondelet and Durand, whose books contain in essence that part of the legacy of the later eighteenth century considered most useful in their own day. Jean-Baptiste Rondelet was a native of Lyon, trained in Paris by Blondel and Soufflot, who took over from Brébion and Soufflot's nephew the responsibility for the completion of Ste-Geneviève. Rondelet published a lengthy study of the church in 1797 and in 1806 he was to

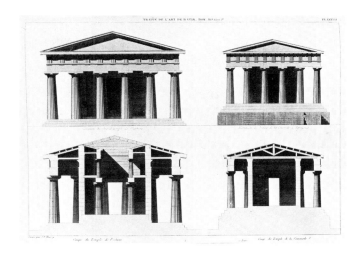

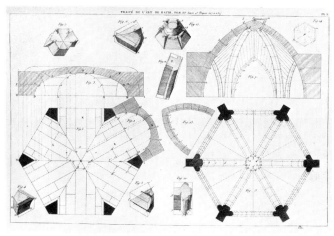

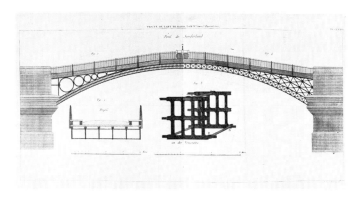

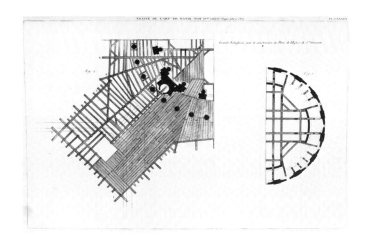

341 Plates from Rondelet's *Traité*, 1802–17, Greek temples, Gothic vaults, the bridge of Coalbrookdale, the scaffolding of the dome of Ste-Geneviève, primitive cabins. Rondelet's practical guide to the 'art' of building includes an analysis of how primitive cabins *(54)* were really built

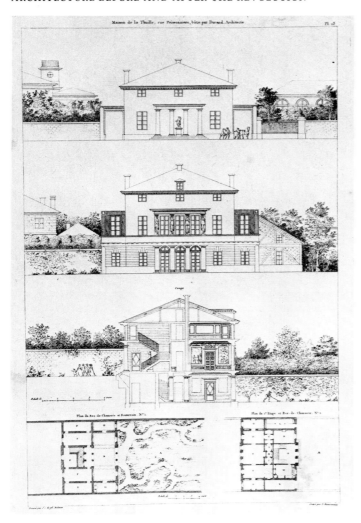

342 The house of M. Lathuille, rue du Faubourg-Poissonnière, Paris, elevations, section and plans (engraving from Krafft and Ransonnette). One of several small houses constructed by Durand (1788)

is less in evidence than the 'pratique' since for Rondelet architecture was less an imaginative than a practical art, while theory meant a sound knowledge of mathematics and physics: 'the essential aim of the art of building is to construct solidly through the employment of the right quantity of chosen materials carried out with art and economy'.

His treatise is thus concerned largely with building materials and their capacities, a subject in which the author far surpassed Patte's addition to the *Cours* of Blondel and Le Camus de Mézières' treatise of 1781. As heir to the work of Soufflot, Rondelet explored both Greek and Gothic building methods in his book, and he showed plank by plank the type of scaffolding used to construct the dome of Ste-Geneviève *(341)*. He discussed iron as a building material, illustrating early iron bridges constructed in England, including Coalbrookdale, and the iron roof trusses that Soufflot and Brébion had employed at the Louvre, as well as those of Victor Louis at the Théâtre-Français. Practical to the last, Rondelet showed in his discussion of wooden buildings how a primitive cabin was really constructed, not of columns as Laugier had supposed *(54)*, but of logs laid one upon the other *(341)*.

While all the practical aspects of architecture were covered by Rondelet, the principles of architectural design were outlined in the yet more influential treatise of Durand, the *Précis des leçons d'architecture données à l'Ecole Polytechnique* (1802–05), which became the standard training manual for generations of architects both in France and abroad, where it served in the absence of any schools comparable to those which had flourished in Paris before and after the Revolution. Born in 1760, Durand had already studied architecture under Pierre Panseron when he became one of Boullée's assistants and received a salary that enabled him to enter for the Prix de Rome competitions, in which he was placed second in 1779 and 1780. Durand then worked mainly as a draughtsman and produced one of the many collections of views of important Parisian buildings, roundels that include several of the early works of Boullée *(145)*.

Durand was also responsible for the construction of several small private houses of which the best known, recorded by Krafft, was the Maison Lathuille in the rue du Faubourg-Poissonnière *(342)*. Simple and block-like in character, the house had an uncomplicated rectangular plan incorporating a staircase directly accessible from the vestibule. As in the work of Belanger and Brongniart, the decoration seems shrunken in relation to the scale of the building; the choice of ornament on the garden side included caryatids of an order only rarely encountered in France, deriving from the Doric Temple of Apollo at Delos, which is fluted only at the top and bottom of the shaft.

In addition to his drawings and buildings Durand was also actively engaged on the drafting of competition projects and together with J.-T. Thibault, another of Boullée's protégés, he submitted a total of eleven designs for public schemes proposed in 1793 by the Convention. None of these designs was carried out, but probably as a consequence Durand was appointed professor of architec-

put the finishing touches to the architecture of the building when he stabilized the piers of the crossing. Working on the latest stages of Soufflot's masterpiece, Rondelet was confronted with problems of engineering which led him to study at length building techniques and materials and which took him to Italy in 1783 at the expense of the state to investigate methods of antique engineering. As one of the members of the Commission des Travaux Publics he was instrumental in the creation of the Ecole Polytechnique, and shortly after its foundation he became the professor of stereotomy at Le Roy's Ecole Speciale, where he taught before and after its incorporation into the Ecole des Beaux-Arts and until his death in 1829.

Rondelet's masterpiece, the *Traité théorique et pratique de l'art de bâtir*, was first published in four volumes in 1802–17, and by 1861 it had run to as many as eighteen editions. In the book the 'théorique' promised by the title

ture at the Ecole Polytechnique, where he was active until shortly before his death (1834). In 1800 Durand published a *Recueil et parallèle des édifices de tout genre*, where instead of recent building in Paris the author surveyed the whole history of architecture, tabulating buildings on a common scale according to their function, beginning with Egyptian and Greek temples which are crowded on the title page *(343)*. These are followed by Gothic churches and buildings of every conceivable type.

Geometry is the basis of Durand's designs in the *Précis des leçons d'architecture*, and his illustrations, showing how buildings are to be laid out on a grid, resemble endless simple geometrical problems *(344)*. Not the least reason for the popularity of Durand's book lay in its value as a pattern book, covering every aspect of building design, just as earlier Durand had covered the history of building types. Function and economy he stressed to the extent that his recommendations remained notionally classical only in their simplification of form. The obsession of the later eighteenth century with columns and lintels Durand rejected in favour of the more practical arcading methods of the early Renaissance, which were taken up extensively in Germany in the early nineteenth century.

The overwhelming interest in classical antiquity of the later eighteenth century was replaced in the thinking of Rondelet and Durand by new priorities – geometry, economy, structure, function – but it was only gradually that classicism relinquished its hold on the minds of architects. Parisian buildings of the time of Napoleon were to this extent directly descended from their eighteenth-

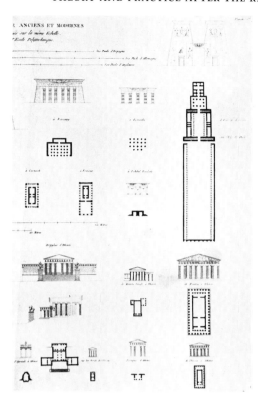

343 Title-page of Durand's *Recueil*, 1800, detail. Durand's survey of the history of architecture, according to function, beginning with Egyptian and Greek temples

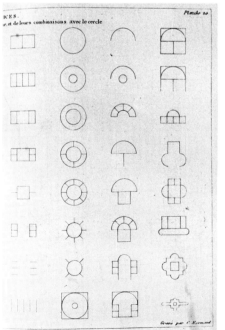
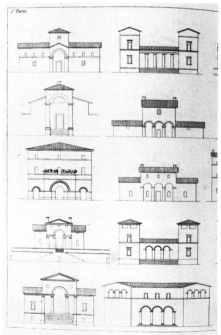
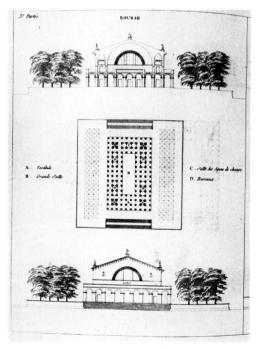

344 Plates from Durand's *Précis*, 1802–05. Durand's patterns for buildings derive from his simple geometrical diagrams ('Ensembles d'Edifices')

345 The church of the Madeleine, Paris. The present building was begun in 1806 by Ledoux's pupil, Pierre Vignon, who changed the designs of Contant d'Ivry (58) and Couture (59)

346 The Chambre des Députés, Paris, the river façade. The Palais-Bourbon of the Prince de Condé was taken over as the seat of the Revolutionary government, and the river portico, facing the Place de la Concorde, was begun by Bernard Poyet in 1808

century precursors even if they look forward to the later nineteenth century in displaying a much greater degree of straightforward imitation.

This is especially apparent in the group of buildings begun by Napoleon in 1806 when at the height of his power after the battle of Austerlitz, the most flagrant instance being the church of the Madeleine as finally designed in 1807 by Ledoux's pupil, Pierre Vignon (345). The river façade of the Chambre des Députés which distantly faces the Madeleine across the Seine has the same monolithic character (346). The Palais-Bourbon, where the Prince de Condé had lived, was adapted as the seat of government in the mid-1790s by Jacques-Pierre de Gisors and Etienne Leconte, who added a semicircular debating chamber at the back of the palace based upon the amphitheatre of Gondoin's Ecole de Chirurgie; a huge Corinthian frontispiece, which masks the buildings of the Palais-Bourbon, was begun in 1808 by Poyet. Even Gondoin, Brongniart and Chalgrin in their work for Napoleon were unable to prevail against the pressure towards mere imitation. The Colonne Vendôme, constructed in honour of the Grande Armée (the original was destroyed during the Commune), is based upon Trajan's column, and even the Bourse (now extended and altered) became yet another of the giant Corinthian temples of the Napoleonic capital. And Chalgrin too, though he had

transformed the Luxembourg palace under the Consulate without loss of stylishness, could scarcely make of the Arc-de-Triomphe much more than an inflated derivation of an antique arch.

Napoleon appears in a more sympathetic light in his extensive patronage of social and educational buildings and in the more intimate work carried out for him by his two personal architects, Percier and Fontaine. The latter were both pupils of Antoine-François Peyre, and both winners of the Prix de Rome, and worked in collaboration until Percier retired from practice in 1814. They became Napoleon's official architects in 1801 and worked for him at all his different residences, especially at Malmaison and the Tuileries. Indeed they excelled as decorators and furniture designers rather than as architects *(347)*. Colour and linear pattern play the predominant part in their interiors, the ornaments being small and placed largely in isolation in the manner that originated with the revival of grotesque ornament in the later eighteenth century.

The building that is usually regarded as their surviving masterpiece is the Arc du Carrousel *(348)*, standing in isolation near the Louvre, which was built in 1806–08 as the gateway to the Tuileries. A late survival from the tradition that began with Peyre's design for the Hôtel de Condé, the arch is a reduction of one of the more elaborate arches of Rome, the Arch of Septimius Severus. Intricately

347 The Château of Malmaison, the library, *c.* 1800. One of the many interiors designed for Napoleon by his official architects, Charles Percier and Pierre Fontaine

348 The Arc du Carrousel, Paris, 1806–08. Built by Percier and Fontaine as the main gateway to Napoleon's Paris residence, the now destroyed palace of the Tuileries

349 The rue de Rivoli, Paris, facing the Place de la Concorde. Begun by Percier and Fontaine in 1802, the rue de Rivoli, the first of the ambitious urban transformations of nineteenth-century Paris, opens at the corner of the Place de la Concorde beside the Hôtel de St-Florentin

coloured and decorated like the interiors by the two architects, the arch partakes of the character of a piece of furniture, and it served originally the function of a pedestal on which the bronze horses looted from St Mark's in Venice were placed.

The architectural style of Percier and Fontaine is better illustrated by their work on the construction of the rue de Rivoli, which was begun in 1802 near the rue de Castiglione, the road leading from the Place Vendôme to the Tuileries gardens. The road begins at the Place de la Concorde, beside the Hôtel de St-Florentin *(349)*, which determined the main levels of the façades. The character of the street, compared with the side elevation of the Hôtel de St-Florentin, has the geometrical precision and shrunken ornamentation that distinguishes the furniture and decoration of Percier and Fontaine. The most ambitious architectural project of the two architects was their design for the palace of Chaillot, dating from 1811 and intended for Napoleon's son, the King of Rome *(350)*. A modern

Versailles, equipped with a huge garden of the most formal kind, the great palace was to be exactly symmetrical about its main axis, resembling a museum plan in its long series of identically fashioned rooms and scarcely less geometrical than one of Durand's architectural prescriptions.

At the time when the palace of Chaillot was designed most of the great architects of the later eighteenth century were already dead. Only Gondoin and Belanger survived the reign of Napoleon and witnessed the return of the Bourbon monarchy. Architects of the transition between the Renaissance tradition and the historical and functional styles of the nineteenth century, they and their contemporaries have been appreciated as exponents of the 'Neo-classicism' of their age, or as prophets of future developments in architecture, even into the present century, but only rarely are they admired for what they were in themselves, artists of the Enlightenment who responded with such deep and varied sensitivity to the intellectual, aesthetic and social pressures of their time.

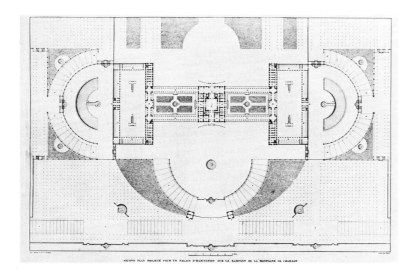

350 Project for the Palais de Chaillot, Paris, plan (engraving from Percier and Fontaine). The second of Percier and Fontaine's projects for a palace for the son of Napoleon, at Chaillot

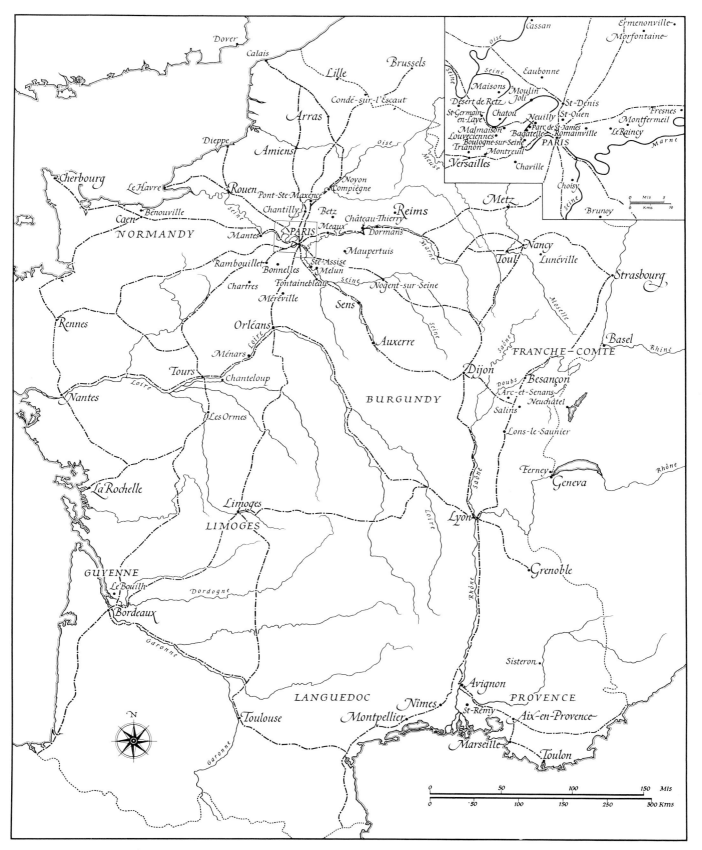

Inset (Paris region)

Cassan
Ermenonville
Morfontaine
Oise
Seine
Seine
Éaubonne
Maisons
Moulin Joli
St-Denis
Désert de Retz
St-Germain-en-Laye
Chatou
Neuilly
St-Ouen
Fresnes
Montfermeil
Malmaison
Parc de St-James
Bagatelle
Romainville
Le Raincy
Louveciennes
Boulogne-sur-Seine
PARIS
Marne
Trianon
Montreuil
Versailles
Chaville
Choisy
Brunoy
Meuse

Mls 5
Kms 10

Main map

Dover
Calais
Lille
Brussels
Condé-sur-l'Escaut
Arras
Dieppe
Amiens
Oise
Metz
Cherbourg
Le Havre
Noyon
Compiègne
Reims
Rouen
Pont-Ste-Maxence
Betz
Château-Thierry
Chantilly
Meaux
Dormans
Bénouville
PARIS
Caen
Mantes
Seine
Maupertuis
Nancy
NORMANDY
Ste-Assise
Lunéville
Toul
Rambouillet
Bonnelles
Melun
Strasbourg
Chartres
Fontainebleau
Nogent-sur-Seine
Moselle
Méréville
Seine
Marne
Rennes
Sens
Seine
Orléans
Auxerre
Basel
Loire
FRANCHE-COMTE
Rhine
Ménars
Dijon
Saône
Tours
Chanteloup
Besançon
Doubs
Nantes
Loire
Arc-et-Senans
Neuchâtel
BURGUNDY
Salins
Les Ormes
Lons-le-Saunier
La Rochelle
Ferney
Geneva
Rhône
Limoges
Saône
Lyon
LIMOGES
Loire
Grenoble
GUYENNE
Le Bouilh
Dordogne
Bordeaux
Rhône
Garonne
Sisteron
Avignon
PROVENCE
LANGUEDOC
Nîmes
St-Rémy
Aix-en-Provence
Toulouse
Montpellier
Garonne
Marseille
Toulon

N

50   100   150 Mls
50   100   150   250   300 Kms

Map of late eighteenth-century France, showing main towns and roads, and sites mentioned in text.
Based on the *Carte des Postes* of 1774

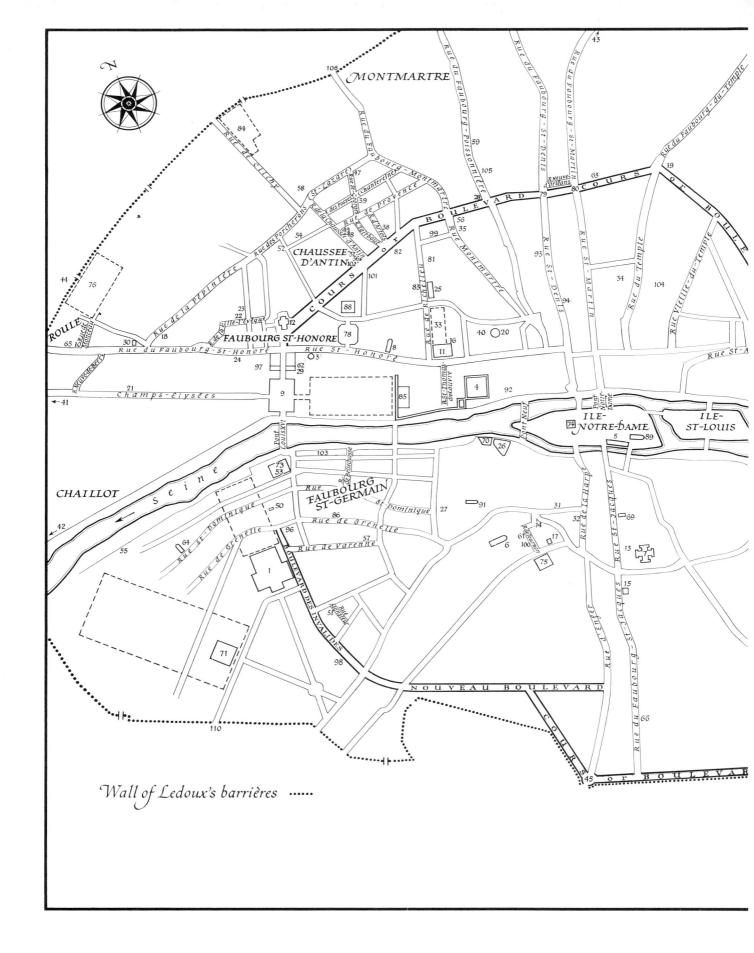

Wall of Ledoux's barrières ......

Map of late eighteenth-century Paris, showing roads, buildings and sites mentioned in text. Based on the *Plan Routier* of 1792

KEY
Numbers at left refer to the map; the sequence follows the order of the illustrations, which are numbered in italics at right

BUILDINGS AND PROJECTS ILLUSTRATED IN TEXT

1 Invalides, *13*
2 Visitation, *14*
3 Assomption, *15*
4 Louvre, 16
5 Hôtel-Dieu, *20*
6 St-Sulpice, Place St-Sulpice, *23–24, 171*
7 Ste-Geneviève, *34, 89–94, 96–101*
8 St-Roch, *35–36*
9 Place Louis XV (Place de la Concorde), *42–45*
10 House of Marigny, site of, *53*
11 Palais-Royal, *56, 136*
12 Madeleine, *58–59*
13 Ecole de Droit, *95*
14 Hôtel de Condé, site of, *108*
15 Visitation, site of chapel, *111*
16 Hôtel de Voyer, site of, *116–117*
17 Comédie-Française (Théâtre de l'Odéon), *124–130*
18 House of de Wailly, site of, *132–133*
19 Hôtel de Chavannes, site of, *135*
20 Halle au Blé (Bourse de Commerce), *138–139, 304*
21 Colisée, site of, *140*
22 Hôtel Alexandre, *141*
23 Hôtel de Monville, site of, *142–143*
24 Hôtel de Brunoy, site of, *144–145*
25 Bibliothèque du Roi (Bibliothèque Nationale), *146*
26 Hôtel des Monnaies, *148–154*
27 Hôpital de la Charité, site of, *155*
28 House by Trouard, *159*
29 Hôtel de St-Florentin, *165–168*
30 St-Philippe-du-Roule, *169–170*
31 Ecole de Chirurgie, *176–180, 182–183*
32 Old Anatomy Theatre, *181*
33 Palais-Royal garden, *199–200*
34 Hôtel d'Hallwyl, *204–209*
35 Hôtel d'Uzès, site of, *211–215*
36 Hôtel de Montmorency, site of, *221*
37 Hôtel Guimard, site of, *226–227*
38 Hôtel du Barry, intended site, *233*
39 Hôtel de Thélusson, site of, *247–248, 250*
40 Hôtel des Fermes, site of, *251*
41 Barrière de l'Etoile, site of, *254*
42 Barrière des Bonshommes, site of, *255*
43 Barrière de la Villette, *256*
44 Barrière de Monceau, *257*
45 Barrière d'Orléans (d'Enfer), *258*
46 Barrière du Trône, *259–260*
47 Hosten houses, site of, *265–267*
48 Hôtel de Montesson, site of, *280*
49 House of the Duc d'Orléans, site of, *281–282*
50 Hôtel de Monaco, *283–284*
51 Hôtel de Bourbon-Condé, *285–286*
52 Capuchin monastery of the Chaussée-d'Antin (Lycée Condorcet), *288–290*
53 Hôtel de Brancas, site of *292–293*
54 House by Belanger, *302–303*
55 Hôtel de Salm, *305–307*
56 Hôtel de Montholon, *308–309*

57 Hôtel de Gallifet, *313–314*
58 House of M. Vassale, site of, *315*
59 Hôtel de Titon, *318*
60 House of Beaumarchais, site of, *319–320*
61 Rue de Tournon apartment house, *321*
62 Infantado stables, site of, *322*
63 Opéra 'provisoire', site of, *323*
64 St-Christophe, Gros-Caillou, *324–325*
65 Hospice Beaujon, *327*
66 Hôpital Cochin, *328*

OTHER PRINCIPAL MONUMENTS

67 Arsénal
68 Bastille, site of
69 Collège de France
70 Collège des Quatre-Nations
71 Ecole Militaire
72 Jardin des Plantes
73 Palais-Bourbon (Chambre des Députés)
74 Palais de Justice
75 Palais du Luxembourg
76 Parc Monceau
77 Père Lachaise
78 Place Vendôme
79 Porte St-Denis
80 Porte St-Martin
81 Théâtre Feydeau, site of
82 Théâtre-Italien (Opéra-Lyrique)
83 Théâtre-National (des Arts), site of
84 'Tivoli', site of
85 Tuileries

OTHER ECCLESIASTICAL BUILDINGS

86 Abbaye de Panthémont
87 Abbaye de St-Antoine-des-Champs (Hôpital St-Antoine)
88 Capuchin monastery of the rue St-Honoré, site of
89 Notre-Dame
90 Notre-Dame-de-Bonsecours
91 St-Germain-des-Prés
92 St-Germain-l'Auxerrois
93 St-Sauveur, site of
94 St-Leu-St-Gilles
95 Ste-Marguerite

OTHER MAJOR HÔTELS

96 Hôtel de Châtelet
97 Hôtel Grimod de la Reynière
98 Hôtel Masseran
99 Hôtel de Montmorency-Luxembourg, site of
100 Hôtel de Nivernais
101 Hôtel de Richelieu, site of
102 Hôtel de Ste-Foix, site of
103 Saiseval houses, site of
104 Hôtel de Soubise
105 Hôtel Tabary, site of

OTHER MAIN BARRIÈRES

106 Barrière de Montmartre, site of
107 Barrière de Belleville, site of
108 Barrière de Charonne, site of
109 Barrière d'Italie (Fontainebleau), site of
110 Barrière de l'Ecole Militaire, site of

Notes to the text

Numbers on left of note entries denote page numbers of text. Full details of works which appear in the notes in a shortened form are given in the general bibliography and list of abbreviations, pp. 279–82 below.

Introduction

9 Historical background: the references in this and the following paragraphs are based mainly on Cobban, Lough and the memoirs quoted below.

10 Mme de Pompadour: see especially Emile Campardon, *Madame de Pompadour et la cour de Louis XV au milieu du dix-huitième siècle*, 1867.

Choiseul: Gaston Maugras, *Le Duc et la Duchesse de Choiseul*, 1902; his interesting, unsuccessful and little-known experiment in town-planning at Versoix in Switzerland is mentioned in Maugras, 321ff., and also referred to in Ledoux's prospectus for his *Architecture*, see ch. 12 above. For his collection see Levallet in *BSHAF*, 1925, 201–11; Dacier in *GBA*, 1949, 2, 47–74; Scott, 42–53; and Eriksen, 1974, 165–7.

The reaction against the Rococo: quotation from Créquy, 6, 214; and see especially F. Kimball in *GBA*, 1954, 2, 57–64; Herrmann, 1962, 221–34; Gallet in *GBA*, 1966, 1, 145–68; Gallet, 1972, 37–62; Honour, 17–42; and Eriksen, 1974, 25–9.

Turgot: see Dakin, 153 and *passim*.

D'Angiviller: see Silvestre de Sacy, 1953; the close physical resemblance between d'Angiviller and Turgot is mentioned by Croÿ, 3, 140.

The Bordeaux theatre: see ch. 9 above; on the Louvre, *AAF*, 1927, 408, and Pevsner, 120 and ch. 8 (museums in general).

Finances and bankers: quotations from Mercier, *Tableau*, 1, 162, and 7, 89 (see also 8, 190); Bosher, 35, 67, 74ff., 85ff.; Thiéry, *Almanach*, 78ff., and editions of the *Almanach royal*; Cobban, 1, 58–9.

11 The development of Paris: especially Gallet, 1972, 1–8; Rosenau, 1970, ch. 2; Hautecoeur, *Histoire*, 4, 116–33; the attractive illustrated survey by Gaxotte, 1968; and M. Foucquier, *Paris au XVIIIe siècle*, n.d. For the different roads see J. Hillairet, *La Rue de Richelieu*, 1966; R. Hénard, *La Rue Saint-Honoré*, 1908, chs 8 and 14; A. Detrez, *Le Faubourg Saint-Honoré*, 1953; Bonnardot; A. Chastel and J. M. Pérouse de Montclos in *MHF*, 1966, 176–249 (projects for the Louvre and the Tuileries); *BM*, 1969, 69–106 (the quartier des Halles). Collections of contemporary engravings include those of Gaitte (BHVP, Rés 102, 530) and the weaker plates by Janinet (BHVP, Fol. 93, 142). Detailed plans of the main late eighteenth-century developments are in AN, F31, 73 (Roule and the Tuileries), 75 (Chaussée-d'Antin) and 77 (Faubourg-Poissonnière); the topographical collection of the BN, Est. contains many projects for houses of the time, especially Va 285 (Chaussée-d'Antin).

The Palais-Royal: see ch. 9 above; the speculation of the royal princes is discussed by Hautecoeur, *Histoire*, 4, 102–16.

Disapproval of speculation at the Academy: see especially the *Autobiographie* of Cherpitel.

Superfluity of architects: Quatremère, 1834, 298 (life of Heurtier). The *Almanach historique . . . des architectes, peintres, sculpteurs . . .*, 1776, gives a list of architects and their addresses.

The aristocracy: see Créquy, 7, 66ff. (renegade peers), and financiers in 5, ch. 8.

Social life: Créquy, 6, 219; also Ségur, 1, 64; for the social position of the architect see especially Gallet, 1972, 18–25.

Freemasonry: see Thiéry, *Almanach*, 248ff. and *Paris*, 1, 278–9; Britsch, 229–51; Mornet, 1933, 357–88 and 323–5 (bibliography); Bord; Le Bilhan; Vidler; and see under Ledoux, ch. 10 above.

Walpole and Blaikie on Paris: Walpole, 6, 351 (19 November 1765); Blaikie, 24 (on lighting see also Lavoisier, 3, 1ff.).

The *barrières*: see ch. 12 above.

Guides: especially Thiéry (quotation from *Paris*, 1, xxxii–iii) and his main rival, Dulaure, whose guide is arranged in alphabetical order, however.

Mrs Thrale on Paris: Thrale, 93, 95 and 119.

Necker: see Jean Egret, *Necker, Ministre de Louis XVI, 1776–1790*, 1975.

12 Anglomania: quotations from La Tour du Pin, 98; Walpole, 6, 341 and 335.

Versailles and the patronage of Artois and Provence: see chs 8, 13 and 14 above.

Diderot on architecture: quoted from Diderot, *Letters to Sophie Volland*, 11f.

Voltaire's buildings: see Voltaire XLIV (1959), no. 8532, 23 (8 Oct. 1760); his architect at Ferney was Lenoir, for whom see chs 6 and 14 above.

Chinese influence: see H. Cordier, *La Chine en France au XVIIIe siècle*, 1910; A. Reichwein, *China and Europe, Intellectual and Artistic Contacts in the Eighteenth Century*, 1925, 111–26; H. Honour, *Chinoiserie, The Vision of Cathay*, 1961. For gardens in particular see Sirén; Erdberg; *JF*, 141–4; Wiebenson, 1978; and ch. 4 above.

13 The influence of England: an unconvincing account, relying on minor works, is given by F. Kimball in *GBA*, 1931, 1, 29–44 and 231–55. Contacts with England are discussed by Boyer, 1945–46. On the intangible subject of Palladianism see especially Gallet, 1972, 54–7, and 1975; D. Rabreau in *Bolletino del centro internazionale di studi di architettura, Andrea Palladio*, XIII, 1970, 206ff.; Eriksen, 1974, 139–44.

Croÿ on travellers to England: Croÿ, 1, 304.

Opinions of English architecture: Jean-André Rouquet, *The Present State of the Arts in England*, 1755, 95 (see *CL*, I, 375 on the authorship). The second quotation noted by Gallet, 1975, 43, from Pigneron's edition of Milizia, 1773. A French guide to England is [G.L.] Le Rouge's *Curiosités de Londres et de l'Angleterre*, 1766 (second ed.).

D'Holbach in England: Diderot, *Letters to Sophie Volland*, 145–6.

14 The rôle of Hawksmoor: the views of Kaufmann, 1968, 19–20, seem largely to reflect the author's simplified approach to buildings.

English opinions of the French: quotations from Thrale, 95, Thicknesse, 2, 151, and 1, 6–7; see also Moore, 1, 29, and Pujoulx, 171–4 and 186–96 (prostitution). For visitors to France see A. Babeau, *Les Voyageurs en France de la Renaissance à la Révolution*, 1928.

Interior decoration: quotation from Mercier, *Tableau*, 2, 181; see also Hautecoeur, *Histoire*, 4, 455–509; Gallet, 1972, 109–37.

The house of Laborde: quotation from Walpole, 6, 374–5; later owned by the Duc de Choiseul, the house is described by Thiéry, *Paris*, 1, 187. The patronage of Laborde is discussed by Boyer in *BSHAF*, 1954, 214–26, 1961, 137–52 (with the history of the house), and 1967, 141–52 (the collections of his son). See also Thirion, 278ff.; Gallet, 1972, 169 (Le Carpentier).

Population of Paris: estimated at about 500,000 in the mid-century, with Lyon at 160,000 and Bordeaux at 100,000 (Cobban, 1, 48).

Calonne: Ségur, 2, 16; see also note on Calonne, ch. 12 below; C. Ballot, *L'Introduction du machinisme en France*, 1923, 9ff.; *Le Provincial à Paris*, 171–2; on his houses Thiéry, *Paris*, 1, 168 and 172, and Scott, 86–91 (his collection).

15 Napoleon's Paris: see chs 13 and 15 above.

16 French and Italian music: quotation from Mercier, *Tableau*, 1, 162; also Marmontel, 2, 105ff., and Créquy, 6, 112–19.

Piranesi: see ch. 4 above.

Bouchardon: see especially Levey, 57–8.

17 Bernini in Paris: see Paul Fréart de Chantelou, *Journal du voyage du Cavalier Bernin en France*, ed. L. Lalanne, 1885.

PART ONE
Chapter 1

19 Opinions of Soufflot: quotations from the *Nécrologie*, 1781, 201–2, Quatremère, 1830, 2, 337, and Laugier, 1765, 182.

Soufflot: especially the thorough, but largely unillustrated monograph by Monval, based on the extensive documentation of the Maison du Roi in the AN. Short contemporary obituaries appeared in the *Journal de Paris*, 16 Sept. 1780 (vol. 2 of *Abrégé*, 1134ff.), by Renou, and in the *Nécrologie*, 1781, 191ff. (reprinted in *RUA*, 1861, 135–9), by a M. Castilhon; a notice by the architect, probably a pupil of Soufflot, Philippe Bienaimé (mentioned in early editions of the *NBG*), seems to be undiscoverable. For the literature before 1937 see Thieme Becker, 31; more recently Hautecoeur, *Histoire*, 3, 595ff., and 4, 188–205; Petzet; and Gallet, 1972, 185.

Soufflot's epitaph: see ch. 5 above.

Soufflot at Fresnes: Antoine-Nicolas Duchesne, *Relation du voyage à Reims (1775)*, ed. H. Jadot, 1902, 119, refers to Soufflot, saying that he had made drawings at Fresnes 'dans sa jeunesse' (this may possibly have been in the 1740s, when he was working at Lyon).

20 French architecture in the late seventeenth century: for a general survey see Anthony Blunt, *Art and Architecture in France 1500–1700*, 1973 revised ed., chs 7 and 8.

Soufflot in Rome: *CD*, IX, 146 (also IX, 128).

22 Roman architecture in the early eighteenth century: general survey by Rudolf Wittkower, *Art and Architecture in Italy 1600–1800*, 1973 ed., ch. 16; Oechslin, 1972.

Carlo Fontana: E. Coudenhove-Erthal, *Carlo Fontana*, 1930; Braham and Hager; Hager in *JWCI*, 1973, 319ff. (Colosseum church project).

Panini: Ferdinando Arisi, *Gian Paolo Panini*, 1961.

French architecture in the early eighteenth century: Hautecoeur, *Histoire*, 3; Gallet, 1972, and in *GBA*, 1966, 1, 145–68; and Kalnein, chs 4, 5 and 6.

24 Servandoni: a modern, well illustrated monograph is seriously needed. Books by and attributed to Servandoni are listed in the BN catalogue. Contemporary obituaries appeared in the *Nécrologie*, 1775, 223–36 (reprinted in *RUA*, 1860–61, 115–18), and in Pigneron's edition of Milizia, 459–70; see also Thiéry, *Paris*, 1, 391ff., and Quatremère, 1830, 2, 285ff. For more recent literature, H. de Chennevières in *Revue des arts décoratifs*, 1880–81, 22–7, 170–6, 403–6 and 429–35; Chavret, 362–5; J. Bouché in *GBA*, 1910, 2, 121–46; Thieme Becker (1936), with bibliography; Gallet, 1972, 184; and Roland-Michel, *PF*, 329–34. For the stage work, Decugis and Reymond, 90–5; P. Bjurström in *RSHT*, 1954, 150–9; and C. di Matteo in *IHA*, 1971, 40–3. For St-Sulpice, E. Malbois in *GBA*, 1922, 2, 283–92; Lemesle, 37–8, 48–51 and 58; Middleton, 1962, 278–80; B. Sydhoff in *IHA*, 1963, 85–90 (with bibliography).

Early nineteenth-century praise of St-Sulpice: Quatremère, 1830, 2, 292.

25 Blondel on Servandoni: quoted by Middleton, 1962, 280.

The Academy in the late eighteenth century: *PV* (ed. Lemonnier), and Lemonnier in *RAAM*, 1927, 1, 11–26 and 173–8; Thiéry, *Paris*, 1, 332ff.; *AAF*, 1853, 419–24 (list of architects), and 1857–58, 273–333 (list of prize-winners, by M. A. Duvivier); AN, 01 1930 and 1073 (documentation); M. Rousseau in *BSHAF*, 1935, 275–98; M. Aulanier in *BSHAF*, 1961, 215–24 (premises in Louvre); and W. Bouleau-Rabaud in *GBA*, 1966, 2, 355–64. See also Herrmann, 1958 (difficulties of Desgodetz), and Chaffee, 61–5 (summary and outline of Academy teaching procedures). For the Prix de Rome drawings, engraved only from 1779, see Rosenau in *AH*, 1960, and Allais, Detournelle and Vaudoyer, *Grands Prix d'architecture (1791–1805)*, 1806. The earlier drawings have now been photographed by the Inventaire and a catalogue is being prepared. For Academies in general see N. Pevsner, *Academies of Art*, 1940, chs 3 and 4.

The Accademia di S. Luca: drawings catalogued in Marconi, Cipriani and Valeriani.

Perrault: see especially Wolfgang Herrmann, *The Theory of Claude Perrault*, 1975.

Desgodetz: Herrmann, 1958.

26 Thicknesse on Lyon: Thicknesse, 1, 51, and 2, 93.

Lyon in the eighteenth century: principally, Kleinclausz, *Lyon*, 2, 137ff., and *Lyon: des origines à nos jours*, 1925, 37ff.; Monfalcon, 2, 862ff.; and C. Bréghot du Lut and A. Péricaud, *Notice topographique sur la ville de Lyon*, 1834.

The work of Soufflot in Lyon: see Monval, 84–95; [Bréghot du Lut], *Mélanges biographiques et littéraires*, 1828, 127ff. The work of an early follower, Toussaint Loyer, is illustrated by Eriksen, 1974, pls 32–4; for Léonard Roux see ch. 8 above.

Natoire's letters: *CD*, X, 303 (see also XI, 327–8, and in *AAF*, 1853, 259 and 300).

Soufflot's discourses: quoted in Petzet, 131–47.

The Loge-au-Change: Cochard, 1817, 266, and Monfalcon, 2, 862; Pevsner, 1976, ch. 12 (exchanges).

The Hôtel-Dieu: Kleinclausz, 2, 181ff.; Cochard, 1817, 64ff.; Monfalcon, 2, 861; *Statuts et règlemens généraux de l'Hôpital . . . et Grand Hôtel-Dieu de la ville de Lyon*, 1757. A project by Servandoni is mentioned by Pigneron, 463n. For hospitals in general see Pevsner, 1976, ch. 9; and ch. 14 above.

28 Soufflot joins the Academy: *PV*, 6, 130 (23 November 1749); he was promoted in 1755, *PV*, 6, 247 (10 December). A project by Soufflot for the 1753 Place de la Concorde project is illustrated in the 1973 Hermitage exhibition catalogue, 35 (no. 97).

Mme de Pompadour and the arts: Dufort, 1, 98.

29 Le Blanc: Monod-Cassidy (detailed biography); Eriksen, 1974, 226–32 (quotations); Zmijewska, 45–50 (art criticism). On Le Blanc's *Lettres d'un françois* see *CL*, 1, 375 ('dont le ton dur et insolent a toujours déplu aux honnêtes gens').

Cochin: S. Rocheblave, *Charles-Nicolas Cochin . . . (1715–1790)*, 1927; Eriksen, 1974, 233ff. (quotations); Zmijewska, 94–8 (art criticism); and Cochin's own *Oeuvres diverses*, 1771.

Marigny in Italy: Monval, 96–107; Marquiset, 25–36; Cochin, *Voyage d'Italie*, 1758 (3 vols); Mme de Pompadour's unenlightening letters to Marigny are in *Correspondance de Mme de Pompadour avec son père, M. Poisson et son frère, M. de Vandières*, 1878; a brief account of the journey by H. Roujon is in *L'Ami des monuments et des arts*, 1899, 323ff., and 1900, 11; for caricatures by Ghezzi of the travellers see M. N. Benisovich in *Apollo*, 1967, 344–5.

Soufflot at the Accademia di San Luca: his presentation drawing has recently been rediscovered by Werner Oechslin.

30 Paestum: Dumont's *Les Ruines de Paestum*, 1764 (dedicated to Marigny); see also S. Lang in *JWCI*, 1950, XIII, 48–64, and A. Blunt, *Neapolitan Baroque and Rococo Architecture*, 1975, 165–6.

Soufflot in Viterbo: Monval, 106; for his indigestion see Marquiset, 36, and ch. 5 above.

Cochin and Bellicard: *Observations sur les antiquités de la ville d'Herculanum*, 1754 (see also *CL*, 1, 196–7); for Bellicard, Erouard and Oechslin in *PF*, 52–5.

Cochin's 'Lycurgus blessé': see *Diderot Salons*, 1, 105 and 138.

Rue Champfleuri: 'brevet de logement' for Soufflot and Cochin, *NAAF*, 1873, 110–11.

Soufflot's appearance in *Correspondance littéraire*: *CL*, 1, 91.

The Lyon theatre: Monval, 118–23 (Soufflot's opinion, 122); Cochard, 1817, 165, and 1829, 349; Monfalcon, 2, 860–1; Hautecoeur, *Histoire*, 4, 187; Pevsner, 1976, 63ff. and 76.

The ellipse: the shape was especially recommended by Patte, 1782, 16.

Acting: Marmontel attributes the change to more realistic acting to Mlle Clairon (and see also ch. 13 above for the role of the Comte de Lauraguais); according to Kleinclausz, Soufflot's theatre opened with a performance of *Bérénice* with Clairon in the title role but Monval gives *Britannicus* as the opening play. On theatrical changes in general see Bapst; M. Barton, *Garrick*, 1948, 187 and *passim*; and D. Lynham, *The Chevalier Noverre*, 1950, for the activity of Noverre at Lyon.

32 The Bâtiments du Roi: in order of seniority under Gabriel, until 1775 (see ch. 5 above), were three Intendants and Ordonnateurs, and three Contrôleurs-généraux (*Almanach royal*, for example, 1760).

The *cordon noir*: Grandmaison, 47–50, and J. J. Guiffrey in *Revue historique nobiliaire et biographique*, 1873, 23–6.

Mme Geoffrin: Pierre de Ségur, *Le Royaume de la rue Saint-Honoré*, 1897, and Aldis. For Mme Geoffrin's influence on Marigny, Dufort, 1, 115. According to Gallet, 1964, 37, Soufflot had made a design for the gateway of M. Geoffrin's glass factory; since the husband died in 1750, he may have been in contact with the Geoffrins before his Italian journey.

Diderot and Marmontel on Soufflot: Marmontel, 1, 266; Diderot, *Correspondance*, 6, 24 (18 January 1766: 'Elle [Mme Le Gendre] descendit dans une petite salle à manger ou elle fut exposée aux alternatives du froid et du chaud et au bruit continu de la redoutable poitrine de Soufflot, qui ne cessa pas de tonner trois ou quatre heures de suite à ses oreilles délicates').

Marmontel on Caylus: Marmontel, 1, 267.

The Comte de Caylus: notice in the *Nécrologie*, reprinted in *RUA*, 1860–61, 106–10; Thiéry, *Paris*, 1, 407–8; S. Rocheblave, *Essai sur le Comte de Caylus*, 1889; the introduction to Caylus' own *Vies d'artistes du XVIIIe siècle* (ed. A. Fontaine), 1910; J. Seznec, *Essais sur Diderot et l'antiquité*, 1957, 79–96 ('Le Singe antiquaire'); J. Babelon, *Choix de bronzes de la collection Caylus*, 1928; Żmijewska, 79–85 (his art criticism).

The Abbé Barthélemy: M. Badolle, *L'Abbé Jean-Jacques Barthélemy (1716–1795) et l'Hellénisme en France dans la seconde moitié du XVIIIe siècle*, n.d.

Barthélemy on Soufflot: Barthélemy, 5.

Soufflot in Paris: see Monval, 131–50; the architect's letter books are AN, 01 1542, 1543, 1552 and 1555. For Bordeaux and Reims, where the architect was Sophie Volland's brother, see AN, 01 1904; Lavedan, 1941, 319. For Notre-Dame, AN, 01 1690, and Thiéry, *Paris*, 2, 88 and 109. For the Louvre, Monval, 151–235; Christ, 79ff.; Hautecoeur, *Histoire*, 4, 196–8; chapter 5 above.

Perrault's projects for Ste-Geneviève: Petzet in *BM*, 1957, 81–96, and R. Strandberg in *BSHAF*, 1971, 45–59.

33 Soufflot's Ste-Geneviève: see the bibliography in Mathieu, 387–97; Jean Rondelet, *Mémoire historique sur le dôme du Panthéon français*, An V (1797); A. Rondelet, *Notice historique sur l'Eglise de Sainte Geneviève*, 1852; Piganiol, 6, 98–105; Thiéry, *Paris*, 2, 240ff.; Monval, 423, 515; Petzet; Hautecoeur, *Histoire*, 4, 188–96; Middleton, 1963, 105–18; Braham, 1971; Chevallier and Rabreau.

St.-Roch: J.-P. Babelon, *L'Eglise de Saint-Roch à Paris*, 1972, with bibliography. For the comparable later eighteenth-century cathedrals of Versailles and La Rochelle see P. Moisy in *GBA*, 1952, 1, 89–102.

The complexity of the portico: criticized, for example, by Legrand and Landon, 1, 113.

36 Bernini's designs for S. Andrea al Quirinale: H. Brauer and R. Wittkower, *Die Zeichnungen des Gianlorenzo Bernini*, 1931, 110–13. Statues on towers and columns, as opposed to domes, were commonplace.

Brébion's opinion: memoir quoted in Petzet, 147.

Chapter 2

37 Blondel: contemporary obituaries by Franque in *Journal des beaux-arts et des sciences*, 1774, 1/2, 559–70, and in the *Nécrologie*, 1775, 223–36 (reprinted in *RUA*, 1860–61, 409–13); short biography by A. Prost, *J.-F. Blondel et son oeuvre*, 1860. More recently, J. Lejeaux in *RAAM*, 1927, 2, 223–34 and 271–85; Thieme Becker (1910), with bibliography; Pariset in *AAHA*, 1927, 171–6 (see also *NAAF*, 1878, 73); Hautecoeur, *Histoire*, 3, 598ff.; R. Middleton in *JSAH*, 1952, 16–19; *CA*, March 1967, 74–81; Eriksen, 1974, 251–4. For the work of Blondel's son, Georges-François, see J. Lejeaux in *BSHAF*, 1935, 85–9; J. Harris in *The Connoisseur*, 1964, 155ff.; and J. F. Méjanes in *PF*, 58.

Chambers in Paris: see Harris, 1963, in *GBA*, 1966, 51–4, and 1970, 4–6, 14; Eriksen, 1974, 139–41.

38 Blondel on seventeenth-century architects: *Discours sur . . . l'architecture*, 1747, 4.

Gabriel: earlier literature, including the monographs by Gromort, *Jacques-Ange Gabriel*, 1933, and Fels, *Ange-Jacques Gabriel*, 1924 (2nd ed.), is superseded by Tadgell, 1978, where the links between Blondel and Gabriel are thoroughly analysed. See also Quatremère, 1830, 2, 311–20; Hautecoeur, *Histoire*, 3, 548ff.; Gallet, 1972, 161–2; and P. Vitry in *AAF*, 1913, 307–8 (bust of Gabriel by Lemoyne).

39 Mansart's house: see Maurice Dumolin, *Etudes de topographie parisienne*, 3 (1931), 369.

Gabriel and the king collaborate: Croÿ, 1, 213, 224, 232.

Marigny and Gabriel: see Rabreau in *BM*, 1972, 360; *Mémoires secrets*, 20, 13 (which also mention a quarrel about the garden of the Hôtel de Pompadour, 18, 323, 8 October 1767); see also Tadgell, 4–7; and under de Wailly, ch. 6 above.

Place de la Concorde: Tadgell, 175–81; S. Granet in *GBA*, 1959, 1, 153–66, 1962, 1, 233–40, 1961, 107–13, and in *VU*, 1962, 161–218; also Thiéry, *Paris*, 1, 96f.; E. Lambert in *BSHAF*, 1938, 85–97; P. Lavedan in *VU*, 1956; and M. de Pradel de Lamaze, *Guide historique de l'Hôtel de la Marine*, 1956. For the Ecole Militaire, Laulan; Tadgell, 181–94; and A. Mayeux in *L'Architecture*, 1929, 23–7.

41 Le Vau's drawing for the colonnade: see M. Whiteley and A. Braham in *GBA*, 1964, 2, 347–62.

Criticism of the Place: Laugier, 1765, 25; Landon, *Annales*, 10 (1805), 61 (also Blondel, 1774, 2, 205ff.); Ledoux, 108; satirical epigram quoted by C. P. Gooch, *Louis XV*, 4th ed., 1966, 246.

42 Versailles: see especially Tadgell, 84–119, and in *AR*, March, 1975, 155–64; Racinais (interiors). Fontainebleau: Y. Bottineau, *L'Art d'Ange-Jacques Gabriel à Fontainebleau*, 1962; Tadgell, 127–40. Compiègne: *Bulletin de la Société historique de Compiègne*, 1944, 67–134; Tadgell, 140–51.

Petit Trianon: Tadgell, 124–7.

The Versailles Opéra: Tadgell, 119–24; also P. Pradel in *GBA*, 1937, 1, 109–25; *MHF*, 1957, 3–48; P. Verlet in *RHT*, 1957, 133–54; A. Japy, *L'Opéra royal de Versailles*, 1958; A. Gruber in *RA*, 13, 1971, 87–97 (unreasonably diminishing Gabriel's role).

43 Gabriel's letters on the Opéra: in *Mercure de France*, August 1770, 174ff. and September 1770, 2, 181ff.

Opinions of the Opéra: Croÿ, 2, 390 and 404ff.; Thrale, 131.

The Frederikskirke: Elling; Meldahl; Tadgell, 203–7; and see further under Jardin, ch. 3 above.

44 Marigny: quotation from *Notice nécrologique* in *Journal de Paris*, May 1781 (noted by Scott, 26); see also Marquiset; Bord, 284 (freemasonry); E. Plantet, *La Collection des statues du Marquis de Marigny*, 1885, 1–109; also *NAAF*, 1874, 367–72; *NAAF*, 1873, 388–404 (sale).

Opinions of Marigny: Créquy, 4, 55; Oberkirch, 2, 35.

Marigny's drinking: Dufort 1, 115. As Mlle Monique Mosser kindly informed me large quantities of wine appear in the inventory of Ménars.

45 Marmontel on Marigny: Marmontel 1, 200, 223.

Goût-grec: *CL*, 3, 224; see also Walpole, 6, 400 (19 January 1766), and ch. 3 above.

Roslin's portrait: Eriksen, 1962, and 1974, 35–6.

Marigny's statements on taste: Eriksen, 1962, 97–8; and *CD*, 11, 437–8 (1 September 1762).

46 Ménars and its park: Monval, 402–21; and especially Mosser, 1973; also Ganay in *RAAM*, 1935, 1, 157–74; F. Lesueur in *Mémoires de la Société des sciences et lettres de Loir-et-Cher*, 1912, 1–256; and Dupré in *Mémoires de la Société des sciences et lettres de Blois*, 1860, 99–177. For Soufflot's visits, P. Ratouis de Limay, *Un Amateur orléanais au XVIIIe siècle: Aignan-Thomas Desfriches (1715–1800)*, 1907, 66–8 (reference kindly supplied by Robin Middleton).

Marigny's Chinese pavilion: Monval, 417–18; Mosser, 284.

47 Marriage of Marigny: Marquiset, 135; and Baron de Maricourt, *Madame de Souza et sa famille*, 1907 (Marigny's daughter).

Marigny's house: Thiéry, *Paris*, 1, 64; AN, 01 1252 (Marigny's personal papers); Marquiset, 111ff. and 141; Hautecoeur, *Histoire*, 4, 198–9; Gallet, 1972, 29.

Marigny on Italian art: *CD*, 10, 336.

Chapter 3

48 Laugier: see especially Hermann, 1962 (and review by D. Nyberg in *AB*, 1964, 107ff., stressing the relative unimportance of Lodoli for Laugier); and Middleton, 1963, 97–104; also Kaufmann, 1968, 134; Zmijewska, 89–90 (art criticism); and *CL*, 6, 233–4 (obituary).

49 Cordemoy's ideas for churches: especially the second (1714) edition of his book where his ideas developed in response to the criticism of Frézier (Middleton, 1962, 280–90).

Reactions to Laugier: *CL*, 1, 88 and ff.; Blondel, 1774, 2, 13; and see also G[uillaumot], *Remarques sur un livre*, 1768.

Medieval cathedrals: Oberkirch, 1, 216; Thicknesse, 1, 30; Thrale, 69. See especially the survey in Middleton, 1962, 310–20.

Ste-Croix: Chenesseau, 271ff., and see under Trouard, ch. 8 above.

St-Vaast: A. de Cardevaque and A. Terninck, *L'Abbaye de Saint-Vaast*, 1865–68, 2, 57ff.; A Leclercq, *Les Cathédrales d'Arras et leurs évêques*, 1933; Evans, 50.

50 Contant d'Ivry: Contant's own *Oeuvres d'architecture*, 1769 (review in *Mercure de France*, July 1770, 2, 166); *NAAF*, 1885, 76–7 (death); Thieme Becker (1912), with bibliography; T. H. Lunsingh Scheurleer in *BSHAF*, 1934, 291–8 (Hôtel de Thiers); Hautecoeur, *Histoire*, 3, 588ff.; Middleton, 1963, 92–4.

The Palais-Royal: Champier and Sandoz, 1, 313–22; T. Sauvel in *BM*, 1962, 185–90; E. Dupézard, *Le Palais-Royal de Paris*, 1911; *NAAF*, 1872, 96 (household of Duc d'Orléans; for Croÿ's friendship with Contant, Croÿ, 1, 182).

The Abbaye de Panthémont: Thiéry, *Paris*, 2, 568 (Soufflot used brick vaults of a similar kind for the sacristy of Notre-Dame, Middleton, 1963, 92), F. Rousseau, *MSHP*, 1918, 171–227.

The Madeleine: AN, 01 1688 (documents and drawings); Gruel, 1910, 28–33, and in *BSHAVIIIAP*, 1900, 107–18; Kreiger, 251–7; Bonnardot, 36–9; Gallet in *BMC*, 1965, 1, 14–19 (Contant's model); and Couture, *Autobiographie*. See ch. 15 above for the later history. (The projects for Ste-Geneviève by Desboeufs (1753), which Soufflot was said to have plundered for his own design (*Mémoires secrets*, 6, 327, and 24, 229, 4 and 24 October 1772), are yet more old-fashioned than Contant's projects for the Madeleine.)

52 Legeay: Kaufmann, 1952, 450–3; Harris, 1967, 189–93; Pérouse de Montclos, 39–46; Erouard and Arrizoli in *PF*, 179–200, and in *PF Colloque*, 199–208; *CD*, 9, 382 and 386.

Cochin on Legeay: Cochin, 1880, 142.

53 De Troy on Legeay: *CD*, 10, 1.

Legeay in Berlin: Pérouse de Montclos, 39–41; Colombier, p. 60 and pls 213, 217–18 (St Hedwig's).

54 Legeay in Paris: Viel de St-Maux, 58, n. 29 (also quoted in Pérouse de Montclos, 41).

56 Dumont: *CD*, especially 9, 426, and 10, 109; Dumont's *Autobiographie*; Hautecoeur, *Histoire*, 3, 594ff.; Gallet, 1972, 159; Erouard and Oechslin in *PF*, 143–6. Amongst Dumont's own collections of engravings are *Détails des plus intéressantes parties d'architecture de la Basilique de Saint Pierre*, 1763, *Etudes d'architecture de différents maîtres italiens* (with dated engravings of 1778), and *Suite de projets détaillés des salles de spectacle* (dated engravings of 1772–75).

Jardin: the basic study is P. Lespinasse in *RAAM*, 1910, 2, 111–22 and 227–38; also C. Elling, *Jardin i Rom (Studier fra Sprog- og Oldtidsforskning*, 193), 1943 (French translation in *PF Colloque*, 181–94); also *CD*, 10, especially 163; Jardin's own *Plans, coupes et élévations de l'Eglise Royale de Frédéric V à Copenhague*, 1765; Grandmaison, 77–8 (ennoblement in 1768), and *NAAF*, 1889, 232–4, and 1895, 340–3; Thieme Becker, 18 (1925); Hautecoeur, *Histoire*, 4, 209–12; Gallet, 1972, 166; Braham, 1972, fig. 22 (Prix de Rome drawing); Erouard in *PF*, 155–9.

Jardin in Copenhagen: Elling; Meldahl; the drawings for the Frederikskirke are in the Rigsarkivet, Copenhagen, Kortsamlingen, 341. *NAAF*, 1878, 35, and 1895, 113ff. (his *congé*).

58 Comments on Jardin's Frederikskirke projects: Elling, 31–2; *CD*, 11, 118; and *PV*, 7, 133 (24 January 1763).

Jardin's later career: see *PV*, 8, 316 (9 December 1777), and Thiéry, *Paris*, 2, 198 (park of Mme Vieillard); Gallet, 1972, 166.

Petitot: see Marco Pellegri, *Ennemondo Alessandro Petitot, 1727–1801*, 1975; Grandmaison, 60–2 (his *cordon noir*, 1760); Gruber in *GBA*, 1971, 2, 355–70; Erouard, Oechslin and Arrizoli in *PF*, 250–60.

Barreau: Pariset, 1962; Gallet, 1972, 141.

Le Lorrain: Harris, 1967, 193–5; R. P. Wunder in *Apollo*, 1967, 354–9; Eriksen, 1974, 44–8 and 201–2; Erouard and Oechslin in *PF*, 201–15; Rosenberg in *RA*, 40–1, 1978, 173–202; *NAAF*, 1878, 33 (his *congé* for Russia, 1758).

De Troy's opinion: *CD*, 9, 445, and 10, 172, and 81–2.

Le Lorrain and Åkerö: Eriksen in *Konsthistorisk Tidskrift*, December 1963, 94–120.

La Live and his houses: Dufort, 1, 86–7; Thirion, 262; Eriksen, 1961 (his furniture), 1963, 344–51, 1974, 48–51, 97–8, 115–16, 195–7, and pls 305–7; Scott, 72–7. La Live owned a view by de Machy of the interior of Ste-Geneviève (*Diderot Salons*, 1, 1761, 130); Réau in *BSHAF*, 1920, 222–34 (tomb of Mme de la Live).

60 Opinions of the furniture: Cochin, 1880, 143; *Catalogue historique de peinture et sculpture française de M. de la Live*, 1764.

Neufforge: Thieme Becker, 25 (1931), with bibliography; Kaufmann, 1968, 151–4; Eriksen, 1974, 207.

Presentation of *Recueil* to Academy: *PV*, 6, 305 (September 1757), and 7, 282 (15 June 1767).

61 Opinions of Neufforge: Blondel, 1774, 2, 316, speaks of the 'pesanteur' of his style.

Chapter 4

63 Piranesi: Henri Focillon, *Giovanni Battista Piranesi*, 1918, and John Wilton-Ely, *The Mind and Art of Giovanni Battista Piranesi*, 1978 (with up-to-date bibliography); for Piranesi and France, Méjanes, Arrizoli and Brunel in *PF*, 271–301; and *PF Colloque*, *passim*; Marigny's acquisition of works by Piranesi, *CD*, 11, 139, 176, 413, 417, 514.

Piranesi and Roman vaulting: Karl Lehmann in *Piranesi* (exhibition catalogue), Smith College of Art, Northampton, Mass., 1961, 89.

64 Review of Cochin and Bellicard: *CL*, 1, 196–7.

Le Roy: obituary by Dacier in *Histoire et mémoires de l'Institut royal de France, Classe d'histoire et de littérature ancienne*, 1815, 1, 267–84; Wiebenson, 1969, 33–4; Mosser in *PF*, 220–4; BN Catalogue for Le Roy's publications; M. Whiffen in *AR*, 1959, 119–20 (English edition of the *Ruines*, 1758).

Le Roy's reputation: for example Belanger in his life of de Wailly, *Journal de Paris*, 27 Brumaire, An VII, 260–2.

Prix de Rome drawings: see *PF*, figs 116, 116 *bis*.

Stuart and Revett: L. Lawrence in *JWI*, 1938–39, 2, 128–46; Summerson, 239–40; Wiebenson, 1969, 1–18.

Le Roy in Rome: *CD*, 10, 23, 413 and 503, and 11, 15.

Reactions to the *Ruines*: Cochin, 1880, 78–9.

66 Le Roy's defence against Stuart and Revett: *Observations sur les édifices des anciens peuples, précédées de réflexions préliminaires sur la critique des Ruines de la Grèce, publiée dans un ouvrage anglois, intitulé les Antiquités d'Athènes*, 1767.

Piranesi's reaction: see J. Wilton-Ely, *The Mind and Art of Giovanni Battista Piranesi*, 1978, ch. 4.

Le Roy at the Academy: he was a possible candidate for the post of Secretary in 1768, when Sedaine was appointed (*CL*, 5, 479).

Le Roy's brochure on churches: *Histoire de la disposition et des formes différentes que les Chrétiens ont données à leurs temples, depuis le règne de Constantin le Grand, jusqu'à nous*, 1764 (note on Laugier, 73). Le Roy discusses the church of Ste-Geneviève and the Madeleine (76ff.) in very simple terms, saying that both derived from the Versailles chapel and the Louvre colonnade.

Le Roy on shipping: *La Marine des anciens peuples*, 1777; *Les Navires des anciens*, 1783; *Nouvelles Recherches sur le vaisseau long des anciens*, 1786; *Lettres à M. Franklin sur la marine*, 1790 (2nd ed.); and in *MINSA*, I (An VI), 497ff., and III (An XI), 141ff.

Mrs Thrale on Le Roy: Thrale, 117.

St-Non: see Louis Guimbaud, *Saint-Non et Fragonard*, 1928, 151–68; *Le Voyage pittoresque des Royaumes de Naples et de Sicile*, 1781–86; Hautecoeur, *Histoire*, 3, 17; Renard, *Autobiographie*; *PV*, 9, 68 (25 February 1782), and 9, 133 (7 June 1784).

Houel: on *Le Voyage pittoresque des Iles de Sicile* (1782–87) see Hautecoeur, *Histoire*, 3, 17, and Méjanes in *PF*, 151–3 (with bibliography).

Clérisseau: the literature before 1967 is tabulated by T. McCormick in *The American Association of Architectural Bibliographers*, 1967, 11–16; for the work at Metz see note below. See especially Hautecoeur, 1912, 40–4; J. Fleming in *The Connoisseur*, 1960, 186–94; McCormick and Fleming in *The Connoisseur*, 1964, 2, 239–43; McCormick in *JSAH*, 1963, 3, 119–26, and in *Arts in Virginia*, 1964, 2, 3–13. Clérisseau's extensive library, which included Ledoux's *Architecture*, was catalogued and sold 11–16 November 1820. For the Hôtel de la Reynière see note on ch. 8 below.

Clérisseau in Rome: *CD*, 10, 399, 457, 461ff.

Clérisseau's work at Metz: J. Lejeaux in *L'Architecture*, 1928, 115–21, and in *RAAM*, 1928, 1, 225–31 and 2, 125–36, and 1932, 2, 3–16.

67 Jean-Benjamin de La Borde: see ch. 11 above; Visme, 104ff.

Ecole des Ponts et Chaussées: the basic study is by Dartein in *APC*, 1906, 2, 5–143; the documentation at the Ecole is listed in the *Catalogue des livres*, 2 vols, 1894, and the *Catalogue des manuscrits*, 1886; see also Thiéry, *Paris*, 1, 586ff.; Tarbé de St-Hardouin, 7ff.; Dakin, *Turgot*, 63; Ardascheff, 303; editions of the *Almanach royal*.

Perronet: see Dartein in *APC*, 1906, 4, 5–87; lengthy obituary by P. C. Lesage, *Notice pour servir à l'éloge de M. Perronet*, 1805, and Prony in *Institut royal de France, Séance publique annuelle des Quatre Académies*, 24 April 1829, 53–76; also Grandmaison, 70–1 (ennoblement, 1763); Chavret; Tarbé de St-Hardouin, 28ff.; B. du Montgolfier in *BMC*, June, 1969, 14–15 (bust by Masson).

Roads and bridges: Thiéry, *Paris*, 1, xxxix; Young, 39; see also Patte, 1769, ch. 5.

68 Pont Louis XVI: Dartein in *APC*, 1906, 4, 88–148; B. Fillon and J. Cousin in *NAAF*, 1872, 371–7; M. A. Levent in *BMC*, June 1954 (model at the Musée Carnavalet on loan from the Ecole des Ponts et Chaussées).

69 Blaikie and Young on Perronet's bridges: Blaikie, 130; Young, 88, 77 (Pont-Ste-Maxence), 15 (Orléans).

Architects of the Ecole. Le Masson: see the sale of his collection, with biography, 10–12 March 1830; Gallet, 1972, 171; Tarbé de St-Hardouin, 54ff. Gauthey: *Oeuvres de M. Gauthey*, 3 vols, 1809–16; Tarbé de St-Hardouin, 45ff.; Hautecoeur, *Histoire*, 4, 205–7; Y. Beauvalot in *MCADCO*, 27, 1970–71, 227–59 (his influence in Burgundy).

Hue and the La Rochelle Bourse: Moulin, 64–71.

70 Young at Chanteloup: Young, 67.

Blaikie on Le Nôtre: Blaikie, 192 (comment made at Compiègne, 1785).

Diderot: quoted by Guéhenno 1, 176; see also Mornet, 1907, 183–217; Paul van Tieghem, *Le Sentiment de la nature dans le préromantisme européen*, 1960; for Laugier's views see Herrmann, 1962, 140–7.

Gardens: most recently the exhibition *JF*, but without bibliography, and Wiebenson, 1978. In general see Ganay, 1933, in *GBA*, 1932, 2, 183–97, 1955, 1, 287–98, and in *RAAM*, 1934, 2, 63–80 (and further references below); H. F. Clark in *JWI*, 1943 (6), 156–89; Hautecoeur, *Histoire*, 5, 3–50; Langner, 1963; D. Wiebenson in *JSAH*, 1968, 136–9; Gallet, 1972, 101–3. Chinese influences, see note on Introduction above.

Lunéville: B. Scott in *Apollo*, 1968, 100–7; Wiebenson, 1978, 10–14, 130 (bibliography).

Gardens in England: survey in Summerson, 276–7; Kimball, 1931, 29ff.; Wiebenson, 1978, 39–63 (theory).

Mrs Thrale's comment: Thrale, 87.

Watelet and Moulin Joli: *JF*, 52; M. Henriet in *GBA*, 1922, 173–94; *CL*, 1, 387 and 2, 370; Wiebenson, 1978, 15–19, 131 (bibliography).

Contemporary literature on gardens: *JF*, 80–1; [J. Morel], *Théorie des jardins*, 1776; Walpole, *Essay on Modern Gardening*, 1770 (French translation, 1784, by the Duc de Nivernais); G. C. L. Hirschfeld, *Theorie der Gartenkunst*, 1775 (French translation, 5 vols, 1779–85); Ligne, 1781; other sources are listed by Wiebenson, 1978, 123–7.

72 Tivoli: Thiéry, *Paris*, 1, 140ff.; Mercier, [1797], 4, 232–8; Ligne, 176; *JF*, 52. Boutin: Swarte, 46; Pariset, 1961, 82–5; *CD*, 11, 12 (in Italy, 1753) and 14; Vigée Lebrun, *Memoirs*, 183–5; Thirion, 273ff.; Oberkirch, 3, 296.

Ermenonville: Gerardin's (*sic*) own *De la composition des paysages*, 1777; Blaikie, 156–7, 186, 217; Oberkirch, 3, 12; Young, 76; Laborde, s.v. Ermenonville; Croÿ, 1, 182 (Contant working there in 1752); Langner, 1963; *ACF*, 1; Sirén, 125–32; Wiebenson, 1978, 81–8, 130 (bibliography). Girardin: A. Martin-Decaen, *Le Dernier Ami de J.-J. Rousseau, Le Marquis René de Girardin (1735–1808)*, 1912; Gallet, 1972, 177 (s.v. Morel).

Morfontaine: Blaikie, 157; Young, 76; Laborde (s.v. Morfontaine); Wiebenson, 131 (bibliography). Le Pelletier de Morfontaine: Ardascheff, 177; Thiéry, *Paris*, 1, 601ff. (his Paris house); Vigée Lebrun, *Memoirs*, 196ff.

Monceau: Carmontelle, *Jardin de Monceau*, 1779; Thiéry, *Paris*, 1, 64ff.; E. Dacier in *SIP*, 1910, 49–63; Sirén, 121–5; *JF*, 85–8; Wiebenson in *MHF*, 1976, 5, 16–19, and 1978, 91–6, 131 (bibliography).

The Duc de Chartres: see note on Louis, ch. 9 below.

Other early gardens: Duc d'Harcourt: Ganay in *RAAM*, 1923, 1, 59–64; Young, 103; Soulange Bodin, 1, 46–58. Princesse de Montmorency: see under Ledoux, ch. 10 above. Prince de Croÿ: Croÿ, 1, xxxi (Croÿ himself was politically anti-English: Croÿ, 1, xxix).

Blaikie on Henri: Blaikie, 143; on botany and gardens, see *JF*, 114–120.

Young on Rousseau and du Barry's garden: Young, 74 and 28.

Walpole on Tivoli: Walpole, 8, 65 (5 August 1771).

Vigée Lebrun's opinions: *Memoirs*, 107–10.

Le Rouge: see Sirén, 107–11; Wiebenson, 1978, *passim*.

Rousseau's tomb: T. Bodkin in *GBA*, 1936, 2, 156–66; *JF*, 147–8; Wiebenson, 1978, 82, 87.

Chapter 5

73 Later development of Ste-Geneviève: Petzet, 43–58; Mathieu, 181–283; Middleton, 1963, 106–15; Braham, 1971. For other drawings, not necessarily rightly dated or rightly attributed, see Lavedan in *BSHAF*, 1954, 34–6, S. Damiron in *BSHAF*, 1960, 27–32, and Rabreau in *BM*, 1972, 361–2.

Grimm on the first project: *CL*, 2, 199.

The drawings for the crypt: Braham, 1971, 585–6. On the subject of the Greek Doric in general see Pevsner and S. Lang in *AR*, 1948, 271–9, and Wiebenson, 1969, 67–70 (appearance in France).

74 De Machy's painting: see *Diderot Salons*, 1, 130, and B. du Montgolfier in *BMC*, 1955, 1, 8–10.

75 Grimm on the crypt: *CL*, 4, 91.

Pilon's sculptures: see Monval, 481–2; Chevallier and Rabreau, 41.

Créquy *Souvenirs* on Valois tombs: Créquy, 1, 29.

77 The dome of 1764: engravings of the project published by Piganiol, 6, 98–105. Disapproval for the dome was voiced by Laugier, 1765, 26.

Ecole de Droit: Thiéry, *Paris*, 2, 243; Mercier, *Tableau*, 2, 18–19; Monval, 463; drawings in AN, N III Seine 543.

The Tuileries theatre: Thiéry, *Paris*, 1, 391; Monval, 173–80; AN, 01 1680 (correspondence on Tuileries).

The Gobelins factory and Soufflot's furniture designs: J. Mondain-Monval, *Correspondance de Soufflot . . . concernant la manufacture des Gobelins*, 1918; Monval, 317–47; E. Harris in *Apollo*, 1962, 100; F. Watson in *Apollo*, 1967, 239; Eriksen, 1974, 61.

Criticism of Tuileries theatre: *Mémoires secrets*, 2, 11 and 20 (24 January and 7 February 1764); *CL*, 4, 91–93; *Arnoldiana*, 126–7.

Soufflot's Opéra design: Monval, 175–6 (the drawings he mentions – one illustrated in Pérouse de Montclos, pl. 73 – are probably the work of Antoine, see ch. 7 above).

The Louvre staircase: Bannister, 231ff.; Christ, 82. An earlier project for a staircase in the Louvre is illustrated by Hautecoeur, *Histoire du Louvre* 1928, 74 (drawings in the Louvre, Cabinet des Dessins).

Minor works: AN, 01 1552, 29 June 1764 (Prince de Tingry's apartment); *NAAF*, 1891, 171, 204; *AAF*, 1927, 291; *BSHAF*, 1923, 387 (letter for M. St-Far).

78 Patte: see Mathieu; Petzet, 67–8, and *passim*; Middleton, 1963, 108–17; Cochin, 1771, 3, 130ff. According to the *Mémoires secrets*, Patte was little known in 1770 (19, 299–300, 23 January 1771). On his relation to the *Encyclopédie* see Wilson, *Diderot*, 360.

Grimm on Patte: *CL*, 6, 446, and 7, 34–6.

The weight of Soufflot's dome: Legrand and Landon, 1, 110, n.1, give the weight on each pier as $7\frac{1}{2}$ million pounds.

Churches discussed by Soufflot at the Academy. S. Agostino, Piacenza: *PV*, 7, 121 (22 November 1762). St-Jean, Liège: *PV*, 7, 119 (6 September 1762). Toussaint, Angers: *PV*, 7, 189 (3 December 1764). St-Mary-le-Bow, London: *PV*, 8, 78 (2 July 1770). St-Etienne-du-Mont: *PV*, 8, 146–8 (8 March 1773). S. Maria della Salute, Venice: *PV*, 8, 214–15 (20 February 1775). Other drawings he brought to discuss were of a Roman aqueduct, *PV*, 8, 198 (11 July 1774), the temple of Minerva Medici, *PV*, 8, 341–2 (23 March 1778), and a fountain by Bernini, *PV*, 8, 534 (30 June 1778).

Patte in London: Mathieu, 183.

Drawing of diagonal section: Braham, 1971, 590.

79 The dispute of 1776: especially Middleton, 1963, 113; Mathieu, 246ff.

Changes of 1775: *Almanach royal*; J. Monval, 47–51; Marquiset, 176; Silvestre de Sacy, 1953, 62ff.

Mique: see ch. 14 above.

Soufflot's epitaph: quoted in Quatremère, 1830, 2, 346.

Soufflot and Voltaire: Voltaire, 85 (1963), 219, no. 17426; *NAAF*, 1878, 126–7 (*congé* for Lyon, 1773).

Obituary in *Journal de Paris*: Abrégé, 2, pt. 2, 1789; *NAAF*, 1880–81, 244–5 (burial in Ste-Geneviève).

Soufflot's pupils and followers. Soufflot 'le Romain': ch. 14 above. Brébion: Gallet, 1972, 146. Rondelet: ch. 15 above. De Bourge: see his *Autobiographie*. Etienne Le Roy: Gallet, 1972, 173. Etienne de Montgolfier: Gallet, 1972, 177 (the architect of the Château d'Aiguillon). Raymond: Gallet, 1972, 183.

Lequeu: volume presented to BN, Est., Ha 41; on Lequeu himself see ch. 14 above.

Soufflot's executors: for Vernet in general see P. Conisbee, catalogue of Vernet exhibition, Kenwood House and Musée de la Marine, Paris, 1976–77; for Chalgrin and his wife see ch. 8 above.

80 Soufflot's house and his collection: Monval, 59–63, 67–71; copy of sale catalogue BI, Duplessis 281; *NAAF*, 1885, 108–12 (sealing of the house); *PV* of the Academy of Painting, 6, 141, and 8, 372.

Bertin: *DBF*; Thiéry, *Paris*, 1, 134 (his house in Paris and his collection). His estate at Chatou: Monval, 419–21; Ganay, 1933, 56; Hautecoeur, *Histoire*, 4, 202–3; *JF*, 78. His Chinese collection shown by Soufflot to the Academy: *PV*, 8, 242 (27 November 1775).

81 Gift of the *Encyclopédie*: *PV*, 8, 387 (30 August 1779).

Succession of Brébion: Monval, 479. He was chosen, according to the *Mémoires secrets* (16, 40), because he would not interfere with Soufflot's ideas. Brébion supposedly died in 1775, but he is listed (*AAF*, 1927, 195) as Inspecteur du Louvre in 1779.

Quatremère and the Panthéon: Schneider, 33–49; Middleton, 1963, 117.

Quatremère's opinions: 1830, 2, 341–2.

82 Projects for the Panthéon: de Wailly's design published in *La Décade philosophique*, An VI, 1, 537 (noted by Kaufmann, 1968, 148, 259), and his pyramidal project mentioned by Chennevières in *GBA*, 1880, 2, 306n. Other projects: see the list of publications in Mathieu, 387–97; Biver, 26; Mercier [1797], 1, 179–84, speaks of the dome with great irony.

Rondelet: see ch. 15 above.

The decorations of the Panthéon: Monval, 479–83; Chennevières in *GBA*, 1880, 1, 296–306 and 501–511.

PART TWO

Chapter 6

83 Peyre: see his own *Oeuvres d'architecture*, 1765 and 1795, the second edition with short life by his son and collected essays by Peyre; *BU*; *NBG*; Thieme Becker, 26 (1932); Hautecoeur, *Histoire*, 4, 225–31; Kaufmann, 1968, 143–4; Gallet, 1972, 181; 1971 Hermitage exhibition, 30; M. Mosser in *PF*, 266–70. His portrait in the Ecole des Beaux-Arts (pl. 102 above) published by Gallet, 1975, 44.

Peyre in Rome: *CD*, 10, 447, 452 (letter recording connection with the Princesse de Conti), 453, and 11, 81 and 112; *De Wailly*, 10 (drawings made in Rome).

Peyre's *Oeuvres d'architecture*: shown to the Academy 10 December 1765 (*PV*, 7, 232); his paper on the planning of houses shown on 27 April 1770, and published in the *Mercure de France* and in the second edition of the *Oeuvres*, 1795.

84 Accademia di San Luca competition drawings: see Marconi, Cipriani and Valeriani.

85 Work in Paris: AN, 01 629 (10) (*devis* for Opéra at Tuileries).

Neubourg house: Thiéry, *Paris*, 2, 203; Legrand and Landon, 2, 4, 21; Krafft and Ransonnette, 38 (1762). The family: Bosher, index; Couture, *Autobiographie* (work at the Château of La Moustière (Berry) for M. Le Prêtre, 'trésorier des troupes de la maison du Roy'); Thiéry, *Paris*, 2, 207 (tomb of son of family in St-Hippolyte).

87 Hôtel de Condé: Peyre showed his projects to the Academy in 1763 (25 April, *PV*, 7, 143).

The Prince de Condé: Piépape, 2, 65ff. and 81 (charitable activities); Emile Lesueur, *Louis-Henri-Joseph de Bourbon, Le Dernier Condé*, 1937 (especially for his later life); Macon, 98ff.; Croÿ, 1, 267. For his patronage in general see Hautecoeur, *Histoire*, 4, 113–16, and Eriksen, 1974, 80–1 and 168–9.

Chantilly in the eighteenth century: Mérigot, *Promenades ou itinéraire des jardins de Chantilly*, 1791; Thicknesse, 2, 175; Young, 10; Gustave Macon, *Chantilly et le Musée Condé*; Ernest de Ganay, *Chantilly*, n.d. (short guide), *Chantilly au XVIIIe siècle*, 1925 (more thorough), and in *RAAM*, 1928, 1, 93–110 (the gardens); de Broglie in *GBA*, 1950, 2, 309–24 (hameau and laiterie), and 1961, 1, 155–66 (theatre); Erdberg, 154 (gardens); Bellisard, *Autobiographie*; Gallet, 1972, 173 (s.v. Jean-François Le Roy); and Wiebenson, 1978, 129–30 (further bibliography).

Drouais' portrait: see C. Gabillot in *GBA*, 1905, 2, 388–90, and sale catalogue, Parke-Bernet, 8 May 1947 (lot 58).

88 The Palais-Bourbon: see especially Pérouse de Montclos, 1969, 67; also Boyer, 1935 (background); Piépape, 2, 63–4; Macon, 122ff.; Henri Coutant, *Le Palais-Bourbon au XVIIIe siècle*, 1905; Pariset, 1962, 80–2; Bellisard and Renard, *Autobiographies*; Gallet, 1972, 142 (Belisard) and 172 (Lemonnier).

Duc de Nivernais: Vigée Lebrun, *Memoirs*, 112; Créquy, 6, 84–5; Du Barry, 2, 124; Thiéry, *Paris*, 2, 426–7 (his hôtel); *CD*, 16, 315, 338 and 344 (embassy in Rome); A. F. Blunt in *Master Drawings*, 1973, 363.

Walpole on Nivernais: Walpole, 6, 407–8, and R. W. Ketton-Cremer, *Horace Walpole*, 1964, 226.

89 Opinion of Nivernais' house: Vallentin, *Mirabeau*, 72.

Church of the Visitation: *PV*, 7, 273 (27 April 1767) (showing of drawings at the Academy); Thiéry, *Paris*, 2, 245–6.

Peyre's death: not 1788, as sometimes said, but 1785 (*PV*, 9, 161, 16 August 1785). In August 1780 he had shown to the Academy a letter on the gardens of Ermenonville (*PV*, 9, 55). For his wife, the sister of

Moreau, see Vigée Lebrun, *Souvenirs*, 2, 205, and see note on Moreau (ch. 6 below) on her marriage to the poet, Ducis.

Charles de Wailly: born 9 November 1730 (Arch. de la Seine), died 12 Brumaire, An VII (2 November 1798: AN, Min. Cent., XII, 783). Contemporary lives by Andrieux in *MINSA*, 3 (An IX), 36–42; Joseph Lavallée, *Notice historique sur Charles Dewailly*, An VII; Clément in *Mercure de France*, 10 Fructidor, An VII, 27–8 (and in *Gazette nationale*, 64, 4 Frimaire, An VII, 261–2) and by Belanger in *Journal de Paris*, 27 Brumaire, An VII, 260–2. Later accounts in *BU* and *NBG*; Thieme Becker, 35 (1942) with bibliography; Kaufmann, 1968, 145–8; Hautecoeur, *Histoire*, 4, 232–42; Gallet, 1972, 157–8; Mosser in *PF*, 132–40; Braham, 1972; Rabreau, 1972, 1977; also Le Bilhan, *Francs-maçons*, 485; Stein, *Pajou*, 27 (bust by Pajou, 1789). The exhibition catalogue, *De Wailly*, 1979, goes far to satisfy the demand for a comprehensive monograph.

Drawings by de Wailly: Clément de Ris in *GBA*, 1880, 2, nos 391–6; Mireur, s.v. De Wailly; A. Voronikhine in *Hermitage Bulletin*, 1971, 33–8, and 1971 Hermitage exhibition, 16–17; Musée des Arts Décoratifs exhibition, 1880; *De Wailly*, 1979; and in de Wailly sales, see note below. Documents: BN, Ms NAF 2479 (letters).

'The Palladio of his century': *Mercure de France*, 10 Fructidor, An VII, 28.

Peyre on Servandoni: *Oeuvres*, 1795, 8.

90 Position of Moreau: *CD*, 10, 469–70 (request to share prize) and 476 (letter of Mme Beausire, Moreau's aunt).

De Wailly in Rome: *CD*, 11, 8 (*brevet*), 31–2 (money), 58 (arrival), 112 (drawing of fountain), 140 (good conduct), 142 (return): *De Wailly*, 19–21.

Explorations in Rome: Barthélemy, 207 (also quoted in Gallet, 1975, 44); *CD*, 11, 172–3. A drawing by de Wailly of Caylus' tomb (the famous 'cruche étrusque') is in BN, Est., Va 223a (35) (noted by Rabreau and Gallet, n. 44).

91 Work at Versailles: Gabriel's letters, see ch. 2 above; *De Wailly*, 49; Lavallée, 47 (his dislike of Versailles). In 1772 Peyre and de Wailly are said to have been the architects of Fontainebleau (Champollion-Figeac, 429).

De Wailly at Ménars: Mosser, 1973, 273–6, 281ff.; *De Wailly*, 42–3. Two drawings by de Wailly appear in Marigny's sale, one of them of Ste-Geneviève.

Election to the Academy: Marionneau in *RSBAD*, 1894, 468–509; *PV*, 7, xxiv–ix, 276–318 *passim*; *Mémoires secrets*, 3, 273–4 (8 October, 1767), mention the modesty of de Wailly, but for a different opinion, by Pâris, see *De Wailly*, 22.

Furniture designs, etc.: Eriksen, 1974, 69–70; Rabreau and Gallet, 40–1.

Early pupils. Bajenev: *CD*, 11, 448; Hautecoeur, 1912, 29–30. *RSBAD*, 1897, 699 (de Wailly's Russian contacts). De Bourge was another early pupil; see his *Autobiographie*. List of pupils in *De Wailly*, 100–5.

The choir of Amiens: Laugier, 1765, 145; J. Foucart-Borville in *BSHAF*, 1974, 130–8; also A. P. M. Gilbert, *Description historique de l'église de Notre-Dame d'Amiens*, 1833, 285ff.; *De Wailly*, 47.

The Voyer family: Créquy, 1, 134; also *DN*; Genlis, 9, 108–9 (Mme de Voyer): Thiéry, *Paris*, 1, 40 and 598–9 (properties).

Marquis de Voyer (1722–82): Dufort, 1, 390 ('foremost connoisseur'), 116 (habitué of Mme Geoffrin); Britsch, 397 (his anglomania); Croÿ, 1, 73 and *passim* (Voyer a supper guest of the king, 1746–51); *Index biographique . . . Académie des Sciences*, 395.

Château of Les Ormes and work for the Marquis d'Argenson: Mosser in *PF*, 132; *De Wailly*, 43–44; also, Young, 64.

Hôtel de Voyer: Thiéry, *Paris*, 1, 287–8; J. Mayor in *GBA*, 1914, 2, 333 (but with wrong date); Harris, 1963, no. 10 (the redating suggests that Chambers' drawings of the hotel are not later than the other drawings); *De Wailly*, 44–5.

Le Roy on the Hôtel de Voyer: *Observations sur les édifices . . .*, 1767, 10.

Visit of Mrs Thrale and Dr Johnson: Thrale, 116, 118, Johnson, 178–9, 172.

94 Montmusard: E. Fyot in *MCADCO*, 18, 1922–26, 222ff.; Braham, 1972, 677–8; *De Wailly*, 42; Bibliothèque Municipale de Dijon,

Estampes 5011 and Ms 989 PF and 1606 (documents and drawings). Full publication by Y. Beauvalot in *Les Cahiers du vieux Dijon*, 6, 1978. On the development of châteaux in general see Hautecoeur, *Histoire*, 4, 407–19. (See also *RAAM*, 1924, 2, 257 for influence of Montmusard on Pâris.)

Lenoir's early years: Lenoir, *Autobiographie*; *CD*, 10, 450 (stay in Rome); Monod-Cassidy, 6–9 (Président Jean Bouhier).

The Fyots: *DN*, 8, 747–51. Beauvalot in *Les Cahiers du vieux Dijon*, 1974–75, 31–43 (patronage of Lenoir).

95 De Wailly at Dijon: *PV*, 7, 140, 142 (21 March, 11 April 1763).

96 Salon of 1771: *PV* (Academy of Painting), 8, 69; *Mercure de France*, October 1771, 1, 190, October 1773, 1, 175; *Diderot Salons*, 4, 204 (comments on the model).

Versailles, Reposoir: AN, 01 1861; Gallet, 1972, 157; Braham, 1972, 681; *De Wailly*, 47. Also Vaysse de Villiers, *Tableau descriptif . . . de Versailles*, 1828 (2nd ed.), 26; H.-J. Messines, *Eglise réformée de Versailles*, n.d., 79 (with date, 1769); Le Roi, 53.

Comédie-Française: AN, 01 846, Comédie-Française, *liasse* 38–9; Thiéry, *Paris*, 2, 376ff.; Peyre fils, *Projets de reconstruction de la Salle de l'Odéon*, 1819; Legrand and Landon, 2, 3, 91ff.; Donnet, chs 2 and 11; *Encyclopédie, Suite . . . des planches*, 60–7; La Ferté, 314–15 (Mme du Barry sees projects). Recent literature: Gallet, 1965; Braham, 1972, 681–3; and, the most detailed study, Steinhauser and Rabreau. Also Claude Alasseur, *La Comédie-Française au 18e siècle*, 1967 (general background), and Raymond Genty, *Les Souterrains de l'Odéon*, 1945.

Theatres in Paris: Donnet; Hautecoeur, *Histoire*, 4, 160–2 and 430–51; Patte, 1782, especially 120ff. (review of recent books); Max Aghion, *Les Théâtres de Paris au XVIIIe siècle*, n.d. (1926?); John Lough, *Paris Theatre Audiences in the Seventeenth & Eighteenth Centuries*, 1957. Also Maurice Albert, *Les Théâtres de la foire (1660–1789)*, 1900, and *Les Théâtres des boulevards (1789–1848)*, 1902; Decugis and Reymond (stage scenery).

97 De Wailly abroad: *NAAF*, 1878, 124–6 (Pisa and Genoa, 1772).

Visit to Voltaire: Voltaire, *Correspondance*, 80, 136 (18 November 1771).

98 Third journey to Italy (with Antoine) and start of Comédie: *PV*, 8, 344 (27 April 1778); *NAAF*, 1878, 50, 124–6 (*congé* and letter from Pisa); *AAF*, 1907, 417–19 (work begins 8 May 1779).

The building of the Comédie and the Place: Steinhauser and Rabreau, 12–14, 18–21; Gallet, 1972, 186 (s.v. Thunot).

The Brussels theatre: BN, Est., Vg 79 (album of de Wailly's drawings); Brussels, Bibliothèque Royale Albert Ier, MS II 2135 (paper by de Wailly); V. G. Martiny in *Etudes sur le XVIIIe siècle*, Brussels, 1977, 87–99; *De Wailly*, 67–8.

The Théâtre-Italien: *PV*, 9, 126 (8 March 1784); *Mercure de France*, May 1784, 40, and *La Décade philosophique*, 10 Floréal, An VI, 3, 237ff. (de Wailly's letters); and see under Heurtier, ch. 14 above.

The manuscript of Peyre and de Wailly: Braham in *The National Trust Year Book*, 1976–77, 38–53.

Mrs Thrale at the Tuileries theatre: Thrale, 96 and 98.

De Wailly's presentation drawings: Gallet, 1965.

100 The interior of the Comédie-Française: Steinhauser and Rabreau, 35–40; Pevsner, 1976, 78–9 (partitions); Patte, 1782, 105, claimed that Slotdz was the first to dispense with separate boxes in the *Salle provisoire* at the Versailles stables (1745). The method of lighting was based on a process invented by Lavoisier (*Mémoires secrets*, 18, 187–88, 1 December 1781).

101 Mme d'Oberkirch on *Figaro*: Oberkirch, 2, 216.

102 Later projects for the theatre: Steinhauser and Rabreau, 31–4.

Opinions of the theatre: *CL*, 11, 88–91; Oberkirch, 1, 275–6; Croÿ, 4, 249.

Marriage of de Wailly: AN, Min. Cent., LXXXVI (817), 31 August 1781; for his activities as a freemason see Vidler, 84; Gallet, 1972, 24; *De Wailly*, 23–4.

103 Hôtel de la Villette: Gallet, 1972, s.v. de Wailly; *De Wailly*, 45–6.

House of Mme Denis: Thiéry, *Paris*, 1, 189; *PV*, 9, 44–5, 23 April 1781; for his activities as a freemason see Vidler, 84; Gallet, 1972, 24; Voltaire, *Correspondance*, 98, 202 (letter to Chalgrin, 3 May 1778); *De Wailly*, 45.

Palazzo Spinola: drawings in the Musée des Arts Décoratifs; *Encyclopédie, Suite . . . des planches*, 1, 56–8; *PV*, 8, 283 (2 December 1776) and 8, 296 (25 February 1777) (engravings shown to Academy); Réau in *L'Architecture*, 1932, 219ff.; Lossky in *Urbanisme et architecture, Etudes écrites et publiées en l'honneur de Pierre Lavedan*, 1954, 245ff.; Maltese in *Neoclassicismo*, 77ff.; Braham, 1972, 683; *De Wailly*, 82–3.

Chapelle de la Vierge: quotation from *Journal de Paris*, 25 August 1778 (*Abrégé*, 2, 325ff.). For the church see under Servandoni, ch. 1 above; E. Malbois in *GBA*, 1924, 1, 215–22; Lemesle, 33–6 and 47–8; *De Wailly*, 48–9. For de Wailly's pulpit see Rabreau and Gallet; G. Gailland in *BSHAF*, 1957, 55–9; Gallet in *BMC*, November 1972, 23–6.

The crypt chapel in St-Leu-St-Gilles: drawings exhibited at 1773 Salon; Thiéry, *Paris*, 1, 501; Legrand and Landon, 1, 145; M. Vimont, *Histoire de l'église et de la paroisse Saint-Leu-Saint-Gilles à Paris*, 1932, 7; Boinet, 1, 297ff.; Braham, 1972, 683–4; *De Wailly*, 48.

De Wailly's house: Krafft and Ransonnette, 43–4 (showing 5 houses, 1778); Thiéry, *Paris*, 1, 78; Stein, *Pajou*, 27–8; Braham, 1972, 684 (documentation); *De Wailly*, 46–7; Gallet, 1972, 104–8 (artists' houses in general).

104 De Wailly's sales: 24 November 1788; AN, Min. Cent., XII (785), 27 Nivôse, An VIII (inventory); Comtesse de Fourcroy (de Wailly's widow), 16–17 March 1810, and 2 April 1839.

Plan for development of Paris: *PV*, 9, 205 (3 July 1787); BN, Cartes et Plans, GeC 4384 (noted by C. du Bus in *Chronique des arts*, 1914, 60–1, and illustrated by Rabreau, 1977, 36–7).

Relations with Catherine the Great: A. Voronikhine in *Hermitage Museum Report*, 33, 1971, 33–8 (drawings for a 'Pavillon de Minerve', 1773); Andrieux, 41 (refusal of Directorship of Leningrad Academy; Réau, *Le Monde slav*, 1928, 178, suggests that the invitation to St Petersburg was made in 1773).

Later work: Projects for Belgium: *De Wailly*, 87; for the Brussels theatre see note above; *NAAF*, 1878, 64 (*congé* for Brussels, 1787), and 1880–81, 96–103 (negotiating sale of painting to d'Angiviller); P. J. Goetghebuer, *Choix des monumens . . . du royaume des Pays-Bas*, 1827, 27a, 35; Réau, 1924–33, *Belgique et Hollande*, 27f. and 195; X. Duquenne in *Revue du personnel de la Banque Nationale de Belgique*, 9 September 1976, 5–31 (Château of Laeken), and *Le Château de Seneffe*, 1978. Projects for Kassel: see *W. Strieders Wilhelmshöhe*, 1913, figs 5–7; *Die Bau- und Kunstdenkmäler im Regierungsbezirk Cassel*, 6, 1923, 313 (1782), and 4, 1910, 303–7; Colombier, 233–8; Braham, 1972, 684–5; *De Wailly*, 86–7. Projects for Russia: see de Baye, *Kouskovo*, 1905, 23ff.; Réau, *Le Monde slav*, 1928, 258ff. Port-Vendres: see *PV*, 9, 45 (23 April 1781), and *Mercure de France*, May 1781, 141; La Borde, 3, 1, 18–20; S. Pressouyre in *MHF*, 1965, 199–22; Gaston Vidal, *Port-Vendres*, 1969; *De Wailly*, 72–3. Projects for Paris: see J. Wilhelm in *BMC*, 1963, 1, 5–10 (project for Salon Carré); J. Babelon in *Journal des savants*, June, 1964, 99. According to Gallet, 1972, 61, de Wailly designed the architecture for David's *Les Horaces*.

Revolutionary activities: a Jesuit church in Brussels was converted by de Wailly into a 'Salle d'Assemblée des Amis de la Liberté' (BN, Est., Qb 1, 12 January 1793).

105 The Théâtre des Arts: *La Décade philosophique*, An VII (30 Ventôse), 2, 559ff.; G. Gailland in *BSHAF*, 1954, 80–4; entire scheme published by Rabreau, 1977; *De Wailly*, 68–72.

De Wailly's view of recent architecture: quoted by Belanger in his obituary.

Moreau: Thieme Becker, 25 (1931), with bibliography; Hautecoeur, *Histoire*, 4, 233; Gallet, 1961 (the major article on Moreau), and 1972, 177. Also Grandmaison, 83–5, and *Mémoires secrets*, 7, 48 (24 August 1773) (ennoblement); Bord, 359 and 381 (freemasonry).

Ville de Paris: for the Beausire family, see D. Labarre de Raillicourt in *BSHAF*, 1958, 83–7; Gallet, 1972, 141–2. Destouches was Beausire's son-in-law and Moreau apparently succeeded him in the post of 'Maître des Bâtiments': Hautecoeur, *Histoire*, 4, 233; Gallet, 1972, 157.

Moreau at the Academy: he became a member in 1762 and joined the first class in 1776 (*PV*, 8, 267).

Works for Paris: plan of the Seine embankments, BN, Est., Ve 36; Thiéry, *Paris*, 2, 59 (Pont Notre-Dame).

Fête decorations of Moreau: For the fête of 1771 see Du Barry, 1, 335; Croÿ, 2, 418ff.; Créquy, 6, 62ff. For the fête of 1781–82 see Croÿ, 4, 238; *PV*, 9, 59 (10 December 1781); Lemonnier in *BSHAF*, 1913, 36–9. In general see Gallet, 1961; Gruber, 20–2, 84–6, 105–6, 117–27 and 134–5. For illustrations of fêtes see Gabriel Mourey, *Le Livre des fêtes françaises*, 1930, 191–288.

The Hôtel de Chavannes: Laugier, 1765, 88–9; Thiéry, *Paris*, 1, 610; Gallet, 1961, and 1972, 118 (heating).

106 Palais-Royal: *IGRAF*, 1, 62ff.; Thiéry, *Paris*, 1, 327; Laugier, 1765, 97; and see under Contant, ch. 3 above.

Palais-Royal theatre: Donnet, ch. 13 (with elevation and plan); René Fargue in *SIP*, 1908, 10–26; also Mercier, *Tableau*, 3, 35 ('Commode et magnifique, malgré ses défauts'); Thiéry, *Paris*, 1, 217; *Mercure de France*, 1770, 2, 141–2 (description); *CL*, 7, 450–1; Thrale, 115 (mentioning standing in pit); Oberkirch, 1, 247 (fire).

Folie Favart and other works: Gallet, 1975, 46–7. St-Eustache: Gallet, 1961, 8–9; Thiéry, *Paris*, 1, 423. Gouteau house: Krafft and Ransonnette, 51 (1771). Fontaine des Haudriettes: Thiéry, *Paris*, 1, 592.

Screen of Palais-Royal: *PV*, 7, 172–4 (7 and 14 May 1764).

Comédie-Française: Gallet, 1961, 7–8, and see under de Wailly, ch. 6 above.

107 Moreau's *Mémoire*: BI Duplessis 95, together with Poyet's reply; Poyet himself was attacked in a pamphlet, see *Bonhomme* in General Bibliography.

Death of Moreau: Gallet, 1961, 12, 15. For Mme Peyre, Moreau's sister, later married to Ducis, the poet and translator of *Othello* into French, see also Vigée Lebrun, *Souvenirs*, 2, 205.

Chapter 7

109 Le Camus de Mézières: bibliography of his writings in BN catalogue; Thiéry, *Paris*, 2, 253; Thieme Becker, 22 (1928), with bibliography; Kaufmann, 149–60; Gallet, 1972, 23 and 168–9; Bord, 366 (freemasonry); G. Saisselin in *The British Journal of Aesthetics*, 1975, 239–53 (his theories); and *De Wailly*, 23.

The Halle au Blé: Le Camus de Mézières, *Recueil des differens plans et dessins concernant la nouvelle Halle aux Grains*, 1769; Thiéry, *Paris*, 1, 413ff.; Pujoulx, 214–18; Legrand and Landon, 2, 3, 29; Landon, *Annales*, 11 (1806), 17; Wiebenson, 1973, 262–3, and Boudon, 276–86 (main recent studies). Also AN, N III Seine 233 (drawings).

Corn laws: see, for example, Henry Higgs, *The Physiocrats*, 1897.

Laugier's opinion: Laugier, 1765, 196.

Fontana's granary: Braham and Hager, 152–6.

110 Legrand: bibliography of his writings in BN catalogue, including the *Essai sur l'histoire générale de l'architecture*, 1809 (2nd ed.), with life by Landon, 7–12; Thieme Becker, 22 (1928), with bibliography; and Landon, *Annales, Salon de 1808*, 1, 18; Kaufmann, 1968, 158–9; Gallet, 1972, 171; D. Genoux in *BSHAF*, 1966, 193–8 (bust of Legrand by Roland); Normand, pl. 60 (tomb).

Markets: Thiéry, *Almanach*, 261ff.

Dome of Halle au Blé: Wiebenson, 1973, 264–5 and 275–6; Adhémar in *L'Architecture*, 1933, 249–52; quotation from Young, 81–2.

Molinos and his work with Legrand: see note on Legrand above; Chavret, 261–2. Théâtre Feydeau: Donnet, 96–107; Krafft, 1838, 92–3; Legrand and Landon, 3, 3, 95; Rabreau, 1975. Hôtel Marboeuf: Krafft and Ransonnette, 81 (1790), and D. Genoux in *BSHAF*, 1966, 193–8. Epinay garden: Krafft, 1812, 71. Also Landon, *Annales* (1803), 39–40 (greenhouse of Jardin des Plantes), 12 (1806), 63 (mortuary), 13 (1807), 31 (Halle aux Draps); Thiéry, *Paris*, 1, 497; *JF*, 55; *NAAF*, 1874, 353–9 (Ecole de Mosaïque project, 1785).

111 The Colisée and 'Wauxhalls' in general: see especially Gruber in *BSHAF*, 1972, 125–43; Hautecoeur, *Histoire*, 4, 451–4.

Louis-Denis Le Camus: Gallet, 1972, 168; Mosser in *PF*, 171–2. The Quartier Italien: Thiéry, *Paris*, 1, 186; Boyer, 1962. Chanteloup: Jehanne d'Orliac, *Chanteloup du XIIIe au XXe siècle*, 1929; E. André in *BSHAF*, 1935, 21–39; *ACF*, vol. 12; Wiebenson, 1978, 129 (further bibliography).

Opinions of the Colisée: see Blaikie, 136–7; Thrale 95–6; Mercier, *Tableau*, 3, 20–1; also Walpole, 8, 62, 31 July 1771 ('a most gaudy Ranelagh'); Croÿ, 2, 444; Bonnardot, 91–4.

The Hôtel de Beauvau: Thiéry, *Paris*, 1, 81; Bonnardot, 51.

Boullée: contemporary notices by Villar (*MINSA*, 3 (An IX) 43–51), and Anon, BN Mss, Fonds français, 9153, fo 38; Institut National, *Funérailles du citoyen Boullée* BL 733d). The basic modern book is Pérouse de Montclos, 1969 (shortened English ed., 1974). Boullée's treatise first edited by Rosenau, 1953, and by Pérouse de Montclos, 1968. Also Thieme Becker, 4 (1910); Kaufmann in *AB*, 1939, 213–37, 1952, 436–73, and 1968, 160–2; Rosenau in *AR*, 1952, 387–402, and *GBA*, 1964, 1, 173–90; H. Leclerc in *RHT*, 1965, 151–9; exhibition, *Visionary Architects*, 1968, 13–65; Klaus Lankheit, *Der Tempel der Vernunft. Unveröffentlichte Zeichnungen von Boullée*, 1968; A. M. Vogt, *Boullées Newton-Denkmal*, 1969; Rosenau, 1976 (with translation of Boullée's treatise); Mosser in *PF*, 59–65.

Legeay and Boullée: Villar, 43.

Palais-Bourbon and Chaville: Pérouse de Montclos, 67, 82–6; Rice, 96–9; Croÿ, 1, 321, and 3, 441–2, and Créquy, 6, 80 (Mme de Tessé).

Hôtel Alexandre: Pérouse de Montclos, 71–3; Thiéry, *Paris*, 1, 89, and *Almanach*, 78 (bank of Alexandre); BL Album 25.

112 Hôtel de Monville: Pérouse de Montclos, 73–7; Thiéry, *Paris*, 1, 88; BL Album 1, 24, 26–7; Thrale (and Johnson), 113, 169.

113 Hôtel de Brunoy: Pérouse de Montclos, 105–8; Krafft and Ransonnette, 1 (1772); Thiéry, *Paris*, 1, 90; BL Album, 8, 10.

115 Marquis de Brunoy: Thirion, 462ff.; Dubois-Corneau, 141ff.; Créquy, 4, 103n. Mme de Brunoy: Vigée Lebrun, *Souvenirs*, 1, 134 (visits with Monville to Mme du Barry).

Boullée's public works: Pérouse de Montclos, 131–42, 143–6 (project for Versailles, see also ch. 14 above); *PV*, 9, 22 (24 July 1780) (report on prison project for Necker); Laulan, 57.

Boullée's *Essai*: Villar, 45–6; for bibliography see main note for Boullée above. Diderot's *The Nun*: L. G. Crocker, *The Embattled Philosopher*, 1955, 266.

Bernini's Louvre project: L. Mirot in *MSHP*, 1904, 161ff.

Boullée's library: Pérouse de Montclos, 166–7; Rosenau, 1953, 18–19; Pevsner, 1976, ch. 7.

116 The Newton memorial: see references in general note on Boullée above, and Rosenau in *AB*, 1968, 65–6; Pérouse de Montclos, 200–4; Vogt in *ANCE*, 502–3; Oechslin in *GBA*, 1971, 1, 218–23; also Cambry, *Rapport sur les sépultures*, An VII (influence on Molinos). The metaphor of the globe with star-shaped apertures may have been suggested to Boullée by the Sèvres porcelain writing-set of Mme Adelaide (Wallace Collection).

117 Boullée and his pupils: quotation from Villar, 50; Pérouse de Montclos, 209–18. Prix de Rome projects, see under Academy, ch. 1 above (especially Rosenau, 1960).

Antoine: contemporary lives by Renou, n.d., and Lussault, 1801, and in *Plans . . . de l'Hôtel des Monnaies* (see next note); Quatremère, 1830, 2, 321–8; Thieme Becker, 1 (1907), with bibliography; Kaufmann, 1968, 144–5; Hautecoeur, *Histoire*, 4, 247–60; Gallet, 1972, 139–40; a catalogue of the drawings, BN, Est., Yb3 32, is now apparently missing.

The Monnaie: *Plans des divers étages, . . . de l'Hôtel des Monnaies, à Paris*, 1826; *Journal de Paris*, 1 April 1777 (*Abrégé*, 2, 304ff.); Thiéry, *Paris*, 2, 473; Legrand and Landon, 2, 3, 81; Fernand Mazerolles, *L'Hôtel des Monnaies (Les Grands Institutions de France)*, 1907; Mosser, 1971.

Theatre project: Mosser, 1971, 96, and Pérouse de Montclos, pl. 73. Antoine's letters in *Mercure de France*, April 1770, 1, 197–9 and 2, 198–200.

Election of Antoine to Academy: *PV*, 8, 278 (11 August 1776) (promoted to first class).

Journey to Italy: *NAAF*, 1879, 49 (1777), and 139–40; *PV*, 8, 344 (27 April 1778); BI Ms 1913 (account of journey, identified by Gallet, 1972, 140).

Boullée's Monnaie projects: Pérouse de Montclos, 58–60 (Dulin was also a competitor, see his *Autobiographie*).

120 Lussault's opinion of the Monnaie: Lussault, 13.

Antoine and the *Encyclopédie*: Renou, 8–9.

Drawings for the Monnaie: BN, Est., Hd 625.

Houses by Antoine: Gallet, 1972, 139; and in *MSHP*, 1972, 275–8;

Thiéry, *Paris*, 2, 566. Pariset, 1962, 83 (Château of Herces, E.-et-L., for Boutin, 1772). The Alba Palace, Madrid: see J. M. Pita Andrade in *Neoclassicismo*, 93ff. (Antoine not mentioned).

The Palais de Justice: Mercier, *Tableau*, 8, 194; Thiéry, *Paris*, 2, 22 and 690–1; Legrand and Landon, 2, 2, 55; Stein, 65–74; Gallet in *BMC*, 1963, 1, 2–4. Also P. Brachet in *VU*, 1962, 181ff. (work of Jacques V. Gabriel). For Antoine's project for the Louvre see Boyer in *BSHAF*, 1959, 173–5.

122 The Visitation at Nancy: Thiéry, *Paris*, 2, 482 (as just completed, 1787); Evans, 99.

Portail of the Charité: Thiéry, *Almanach*, 271, and *Paris*, 2, 523; *Mémoires secrets*, 18, 87–8 and 23, 277 (10 October 1781 and 1 November 1783). For Boullée's projects and their dating see Pérouse de Montclos, 60–1.

Antoine's intervention in the *barrières*: Renou, 11–12; and see under Ledoux, ch. 12 above.

Chapter 8

123 Churches of the later eighteenth century in France: Hautecoeur, *Histoire*, 4, 329–69; Herrmann, 1962, 102–30 and 245–6; Middleton, 1962–63; P. Heliot in *GBA*, 1951, 1, 111–28.

Atheism: Walpole, 6, 532; Thrale, 84; and see Mornet, 1933, 137–41 and 270–7.

Roux and St-Vincent: *Almanach historique*, 234–5; Chavret, 351–2.

124 Desgodetz: especially Herrmann, 1958.

Potain: Thieme Becker, 27 (1933), with bibliography; Hautecoeur, *Histoire*, 4, 207–9; Gallet, 1972, 182; *AAF*, 1927, 337 (1787, working at Fontainebleau, and reference to his son-in-law, the sculptor, Roland, who worked with Legrand and Molinos, see ch. 7 above).

Potain in Italy: *CD*, 9, 338, 357, 385, 483 (an accident), 10, 68, 73, 87 (grant from Gabriel to study theatres), 93, 108.

Assistant of Gabriel: see Gabriel's letter in *Mercure de France*, August 1770, 174ff.

Work on orders: *PV*, 7, 1–5 (8 January 1759) and 7, 237, 241–2 (27 January and 10 March 1766) (*PV*, 7, 106, his promotion to the first class at the Academy, 19 June 1762).

Work at Ménars: Mosser, 1973, 285–8.

Theatre project: Hautecoeur, *BSHAF*, 1924, 30–1; [C. N. Cochin], *Projet d'une salle de spectacle*, 1765; AN, 01, 1073 (110).

125 Rennes cathedral: AN, 01 1904; *PV*, 7, 114 (26 July 1762), 7, 138–9 (7 March 1763), 7, 217 (17 June 1765) and 9, 150–1 (28 February 1785).

St-Louis at St-Germain-en-Laye: *PV*, 7, 217 (17 June 1765); Patte, 1769, 205–10; AN, 01 1718 and 1720B (site plan showing existing church); Herrmann, 1962, 113. Drawings for the church in the Marigny sale, 1782.

Death of Potain: reported to the Academy on 10 January 1791 (*PV*, 9, 289); Chalgrin succeeded him in the first class (*PV*, 9, 297, 21 February).

126 Trouard: Thieme Becker, 33 (1939), with bibliography; Hautecoeur, *Histoire*, 4, 219–20; Gallet, 1970, 66–8, 1972, 186, and 1976, 201–7; Granges de Surgères, *BSHAF*, 1893, 194 (inventory of father, a Marbrier du Roi).

Trouard in Italy: *CD*, 11, 31 and 57 (arrival in Rome, 6 November 1754) and 191.

At the Academy: *PV*, 7, 320 (7 December 1767) (competes for a place), and 8, 42 (27 February 1769) (elected, in preference to Chalgrin).

Work at Ménars: Mosser, 1973, 291.

Trouard and the Economats: Gallet, 1976, 206–7; Chenesseau, 271ff.; Bosher, 31.

Trouard's collection: sale catalogue 22 February 1779 (BN, Est., Yd 2101 (2)); one of his Chardins mentioned in *Diderot Salons*, 1, 31 (1759).

The crisis of the 1770s: Chenesseau, 289ff.; Gallet, 1976, 207; AN, 01 1834, 355ff.

St- Symphorien: Duchesne (1804), 157–8 (1764–70); Le Roi, 580–1,

315 (caserne), 500 (catechism chapel); J. Guillaume in *MHF*, 1971, 4, 53–7; P. Quarré in *BSHAF*, 1970, 115 (views of the church).

128 Chalgrin: no modern monograph; contemporary lives by Quatremère, 1834, 1–22, based on his *Notice historique sur . . . M. Chalgrin*, 1816, and by Chalgrin's pupil Charles-François Viel, *Notice nécrologique*, 1814; *BU*; *NBG*; Thieme Becker, 6 (1912), with bibliography; Hautecoeur, *Histoire*, 4, 212–19; Kaufmann, 1968, 169; Gallet, 1972, 149; *DBF*, 8 (1959). Chalgrin's so-called 'Livre d'architecture', supposedly published in addition to his books on the church of St-Philippe and the Arc-de-Triomphe, may be the volume in BHVP (Fo 19 790) which contains several unpublished engraved projects for Bordeaux.

129 Chalgrin in Rome: *CD*, 11, 264, 296, 320 and 341 (correspondence with Soufflot), 437–8 (criticism by Marigny), 442, 469.

Work with Moreau: Viel, 17 (1766).

Chatou: Viel, 17; see under Soufflot, ch. 5 above, for Chatou and Bertin.

Hôtel de St-Florentin: Cochin, 1771, 3, 139 (staircase); Thiéry, *Paris*, 1, 104; Gallet, 1972, 22 (foundation ceremony); Couture, *Autobiographie*, mentions project made for house for La Vrillière, suggesting the possibility of a competition for the building. For ironwork in general, Hautecoeur, *Histoire*, 4, 518–27; Gallet in *Médecine de France*, 1968, 25–40 (reprinted in *BSHP*, 1970, 21–4).

The Comte de St-Florentin: Du Barry, 1, 146; Dufort, 1, 67, 105; McKie, 54; Créquy, 5, 139; portraits of St-Florentin, see A. Doria in *BSHAF*, 1932, 290–331, and 1933, 243–5.

Hôtel de Langeac: Rice, 51–4, and *The Hôtel de Langeac*, 1947; Thiéry, *Paris*, 1, 54.

House of Grimod de la Reynière: the approximately matching house to the west of the Place de la Concorde is the one built by Nicolas Barré for the financier Grimod de la Reynière, where Clérisseau worked on the decoration; see Thiéry, *Paris*, 1, 103; L. Réau in *BSHAF*, 1937, 7–16; E. Croft-Murray in *Apollo*, 1963, 377–83; for Clérisseau see ch. 4 above.

132 St-Philippe-du-Roule: Quatremère, 1834, 10ff.; Thiéry, *Paris*, 1, 75ff.; Legrand and Landon, 1, 127; Landon, *Annales*, 10 (1805), 85; *PV*, 9, 168 (21 November 1785) (drawings presented to Academy); Bonnardot, 40–2 (illustrating thirteenth-century chapel there, acquired for demolition, 1769).

Model of vault: formerly at the Ecole des Ponts et Chaussées, Thiéry, *Paris*, 1, 589.

133 Criticism of belfry: Thiéry, *Paris*, 1, 77.

Ecclesiastical works. Gros Caillou: Cherpitel, *Autobiographie*; Thiéry, *Paris*, 2, 618. Rue Lhomond chapel: Thiéry, *Paris*, 2, 225; Legrand and Landon, 1, 176. St-Sauveur: Thiéry, *Paris*, 1, 506–8; *Bonhomme*, 24; Quatremère, 1834, 7; and see under Poyet, ch. 14 above.

Chalgrin's travels: to Besançon, about 1770, see Tournier, 1943, 25; for projects for Bordeaux see first note on Chalgrin above.

Hall of 1770: Gruber, 74–82; Croÿ (2, 423ff.) compared Chalgrin's hall favourably with the one by Louis (see ch. 9 above) as being less fussy.

135 Works for Monsieur: Hautecoeur, *Histoire*, 4, 102–5 (his patronage). Brunoy: Dulaure, 1, 36–8; R. Dubois-Corneau, *Le Comte de Provence à Brunoy (1774–1791)*, 1909. Work for Madame at Versailles: *MHF*, 1957, 156; *CA*, 1964, 88–95; Scott, in *Apollo*, 1972, 390–9. Work for the mistress of Monsieur, Mme de Balbi, at Versailles: Ganay, 1933, 73–4; J. Robiquet in *BSHAF*, 1920, 219–21; *JF*, 118–19. For Monsieur himself: Gerard Walter, *Le Comte de Provence*, 1950; Oberkirch, 2, 257; Vigée Lebrun, *Souvenirs*, 1, 71; Créquy, 5, 35; *NAAF*, 1872, 102 (his household).

Intendant to Comte d'Artois: *NAAF*, 1872, 104; Duchesne, 1909, 121; Stern, 1, 54.

Viel's work for Chalgrin: Viel, 18.

Election to Academy: *PV*, 8, 74 (7 May 1770); in May 1786 Trouard also overtook Chalgrin for membership of the first class (*PV*, 9, 183).

Chalgrin's wife: Dubois-Corneau, 220–1 (marriage); C. Stryienski, *Deux Victimes de la Terreur*, 1899, 147ff. (execution of Mme Chalgrin, who had been separated from her husband since 1782); Vigée Lebrun, *Memoirs*, 29–30, 73–6 (her Greek supper).

Relations with Voltaire: see under de Wailly, ch. 6 above; Gallet, 1972, 24.

Chalgrin's manner and appearance: Quatremère, 1834, 21.

Work at St-Sulpice: Thiéry, *Paris*, 2, 429ff.; Legrand and Landon, 1, 126; Lemesle, 51–2. Projects shown by Soufflot and Patte: *PV*, 7, 322 (22 December 1767), and 8, 2, 7–9 (11 January and 7 March 1768); Patte, *Mémoires*, 1769, ch. 8. Oudot de Maclaurin: Gallet, 1972, 175; Landon, *Annales*, 10 (1805), 15 (attribution of door of cemetery of St-Sulpice); *RSBAD*, 1882, 275 (work at Cramayel); Gallet, 1972, 168 (Laurent succeeds Servandoni).

Furnishing of St-Sulpice: Blondel, 1752–56, pl. 167, showing the columns of the organ case already in place; for de Wailly's pulpit see ch. 6 above.

Collège de France: contemporary description in *Journal des beaux arts et des sciences*, 1775, 1/2, 147ff.; Thiéry, *Paris*, 2, 303ff.; BN, Est., Ha48 (volume of Chalgrin's drawings).

136 Palais du Luxembourg: Legrand and Landon, 2, 2, 61; Gustave Hirschfeld, *Le Palais du Luxembourg*, 1931; *AAF*, 1927, 234 (sculpture by Mouchy transferred there).

Decorations for Napoleon: Guerrini, 67, 79; Viel, 19.

Arc-de-Triomphe: Guerrini, 192, 291; G. Vauthier in *BSHAF*, 1920, 6–21; AN, F13 203, 206 (documentation); and see further, ch. 15 above.

Chapter 9

137 Gondoin: the main early source is Quatremère's life, 1834, 192–213, based on his *Notice historique . . . de M. Gondoin*, 1821, and the abbreviated version in the *Vies*, 1830, 2, 329–36; also Thieme-Becker, 14 (1921), with bibliography; Hautecoeur, *Histoire*, 4, 242–7; Kaufmann, 1968, 167–8; Gallet, 1972, 163.

Opinions of the Ecole de Chirurgie: Thiéry, *Paris*, 2, 364; *PV*, 9, 9 (13 March 1780); Quatremère, 1834, 201.

Gondoin in Rome: quotations from Quatremère, 1834, 203; also *CD*, 11, 398; *NAAF*, 1878, 45 (*congé*); the rules of the Academy competitions were relaxed on other occasions for protégés of the king, for example in the case of Charpentier, the son of the Marly gardener (*CD*, 11, 427).

138 Gondoin in London: *NAAF*, 1878, 76, 3 September 1766 (letter complaining that the air was bad for his health).

Gondoin's furniture: Verlet in *CA*, May 1958, 92ff.; M. Jaillot in *GBA*, 1964, 1, 307 (decoration of room at Versailles); Eriksen, 1974, 186–7.

La Martinière (1696–1783): quotation from Besenval, 144; see also Croÿ, 1, 197; Du Barry, 3, 328–9; life by L. Desaivre, 1895.

Status of surgery: quotation from Mercier, *Tableau*, 8, 116.

139 Early projects for the Ecole: Gallet, 1972, 140, mentions one of 1770 by Arnould; Belanger, *Autobiographie*, mentions a project of 1774 for a site on the Quai de la Tournelle.

The Ecole de Chirurgie: *Mémoires secrets*, 7, 81–2 (17 October 1773), 7, 285 (15 December 1774); contemporary description in *Journal des beaux arts et sciences*, 1774, 1/2, 185–90; *PV*, 8, 166 (16 August 1773) (the Academy see the projects); Gondoin's own *Description des Ecoles de Chirurgie*, 1780; Thiéry, *Paris*, 2, 361–5; Legrand and Landon, 2, 3, 63–7; J. Adhémar in *L'Architecture*, 1934, 105–8; P. Huard and M. J. Imbault Huard in *BSHP*, 1972–73, 109ff. (and publishing portrait of Gondoin by Houdon).

140 Straightness of façade: see Landon, *Annales*, 5 (1803), 119–27; Poisson, 1970, 342 (Bienfaisance replaces the figure of the king in the main relief).

Opinions quoted: Peyre, *Oeuvres d'architecture*, 1795, 17; Blondel, 1774, 2, 105; also Blaikie, 102–3.

144 Cordelier site prison: project by Moreau of 1780 (*PV*, 9, 1–3, 10 January).

145 Other pre-Revolutionary works by Gondoin: intervention in Palais de Justice: Stein, 69. Some châteaux in Normandy falsely attributed; see Hautecoeur, *Histoire*, 4, 246–7.

Vives-Eaux: Quatremère, 1834, 206–8 (the site is apparently still undiscovered).

The Colonne Vendôme: Hirschfeld, 84–95; *NAAF*, 1889, 244 (ennoblement, 1816).

Louis: no known contemporary life, except Louis' *Autobiographie*, and no modern monograph, but much material recently published by Pariset. The volumes of drawings, formerly believed to have been burnt in a fire at Bordeaux, survive only partially damaged (typescript catalogue). Monographs by Gaullieur l'Hardy (1828), and Marionneau (1881), and, on the theatres, Prudent and Gaudet (1903); also Marionneau in *Réunion des Sociétés savantes des Départements. Section des beaux-arts*, 24–27 April 1878, 1879, 151–67; M. de L., in *RHB*, 1920, 1, 18–29 (portraits); P. Courteault, *RHB*, 1921, 1, 14–23 (last years); Thieme Becker, 23 (1929), with bibliography; Hautecoeur, *Histoire*, 4, 270–87; Kaufmann, 1968, 145; Gallet, 1972, 169–70; Pariset, 1950–57 (Mme Louis), 1959, 1968, 1973, and in *Actes du 82 Congrès des Sociétés savantes*, 1957 (summary in *BM*, 1959, 298); Mosser in *PF*, 225–30. For articles on Louis' work at Warsaw and Bordeaux see further below.

Louis at the Academy: competitions of 1748, etc. (*PV*, 6, 102 to 241–42). Louis was a candidate for election on many occasions between 1767 and 1780.

146 Louis in Rome: *CD*, 11, 132ff. (*brevet*); 307 ('peu docile'); Pariset, 1959, 41–7 (drawings made for Caylus); *PV*, 7, 28 (10 December 1759) (drawings shown to Academy).

Early chapels: Laugier, 1765, 114; Thiéry, *Paris*, 1, 649–50, 654; Y. Christ in *CA*, February 1958, 18–21 (Ste-Marguerite); Pariset, 1973, 84–5; Pariset in *RHB*, 1959, 289–94 (Chartres choir); J. Foucart-Borville in *BSHAF*, 1974, 139–44 (Noyon choir, *c.* 1766–79).

Decorations for fêtes: Gruber, 77–9.

Works for Warsaw: Pariset in *RHB*, 1956, 281–97; S. Lorentz, 1958; Pariset, 1959, 47–55 (furniture); B. Krol in *RSHT*, 1960, 36–7 (palace theatre); also Réau in *AAF*, 1931–32, 225–48 (French works of art in Poniatowski's collection). Louis' *congé* for Poland: *NAAF*, 1878, 74–5 (application unnecessary).

Views of Poniatowski and about him: Lorentz, 10, 11; Ségur, 2, 163 and ff.

147 Louis' full name: Eriksen, 1974, 203.

Festival hall: Gruber, 81–2, and see under Chalgrin, ch. 8 above.

148 La Coré: Ardascheff, 142–3, 322–3, 369 and 377; Croÿ, 1, 319.

The Besançon Intendance: the basic study of Ganay in *RAAM*, 1926, 1, 217–25 and 295ff.; Castan, 217ff.; also *CA*, November 1967, 106–11. The false date of 1776 for the design of the Intendance appears to derive from Marionneau, 434–6. The other particularly imposing Intendance of the period is that of Châlons; see F. Berland, *L'Hôtel de l'Intendance de Champagne*, 1928.

Richelieu: Estrée, 1921, and *Le Maréchal de Richelieu (1696–1788)*, 1917, especially 103ff. (patronage) and 226 (relations with Louis); Académie des Sciences, Index; an amusing book in English is Hugo Cole's *First Gentleman of the Bedchamber*, 1965. Richelieu's patronage: Gallet, 1972, 97–8, and 164 (Goupy); Estrée, 1921, 297ff.; Eriksen, 1974, 218–89.

Opinions of Richelieu: Walpole, 6, 372 (in 1765); Du Barry, 1, 89; Créquy, 2, 202.

Louis' project for the Comédie: La Ferté, 315–18.

Hôtel de Richelieu: Pariset, 1973, 88–90; Thiéry, *Paris*, 1, 149; Wilhelm in *BMC*, 1967, 1, 2–14 (decorations in his Place des Vosges house).

Eighteenth-century Bordeaux: Pariset, 1968 and see further below.

Bordeaux theatre projects by Soufflot: *PV*, 6, 329 (1 August 1758}.

Barreau at Bordeaux: Pariset, 1962, 85–99.

Louis' theatre: Louis' own *Salle de spectacle de Bordeaux*, 1782; Marionneau, 103–431, and *Douze lettres de Victor Louis, 1776–1777*, 1858; Prudent and Gaudet, 19–27; Arnaud Detchéverry, *Histoire des théâtres de Bordeaux*, 1860, 33ff.; *Description historique de Bordeaux*, 1785, 154ff. (giving the original colours); Bordeaux 1973 exhibition, 425–9; Pariset, 1968, 591–616; Courteault in *RHB*, 1914–17 (Lhote's project); Ardascheff, 185ff. (Dupré de St-Maur).

150 Social life of Louis: Prudent and Gaudet, 51 (Louis' *Prince dupé* given at the Orléans theatre); Genlis, 1, 357 (Mme Louis plays at Mme de Genlis' Salon); Wilson, 595 (Mme Louis plays at Diderot's birthday party); Pariset, 1950–57, 270–9 (relations with Diderot's daughter); *Mémoires secrets*, 22, 42 (17 January 1783) (journey with Grétry).

Louis' difficult character: Diderot, *Correspondance*, 15, 256 (28 July 1781); *Mémoires secrets*, 23, 207–8 (27 September 1783).

152 Masonry of the theatre: Marionneau, 351–2 ('clou' of Louis); diagrams of the masonry in Gaullieur l'Hardy.

Gabriel's Louvre staircase: Tadgell, fig. 169.

153 Opinions of theatre: Patte, 1782, 115, 117; Young, 58–9.

Louis and the activities of his followers in Bordeaux: especially Pariset, 1968, 616–45; Courteault, 1932; Lavedan in *AAF*, 1950–57, 293–6. Pariset in *Annales du Midi*, 1964, 543–54 (Combes, for whom see also Pariset in *RHB*, 1973 (extract paginated 1–90)); M. Mosser in *PF*, 101–2; *MHF*, 1972, 2, 60–1 (Château Raba); Boyer, 1933 (Salle pour les Assemblées); J.-P. Mouilleseaux, in *MHF*, 1975, 2, 66–73, and his catalogue *Architectes bordelais et néoclassicisme, Les Sources de l'histoire de l'architecture aux Archives Municipales de Bordeaux*, 1970.

Le Bouilh: Ganay, 1948–53, 2, 33–4; Pariset, 1973, 90–1; M. Binney in *Country Life*, 13 January 1977, 70–3; La Tour du Pin, 179 (commissioning of château by her father-in-law).

Duc de Chartres: especially Britsch, *passim*, 361 (education of children) and 403 (approval of George III); Eriksen, 1974, 65 and 165 (patronage); Gallet, 1975, 181 (Piètre), and in *BMC*, June, 1960, 8–15; Piètre, *Autobiographie*.

154 The Palais-Royal: Thiéry, *Paris*, 1, 236–9; Mercier [1797], 3, 93–128; Britsch, 311–51 (330, trees); Champier and Sandoz, 1, 411–34; AN, R4 283 (documentation); Rice, 14–15 (circus).

157 Limited admission for lower classes: Britsch, 330.

Opinions of the Palais-Royal: Oberkirch, 2, 234 (unpopularity of felling of trees), 235 (derivation from 'Place St. Marc'); Thrale, 198.

Freemasonry: especially Britsch, 229–57; Genlis, 3, 12 (contingent of freemasons for opening of Bordeaux theatre).

Thiéry on Palais-Royal: Thiéry, *Paris*, 1, 265, 266.

Later theatres: Thiéry, *Paris*, 1, 733; Legrand and Landon, 2, 3, 87 and 89; Landon, *Annales*, 11 (1806), 131; Donnet, chs 4, 8, 14 and 21; Prudent and Gaudet, 29–46, 47–58; Bannister, 234.

PART THREE
Chapter 10

159 Ledoux: apart from the *Autobiographie* (in full in Gallet, 1979, 134–6), there are contemporary biographies by J[acques] C[ellerier], 1806 (BI, Duplessis 1332); a short notice in *Annales de l'architecture et des arts*, 41 (20 November 1806), 665–7; Landon, *Annales, Salon de 1808*, 1, 10–14, identifying J.C. as Cellerier; notice by Ramée in vol. 2 of the *Architecture* (1847); *BU*, 8 (1813). 'Les bizarreries de Ledoux', *Le Magazin pittoresque*, 1859, 27–9. Kaufmann in Thieme Becker, 22 (1928), in *Zeitschrift für bildende Kunst*, 1923–30, 38–46, *Von Ledoux bis Le Corbusier*, 1933, in *Parnassus*, October, 1936, 16–18, and in *JSAH*, 1943, 12–20; also, 1952, 474–537, and 1968, 162–7. Rosenau in *B Mag*, 1946, 163; Hautecoeur, *Histoire*, 4, 270–87; Gallet, 1972, 169–70, 1970, and 1974–75; M. Mosser in *PF*, 173–8; *Visionary Architects*, 1968, 66–149. Levallet-Haug, 1934, is in many ways still the best monograph, though now partially out of date; Marcel Raval and J.-Ch. Moreau, *Claude-Nicolas Ledoux*, 1946, provides a useful corpus of illustrations, though the bibliography is unreliable. Gallet, 1979, gives much new information on Ledoux's work in Paris, and an excellent bibliography. Other recent literature has stressed the visionary character of Ledoux's work: Yvan Christ, *Projets et divagations de Claude-Nicolas Ledoux*, 1961, and (with Ionel Schein), *L'Oeuvre et les rêves de Claude-Nicolas Ledoux*, 1971; Bernard Stoloff, *L'Affaire Claude-Nicolas Ledoux*, 1977. One certain portrait of Ledoux is known (pl. 201 above), in addition to the engraved frontispiece of the *Architecture*; the pendant showing Mme Ledoux and the younger daughter (pl. 224 above) has been rediscovered by Gallet (1974–75, fig. 25); a sketch by Marguerite Gérard, now in the Musée Cognac-Jay, supposedly shows Ledoux at full-length, while a family group in the Baltimore Museum of Arts supposedly showing the Ledoux family must represent another architect and his family.

Quotations from Cellerier and Ledoux: C[ellerier], 15, 4; Ledoux, *Architecture*, 16.

160 Expedition with Beckford: Oliver, 171–82.

The engravings and their chronology: see Herrmann, 1960, and Langner, 1960. As well as the engravings in the *Architecture*, two other volumes are known containing engravings which differ from the published collection, one in the Bibliothèque Doucet, Fol. Rés. 169, and one formerly (?) in the Carlhian collection.

Père Coffin: *DBF*; Aldis, 100.

The Café Godot (or Militaire): Fréron in *L'Année littéraire*, VI, 282 (noted by Kaufmann); and Gallet in *BMC*, June 1972, 12–17, and 1979, 63–5.

161 Eaux et Forêts: see *Almanach royal*, for example, 1760; Gallet, 1972 (Daviler); Lenoir, *Autobiographie*; Thiéry, *Paris*, 2, 45 (administration).

Earliest works: Gallet, 1970, 68–71, and 1979, 12–19.

Maupertuis: Ledoux, *Autobiographie*; Rivière, 46ff. (the château of 1711?), 22ff. (the owner); Vigée Lebrun, *Memoirs*, 110–11 (size of new château); Gallet, 1979, 68–9.

Montesquiou and the Hocquart family: Thirion, 395; Du Barry, 2, 158–9; Britsch, 436 (relations with Orléans circle); Créquy, 7, 87 (Président Hocquart); Bosher, index.

Gardens of Maupertuis: see under Brongniart, ch. 13 above.

The Hôtel Hocquart: see Gallet, 1974, 132 (plan), and 1979, 66–7.

Other early patrons of Ledoux: Gallet, 1974–75, for his relations with members of the Lamoignon family and the case brought by Ledoux against his patrons. The Baron de Thiers may have been the owner of the house where Contant had already worked (*BSHAF*, 1934, 291–8).

Hôtel d'Hallwyl: Ledoux, *Autobiographie*; Thiéry, *Paris*, 1, 594; Levallet-Haug, 39–41; Gallet, 1970, 72–3, 1974–75, 140, and 1979, 68–73; Lüthy, 2, 373; Aldis, 164 (d'Alembert living nearby); A. de Champeaux in *GBA*, 1892, 1, 252 (panels from the hôtel). See also Herrmann, 1960, 202–3, and Langner, 1960, 145–6.

163 The Comte d'Hallwyl: see Oberkirch, 1, 261; *Dictionnaire historique et biographique de la Suisse*

164 Watersellers: see Mercier, *Tableau*, 1, 90.

Hôtel d'Uzès: Blondel, 1774, 1, 255–6; Thiéry, *Paris*, 1, 461; Krafft and Ransonnette, 75–6 (1767) and Krafft, 1838, 25–6; Levallet-Haug, 41–3; Gallet in *BMC*, 1969, 2, 2–23, 1970, 73–85, and 1979, 73–6; Viel de St-Maux, 58, n.29 (Legeay's approval of the gateway). See also Herrmann, 1960, 198–201; AN, N III Seine 1265 (drawings).

Duc d'Uzès: L. d'Albiousse, *Histoire des Ducs d'Uzès*, 1887, 237ff.; Croÿ, 1, 194 (presence at king's table); *DBF*, s.v. Crussol, François-Emmanuel; Gallet, 1972, 184 (Rousset works on town hall of Uzès).

Uzès and Voltaire: Voltaire, 20, no. 3970 (27 August 1751), for first exchange of letters.

166 Bonnelles: Sirén, 158 (with illustration); Erdberg, 151 and fig 67.

167 Bénouville: Soulange Bodin, 1, 16–22, and in *BSHAF*, 1925, 166; Levallet-Haug, 43–6; Gallet, 1972, 157 (s.v. Devilliers de Maison Rouge). Professor Langner kindly pointed out to me the existence of the earlier château on the site.

Marquis de Livry and his father: *CD*, 10, 388 (Natoire's work for Livry); Croÿ, 1, 73 etc. (relations with king); Dubois-Corneau, 277 (suppression of post of Maître d'Hôtel).

Engravings of Bénouville: see Herrmann, 1960, 192–8, and Langner, 1960, 137–43.

169 Hôtel de Montmorency: Croÿ, 3, 76; Thiéry, *Paris*, 1, 146–7; Langner, 1960, 146; Krafft and Ransonnette, 40 (1772); BL Album, 6–7; Levallet-Haug, 46–7; Langner, 1960, 146; Gallet, 1970, 85–6 (publication of the contract and its drawings, AN, Min. Cent., LII (477), 5 January 1770), and 1979, 76–8.

171 The Logny family: *DN*, 14, 399–401.

Duc de Montmorency-Luxembourg: see especially Lestrade, *Autobiographie*, for the architectural pretensions of the Duc de Montmorency; Créquy, 1, 30–1; Britsch, 229–30 (the masonic lodge Montmorency-Luxembourg).

The Hôtel de Montmorency, rue St-Marc: Thiéry, *Paris*, 1, 448–53; Perlin, *Autobiographie*; Gallet, 1972, 169 (s.v. Le Carpentier).

Princesse de Montmorency and her garden at Boulogne-sur-Seine: Croÿ, 2, 272 and 316 (her visit to England and garden, before 1767), and 440 (her relations with Mme du Barry); Ligne, 176–7; Duc de Choiseul, *Mémoires*, 1904, 230 (her ambitions for her husband).

172 Ledoux in England: Gallet, 1975, 48; for Clive, *DNB* (a drawing of a house of his, 'Clermont', appears in Belanger's 'English' sketchbook, see ch. 13 above).

Ledoux's family: the dossier of Ledoux's arrest, AN, F7 4774, gives details of his wife, father-in-law and his daughters, and further details about them and their properties are given in legal papers in AN, Min. Cent. (especially XXVIII (560), 7 January 1793, see further below).

Ledoux's house: see preceding note; Oliver, 173 (Beckford's opinion); Gallet, 1974–75, 141.

Chapter 11

173 The Hôtel Guimard: Thiéry, *Paris*, 1, 145–6; BL Album, 6, and 16–18; Krafft and Ransonnette, 49 (1770); Levallet-Haug, 26–8; Gallet, 1970, 92 (n. 62), and 1979, 82–6.

Mlle Guimard and her lovers: Campardon, 1, 366–90; E. de Goncourt, *La Guimard*, 1893; *Arnoldiana*, 190–1 (her lovers); Vigée Lebrun, *Memoirs*, 95; Du Barry, 1, 61–2. The Prince de Soubise: quotation from Besenval, 232; see also Du Barry, 1, 38; Cellerier, *Autobiographie* (work for Soubise, and for the L'Hôpitals); La Borde: Visme, especially 60–2; Thirion, 300 and 432ff.; Du Barry, 1, 68; Dufort, 1, 4–5. Another of Mlle Guimard's lovers, the Bishop of Orléans, was Trouard's patron in the department of the Economats (see ch. 8 above).

Sale of the house: Thiéry, *Paris*, 1, 719.

174 Guimard's house at Pantin: Thirion, 432; Visme, 60, 77.

Grimm's opinion: *CL*, 8, 167 (March 1773).

House projects of Mlles Dervieux and Arnould: see under Brongniart and Belanger, ch. 13 above.

Visit of Joseph II and Paul I to the Hôtel Guimard: Ledoux, *Architecture*, 32n., and see note on ch. 12 below.

175 Walpole's description: Walpole, 8, 76 (25 August 1771).

Blondel's comments: Blondel, 1775, 2, 109ff.

176 Rue du Faubourg-Poissonnière houses: Thiéry, *Paris*, 1, 486; Krafft and Ransonnette, 20 and 32; Levallet-Haug, 29–32; Gallet, 1972, 169–70.

Other houses: especially Gallet, 1979, 81, 97–102. Hôtel de Valentinois: Thiéry, *Paris*, 1, 143. Work on the Hôtel de Cramayel, 1775: BHVP, NA Mss 182, 437 (Ledoux also worked at the Château of Cramayel, as did Maclaurin (*RSBAD*, 1882, 275). Cramayel was the brother-in-law of J.-B. de La Borde, one of Mlle Guimard's lovers; Visme, 17). Hôtel de St-Germain: Thiéry, *Paris*, 1, 143; Krafft and Ransonnette, 25 (1772); Gallet, 1974–75, 140.

Mme du Barry: quotation from Cobban, 5, 94; see especially the memoirs attributed to her (Du Barry in general bibliography); on her patronage in general, Eriksen, 1974, 74, 91–2 and 123–4, and on her tastes, Du Barry, 1, 28ff., and 2, 182–3 and 251–2. Also Ch. Davillier, *Les Porcelaines de Sèvres de Mme du Barry*, 1870; La Ferté, 314–15 (her intervention in the commissioning of the Comédie-Française); D. Wildenstein in *GBA*, 1962, 2, 365–77; F. M. Biebel in *GBA*, 1960, 2, 207–26 (portraits); Scott, 60–71.

Louveciennes: BL Album, 2–3 and 20–1; *Mémoires secrets*, 21, 113 (30 September 1771), and 24, 184–7 (20 July 1772); Krafft, 1812, 1; AN, 01 1496 (documentation); *AAF*, 1851–52, 270–2, and 1858–60, 270–1 (sculptural decoration), and 1927, 356; Levallet-Haug, 17–26; Cailleux in *RAAM*, 1935, 1, 213–24 and 2, 35–48; *ACF*, vol. 1; Gallet, 1979, 86–92. A positive error in Du Barry (1, 281) is the statement that the pavilion was constructed for the former owner of the site, the Duc de Penthièvre, who had died there in 1768 (Britsch, 94). Ledoux's work at Pont-aux-Dames for Mme du Barry, after her disgrace, is mentioned in Du Barry, 4, 15.

Mme du Barry and the Abbé Terray: Croÿ, 2, 514, and Dakin, *Turgot*, 155; for her promise of the *cordon noir* to Ledoux, see AN, F7 4774.

Presentation at court: especially Croÿ, 2, 365ff.

177 Du Barry in prison: Créquy, 5, 128.

Her attitude to Mlle Guimard: Du Barry, 1, 61–2.

Roofs of château and basement of the pavilion: Langner, 1960, 148–50, and Gallet, 1972, 118.

178   The stables of Mme du Barry: Levallet-Haug, 47–50, and in *Revue de l'histoire de Versailles*, 1933, 6–11; Langner, 1960, 144–5; Gallet, 1979, 92–6.

180   Eaubonne: A. de Visme, *Essai historique sur Eaubonne*, 1914 (no references); Krafft, 1812, 8; *Tableau pittoresque de la Vallée de Montmorency*, n.d., 5; Levallet-Haug, 28–9, 32–4; Raval and Moreau, 52; *ACF*, vol. 2; Langner, 1960, 146–8; Gallet, 1979, 78–81.

St-Lambert's works: quoted in R. Fargher, *Life and Letters in France, The Eighteenth Century*, 1970, 180.

Ledoux and Delille: see ch. 12 above.

181   The saltworks and the ideal town: Pevsner, 1976, ch. 17 (factories); Ledoux, 35ff.; Pierre Boye, *Les Salines et le sel en Lorraine au XVIIIe siècle*, 1904, 12ff. and 23ff.; Cobban, 1, 58–9 (the *gabelle*); Levallet-Haug, 63–75; M. Ozouf in *AESC*, 1966, 6, 1273–304; H. Graham in *Apollo*, 1963, 384–8; *Actualité de Cl. N. Ledoux, Son oeuvre en Franche-Comté, Les Salines royales d'Arc-et-Senans*, 1969; M. Saboya, in *IHA*, 1970, 136–8; *AR*, 1972, 265–9; *MHF*, 1972, 3/4, 22–41; N. Stoloff in *GBA*, 1977, 1, 65–72; Gallet, 1979, 19–28, 138–9. For the ideal town see further below.

Lavoisier's part in the salt trade: *Oeuvres*, 3, 145–88; McKie, 132–5.

182   Ledoux on the saltworks: *Architecture*, 16 and 35.

183   Banded columns: Genoa provided many examples from the sixteenth century, and the fashion became popular especially in Russia in the early nineteenth century (see, for example, Yurova, pl. 69).

184   Kassel: Levallet-Haug, 97–100; Colombier, 236–7; *CA*, October 1967, 72–81. The Prince de Soubise married as his third wife, Anne of Hesse, the sister of the Landgrave Frederick II (Croÿ, 1, 60).

Du Ry on Ledoux: Gerland, 118–21.

185   The Besançon theatre: the basic study is H. Leclerc in *RHT*, 1958, 103–27; also Alphonse Deis, *Esquisse historique sur la création du théâtre de Besançon*, n.d.; Castan, 233–7; Ganay in *RAAM*, 1927, 2, 3–21; Levallet-Haug, 77–91; Gallet, 1979, 28–34, 102–8.

186   Ledoux on the theatre: AN, F7 4774 ('Republican Theatre'); Rabreau, 1968, 134 (moral attitude of Ledoux).

The Marseille theatre: E. Bonnel in *Marseille*, October/December, 1956, 35–41; AN, H1359 (documentation, including memoir of 2 February 1785, no. 112).

The Hôtel de Thélusson: Thiéry, *Paris*, 1, 178–9; Legrand and Landon, 2, 4, 9; Krafft and Ransonnette, 71–2 (1780); Krafft, 1838, frontis.; BL Album, 13–15; Levallet-Haug, 53–9; Girod de l'Ain, 136–9; Lüthy, 2, 404; Langner, 1963, 3–9 (the garden); Gallet, 1972, 10, 21, 1974–75, 172–3, and especially 1979, 34–40; a small photograph of a surviving pavilion in *L'Illustration*, 17 August 1929, 171 (noted by Levallet-Haug); AN, AB XIX 213–15 (documentation).

Mme de Thélusson: Créquy, 5, 102–4; Oberkirch, 3, 207 (confirming the Neckers' hostility to Mme de Thélusson mentioned in the Créquy *Souvenirs*); Girod de l'Ain, 136 (quoting the wishes of the patron for her house, but with no source).

188   Laborde as site owner: Boyer, 1961, 142 (and also owner of the site of Mme du Barry's projected town house).

189   Opinions of the house: *Mémoires secrets*, 17, 161–2 (30 April 1781), and 17, 253 (14 June 1781); Oberkirch, 1, 291 (also 2, 220); see also Mercier, *Tableau*, 8, 193, and Legrand, *Annales*, 6 (1804), 19.

Chapter 12

190   Visit of Joseph II: Croÿ, 4, 36 (Hôtel Guimard), and 43 (Pavilion of Louveciennes).

Visit of Paul I: Johan Georg Wille, *Mémoires et journal*, 1857, 2, 163, 244 (Ledoux's drawings sent to Russia); C[ellerier], 6–7.

The Caisse d'Escompte: R. Bigo, *La Caisse d'Escompte (1776–1793)*, 1927; Thiéry, *Paris*, 1, 294; McKie, 228; Vallentin, *Mirabeau*, 211; Gallet, 1972, 166 (Jalliers de Savault's building of 1789). The engraving of Ledoux's project in the Bibliothèque Doucet volume is

inscribed as 'ordonné en 1778', presumably referring to the project itself.

The Ferme Générale: Thiéry, *Paris*, 1, 319ff.: editions of the *Almanach royal*; Mercier [1797], 6, 177–9; McKie, 57ff. and 133ff.; Bosher, *passim*.

191   The *barrières*: the basic studies are E. Frémy in *BSHP*, 1912, 115–48, and Gallet, 1979, 40–3, 110–28; also Thiéry, *Almanach*, 82; Lavoisier, 6, 155 (their staffing); Levallet-Haug, 113ff.; Vauthier in *BSHAF*, 1929, 65–73; A. Monin, *L'Etat de Paris en 1789*, 1889, 603ff.; AN, T 705–08 (documentation); AN, N III Seine 885 (plans). The exact number of the *barrières* appears to vary from plan to plan (fifty-five are listed by Gallet, 1979, 114–27).

193   Opinions of Beckford and Thiéry: Olivier, 172; Thiéry, *Paris*, 2, 193.

194   The Barrière de Monceau: Blaikie, 116; Langner, 1963, 8.

196   Criticisms of the *barrières*: *Mémoires secrets*, 30, 40–1 (31 October 1785), and entries in October–December 1787; *Reclamation d'un citoyen contre la nouvelle enceinte de Paris*, 1785 (25, resemblance to caverns, etc.); Legrand and Landon, 2, 2, 7, and 2, 3, 53 (Barrière du Trône, etc.).

Ledoux's memoirs: AN, F7 4774 (not apparently known to Frémy).

197   Marmontel's story: Marmontel, 2, 232–3.

Later history: based on Frémy (see general note on the *barrières* above).

Reappraisal of the *barrières*: Landon, *Annales*, 5 (1803), 87 (Italie), 151 (Bonshommes); 6 (1804), 55 (Orléans), 63 (la Villette), 79 (others); 10 (1805), 137 (Etoile); 15 (1807), 51 (Vincennes); also *Bonhomme*, 1788, 21–2.

Aix: Levallet-Haug, 103–10; Berluc-Pérussis; Roux-Alpheran, *Les Rues d'Aix*, 1847, 1, 10 (the old palace), 2, 58 (Ledoux's palace); *PV*, 9, 163 (29 August 1785) (report on Ledoux's projects).

198   The trial of Mme Mirabeau: Vallentin, 171ff.

199   Ledoux's regret at non-completion: Ledoux, *Architecture*, 33, n.2.

200   Prison reform: Lavoisier, 3, 481–98; McKie, 55, 143ff.; Pevsner, ch. 10.

201   Fontana's prison: Braham and Hager, 143ff.

French prison projects: *Autobiographies* of Caron, Cellerier and Couture; *PV*, 9, 223 (17 March 1788) (Lefebvre).

Neuchâtel: Levallet-Haug, 100–1, and note on Pâris, ch. 14 below.

202   The Saiseval houses: Levallet-Haug, 34; Gallet, 1972, 140 (Aubert).

The Hosten houses: Levallet-Haug, 34; Krafft and Ransonnette, 10 (1787); Gallet, 1972, 155 (work of Delarbre); Danloux, *Journal*, 1910, 267; AN, N III Seine 1054 (plans).

203   Ledoux on the Revolution: Berluc-Pérussis, 206.

Patronage of Calonne: Lescure, 2, 187. For Calonne's taste in general see Scott, 86–91.

Death of Mme Ledoux and subsequent sales: AN, Min. Cent., XXVIII (560), 7 January 1793, and 25, 26, 28 and 30 January 1793.

Ledoux's dossier: AN, F7 4774, and F7 3982 (An VII).

204   Disinheritance of daughter and inventory: AN, Min. Cent., XXXIII (841), 12 and 26 November (inventory), 1806.

Cellerier and Ledoux: both were dinner guests at Belanger's house in 1806 (Bibliothèque Doucet, carton 31). Cellerier is identified as the anonymous author, J.C., of Ledoux's biography in Landon's life of Ledoux (see first note on ch. 10 above).

Ledoux's death and funeral: see C[ellerier], 16, and *AAA*, 41, 20 November 1806, 666–7.

Barrière du Trône project: C[ellerier], 13.

Vignon and other pupils: Vaudoyer (*Extrait*), 1 August 1814; Vaultier, 1910; Boyer, 1933, 266–9; J. Mordaunt Crook in *Country Life*, CXLVII, 242–6 (Damesne). Thomas de Thomon was also apparently a pupil (see below, note on ch. 15, for his work in St Petersburg).

The publication of the *Architecture*: Thiéry, *Paris*, 1, 177 n. (intention to publish); C[ellerier], 10 (work in prison); BI, N 41 B ⁎⁎ (copy of the prospectus); Berluc-Pérussis, 219 (Ledoux's opinion of the prospectus).

Delille's references: *L'Imagination*, 1785–94, chant IX. On Delille see, for example, Vigée Lebrun, *Memoirs*, 140ff.

205 Criticism of the *Architecture*: *AAA*, 36 (1 November 1806), 591–4; *BU*, s.v. Ledoux (1819); *Journal des débats*, 9 April, 1804, 4: 'il est tellement figuré, pour ne pas dire emphatique, que nous ne pouvons, à beaucoup près, lui accorder comme littérateur un degré d'excellence égal à celui qu'il possède comme architecte'. The book, according to Nitot Dufresne, quoted by Ratouis de Limay, was the work of a madman (*BSHAF*, 1949, 76–7).

206 The ideal town: Levallet-Haug, 63–75; Rosenau, 1957, 87–93, and in *Urbanisme*, 1935, 281–2; Kaufmann, especially 1952; Herrmann, 1960, 204–9; Langner, 1960, 151–61, and 1963; Gallet, 1979, 44–52; and see note on the saltworks, ch. 11 above.

207 The Institut copy of the *Architecture*: see Ledoux, *Autobiographie*.

209 Marmontel's memoirs: Marmontel, 2, 340.

PART FOUR
Chapter 13

210 Napoleon on Paris: quoted by Biver, 33.

Percier and Fontaine: see ch. 15 above.

Customs house of the rue Chauchat: Krafft, 1838, 51 (as 'Halle de déchargement de l'octroi', by Lusson).

211 Architecture in St Petersburg: Hautecoeur, 1912 (with bibliography).

Belanger's *éloge* of Brongniart: *Journal des arts, des sciences et de la littérature*, 229, 15 June 1813, 355–6.

Brongniart: *Autobiographie*, listing main works; *Nécrologie* in *Journal de l'Empire*, 28 June 1813; biography by Brongniart fils in *Palais de la Bourse*, 1814 (giving no works earlier than the Hôtel de Montesson, see note below); Silvestre de Sacy, *Brongniart* (including information derived from part of a large collection of drawings, of which the other part has only recently come to light, see *JF*); Launay, 16–48 (his family background); Hautecoeur, *Histoire*, 4, 287–302; Kaufmann, 1968, 169–170; Gallet, 1972, 147; Le Bilhan, *Francs-Maçons*, 98.

Brongniart at the Academy: *PV*, 7, 214–16 (May/June 1765) (Brongniart and Belanger in competition); 8, 195 (30 May 1774) (candidacy for membership, Gondoin chosen); 8, 272 (17 June 1776) (projects examined); 9, 59 (10 December 1781) (becomes a member); 9, 68 (25 February 1782) (shows model for pump).

The Hôtel de Montesson and the Pavillon d'Orléans: Krafft and Ransonnette, 29–30 (1770); Thiéry, *Paris*, 1, 145; La Tour du Pin, 87 (workings of the two houses); Silvestre de Sacy, 17–24; Monique Hébert in *GBA*, 1964, 2, 161–76 (changes introduced by Piètre); Britsch, 215, 435–6 (theatre).

Mme de Montesson and the Duc d'Orléans: Lévis, 248ff.; *CL*, 12, 388; Britsch, 156; Du Barry, 2, 137; Hautecoeur, *Histoire*, 4, 109ff. (Orléans' patronage).

214 Other right-bank hôtels: Silvestre de Sacy, 24–41; Thiéry, *Paris*, 1, 189 (Taillepied de Bondy), and 147 (Ste-Foix, built for Bouret de Vézelay); Krafft and Ransonnette, respectively 21 (1781), and 5–6 (1775, with alterations by Happe, 1798); plan before alterations in Gallet, 1964, 28. Hôtel Dervieux: Thiéry, *Paris*, 1, 144; Krafft and Ransonnette, 7 (Brongniart, 1774; Belanger, 1789); Ganay in *GBA*, 1955, 1, 288 (plan showing garden).

215 The Palais-Bourbon: especially Piépape, 2, 62–3; and see under Peyre, ch. 6 above.

Mme de Monaco and her patronage: Walpole, 6, 380; Dufort, 1, 154; Du Barry, 2, 111; Piépape, 2, 57, 62 (relations with Marie Antoinette), 115, 141 (opinion of Goethe). Gardens at Betz: *JF*, 139; *AAF*, 1927, 269; Wiebenson, 129 (bibliography). Brongniart and the Prince de Monaco, Mme de Monaco's husband, were members of the same masonic lodge (Bord, 381).

The Hôtel de Monaco: Thiéry, *Paris*, 2, 581; Krafft and Ransonnette, 69–70 (1784); Silvestre de Sacy, 27–32; Gallet, 1972, 29 (Mme de Monaco's interest in architecture).

216 The Marquis de Montesquiou: quotations from Blaikie, 206, Du Barry, 2, 158–9, and Vigée Lebrun, *Memoirs*, 60; see also under Ledoux, ch. 10 above; Britsch, 436; Silvestre de Sacy, 54–5.

Louise de Condé and her hôtel: Piépape, 2, 108–16, 112 (the hôtel); Thiéry, *Paris*, 2, 564–5; Krafft and Ransonnette, 61 (1781); Silvestre de Sacy, 57–9; Gaxotte, 1966, 362–5.

Other buildings on the left bank: Silvestre de Sacy, 59–62. The Archives of the Order of St-Lazare: Thiéry, *Paris*, 2, 564; Krafft and Ransonnette, 65 (1787). The stables of Monsieur: Thiéry, *Paris*, 2, 564. Bath chamber of the Hôtel de Besenval: Thiéry, *Paris*, 2, 579. The Hôtel de Damas d'Anzelay, rue de Bourgogne: Thiéry, *Paris*, 2, 565.

The grounds of Maupertuis (see under Ledoux, ch. 10 above, for the château): Silvestre de Sacy, 55–6; also Young, 167 (attributed to Blaikie); Vigée Lebrun, *Memoirs*, 110–11; Laborde, 157–8; Rivière, 69ff.; Vidler, 89–91 (giving what seems a largely unjustified reconstruction of the plan of the pyramid, and following the mistaken attribution to Ledoux).

The Capuchin monastery: Thiéry, *Paris*, 1, 138; Legrand and Landon, 2, 3, 51; Cellerier, *Autobiographie* (project of 1778); Britsch, 434–5; Silvestre de Sacy, 44–8 (47, Capuchins as firemen); Charles Collas, *Une Paroisse de Paris, Saint-Louis d'Antin*, 1932; Evans, 119–21 (Capuchins); Créquy, 7, 87 (the governor's palace at Metz).

218 Influence on David: René Crozet in *GBA*, 1955, 1, 211–20.

Brongniart's own house: Silvestre de Sacy, 56–7; Gaxotte, 1966, 371; Laulan, 57 (Brongniart succeeds Boullée).

The Hôtels Masseran and Chamblin: Krafft and Ransonnette, 39 (Masseran, 1784), and 15 (Chamblin, 1789); Silvestre de Sacy, 64–6; Gaxotte, 1966, 372–6.

219 Romainville: Thiéry, *Paris*, 1, 616; Erdberg, 179; Silvestre de Sacy, 63–4.

Brongniart and his family: Launay, 19 (marriage in 1767), 22 (his children); Vigée Lebrun, *Memoirs*, 54, 109–10, 129; Michelle Beaulieu in *RLMF*, 1974, 105–8 (portraits of his children).

Brongniart sale: catalogue by A. J. Paillet, Bibliothèque du Musée du Louvre, N 836–7697 (noted by Silvestre de Sacy; works of Clodion nos 123–46).

Brongniart in Bordeaux: Launay, 33–5 (letters); Pariset in *Bulletin et mémoires de la Société archéologique de Bordeaux*, LXII, 1957–62, 181–239 (summary in *BM*, 1966, 87–8); *FR*, 39, 40 (unidentified fête projects).

Work at Sèvres: Silvestre de Sacy, 133–6.

Mme de Montesson and Napoleon: Silvestre de Sacy, 22.

The Bourse: [Brongniart], 1814 (5, substitution of Corinthian for Ionic order); Landon, *Annales, Salon de 1808*, 2, 67; Silvestre de Sacy, 146–54.

Père Lachaise cemetery: [Brongniart], 1814, 17 (burial of father); Silvestre de Sacy, 144–6.

Belanger (sometimes Bélanger): Belanger's *Autobiographie*; the only obituary is apparently the one by Belanger's pupil, Mlle Loiseau, n.d.; for Belanger's own writings see BN catalogue (including the *Monument d'utilité publique*, 1808 (a Halle aux vins), and the *Notes instructives*, 1814 (see further below), and notes on de Wailly, Brongniart and Cellerier (chs 6, 13 and 14) for his obituaries of these architects; the drawings of Belanger in seven volumes are in BN, Est., Ha, 58–58f; his extensive collections of drawings and books were catalogued for the sales that took place, respectively, 15ff. June and 22ff. June, 1818; there is a detailed modern biography, but insufficiently illustrated, by Stern (1930), with medallion portrait as frontispiece; a caricature of the architect is in BN, Est., N 2 Suppl., Belanger. See also Hautecoeur, *Histoire*, 4, 302–9; Kaufmann, 1968, 170–6; Gallet, 1972, 142; M. Mosser in *PF*, 49–51.

220 Belanger at the Academy: *PV*, 8, 133 (15 June 1772).

221 Early works: see the *Autobiographie*, and Stern, chs 2–8; *PV*, 8, 166, (16 August 1773) (drawings for the Hôtel des Gardes of the Comte d'Artois at Versailles shown to Academy).

Gretten's geological survey: McKie, 42 (Lavoisier's collaboration).

Sophie Arnould: Stern, *passim*; Campardon, 1, 13–36; *Arnoldiana*, especially 43ff.

The Prince de Ligne: Vigée Lebrun, *Memoirs*, 164–6; Ligne's own *Mémoires*, 1827–29; biography by O. P. Gilbert, 1923; Sirén, 138; Scott in *Apollo*, 1969, 454–9, and Ganay in *GBA*, 1948, 1, 367ff. (Beloeil); also Gallet, 1972, 31–2.

The Duc de Lauraguais: quotations from Ségur, 1, 153–5; also *Mémoires de Mademoiselle Sophie Arnould*, ed. Lamothe-Lanjon, 1837, 1, 172ff.; Blaikie, 113 (Lauraguais, his first French patron); Croÿ, 1, 123 and 304 (his travels) 2, 320 (his garden volcano); Stern, 1, 16ff.; Britsch, 114 (his stables at Newmarket); see also Robert Black, *Horse-racing in France*, 1886, 8–10, and Basil Taylor, *Stubbs*, 1971, 207 (his acquisition of Gimcrack); *Index biographique* of the Académie des Sciences, 75; Genlis, 6, 209–10 (he banishes *balcons* from theatres). For Lauraguais' own writings see BN Books Catalogue.

222 Lauraguais' pavilion, and baths in general: Stern, 1, 18–21; Gallet in *BMC*, June 1972, 22; Ronot, 1959 (public bathing establishments); for the bath of the Baron de Besenval see note under Brongniart above.

Grotesque decoration: Hautecoeur, *Histoire*, 4, 481–509.

223 English sketch-book and English patrons: sketch-book in the EBA, 120 D 20 (see *JF*, 59–61). The gallery for Lord Shelburne: Stern 1, 4–6; Gallet in *BMC*, June, 1972, 19–22. Also McKie, 85 (Shelburne and Joseph Priestley meet Lavoisier in Paris, October 1773).

Bagatelle: Thiéry, *Paris*, 1, 25ff.; Mercier [1797], 3, 31–3; Krafft, 1812, 116f.; Stern, 1, 57–75; Duchesne, 1909; J. C. N. Forestier, *Bagatelle et ses jardins*, n.d.; Georges Pascal, *Histoire du Château de Bagatelle*, 1938 (short guide); *ACF*, vol. 3; B. Scott in *Apollo*, 1972, 476–85.

The Comte d'Artois: quotation from Oberkirch, 1, 296; see also Du Barry, 1, 318, and Créquy, 5, 48. *NAAF*, 1872, 104 (Belanger listed as his Premier Architecte); Hautecoeur, *Histoire*, 4, 105–9.

225 Opinions of Bagatelle: Du Barry, 4, 157, 159; Blaikie, 153; Oberkirch, 2, 298.

Claude Baudard de St-James: Vigée Lebrun, *Memoirs*, 185–7; Visme, 134–5 (freemason); Thirion, 232, 458; Bosher, index; Thiéry, *Paris*, 1, 128 (Place Vendôme house, and salon by Belanger); Hermitage 1971 exhibition (table designed for him).

226 The Folie St-James: Thiéry, *Paris*, 1, 33ff.; Krafft, 1812, 97–102; *ACF*, vol. 13; Ganay in *RAAM*, 1922, 1, 392–8; Stern, 1, 131–47; Gallet, 1972, 149 (Chaussard) and 162 (Gallimard); AN, 01 1581 (documentation, also for Bagatelle).

'L'homme du rocher': Oberkirch, 3, 273; see also Thirion, 332; *JF*, 110–13 (rocks in general); Yurova, pl. 260 (grotto at Alexandrovsky, 1820–22).

Blaikie's opinion: Blaikie, 180–1.

Artois' stables and Nouvelle Amérique: Thiéry, *Paris*, 1, 73; Bonnardot, 114–15; Stern, 1, 93–103; Gallet in *BMC*, June, 1969, 16.

Projects for St-Germain: Blaikie, 187; Stern, 1, 84–92.

Méréville: Ganay in *RAAM*, 1923, 2, 310–16, and 1933, 61, 65; Stern, 1, 157–67; Sirén, 153–8; J. de Cayeux in *BSHAF*, 1968, 127–33 (Robert's work there); Boyer, 1961, 146–8; Gallet, 1972, 141 (Barré), and 1975, 53; *JF*, 76; Wiebenson, 1978, 131 (further bibliography).

Santeny: Krafft, 1812, 31 to 36; Erdberg, 180; Stern, 2, 156–9.

Later houses: Krafft, 1812, 2–3; Krafft and Ransonnette, 4, 17–18, 63; Thiéry, *Paris*, 2, 680; Stern, 1, 207–14, and ff. *passim*. Later designs outside Paris: Krafft, 1812, 9–10, 48, 72 and 91; Stern, 1, 220–9.

227 Mlle Dervieux: Campardon, 1, 223–27; for her house, Stern, 1, 198–206, and see note under Brongniart above.

Belanger during the Revolution: Stern, 2, 1–73.

Theatre projects: *PV*, 8, 124 (24 February 1772 Théâtre-Italien project presented to Academy), and 9, 244 (23 March 1789) (his Opéra project for Place du Carrousel discussed); Stern, 1, 123–32; 2, 144–9; Stern, 2, 189–91 (Brussels theatre projects).

228 The abattoir of Rochechouart: Stern, 2, 238–44.

The Halle au Blé: Stern, 2, 233–8; Wiebenson, 1973, 266–79. Belanger on iron: Stern, 2, 187; the first bridge of iron in France was the Pont des Arts in Paris, opened in 1803.

Correspondence with Fontaine and David: quoted by Stern, 2, 250–1, 255.

Belanger's account of architectural administration in the last years of Napoleon: [J. F. Belanger], *Notes instructives pour les architectes et entrepreneurs*, 1814, 10ff. (his difficulties); Stern, 2, 292–304.

Works of 1814 and after: Stern, 2, 261–82, 316–49.

Belanger's death and tomb, etc.: Normand, 6 (tomb by his pupils Hitorff and Lecointe); Stern, 2, 350–7.

Chapter 14

229 Domestic architecture in Paris: Hautecoeur, *Histoire*, 4, 369–406, and especially Gallet, 1964, and 1972, 69–94.

Ségur on Paris: Ségur, 2, 29.

The Hôtel de Salm: Thiéry, *Paris*, 2, 590; Krafft and Ransonnette, 73; Krafft, 1838, 43–4; Legrand and Landon, 2, 2, 89; Landon, *Annales*, 7 (1803), 145, and 8 (1805), 111; H. Thirion, *Le Palais de la Légion d'Honneur*, 1883 (3–60, the Prince de Salm); Henri Torré and Claude Ducourtial, *Le Palais et le Musée de la Légion d'Honneur*, 1963, and the second author in *AAF*, 1969, 9–21; Gallet, 1972, 10; Gaxotte, 1966, 113–17.

The Prince de Salm: see also Croÿ, 1, 180; Créquy, 3, 12–13.

Pierre Rousseau: Gallet, 1972, 183–4; collection of drawings by Rousseau in the RIBA drawings collection; Thiéry, *Paris*, 1, 449, and Ganay, 1933, 55 (the Hôtel de Montmorency and its Chinese pavilion); J. P. Cuzin in *IHA*, 1971, 2, 91 (caricature of Rousseau by Vincent).

231 The Hôtel de Montholon: Thiéry, *Paris*, 1, 462; Krafft and Ransonnette, 67–8 (1786); Gallet, 1964, pls 91–3; BN, Est., Ve 92 (drawings).

Soufflot 'le Romain': Gallet, 1972, 185; *NAAF*, 1892, 127 (marriage): L. Lambeau in *CMVP*, 1902, 65–8 (his house and his relation to Soufflot); CD, 11, 408 (letter to his uncle). Another relation of Antoine, his nephew, Dubois, was also an architect (see Krafft, 1812, 65).

Lequeu: see especially the recent articles by Philippe Duboy, in *MHF*, 1975, 2, 74–8 (with bibliography) and in *Il Piccolo Hans*, 10, 1976, 113–78. Also Kaufmann in *AB*, 1949, 130–5, 1952, 538–58, and 1968, 185–6; Rosenau in *AR*, 1949, 111–16, and 1950, 264–7; Hautecoeur, *Histoire*, 5, 86–91; Gallet, 1972, 172–3; G. Metken in *GBA*, 1965, 1, 213–30; the collected drawings of architecture are BN, Est., Ha 80–80c, together with a manuscript, Vb 43.

232 Lequeu's two château projects: Krafft, 1812, 37–9 and 55–6. On their masonic connotations see Vidler, 89.

The Hôtel de Gallifet: Thiéry, *Paris*, 2, 551; Dumolin in *BSHAVII/XVAP*, 1923, 142; Gaxotte, 1966, 231–5. For Gallifet (?) himself see Vallentin, 133, and Moreau, 1, 11.

233 Etienne-François Legrand: distinguished from Jacques-Guillaume Legrand by Gallet, 1964, 189, and 1972, 171; also Gallet, 1976, 207–9; Chenesseau, 299–311 (and see under Trouard, ch. 8 above). For the Hôtel de Jarnac, see Thiéry, *Paris*, 2, 565, and Krafft and Ransonnette, 31 (1788).

Henry Trou: Kaufmann, 1968, 184; Gallet, 1972, 165–6; Krafft and Ransonnette, 16, 27, 52, 62.

235 Delafosse: Kaufmann, 1968, 154–7; Gallet in *GBA*, 1963, 1, 157–64 (his hôtels), and 1972, 155; G. Levallet in *GBA*, 1929, 1, 158–69; M. Mosser in *PF*, 103–13. For the Titons see *AAF*, 1927, 235–8, and Britsch, 238 (masonic meeting at the Folie-Titon).

236 The Hôtel de Beaumarchais: Krafft and Ransonnette, 23–4, and 86 (1790); Legrand and Landon, 2, 4, 31; Gallet, 1972, 107–8. On Beaumarchais there is a short biography in English, Cynthia Cox, *The Real Figaro*, 1962.

Lemoine 'le Romain': Gallet, 1972, 171.

Raymond and the Hôtel Lebrun: Gallet in *GBA*, 1960, 2, 275–84, and 1972, 183; Normand, 48 (tomb of Raymond).

Apartment houses: Gallet, 1972, 66–7; Hautecoeur, *Histoire*, 4, 385 and 406; Thiéry, *Paris*, 2, 426–7 (rue de Tournon).

238 Stables: Thiéry, *Almanach*, 224ff., and *Paris*, 2, 540, 564, 678.

The Infantado stables: Thiéry, *Paris*, 1, 104; Krafft and Ransonnette, 54 (1786).

Cellerier (also Cellérier): *Autobiographie*; funeral oration by Belanger, 2 March 1814 (BI, Duplessis 2384); Kaufmann, 1968, 160, 183; Gallet, 1972, 148–9; Krafft and Ransonnette, 41–2, 48, 77–8 and 85 (works for the Prince de Soubise); Thiéry, *Paris*, 1, 91 (Hôtel de Saucour), and 2, 687 (Théâtre de l'Ambigu Comique); Krafft, 1838, 96 (Théâtre des Variétés; also Legrand and Landon, 2, 3, 99); *BMC*, 1960, 2, 19 (project for Voltaire); projects with Poyet: AN, N III Seine 409 and 780 (Opéra), and Boyer, 1962, 255 (Comédie-Italienne); *FR*, 16–19 (Fête de la Fédération, 1790).

Heurtier: Quatremère, 1834, 295ff. (2 October 1824); Kaufmann, 1968, 148–9; Gallet, 1972, 166; Croÿ, 4, 128–9.

The Comédie-Italienne: Thiéry, *Paris*, 1, 182; Legrand and Landon, 2, 3, 93; Donnet, ch. 3; Boyer, 1962, 249.

Lenoir: Gallet, 1972, 172; monograph by Martin Meade, in preparation; Thiéry, *Paris*, 1, 224, 656, 657, and 2, 138; *CD*, 10, 450; Evans, 67–8; Boyer, 1962, 246, 252–3 (Comédie-Italienne projects).

The Opéra: especially Thiéry, *Paris*, 1, 534ff.; also Donnet, 108–16; AN, 01 629 (projects for the Opéra).

240 Gros Caillou: Legrand and Landon, 1, 174; O. Zunz in *AESC*, 1970, 4, 1024–65 (development of the area); BN, Est., Ha 68 (Cherpitel's drawings).

Cherpitel: see the sale of his collection 31 January 1810 (BN, Est., Yd 247), with notice of his life; *DBF* (1959); Gallet, 1972, 29 and 150; *CD*, 11, 264, 296, 354, 408–10, 420; Thiéry, *Paris*, 1, 146, and 2, 51, 569 and 580; Legrand and Landon, 1, 144; BL Album, 19, 21 (Hôtel de Châtelet) and BN, Est., Ha 69 (St-Barthélemy); *BMC*, 1967, 1, 16–19.

241 Choir of St-Germain-l'Auxerrois: Thiéry, *Paris*, 1, 405–6; Herrmann, 1962, 97–8. Other choir decorations, see Laugier, 1765, 131ff.; Thiéry, *Paris*, 1, 548 (St-Médéric) and 2, 212 (St-Médard).

St-Sauveur: Thiéry, *Paris*, 1, 506–7; Legrand and Landon, 1, 152; and see under Chalgrin, ch. 8 above.

Poyet: BN catalogue (for his many publications); Vaudoyer, *Funérailles de M. Poyet* (9 December, 1824); Kaufmann, 1968, 159–60; Hautecoeur, *Histoire*, 5, 81; Gallet, 1972, 182; M. Mosser in *PF*, 302–3; Cellerier, *Autobiographie* (theatre project); Thiéry, *Paris*, 1, 227–8 (Chartres' stables) 2, 49 (Pont-St-Michel); Krafft, 1838, 88–9 (Archevêché stables); *Bonhomme* (1788) (contemporary criticism of Poyet, and see also under Moreau-Desproux, ch. 6 above); and see note on Palais-Bourbon, ch. 15 below.

Poyet's hospital: Rosenau, 1970, ch. 5; J. Magnac in *BSHAVIIAP*, 7 (April 1910), 69–79; Landon, *Annales*, 11 (1806), 59.

Poyet at the Academy: he was the winner of the second prize in the 1768 competition (*PV*, 8, 30, 36).

Pavillon de Bellechasse: Gallet in *BMC*, 1967, 1, 15–16, and 1972, 107.

Callet's house: Krafft and Ransonnette, 37 (1775); BL Album, 23; Gallet, 1964, pl. 58.

Prisons: Hautecoeur, *Histoire*, 4, 159–60; Rosenau, 1970, ch. 4; Thiéry, *Almanach*, 390ff.; H. C. Rice in *JSAH*, 1953, 28–30; and see under Ledoux, ch. 12 above.

Beaujon: Thirion, 263ff.; Bosher, 96; Vigée Lebrun, *Memoirs*, 180–3; André Masson, *Un Mécène bordelais: Nicolas Beaujon, 1718–1786*, 1937; Gallet, 1972, 35.

Beaujon's charterhouse, chapel and hospice: Thiéry, *Paris*, 1, 56ff.; Legrand and Landon, 1, 131, and 2, 3, 79; Krafft and Ransonnette, 46–7 (1781, charterhouse); Krafft, 1838, 80–3; Bonnardot, 68–73; Oberkirch, 2, 30.

242 Girardin: Gallet in *GBA*, 1962, 1, 29–42 (Château of Les Boulayes), and 1972, 163.

Hospitals in general: Pujoulx, 309–14; Hautecoeur, *Histoire*, 4, 164–9; Rosenau, 1970, ch. 3, and in *AR*, 1966, 253–58; Pevsner, 1976, ch. 9.

Lavoisier's report: McKie, 151 (1787).

Viel: Pérouse de Montclos, 1966; Thiéry, *Paris*, 2, 263.

Hôpital Cochin: Thiéry, *Paris*, 2, 264; Landon, *Annales*, 7 (1803), 19.

243 Viel de St-Maux: Viel de St-Maux, 22, his criticism of Les Invalides, and 47, n. 15, of Blondel; Pérouse de Montclos, 1966; see also Kaufmann, 1968, 161, 167.

Regional architecture: see in general Albert Babeau, *La Ville sous*

l'ancien régime, 1880, 365ff.; Lavedan, 1941, 303ff. and 417ff., *Les Villes françaises*, n.d., 146–74, and in *VU*, 1958, 1–30 (Place Louis XVI); Patte, 1769, ch. 1; Ardascheff, 365ff. (survey of work of Intendants). Aix-en-Provence: see under Ledoux, ch. 12 above; Jean Boyer, *L'Architecture réligieuse de l'époque classique à Aix-en-Provence*, 1972. Aunis and Saintonge: Moulin. Besançon: see under Louis and Ledoux, chs 9 and 11, above; Tournier, 1943, *Maisons et hôtels privés au XVIIIe siècle à Besançon*, 1970, and *Les Eglises comtoises, leur architecture des origines au XVIIIe siècle*, 1954, 308–34; D. Rabreau in *BSHAF*, 1972, 295–324 (Bertrand), for whom see also M. Binney in *Country Life*, 1972, CLII, 634–7. Bordeaux: see under Louis, ch. 9 above; Pariset, 1968. Dijon: see under de Wailly, Cellerier and Lenoir, chs 6 and 14 above; P. Quarré in *BM*, 1970, 57–72 (Palais des Etats). Lorient: H.-F. Buffet in *MSHAB*, 1948, 123–41. Orléans: R.-U. Boitel in *MHF*, 1956, 160–8. Lyon: see under Soufflot, ch. 1 above. Strasbourg. The work of Ixnard: M. Jadot in *CAF*, CV, 1947, 11–42; H. Haug in *AAHA*, 1927, 113–76; R. Lehni in *IHA*, 1970, 60–7.

Lequeulx and Lille: J.-J. Duthoy in *IHA*, 1969, 27–32.

Crucy and Nantes: Granges de Surgères in *NAAF*, 1898 (Nantes artists); J. Merlin in *MHF*, 1955, 161–9; P. Jeulin in *MSHAB*, 1943, 67–113; and for Crucy especially Rabreau, 1968, in *IHA*, 1969, 182–5, and in *Storia delle città*, 1976, 4, 45–66; Crucy's theatre is also described by Young, 115.

245 Versailles under Louis XVI: for the general background see Hautecoeur, *Histoire*, 4, 80–90; Nolhac, 1918, chs 5–7, and in *Mémoires de la Société des sciences morales, des lettres et des arts de Seine-et-Oise*, 17, 1889, 19–124; Francastel in *BSHAF*, 1950, 53–7; Pérouse de Montclos, 143–6 (the drawings for the reconstruction of the château); M. Jaillot, *GBA*, 1964, 1, 289–354.

P.-A. Pâris: for fêtes in general see under Moreau-Desproux, ch. 6 above; A. Gruber in *BSHAF*, 1973, 213–27; also A. Estignard, *A. Pâris*, 1902; J. Brochet, *Adrien Pâris (1745–1819)*, 1921; Hautecoeur, *Histoire*, 4, 309–14; Gallet, 1972, 179; Arrizoli in *PF*, 244–5; *PV*, 9, 49 and 68 (11 June and 25 February 1782); Decugis and Reymond, 103–11 (stage decorations, for which see also *CA*, January 1968, 68–75); Grandmaison, 107–8 (*cordon noir*), and in *NAAF*, 1889, 239; Chenesseau, 315ff.; Ganay in *RAAM*, 1924, 2, 249–64; Haug-Levallet in *BSHAF*, 1933, 88–99 (Neuchâtel works); Ronot, 1959; *IGRAF*, 5.

Richard Mique: brief life by P. Morey, *Richard Mique*, 1868; Alfred Hachette in *Revue historique*, 1920, 1–54 (family lawsuit), and his *Le Couvent de la Reine à Versailles*, 1923 (with biography); Gallet, 1972, 176; Grandmaison, 67–70, and *NAAF*, 1872, 94 (titles and appointments); de Ganay in *RAAM*, 1926, 2, 215–28 (gardens at Bellevue and Versailles); P. Lelièvre, in *Mélanges . . . offerts à Monsieur Frantz Calot*, 1960 (Mique's library), 333–6; D. Meyer in *GBA*, 1965, 2, 223–32 (St-Cloud); Gallet, 1976, 213–15.

246 Appearance of Marie Antoinette: see Vigée Lebrun, *Memoirs*, 52–4. Créquy, 6, 218 (vegetable hairpiece).

Rambouillet: short guides by G. Lenôtre (1948) and Henri Longnon (n.d.); *ACF*, 7; Sirén, 158–62; P. Guth in *CA*, May 1958, 74; Gallet, 1972, 186 (Thévenin); Wiebenson, 1978, 131 (further bibliography).

The Petit Trianon gardens: quotation from Blaikie, 136; Oberkirch, 1, 326; see also Laborde, s.v. Trianon; Pierre de Nolhac, *The Trianon of Marie Antoinette*, 1925; Sirén, 112–15; Croÿ, 4, 217; *JF*, 126–32 (*hameaux* in general).

247 Laborde on parks: Laborde, s.v. Le Raincy.

Fontainebleau: Champollion-Figeac; P. Verlet in *AF*, 1961, 159–68; Y. Bottineau in *GBA*, 1967, 1, 139–58.

Pavillon de Cassan: especially O. Choppin de Janvry in *La Revue française*, 1975, 2; also *JF*, 15.

Désert de Retz: especially O. Choppin de Janvry in *BSHAF*, 1970, 125–48; also Le Rouge, cahier XIII; Krafft, 1812, 63; Sirén, 115–20, and in *AR*, 1949, 327–32; Gallet, 1972, 35 and 141 (Barbier).

248 De Monville: Dufort 1, 54–5; also Thirion, 295ff.; Vigée Lebrun, *Souvenirs*, 1, 134; Genlis, 1, 103–4; *Mémoires secrets*, 17, 350–1 (5 August 1781, at which time the tower house was apparently unbuilt).

249 Blaikie on Monville: Blaikie, 210–11.

Circular house near Naples (?): Christies, Rome, 21 October 1976, lot 90 (with illustration).

Chapter 15

251 Architecture after the Revolution: especially Benoit; *FR*, and the Colloque of the exhibition (especially D. Rabreau, 355–75). Salles d'Assemblée: Boyer, 1933, 1935, and in *BSHAF*, 1956, 80–6, and 1964, 193–9. Palace of the Tuileries: Boyer in *BSHAF*, 1934, 242–63, 1938, 261–77, and 1941–44, 142–84 and 185–258; also Ledoux-Lebard in *BSHAF*, 1947–48, 9–18. Decoration in general: Ledoux-Lebard in *GBA*, 1952, 2, 175–92, and 1955, 1, 299–312.

French architects abroad: Hautecoeur, *Histoire*, 4, 323–7; Colombier; Boyer, 1945–46 (contacts with England); Hans-Andreas Klaiber, *Der Württembergische Oberbaudirektor, Philippe de la Guépière*, 1959.

St-Petersburg: see especially Hautecoeur, 1912.

Nicolas Barré: Gallet, 1972, 141; P. Lavedan in *CAF*, CXIX, 1961, 179–84 (minor works); M. Binney in *Country Life*, CXLIX, 1584–7 and CL, 18–21 (Château of Montgeoffroy); for the Hôtel de la Reynière see under the Hôtel de St-Florentin by Chalgrin, ch. 8 above.

Desprez: Nils G. Wollin, *Desprez en Italie*, 1935, and *Desprez en Suède*, 1939 (review by Kaufmann in *AB*, 1946, 283–4); *CA*, June 1967, 54–61; Hautecoeur, *Histoire*, 5, 81–6; Kaufmann, 1968, 176–8; M. Mosser in *PF*, 121–31.

Dufourny: Vaudoyer, *Notice succincte sur M. Dufourny* (extract from the *Moniteur*, 19 September 1818); Quatremère de Quincy, *Funérailles de M. Dufourny*, 1818, and notice in the *Recueil*, 234ff. (5 October 1822); *AAF*, 1910, 351–413; Meekes, 91–4; Normand, 57 (tomb).

French architects in America: Hitchcock, 5–8; du Colombier in *BSHAF*, 1953, 7–17 (Mangin); J. T. Flexner in *The American Art Journal*, 1970, 2, 1, 30–45 (L'Enfant).

Vallin de la Mothe: Hautecoeur, 1912, 21–4; *CD*, 10, 332, 365, 370, 376–7; *NAAF*, 1878, 75.

Thomas de Thomon: Hautecoeur, 1912, 82–6; G. Loukomski in *Apollo*, 1945, 297 and 304; M. Mosser in *PF*, 341–2. Also de Thomon's own *Description . . . de plusieurs édifices . . . à Saint Petersbourg*, 1819; and Landon, *Annales*, 6 (1804), 101–3 (theatre), and 11 (1806), 91 (Bourse).

Administration of architecture: see especially Gourlier and Questel; Benoit, 178–242; the survey in Chaffee, 65–77; Hautecoeur, *Histoire*, 5, 93–143; *Adresse à l'Assemblée nationale, par les membres de l'Académie d'architecture, soussignés; et projet de réglement pour une Académie Nationale des Arts*, 14 February 1791; T. C. Bruun-Neergaard, *Sur la situation des beaux-arts en France*, 1801.

The Academy and schools of architecture: Chaffee, 65–77; Hautecoeur, *Histoire*, 5, 263–79.

252 The Institut: Albert Soubies, *Les Membres de l'Académie des Beaux-Arts*, 4 vols, 1904–17; the volumes of *MINSA*.

Publications: see also the list of travel books in Hautecoeur, *Histoire*, 5, 267–71, and the *Prospectus* of Legrand.

Rondelet: Vaudoyer, *Funérailles de M. Rondelet*, 29 September 1829; Baltard, *Discours nécrologique*, 1829; Chavret, 340–4; Landon, *Annales*, 13 (1807), 31 (Place Maubert); for Ste-Geneviève see under Soufflot, ch. 5 above; also Vaudoyer, *Extrait*.

Role of Rondelet: Middleton and Watkin, 31–2.

254 Durand: A. Rondelet, *Notice historique sur la vie et les ouvrages de J.N.L. Durand*, 1835; Krafft and Ransonnette, 13 (Maison Lathuille 1788); Kaufmann, 1968, 210–14; Gallet, 1972, 159.

Views of Paris buildings by Durand: BL, 179a 22 (2).

Rôle of Durand: Middleton and Watkin, 30–1; Hitchcock, 1958, 20–42; Legrand's *Essai* was composed as the 'Texte explicatif' of the *Recueil*.

255 Napoleon's Paris: Biver; Guerrini; Georges Poisson, *Napoléon et Paris*, 1964; Hautecoeur, *Histoire*, 5, 143–243; F. Bercé and J. M. Pérouse de Montclos in *MHF*, 1969, 4, 25–79; G. Ledoux-Lebard in *AAF*, 1969, 37–56 (fountains); Lavedan in *BSHAF*, 1951, 81–4 (left-bank developments); B. Foucart and V. Noel-Bouton in *BSHAF*, 1971, 235ff. (Napoléonville); J. Leclant in *RA*, 1969, 5, 82–8, and Pevsner and Lang in *AR*, 1956, 243–54 (Egyptomania). Also Vaudoyer, *Extrait*, and another contemporary survey in C. J. Toussaint, *Traité de géométrie et d'architecture*, 1812, 1, 116–33.

256 The Madeleine: Vautier, 1910; Gruel, 1910, 43ff.; Kreiger, 257ff. For Vignon see under Contant d'Ivry and Ledoux, chs 3 and 12 above, and BN catalogue for his publications.

The Palais-Bourbon: Boyer, 1936; *BSHAF*, 1958, 91–4 (statues), and for Poyet, see ch. 14 above.

257 The Arc-de-Triomphe: Hirschfeld, 45–81; Stern in *Revue des études historiques*, 1919, 390–7; R. A. Wiegert, *L'Arc de Triomphe de l'Etoile*, n.d., and see under Chalgrin, ch. 8 above.

Percier and Fontaine: Marie-Louise Biver, *Pierre Fontaine*, 1964; L. Morel d'Arleux in *BSHAF*, 1934, 88–103; Janet S. Byrne in *The Metropolitan Museum of Art Journal*, 1959, 183–96 (Sacre of Louis XVIII); Hautecoeur, *Histoire*, 5, 156–91; Boyer, 1933, and *BSHAF*, 1962, 257–62; P. Marmottain in *BSHAF*, 1921, 125–30 (Percier's pupils); Hirschfeld, 27–43 (the Arc du Carrousel).

General bibliography and list of abbreviations

Articles and books dealing with a single theme or work are in many cases listed in the notes to the text, pp. 262–78 above.

AAA	Annales de l'architecture et des arts
AAF	Archives de l'art français (see also NAAF)
AAHA	Archives alsaciennes d'histoire de l'art
AB	The Art Bulletin
ACF	Les Anciens Châteaux de France, with notes by J. Vacquier and A. Germain, 14 vols, 1914–32
AESC	Annales: Economies, sociétés, civilisations
AF	Art de France
AH	Architectural History
AN	Archives Nationales, Paris
AN, Min. Cent.	Minutier Central, Archives Nationales, Paris
ANCE	The Age of Neoclassicism, catalogue of 14th Council of Europe exhibition, London, 1972
APC	Annales des Ponts et Chaussées
AR	The Architectural Review

Aldis, Janet, *Madame Geoffrin, her Salon and her Times, 1750–1777*, 1905
Almanach historique et raisonné des architectes, peintres, sculpteurs, [J.-B.-P. Le Brun] 1776
Andrieux, Citoyen, 'Notice sur la vie et les travaux de Charles Dewailly', *MINSA, Littérature et beaux arts*, III, An IX, 36–42
Ardascheff, Paul, *Les Intendants de province sous Louis XVI*, 1909
Arnoldiana, ou Sophie Arnould et ses contemporains, 1813
Aulanier, Christine, *Histoire du Palais et du Musée du Louvre*, 1948 etc.
Autobiographie(s), 'Autobiographies d'architectes parisiens, 1759–1811', ed. H. Ottomeyer, *BSHP*, 1971, 141–206

BHVP	Bibliothèque Historique de la Ville de Paris
BI	Bibliothèque de l'Institut
BL	British Library
BL Album	British Library, Department of Maps, K. Top Suppl. CXXIV
BM	Bulletin monumental
B Mag	The Burlington Magazine
BMC	Bulletin du Musée Carnavalet
BN	Bibliothèque Nationale
BN, Est.	Bibliothèque Nationale, Cabinet des Estampes
BSHAF	Bulletin de la Société de l'histoire de l'art français
BSHAVIIAP	Bulletin de la Société d'histoire et d'archéologie du VIIe arrondissement de Paris
BSHAVIIIAP	Bulletin de la Société d'histoire et d'archéologie du VIIIe arrondissement de Paris
BSHAVII/XVAP	Bulletin de la Société d'histoire et d'archéologie des VIIe et XVe arrondissements de Paris
BSHP	Bulletin de la Société de l'histoire de Paris
BU	Biographie universelle, ancienne et moderne, 45 vols, 1843 (unless earlier editions specified)

Bannister, T., 'The First Iron-framed Buildings', *AR*, 1950, 231ff.
Bapst, Constant, *Essai sur l'histoire du théâtre*, 1893
Barthélemy, Abbé, *Voyage en Italie de M. l'Abbé Barthélemy*, ed. A. Serieys, 2nd ed., 1802
Belanger, François-Joseph, obituary of de Wailly in *Journal de Paris*, 1 Frimaire, An VII (1798), 260–2
Benoit, François, *L'Art français sous la Révolution et l'Empire*, 1897
Berluc-Pérussis, L. de, 'L'Architecte Le Doux et le sculpteur Chardigny à Aix', *RSBAD*, 1902, 189–225
Besenval, *Mémoires du Baron de Besenval (Bibliothèque des Mémoires relatifs à l'histoire de France pendant le XVIIIe siècle*, 4), 1883
Biver, Marie-Louise, *Le Paris de Napoléon*, 1963
Blaikie, Thomas, *Diary of a Scotch Gardener at the French Court at the End of the Eighteenth Century*, ed. F. Birrell, 1931
Blondel, Jacques-François, *Architecture françoise*, 1752–56
——, *Cours d'architecture*, 1771–77
——, *L'Homme du monde éclairé par les arts*, 1774
Boinet, A., *Les Eglises parisiennes*, 1958–61

Bonhomme, *Un Bon-homme aux Etats Généraux sur M. Poyet & les Plagiaires*, 1788
Bonnardot, Hippolyte, *Monographie du VIIe arrondissement de Paris*, 1880
Bord, Gustave, *La Franc-maçonnerie en France*, 1 (1688–1771), 1908
Bordeaux, 2000 ans d'histoire, catalogue of exhibition at Bordeaux, Musée de l'Aquitaine, 1973
Bosher, J. F., *French Finances 1770–1795*, 1970
Boudon, Françoise, 'Urbanisme et spéculation à Paris au XVIIIe siècle: le terrain de l'Hôtel de Soissons', *JSAH*, 1973, 267–307
Boyer, F., 'Projets de salles pour les assemblées révolutionnaires à Paris (1782–1792)', *BSHAF*, 1933, 170–83
——, 'Notes sur les architectes Jacques-Pierre Gisors, Charles Percier, Pierre Vignon', *BSHAF*, 1933, 258–69
——, 'Le Conseil des Cinq Cents au Palais-Bourbon', *BSHAF*, 1935, 59–82
——, 'Le Palais-Bourbon sous le Premier Empire', *BSHAF*, 1936, 91–123
——, 'Amateurs anglais et artistes français au XVIIIe siècle', *BSHAF*, 1954–56, 66–71
——, 'J. J. de Laborde', *BSHAF*, 1961, 137–52
——, 'Un Lotissement à Paris au XVIIIe siècle: de l'Hôtel de Choiseul à la Comédie Italienne', *VU*, 1962, 241–60
Braham, Allan, 'Drawings for Soufflot's Sainte-Geneviève', *B Mag*, 1971, 582–90
——, 'Charles de Wailly and Early Neo-classicism', *B Mag*, 1972, 670–85
Braham, Allan, and Hellmut Hager, *Carlo Fontana. The Drawings at Windsor Castle*, 1977
Britsch, Amédée, *La Jeunesse de Philippe-Egalité (1747–1785)*, 1926
[Brongniart, Alexandre], *Plans du Palais de la Bourse à Paris . . . précédés d'une notice . . . sur quelques autres travaux du même artiste*, 1814

CA	Connaissance des arts
CAF	Congrès archéologique de France
CD	Correspondance des Directeurs de l'Académie de France à Rome, 17 vols, 1887–1908
CL	Correspondance littéraire, philosophique et critique de Grimm et de Diderot, depuis 1752 jusqu'en 1790, 15 vols, 1829–31
CMVP	Commission municipale du Vieux Paris, Procès-verbaux

Campardon, Emile, *L'Académie royale de Musique au XVIIIe siècle*, 1884
Castan, Auguste, *Besançon et ses environs*, 1880
C[ellerier], J[acques], *Notice rapide sur la vie et les ouvrages de Claude-Nicolas Ledoux*, 1806
Chaffee, Richard, 'The Teaching of Architecture at the Ecole des Beaux Arts', *The Architecture of the Ecole des Beaux Arts*, ed. A. Drexler, 1977
Champier, V., *L'Art dans les Flandres françaises au XVIIe et XVIIIe siècles*, 1926
Champier, Victor, and G.-Roger Sandoz, *Le Palais Royal*, 1900
Champollion-Figeac, J.-J., *Le Palais de Fontainebleau*, 1866
Chavret, E.-L.-G., *Lyon artistique, Architectes, Notices biographiques et bibliographiques*, 1899
Chenesseau, Georges, *Sainte-Croix d'Orléans*, 1921
Chevallier, Pierre, and Daniel Rabreau, *Le Panthéon*, 1977
Christ, Yvan, *Le Louvre et les Tuileries*, 1949
Cobban, Alfred, *A History of Modern France*, 1 (1715–1799), 3rd ed., 1968
Cochard, N. F., *Description historique de Lyon*, 1817
——, *Guide du voyageur à Lyon*, 1829
Cochin, Charles-Nicolas, *Oeuvres diverses de M. Cochin . . . concernant les arts*, 1771
——, *Mémoires inédits de Charles-Nicolas Cochin sur le Comte de Caylus, Bouchardon, les Slodtz*, ed. Charles Henry, 1880
Colombier, Pierre du, *L'Architecture française en Allemagne au XVIIIe siècle*, 2 vols, 1955
Cordemoy, J. L. de, *Nouveau Traité de toute l'architecture*, 1714
Courteaut, Paul, *Bordeaux, Cité classique*, 1932
Créquy, Marquise de, *Souvenirs de la Marquise de Créquy de 1710 à 1803*, n.d.
Croÿ, Duc de, *Journal inédit du Duc de Croÿ – 1718–1784*, ed. de Grouchy and Cottin, 1906–07

DBF   *Dictionnaire de biographie française*, ed. J. Balteau, M. Barroux and M. Prévost, 1933–
DN   *Dictionnaire de la noblesse*, de la Chenaye-Desbois and Badien, 19 vols, 1868–76
DNB   *Dictionary of National Biography*

Dakin, D., *Turgot and the Ancien Régime in France*, 1939
Decugis, Nicole, and Suzanne Reymond, *Le Décor du théâtre en France du Moyen-Age à 1925*, 1953
De Wailly, Charles de Wailly, peintre architecte dans l'Europe des lumières, catalogue of exhibition at the Hôtel de Sully, 1979, by Monique Mosser and Daniel Rabreau (introduction by Michel Gallet)
Diderot, Denis, *Correspondance*, ed. G. Roth and J. Varloot, 1955–70
——, *Diderot Salons*, ed. J. Seznec and J. Adhémar, 1957–67
——, *Diderot's Letters to Sophie Volland*, ed. and trans. Peter France, 1972. See also *CL*
Donnet, Alexis, *Architectonographie des théâtres à Paris* (engravings by Orgiazzi), 1821
Du Barry, *Memoirs of Madame du Barri*, 1830–31
Dubois-Corneau, *Pâris de Montmartel (Jean), Banquier de la Cour*, n.d.
Duchesne, A.-N., *Le Cicérone de Versailles*, 1804
Duchesne, Henri-Gaston, *Histoire du Bois de Boulogne. Le Château de Bagatelle*, 1909
Dufort, *Mémoires du Comte Dufort de Cheverny*, ed. R. de Crèvecoeur, 1909
Dulaure, J. A., *Nouvelle Description des environs de Paris*, 1786
——, *Nouvelle Description des curiosités de Paris*, 2nd ed., 1787
Dussausoy, M., *Le Citoyen désintéressé, ou diverses idées patriotiques, concernant quelques établissemens et embellissemens utiles à la ville de Paris*, 2nd ed., 1767

EBA   Ecole Nationale Supérieure des Beaux-Arts, Paris

Elling, C., *Documents inédits concernant les projets de A.-J. Gabriel et N.-H. Jardin pour l'Eglise Frédéric à Copenhague*, 1931
Encyclopédie ou Dictionnaire raisonné des sciences, des arts, et des métiers, 17 vols, 1751–65; *Supplément à l'Encyclopédie*, 1776–77; *Recueil des planches*, 11 vols, 1762–72; *Suite du Recueil des planches*, 1777
Erdberg, Eleanor von, *Chinese Influence on European Garden Structures*, 1936
Eriksen, Svend, 'Marigny and *le goût grec*', *B Mag*, 1962, 96–101
——, 'Early Neo-classicism in French Furniture', *Apollo*, November 1963, 344–51
——, *Early Neoclassicism in France*, trans. Peter Thornton, 1974
Estrée, Paul d', *La Vieillesse de Richelieu (1758–1788)*, 1921
Evans, Joan, *Monastic Architecture in France*, 1964

FR   *Les Fêtes de la Révolution*, catalogue of exhibition at Clermont-Ferrand, Musée Bargoin, 1974

Focillon, H., *Giovanni Battista Piranesi 1720–1788*, 1918
Fontaine, Pierre, see Percier and Fontaine
Furcy-Raynaud, Marc, 'Inventaire des sculptures exécutées au XVIIIe siècle pour la Direction des Bâtiments du Roi', *AAF*, 1927

GBA   *Gazette des beaux-arts*

Gallet, Michel, 'Dessins de Pierre-Louis Moreau-Desproux pour les édifices parisiens', *BMC*, 1961, 2, 6–15
——, *Demeures parisiennes, l'époque de Louis XVI*, 1964
——, 'Un Projet de Charles de Wailly pour la Comédie Française', *BMC*, 1965, 1, 2–13
——, 'La Jeunesse de Ledoux', *GBA*, 1970, 1, 65–92
——, *Paris Domestic Architecture of the Eighteenth Century*, 1972
——, 'Ledoux et sa clientèle parisienne', *BSHP*, 1974–75, 131–73
——, 'Palladio et l'architecture française dans la seconde moitié du XVIIIe siècle', *MHF*, 1975, 2, 43–55
——, 'Louis-François Trouard et l'architecture religieuse dans la région de Versailles au temps de Louis XVI', *GBA*, 1976, 201–18
——, *Ledoux et Paris (Cahiers de la Rotonde, 3)*, 1979 (study accompanying exhibition in the Barrière de la Villette)
See also Rabreau and Gallet
Ganay, Ernest de, 'Fabriques aux jardins du XVIIIe siècle', *RAAM*, 1933, 2, 49–74
——, *Châteaux et manoirs de France*, 1934–39
——, *Châteaux de France*, 1948–53
——, *Les Jardins de France*, 1949 (*Arts, styles et techniques*, ed. N. Dufourcq)
Gaudet, see Prudent and Gaudet
Gaullieur-l'Hardy, L.-G.-H., *Porte-feuille ichnographique de V. Louis*, 1828
Gaxotte, Pierre, *Paris au XVIIIe siècle*, 1968
Gaxotte, Pierre (ed.), *Le Faubourg Saint-Germain*, 1966
Genlis, Comtesse de, *Mémoires inédits de Madame la Comtesse de Genlis*, 1825

Girod de l'Ain, Gabriel, 'Les Thélusson et les artistes', *Genava*, 1956, 117–64
Gourlier and Questel, *Notice historique sur le Service des Travaux et sur le Conseil Général des Bâtiments Civils depuis la création de ces services en l'an IV (1795) jusqu'en 1886*, 1886
Grandmaison, Louis de, *Essai d'armorial des artistes français*, 1904
Grimm, see *CL*
Gruber, A.-C., *Les Grandes Fêtes et leurs décors à l'époque de Louis XVI*, 1972
Gruel, Léon, *La Madeleine*, 1910
Guéhenno, J., *Jean-Jacques Rousseau*, trans. J. and D. Weightman, 1966
Guerrini, M., *Napoleon and Paris*, English ed., 1970
Guiffrey, J.-J., 'Congés accordés à des artistes français', etc., *NAAF*, 1878, 1–156

Hager, Hellmut, see Braham and Hager
Hampson, N., *The Enlightenment*, 1968
Harris, John, 'Sir William Chambers and his Paris Album', *AH*, 1963, 54–90
——, 'Le Geay, Piranesi and International Neo-classicism in Rome', *Essays on the History of Architecture presented to Rudolf Wittkower*, 1967
——, *Sir William Chambers*, 1970
Hautecoeur, Louis, *Rome et la Renaissance de l'antiquité à la fin du XVIIIe siècle*, 1912 (*Bibliothèque des Ecoles françaises d'Athènes et de Rome*, 105)
——, *L'Architecture classique à Saint-Petersbourg à la fin du XVIIIe siècle*, 1912 (*Bibliothèque de l'Institut français de Saint-Petersbourg*, 2)
——, *Histoire de l'architecture classique en France*, vols 3–5, 1950–53
Hermitage, Leningrad, catalogue of exhibition of French architectural drawings, 1971
Herrmann, Wolfgang, 'Desgodetz and the Académie royale d'Architecture', *AB*, 1958, 22–53
——, 'The Problem of Chronology in Claude-Nicolas Ledoux's Engraved Work', *AB*, 1960, 191–210
——, *Laugier and Eighteenth century French Theory*, 1962
Hirschfeld, Gustave, *Arcs de triomphe et colonnes triomphales de Paris*, 1938
Hitchcock, Henry-Russell, *Architecture, Nineteenth and Twentieth Centuries*, 1958
Honour, Hugh, *Neo-classicism*, 1968

IGRAF   *Inventaire général des richesses de l'art de la France*
IHA   *L'Information d'histoire de l'art*

Index biographique des membres et correspondants de l'Académie des Sciences (1666–1954), Institut de France, 1954

JF   *Jardins en France, 1760–1820, Pays d'illusion, Terre d'expériences*, catalogue of exhibition at the Hôtel de Sully, Paris, 1977, by Monique Mosser (introduction by Jurgis Baltrusaitis)
JSAH   *Journal of the Society of Architectural Historians*
JW(C)I   *Journal of the Warburg (and Courtauld) Institutes*

Johnson, Dr, see Thrale
Joyault, E., 'Les Gisors', *BSHAF*, 1937, 270–93

Kalnein, Wend, and Michael Levey, *Art and Architecture of the Eighteenth Century in France*, 1972
Karamzin, N. M., *Letters of a Russian Traveller, 1789–1790*, trans. Florence Jonas, 1957
Kaufmann, Emil, 'Three Revolutionary Architects, Boullée, Ledoux and Lequeu', *Transactions of the American Philosophical Society*, XLIII, 3, 1952
——, *Architecture in the Age of Reason, Baroque and Post-Baroque in England, Italy and France*, 1968 (1st ed., 1955)
Kimball, Fiske, 'Les Influences anglaises dans la formation du style Louis XVI', *GBA*, 1931, 29ff. and 231ff.
Kleinclausz, A., *Histoire de Lyon*, 1939–52
Krafft, J. Ch., *Recueil d'architecture civile*, 1812
——, *Portes cochères et portes d'entrées des maisons et édifices publics de Paris*, 2nd(?) ed., 1838
——, *Choix de maisons et d'édifices publics de Paris et de ses environs*, 2nd(?) ed., 1838
Krafft, J. Ch., and N. Ransonnette, *Plans, coupes, élévations des plus belles maisons . . . à Paris*, n.d. (1802?)
Kreiger, Antoine, *La Madeleine*, 1937

Laborde, Alexandre de, *Description des nouveaux jardins de la France*, 1808
La Borde, Jean-Benjamin de, etc., *Description (générale et particulière) de la France*, 12 vols, 1781–[96]

La Ferté, Papillon de, *Journal de Papillon de la Ferté . . . (1756–1780)*, ed. E. Boysse, 1887

Landon, C. P. (ed.), *Annales du Musée*, and *Salon de 1808*, etc., 32 vols, 1801 etc.

See also Legrand and Landon

Langner, Johannes, 'Ledoux' Redaktion der einigen Werke für die Veröffentlichung', *ZK*, 1960, 136ff.

——, 'Ledoux und die 'Fabriken'. Voraufsetzung der Revolutionsarchitektur im Landschaftsgarten', *ZK*, 1963, 1ff.

La Tour du Pin, Marquise de, *Memoirs of Madame de la Tour du Pin*, ed. and trans. F. Harcourt, 1969

Laulan, Robert, *L'Ecole militaire de Paris*, 1950

Laugier, Abbé Marc-Antoine, *Essai sur l'architecture*, 1753 (2nd ed. 1755)

——, *Observations sur l'architecture*, 1765

Launay, Louis de, *Une Grande Famille de savants: Les Brongniart*, 1940

Lavallée, Joseph, *Notice historique sur Charles de Wailly, architecte*, An VII (1798)

Lavedan, Pierre, *Histoire de l'urbanisme, 2, Renaissance et temps modernes*, 1941

Lavoisier, Antoine, *Oeuvres*, 1862–93

Le Bihan, Alain, *Francs-maçons parisiens du Grand Orient de France (fin du XVIIIe siècle)*, 1966

Le Brun, J.-B.-P., see *Almanach historique des . . . architectes*, etc.

Ledoux, Claude-Nicolas, *L'Architecture considérée sous le rapport de l'art, des moeurs et de la législation*, 1804, 1847

Legrand, J.-G., and C.-P. Landon, *Description de Paris et de ses édifices*, 1806, pt. 1 in vol. 1, pts 2–4 in vol. 2

Lemesle, Gaston, *L'Eglise Saint-Sulpice*, 1930

Le Provincial à Paris, publ. Watin, 1787

Le Roi, J. A., *Histoire des rues de Versailles*, 1861

Le Rouge, G. L., *Détails des nouveaux jardins à la mode*, etc., 20 pts, before 1776–88

Le Roy, Julien-David, *Les Ruines des plus beaux monuments de la Grèce*, 1758

Lescure, M. F. A. de (ed.), *Correspondance secrète inédite sur Louis XVI, Marie-Antoinette, la Cour et la Ville de 1777 à 1792*, 1866

Levallet-Haug, Geneviève, *Claude-Nicolas Ledoux 1736–1806*, 1934

Levey, Michael, see Kalnein and Levey

Lévis, Duc de, *Souvenirs et portraits. 1780–1789*, 1813

Ligne, Prince de, *Coup d'oeil sur Beloeil et sur une grande partie des jardins de l'Europe*, 1781, ed. E. de Ganay, 1922 (*Collections des chefs-d'oeuvre méconnus*)

Loiseau, Mlle A., *Nécrologie* (of Belanger), n.d.

Lorentz, S., *Victor Louis et Varsovie*, catalogue of exhibition held at the Musée Jacquemart André, Paris, and at the Bibliothèque Municipale de Bordeaux, 1958 (reprinted from *RHB*, 1958, 38–64), with introduction by F.-G. Pariset

Lough, J., *An Introduction to Eighteenth-Century France*, 1968 ed.

Lussault, Citoyen, *Notice historique sur défunt Jacques-Denis Antoine*, 1801

Lüthy, M., *La Banque protestante en France de la révocation de l'Edit de Nantes à la Révolution*, 1959–61

MCADCO   *Mémoires de la Commission des Antiquités du Département de la Côte-d'Or*

MHF   *Les Monuments historiques de la France*

MINSA   *Mémoires de l'Institut national des sciences et arts . . . Littérature et beaux-arts*

MSHAB   *Mémoires de la Société d'histoire et d'archéologie de Bretagne*

MSHP   *Mémoires de la Société de l'histoire de Paris*

McKie, Douglas, *Antoine Lavoisier: Scientist, Economist, Social Reformer*, 1952

Macon, Gustave, *Les Arts dans la maison de Condé*, 1903

Marconi, P., A. Cipriani and E. Valeriani, *I Disegni di architettura dell' archivio storico dell'Accademia di San Luca*, 1974

Mariette, J., *L'Architecture française*, 1737–38

Marionneau, Charles, *Victor Louis, architecte du théâtre de Bordeaux. Sa vie, ses travaux et sa correspondance*, 1881

Marmontel, *Memoirs of Marmontel*, English trans. in *Autobiography. A collection of the most instructive and amusing lives*, vols 3 and 4, 1826

Marquiset, Alfred, *Le Marquis de Marigny 1727–1781*, 1918

Meekes, Carroll L. V., *Italian Architecture 1750–1914*, 1966

Meldahl, F., *Frederikskirken i Kjøbenhavn*, 1896

Mémoires secrets pour servir à l'histoire de la république des lettres en France, by Petit de Bachaumont, etc., 1777–89

Mercier, [Louis]-Sebastien, *Tableau de Paris*, 1782–83

——, *Le Nouveau Paris*, [1797]

Middleton, Robin, 'The Abbé de Cordemoy and the Graeco-Gothic Ideal: a Prelude to Romantic Classicism', *JWCI*, 1962, 3/4, 278–320, 1963, 90–123

Middleton, Robin, and David Watkin, *Architettura moderna*, 1977

Milizia, see Pigneron

Mireur, H., *Dictionnaire des ventes d'art*, 1911–12

Monfalcon, J. B., *Histoire de la ville de Lyon*, 1847

Monod-Cassidy, Hélène, *Un Voyageur-philosophe au XVIIIe siècle: l'Abbé Jean-Bernard le Blanc*, 1941 (*Harvard Studies in Comparative Literature*, XVII)

Monval, Jean, *Soufflot*, 1918

Moore, John, *A View of Society and Manners in France, Switzerland, and Germany*, 1780

Moreau, J.-Ch., see Raval

Moreau, Jacob-Nicolas, *Mes souvenirs*, ed. Camille Hermelin, 1898

Mornet, Daniel, *Le Sentiment de la nature en France de J.-J. Rousseau à Bernardin de Saint Pierre*, 1907

——, *Les Origines intellectuelles de la Révolution française (1715–1787)*, 1933

Mosser, Monique, 'L'Hôtel des Monnaies de Paris. Oeuvre de J. D. Antoine', *IHA*, 1971, 2, 94–9

——, 'Monsieur de Marigny et les jardins: projets inédits de fabriques pour Ménars', *BSHAF*, 1973, 269–93

Moulin, Monique, *L'Architecture civile et militaire au XVIIIe siècle en Aunis et Saintonge*, 1972

NAAF   *Nouvelles Archives de l'art français*

NBG   *Nouvelle Biographie générale*, 46 vols, 1855–66

Nécrologie   *La Nécrologie des hommes célèbres de France*, 1767–82

Neoclassicismo, Atti del convengo internazionale promosso dal Comité international d'histoire de l'art, Genoa, 1973

Nolhac, Pierre de, *Histoire du Château de Versailles. Versailles au XVIIIe siècle*, 1918

Normand, Louis-Marie, *Monumens funéraires choisis dans les cimetières de Paris et . . . de France*, 1832, 1847

Nyberg, Dorothy, review of Herrmann, *Laugier*, in *AB*, 1964, 107ff.

Oberkirch, Baroness, *Memoirs of the Baroness d'Oberkirch, Countess of Montbrison*, ed. Count de Montbrison, 1853

Oechslin, Werner, 'Pyramide et sphère', *GBA*, 1971, 1, 202–38

——, *Bildungsgut und Antikenrezeption des frühen Settecento in Rom*, 1972

Ogg, D., *Europe of the Ancien Régime 1715–1783*, 1965

Olivier, J. W., *The Life of William Beckford*, 1932

Ottomeyer, Hans, see *Autobiographie(s)*

PF   *Piranèse et les français*, catalogue of exhibition at Rome, Dijon, Paris, 1976

PF, Colloque   *Piranèse et les français, Colloque tenu à la Villa Médicis, 12–14 Mai 1976*, Collection, Académie de France à Rome, 2, ed. Georges Brunel, 1978

PMGEF   *Petites Monographies de Grands Edifices de la France*

PV   *Procès-verbaux de l'Académie royale d'Architecture, 1671–1793*, ed. H. Lemonnier, 1911

Papillon de La Ferté, see La Ferté

Pariset, François-Georges, 'L'Architecte Victor Louis et la fille de Diderot', *AAF*, 1950–57, 270–9

——, 'Notes sur Victor Louis', *BSHAF*, 1959, 40–55

——, 'L'Architecte Barreau de Chefdeville', *BSHAF*, 1962, 77–99

——, 'Dessins inédits de l'architecte Victor Louis. Notes sur un neoclassicisme ambigu', *Neoclassicismo*, 1973, 83ff.

Pariset, François-George (ed.), *Bordeaux au XVIIIe siècle*, 1968

See also Lorentz

Patte, Pierre, *Monumens érigés en France à la gloire de Louis XV*, 1765

——, *Mémoires sur les objets les plus importans de l'architecture*, 1769

——, *Essai sur l'architecture théâtrale*, 1782

Percier, Charles, and Pierre Fontaine, *Résidences des Souverains*, 1833

Pérouse de Montclos, Jean-Marie, 'Charles-François Viel, architecte de l'Hôpital-Général et Jean-Louis Viel de Saint-Maux, architecte, peintre et avocat au Parlement de Paris', *BSHAF*, 1966, 257–69

——, *Etienne-Louis Boullée (1728–1799), de l'architecture classique à l'architecture révolutionnaire*, 1969 (cited without date in notes)

Petzet, Michael, *Soufflots Sainte-Geneviève und der französische Kirchenbau des 18. Jahrhunderts*, 1961

Pevsner, Nikolaus, *A History of Building Types*, 1976

Peyre, Marie-Joseph, *Oeuvres d'architecture*, 1765, 1795

Piépape, Général de, *Histoire des Princes de Condé au XVIIIe siècle*, 1913

Piganiol de la Force, J. A., *Description de Paris*, 3rd ed., 1765

Pigneron, *Vies des architectes anciens et modernes*, 1773

Poisson, Georges, 'L'Art de la Révolution à Paris. Architecture et décors', *GBA*, 1970, 2, 337–58

Pujoulx, J. B., *Paris à la fin du XVIIIe siècle*, 1801

Prudent, H., and P. Gaudet, *Les Salles de spectacle construites par Victor Louis*, 1903

Quatremère de Quincy, Antoine-Chrysostome, *Histoire de la vie et des ouvrages des plus célèbres architectes*, 1830
——, *Recueil de notices historiques lues dans les séances publiques de l'Académie royale des Beaux-Arts à l'Institut*, 1834
Questel, see Gourlier and Questel

RA   *Revue de l'art*
RAAM   *La Revue de l'art ancien et moderne*
RHB   *Revue historique de Bordeaux et du Département de la Gironde*
RIBA   Royal Institute of British Architects
RLMF   *La Revue du Louvre et des musées de France*
RSBAD   *Réunion des Sociétés des beaux-arts des Départements*
RSHT   *Revue de la Société d'histoire du théâtre*
RUA   *Revue universelle des arts*

Rabreau, Daniel, 'Le Théâtre et la Place Graslin de Mathurin Crucy (1784–1787), à Nantes', *Congrès archéologique de Haute-Bretagne*, 1968, 89–135
——, 'Charles De Wailly dessinateur (1730–1798)', *IHA*, 1972, 5, 219–28
——, 'Le Théâtre Feydeau et la rue des Colonnes (1791–1829)', *100e Congrès national des Sociétés savantes*, 1975, *archéologie*, 255–73
——, 'Un Forum au coeur du Paris révolutionnaire. Le projet de Théâtre des Arts de Charles de Wailly, 1798', *L'Ivre de Pierres*, 1, 1977, 35–48
Rabreau, Daniel, and M. Gallet, 'La Chaire de Saint-Sulpice. Sa création par Charles de Wailly et l'example du Bernin en France à la fin de l'Ancien Régime', *BSHP*, 1971, 115ff.
See also Steinhauser and Rabreau
Racinais, Henry, *Les Petits Appartements des roys Louis XV et Louis XVI au Château de Versailles*, 1950
Ransonnette, see Krafft and Ransonnette
Raval, Marcel, and J.-Ch. Moreau, *Claude-Nicolas Ledoux 1756–1806*, 1956
Reuterswärd, O., 'De sjunkna bagarna hos Ledoux, Boullée, Céllerier och Fontaine', *Konsthistorisk Tidskrift*, 1960, 98–117
Réau, Louis, *Histoire de l'expansion de l'art français moderne*, 4 vols, 1924–33
Renou, Antoine, *Notice des ouvrages et de la vie du C[itoy]en Antoine*, n.d.
Reymond, see Decugis and Reymond
Rice, H. C. Jr., *Thomas Jefferson's Paris*, 1976
Rivière, C., *Un Village de Brie au XVIIIe siècle. Maupertuis*, n.d.
Ronot, Henry, 'Bourbonne-les-bains et les établissements thermaux en France au XVIIIe siècle', *BSHAF*, 1959, 125–33
Rosenau, Helen, *Boullée's Treatise on Architecture*, 1953
——, *The Ideal City*, 1959
——, 'Engravings of the Grands Prix of the French Academy of Architecture', *AH*, 3, 1960
——, *Social Purpose in Architecture, Paris and London Compared, 1760–1800*, 1970
——, *Boullée and Visionary Architecture*, 1976
Rosenblum, Robert, *Transformations in Late Eighteenth century Art*, 1967
Roubo, le fils, *Traité de la construction des théâtres et des machines théâtrales (Description des arts et métiers, XXIII)*, 1777 (Académie royale des Sciences)

SIP   *Société d'iconographie parisienne*

Sandoz, see Champier and Sandoz
Schneider, R., *Quatremère de Quincy et son intervention dans les arts (1788–1830)*, 1910
Scott, Barbara, in *Apollo*, January, 1973 (French collectors of the eighteenth century)
Ségur, Comte de, *Mémoires ou souvenirs et anecdotes par M. Le Comte de Ségur*, 1824
Silvestre de Sacy, Jacques, *Alexandre-Théodore Brongniart, 1739–1813. Sa vie – son oeuvre*, n.d. (1940?)
——, *Le Comte d'Angiviller, Dernier Directeur Général des Bâtiments du Roy*, 1953
Sirén, Osvald, *China and the Gardens of Europe of the Eighteenth Century*, 1950
Soulange-Bodin, Henry, *Châteaux de Normandie*, 1928–29
Stein, Henri, *Le Palais de Justice et la Sainte-Chapelle de Paris*, 1912
——, *Augustin Pajou*, 1912

Steinhauser, Monika, and Daniel Rabreau, 'Le Théâtre de l'Odéon de Charles de Wailly et Marie-Joseph Peyre, 1767–1782', *RA*, 19, 1973
Stern, Jean, *A l'ombre de Sophie Arnould: François-Joseph Belanger, Architecte des Menus Plaisirs, Premier Architecte du Comte d'Artois*, 1930
Summerson, John, *Architecture in Britain 1530 to 1830*, 3rd ed., 1958
Swarte, Victor de, *Les Financiers amateurs d'art aux XVIe, XVIIe et XVIIIe siècles*, 1890

Tadgell, Christopher, *Ange-Jacques Gabriel*, 1978
Tarbé de St-Hardouin, F.-P.-H., *Notices biographiques sur les Ingénieurs des Ponts et Chaussées*, 1884
Thicknesse, Philip, *A Year's Journey through France, and Part of Spain*, 1787
Thieme, U., and F. Becker, *Allgemeines Lexikon der bildenden Künstler*, 1908–50
Thiéry, L.-V., *Almanach du voyageur à Paris*, 1786
——, *Guide des amateurs et des étrangers voyageurs à Paris*, 1787 (abbrev. Thiéry, *Paris*)
——, *Guide des amateurs . . . aux environs de Paris*, 1788
Thirion, H., *La Vie privée des financiers au XVIIIe siècle*, 1895
Thrale, Mrs. *The French Journals of Mrs. Thrale and Doctor Johnson*, ed. M. Tyson and H. Guppy, 1932
Tour du Pin, see La Tour du Pin
Tournier, René, 'L'Architecte Claude-Joseph-Alexandre Bertrand (1734–1797)', *Académie des sciences, belles-lettres et arts de Besançon*, 1943, 13–32

VU   *La Vie urbaine* (Institut d'urbanisme de l'Université de Paris)

Vallentin, Antonia, *Mirabeau*, 1948
Vasi, G., *Delle magnificenze di Roma*, 1747–61
Vautier, G., 'Pierre Vignon et l'église de la Madeleine', *BSHAF*, 1910, 380–422
Vidler, Anthony, 'The Architecture of the Lodges; Ritual Form and Associational Life in the Late Enlightenment', *Oppositions*, 5, 1976, 75–97
Viel, Charles-François, *Notice nécrologique sur Jean-François-Thérèse Chalgrin, architecte*, 1814
Viel de St-Maux, Jean-Louis, *Lettres sur l'architecture des anciens, et celle des modernes*, 1787
Vigée Lebrun, Mme, *Souvenirs of Madame Vigée Le Brun*, English trans., 1879
——, *The Memoirs of Mme Elizabeth Louise Vigée-Le Brun, 1755–1789*, trans. G. Shelly, n.d. (1944?)
Villar, Citoyen, 'Notice sur la vie et les travaux d'Etienne-Louis Boullée', *MINSA, Littérature et beaux-arts*, 3, An IX, 43–51
Visionary Architects, Boullée, Ledoux, Lequeu, catalogue of USA touring exhibition, 1968
Visme, Jacques de, *Un Favori des dieux, Jean-Benjamin de la Borde (1734–1794)*, 1935
Vollmer, Hans, See Thieme and Becker (entries for late eighteenth-century French architects)
Voltaire, *Voltaire's Correspondence*, ed. Theodore Besterman, 1953–65

Walpole, *The Letters of Horace Walpole, Fourth Earl of Orford*, ed. Mrs Paget Toynbee, 1903–05
Watin, see *Le Provincial à Paris*
Watkin, David, see Middleton and Watkin
Wiebenson, Dora, *Sources of Greek Revival Architecture*, 1969
——, 'The Two Domes of the Halle au Blé in Paris', *AB*, 1973, 262–79
——, *The Picturesque Garden in France*, 1978
Wilson, A. M., *Diderot*, 1972

Vaudoyer, Antoine-Laurent-Thomas, *Extrait succinct des travaux de quelques architectes du Gouvernement*, Bibliothèque Doucet, carton 32 (1 August 1814)

Young, Arthur, *Travels in France during the Years 1787, 1788 & 1789*, ed. C. Maxwell, 1950 (French ed. by Henry Sée, 1931)
Yurova, T. (ed.), *Moscow, Monuments of architecture (18th century to first third of 19th century)*, 1975

ZK   *Zeitschrift für Kunstgeschichte*

Zmijewska, Hélène, 'La Critique des Salons en France avant Diderot', *GBA*, 1970, 2, 1–144

PHOTOGRAPHIC ACKNOWLEDGMENTS

J. Alaterre, Pontoise 335
Jean Albert 153
Alinari 19
Jörg P. Anders, Berlin 9
Archives Municipales, Bordeaux 186, 196
Archives Photographiques, Paris 1, 35, 47, 101, 231, 242, 256, 285–6, 306, 313, 346
James Austin 95, 130, 167 (screen), 170, 257, 314, 327, 348
B. T. Batsford Ltd 3
Bibliothèque Nationale, Paris 23, 132, 147 (elevation), 157, 222, 287
British Architectural Library, London 8, 37, 62, 117, 123 (plan), 138 (staircase section), 175, 228, 249
British Library, London 75–6
Bulloz 13, 85, 90, 94, 96, 102, 113, 124–6, 133, 171, 177, 253, 260, 307
J.-L. Charmet 128
Cooper-Hewitt Museum of Design, New York 187
Country Life 39
Courtauld Institute of Art, London 11, 17, 20, 25, 29, 31–2, 38, 53–5, 58, 60, 64–5, 67, 69, 74, 81, 84, 88, 97, 99, 110–11, 116, 122, 123 (section), 138 (site plan, elevation and section), 139, 145, 169, 176, 180–3, 190, 195, 199, 202, 236, 245, 248, 268, 297, 299, 316–17, 328, 341–4, 349
Jacques Delamare 150–1, 154
Documentation Photographique de la Réunion des Musées Nationaux 10, 22, 30, 40, 83, 93, 129, 225, 326, 347
Ecole Nationale Supérieure des Beaux-Arts, Paris 294–5
Fitzwilliam Museum, Cambridge 156
Flammarion 143
R. Fleming and Co. Ltd 42
John Freeman 41, 269
Hélène Fustier 197, 217–18

Giraudon 12, 82, 86, 134, 161, 184, 201, 215, 334, 350
J. Hautefeuille 61, 107, 112, 146, 147 (section), 148, 155, 276, 279, 298, 304, 309–10, 323, 331
J. Heesom 71, 79, 87, 103–6, 108, 144, 203–4, 206, 211, 214, 216, 219, 221, 226–7, 230, 232–3, 235, 237, 244, 247, 250–1, 261–3, 265–6, 270–5, 281–2, 284, 288, 302, 305, 315, 319, 320, 322, 338
Hermitage, Leningrad 114
Inventaire Général des Monuments et des Richesses Artistiques de la France 78, 163, 174, 185, 264
A. F. Kersting 2, 4–5, 16, 100, 345
Roland Liot 166, 168
Marburg 15, 21, 46, 178
Eric de Maré 289
Musée Antoine Lecuyer, St-Quentin 115
Musée des Arts Décoratifs, Paris 131, 292–3
Musée Carnavalet, Paris 92, 135
Musée de Dijon 119
Musée de Picardie, Amiens 296
National Gallery of Art, Washington 7, 73
Nordiska Museet, Stockholm 72
Roger-Viollet 26
Jean Roubier 57
Saml. af Arkitekturtegn, Charlottenborg 48–50, 68
Helga Schmidt-Glassner, Stuttgart 193
Peter Smith 14
Wallace Collection, London 140
Jørgen Watz, Denmark 66

Plate 198 is reproduced by gracious permission of Her Majesty The Queen

Index

Numbers in italics refer to illustrations